W9-APJ-714

ASPECTS OF VERDI

Books by George Martin

The Opera Companion
(1961; 3rd ed., 1982)

The Battle of the Frogs and the Mice:
An Homeric Fable
(1962; 2nd ed., 1987)

Verdi, His Music, Life and Times
(1963; 3rd ed., 1983)

The Red Shirt and the Cross of Savoy:
The Story of Italy's Risorgimento, 1748–1871
(1969)

Causes and Conflicts: The Centennial History
of the Association of the Bar of the
City of New York, 1870–1970
(1970)

Madam Secretary: Frances Perkins
(1976)

The Companion to
Twentieth-Century Opera
(1979; 2nd ed., 1984)

The Damrosch Dynasty:
America's First Family of Music
(1983)

Aspects of Verdi
(1988)

ASPECTS OF VERDI

George Martin

Dodd, Mead & Company
New York

Copyright © 1988 by George Martin

All rights reserved

No part of this book may be reproduced in any form
without permission in writing from the publisher.
Published by Dodd, Mead & Company, Inc.
71 Fifth Avenue, New York, NY 10003
Manufactured in the United States of America
First Edition

1 2 3 4 5 6 7 8 9 10

Library of Congress Cataloging-in-Publication Data

Martin, George Whitney.
  Aspects of Verdi.

  Bibliography: p.
  Includes index.
  1. Verdi, Giuseppe, 1813–1901—Criticism and interpretation.
  I. Title.
  ML410.V4M264   1987   782.1'092'4   87–19907
  ISBN 0-396-08843-0

IN MEMORIAM

Allen T. Klots

Editor at Dodd, Mead

MANZONI on a writer's purpose: "To share with others the final victorious words that we utter to ourselves when things become clearest."

—*Del romanzo storico (On the Historical Novel)*

VERDI in conversation, from notes kept by Arnaldo Bonaventura, a musicologist: "Simplicity in art is everything"; when "form is intricate, contorted and difficult, communication fails, and communication is the aim of art."

—*Ricordi e ritratti (Memories and Portraits)*

CONTENTS

ILLUSTRATIONS

Orchestral examples, *La traviata*

MAPS

PREFACE

As I hope will be evident in these essays, I have written them out of joy in working with the material. Even after thirty years of studying Verdi's music and life, I am like one who has just sighted Halley's comet at its brightest. Others have seen it before, but I cannot contain myself: I must pass the telescope to my neighbor, babbling about where to look, what to see, and how to interpret, all the while interspersing comments on the marvel of it. Hence, this book.

If I were asked to name among Verdi's attributes the chief cause of my enthusiasm, I would say his "vitality," including in the term all its facets: The long life and artistic growth that continued to the end; the vigor and pace of much of the music; the patriotism that still could question his country's actions; the daily work on his farms; and the imagination at the end of life, having started poor and become rich, to build a hospital and to found a retirement home for one hundred poor musicians. Few men have lived so intensely, or in so many spheres of activity: politics, art, agriculture, family, society. Nothing that touched humanity was outside his interest, and to be in contact with him, whether through his works or letters, is like having one's hand on the beating heart of life.

Many composers have made us care about love and death, honor and duty, but Verdi surely was the first to stir concern for the paternal anguish of a hunchbacked pander or for the misery and nobility of a kept woman. But even in matters seemingly far from art—the training of a horse or the use of farm machinery—so direct is the language of his letters that he can, for the moment, spark attention. I have a letter he wrote to a tradesman who had sent him a garden chair, and Verdi, in thanking him, explains why it is not so fully or easily adjustable as those at the spa at Montecatini. As he describes the design of the Montecatini chair, its double seat and "cylindrical marble wheel" that allows it to be easily moved, one begins to care about reclining lounge chairs. The range of his interests makes his correspondence as engaging as any I know.

Many of his letters, of course, deal with weighty matters in politics, art, and human affairs, and here his natural good taste comes to the fore. One of the joys of living with Verdi is the way in which he always prefers the first-rate to the second and so draws one to the best: in literature, to Manzoni, Shakespeare, Hugo and Schiller, each of a different language and culture; in politics, to Mazzini and Cavour; and in music, to Palestrina, Vittoria and Rossini, as well as to many of the great singers among his contemporaries. In later life he was, though he himself never would have made the claim, one of the most cultivated Europeans of his day.

In other ways, too, his instinct for the best shows itself. Thousands of his letters have been published, but I have not read a sentence in one that is mean or snide. He could be very harsh to the person he was addressing, and sometimes quite unfair, but he never was malicious, and he did not gossip or intrigue.

I like, too, the way in which he kept certain events and feelings in life to himself. In all his letters there is not a mention of his experience of love, either physical or spiritual. That was not for public discussion. Presumably he wrote such letters, and presumably one such was the letter his wife asked to have buried with her. But if he wrote them, he also later destroyed them, and I suspect he was wise. Only the likes of Elizabeth Barrett and Robert Browning should risk the publication of love letters. Privacy, after all, is not only the foundation of liberty, but to some extent the basis of personality. Those who tell all, for the most part become less rather than more interesting. Verdi gained, I think, by not publishing tomes on his theories of love, death, and art.

Finally, there is his music, which, after falling somewhat out of fashion, has returned, perhaps better understood and even more appreciated than before. It will be with us for many years yet, and I dare to say that Verdi, because of his vitality and his extraordinary response to all things human, is the most popular composer the world has known. There are some persons, of course, who do not like his music. They are unfortunate, in the way that those who do not like Shakespeare or Tolstoy are unfortunate. Italian opera of the nineteenth century, like Elizabethan drama or the Russian novel, is an art form at its height, and though it produced a number of outstanding composers, the greatest of them, the most rewarding as a man and a musician, is Verdi.

GEORGE MARTIN
New York City

ACKNOWLEDGMENTS
AND
EDITORIAL NOTES

A word about the two short works that I believe are by Verdi and are published here for the first time. As readers will see from the reproductions in facsimile, they are sketchily written, hard to read, and need an expert to transcribe them into music that can be sounded or sung. I am grateful to Marvin Tartak for undertaking the task. He has deciphered other autograph musical manuscripts of this period, and among his works is an edition of Rossini's *Quelques Riens pour Album*, published by the Rossini Foundation, Pesaro, 1982. In unraveling Verdi's music Tartak consulted Joseph Kerman, author, teacher, and musicologist.

Just as difficult to read as the music was the text of the song, "La madre e la patria." I had hoped to discover it in some anthology of Risorgimento songs and poems, but could not, and its resurrection from the grave of Verdi's handwriting has been the work of many persons, chiefly of Michael Rose, but also of myself, Tartak, Richard Macnutt, Andrew Porter, Floriano Vecchi, and William Weaver.

Many of the above also helped me from time to time on other problems, and to them should be added Steven Anderson, Marisa Casati, Frank Dunand, Rodger Friedman, Glendower Jones, Giuseppe Mazzotta, Cynthia Merman, Corrado Mingardi, Peyton Moss, John J. E. Palmer, Pierluigi Petrobelli, Bernard Peyrotte, Irene Sloan, and John P. Sweeney. Institutions which, through their directors or librarians, have been helpful, are the Folger Shakespeare Library, Istituto di Studi Verdiani, Library of Congress, New York Public Library, and Pierpont Morgan Library. And I thank the Casa del Manzoni for permission to reproduce two pictures of Manzoni.

Some of the essays, often shorter and without notes, and in several instances in different form, appeared first in the following books or journals: *The Verdi Companion, The Opera Quarterly, The San Francisco Opera Program,* and the *San Diego Opera Program*. One, on *La forza del destino*, originated in a speech at the Sixth International Congress of Verdi Studies, Irvine, California, 1980; another, on *Don Carlos*, as a speech at the Pierpont Morgan Library, New York City, 1983.

With regard to editorial practice: Verdi in his letters often used dots, parentheses, and underlinings, the last usually for foreign words, quotations, or emphasis, and on occasion for proper names. In quoting his letters I have kept all these and indicated ellipses in my quotations by three dots enclosed in brackets. I also have used brackets to insert any editorial comment of my own. I have given citations in the notes for all letters quoted, and unless otherwise stated there, all translations are my own.

Several of Verdi's more important letters are quoted in more than one essay. Sometimes I have found another letter that makes the point as strongly, but often not; and in the latter case I have let the repetition stand. Though I hope people will read the twelve essays in the order presented, I suspect that many will not; so I have organized each, with its notes, as an independent unit. And perhaps I should add that in the notes there is information and argument as well as citation.

In the Preface and in several of the essays I have quoted or referred to a number of unpublished letters, and in order to make the full texts of these available to others I have collected them, with translations, in Appendix C. Several of the illustrations also publish material for the first time, notably the autographs of "La madre e la patria," "Marcia funebre," and the sketch for *La battaglia di Legnano*. Some of the title pages and wrappers of Verdi's scores, though published, to my knowledge have not been reproduced before, among them the title page and table of contents of the rare Choudens edition of *La forza del destino*. And as far as I know, though I have not made a search, the cover of the first United States edition of the "Ave Maria" (1880) exists only in a single copy, though presumably there are others buried in church or choir libraries.

A few remarks about the organization of the Notes and of the Bibliography precede these sections.

G. M.

POLITICAL ASPECTS

1

VERDI
AND THE
RISORGIMENTO

Great men sometimes can put a personal stamp on an event or episode; besides articulating it, they can help to shape it. Winston Churchill, after the fall of France in World War II, so well expressed Britain's lonely defiance of Nazi Germany that its spirit not only rang round the world but helped to forge the ultimate victory.

Such identification or stamping is easier perhaps for heads of state than artists, for the events with which they are associated are often greater, or at least more particular. Artists, however, have an advantage in another way. If they live long enough and are great enough, they can articulate not just an event or moment in time but an entire era, a civilization with all its social customs and attitudes. Who can watch Molière's plays without feeling the currents that disturbed life in mid-seventeenth-century France? Or hear Bach's cantatas without sensing the spirit of early-eighteenth-century Lutheran Germany?

But such stamping, of course, is reciprocal: the man affects the era, and the era, the man. With Verdi the era was the Risorgimento, a period in Italian political and social history that roughly spans the nineteenth century. At its start Italy, in a phrase of the day, was only "a geographical expression," for the Po valley, peninsula, and islands were divided into more than ten political units, none of them powerful, most of them dominated by foreign powers. At the Risorgimento's end these states were united in a Kingdom of Italy,

moderately powerful, truly independent, and with its capital at Rome. Social-
ly, too, the people were beginning to feel themselves a nation: what divided
them was less important than what they had in common. In place of French,
German, Latin, or local dialect, Italian increasingly was spoken, and in place
of distinct Neapolitan, Venetian, or Roman cultures, one more generally
called Italian was emerging.

Verdi was the greatest artist of this movement. Throughout his work its
values, its issues recur constantly, and he expressed them with great power.
In a country divided by local dialects, customs, and governments his music
provided a bond for all sorts of men and women. In his person—starting life
humbly, living it honestly, even nobly—he became for many a symbol of
what was best in the period. If he and his art were partly shaped by the
Risorgimento, they also in part shaped it.

* * * * * *

Verdi was born, on 9 or 10 October 1813,[1] into a world turned upside down
by the French exuberantly exporting their Revolution. Starting in 1796 a
succession of French armies crossed the Alps to bring Liberty, Equality, and
Fraternity to the Italians and also to rob, tax, and conscript them into the
French armies. In the confusion the ten chief Italian states—a theocracy (the
Papal State), two kingdoms (Sardinia–Piedmont, Naples–Sicily), three
republics (Genoa, Venice, Lucca), and four duchies (Tuscany, Parma, Modena, Milan)—were continually reorganized by the French into new entities;
and by 1813, for easier administration Napoleon had absorbed the greater
part of six of them directly into France. Among these was the former Duchy of
Parma, in which Verdi was born, so that technically he was born a Frenchman.

Within two years, however, the British, Russians, and Austrians had
defeated Napoleon and at the Congress of Vienna assigned the Italian states
to the Austrians to reorganize as they wished. In the subsequent shuffle only
three of the former states—the theocracy and the two kingdoms—were powerful enough to regain any independence. The pope was able to reconstitute
his Papal State across the center of the peninsula. The Bourbons of Naples
regained their dual kingdom of Sicily and Naples, ruling all of Italy south of
Rome. And in the northwest the House of Savoy returned from its island of
Sardinia to its capital on the mainland, Turin. In addition, because the
Kingdom of Sardinia could serve as a buffer between France and Austria,
Vittorio Emanuele I was allowed to add to his mainland province of Piedmont
the former Republic of Genoa. The rest of Italy, chiefly the rich Po valley and
Tuscany, was divided into a kingdom and four duchies, with the Austrian
Emperor ruling the Kingdom of Lombardy–Venetia and obedient relatives

placed in the duchies. The new order reduced the former ten states to eight and eliminated the three republics. The Viennese Habsburgs believed in government by absolute monarchy, and in their Italian possessions wherever possible they rooted out any native or new French ideas about self-govern-ment.

Among the obedient relatives given an Italian throne was the emperor's daughter, Marie Louise, whom in 1810 he had married to Napoleon in an effort to secure peace. After Napoleon's defeat and her refusal to accompany him into exile she became, as Maria Luigia, the figurehead of Austrian rule in the reconstituted Duchy of Parma, a small state between the Po and the Apennines. One of her new subjects was the infant Verdi. Twenty-eight years

ITALY in 1815,
AFTER THE CONGRESS OF VIENNA

Emperor Franz of Austria was King of Lombardo-Veneto and also of Illyria; and his relatives ruled in Parma, Modena and Tuscany. Lucca became part of Tuscany in 1847.

later, when still a somewhat rough country musician, he would dedicate to her, his sovereign, his revolutionary opera *I Lombardi,* and she, an Austrian archduchess and former empress of France, would present to him a jewelled pin. At their meeting with its exchange of incongruous gifts two extremes of experience briefly touched.

The town in which Verdi grew up, Busseto, sits in flat farm country midway between the cities of Parma and Piacenza. In his youth it was a small market town of about 2,000 persons, a neat rectangle of buildings still tightly girdled by medieval walls. At one corner, looking out over tilled fields, was the "Rocca," a small castle, and at each of the others, a squat tower. Not far to the north was the Po. In summer the weather was hot and dry; in winter, cold and damp. Farming was the district's chief activity and source of wealth.

Verdi lived in Busseto until 1832, when he went to Milan to study music, and again from 1836–38, while he held the town post of *maestro di musica:* organist, choirmaster, and director of the local orchestra, band, and music school. During these years he married the daughter of his patron and had two children. Tragically, within a three-year period his wife and children died, and for the next decade in a desolate, desperate manner he pursued his career elsewhere while establishing himself as a European composer. Then he returned (with the woman he later married), bought land, began to farm it, and built a large, comfortable house; thereafter, with only occasional inter-ruptions to travel, compose, or produce an opera, he personally managed the farm until his death on 27 January 1901.

Verdi's youth in a farming community and his return to it helped to keep his role in the Risorgimento primarily artistic. Busseto served as a base from which to follow the issues and events of the day while avoiding the activism of the large cities. Even in the decade that he lived in Milan his constant travels to other cities to stage or conduct an opera insured his position as a spectator. In Milan he had friends who wanted to expel the Austrians from Lombardy and who were, to Austrian eyes, revolutionaries. Verdi was sympathetic to his friends' aims but was too often absent to join their conspiracies. When in 1848 the city rose and in five days of street-fighting drove the Austrian army out, Verdi was in Paris. He hurried back but was too late for the fighting and, when the Austrians retook the city, was not included in their reprisals.

He was fortunate, too, to be a citizen of Parma. Of all the Italian states it was the most lightly governed and, probably as a result, the most peaceful. Where rulers of neighboring states seemed often to seek confrontations with their subjects, Maria Luigia and her successors avoided them. Though Verdi frequently had difficulties with censors elsewhere, he had few in Parma; nor was he ever fined for his opinions, or his land expropriated for his actions, as happened to many in Milan. For an outspoken Italian patriot in the mid-nineteenth century Parma was the easiest state in which to live.

The Risorgimento, like many political and social movements that continue for several generations, began obscurely, passed through several phases, and ended by fading imperceptibly into something quite different. Historians do not agree on a date at which a sense of nationality first appeared among the people of Italy, the moment when Venetians, Romans, Neapolitans began to think of themselves as Italians. It is clear, however, that the sense was greatly stimulated by the French invasions following the Revolution.

The French not only talked endlessly about "We, the French," exciting those they harangued to think of "We, the Italians," but in the name of their Revolution they swept away the remains of Italian feudalism, reorganized the states on a more rational basis, and staffed them with skilled administrators—thereby greatly increasing trade—and ruled, at least at the start, through assemblies to which the Italians sent delegates. The memory of those constituent assemblies survived the later imperialism of Napoleon, and clashed, after the Congress of Vienna, with Austria's desire to impose an absolute monarchy on every Italian state.

The first revolution to shake the peninsula occurred in Naples in 1820. It was the work of a secret society whose members were known as the "Carbonari" (Charcoal-burners) because the society was organized by *vendite* (shops) for the ostensible sale of charcoal. There were "shops" or clubs in every Italian state, but they varied greatly and lacked cohesion. Those in the south had a wide membership and much sociability in the meetings; in the north they tended to be restricted to the educated, to be more purely political in aim and more conspiratorial.

The Neapolitan clubs had members in every branch of the government, including the army, and their "revolution" consisted simply of revealing their numbers and staging an enormous parade through Naples. They demanded a constitution, requesting the king to continue as a constitutional monarch. Faced with a government at a standstill, he agreed. But eight months later, after secret negotiations with the Austrians, he called in an Austrian army that swept aside the constitution and reimposed an absolute monarchy.

A revolution with a similar aim started in Turin but was more quickly crushed, again by an Austrian army called in by the king. And still another revolution planned in Milan was prevented by the arrest of its leaders. Everywhere men went to prison or into exile, and Austria was recognized clearly as the chief obstacle to independence for any Italian state. For many, too, the belief increased that no trust should be placed in kings.

Ten years later, in 1831, there was another Carbonaro revolution. This time the conspirators planned to combine Parma, Modena, and as much of the Papal State as lay east of the Apennines into a constitutional Kingdom of Central Italy. By offering the throne to the Duke of Modena they hoped to persuade Austria to acquiesce, and they looked to France, at the time a constitutional monarchy, for diplomatic and even military support.

Though the Duke of Modena had agreed to accept the throne, on the eve of the revolution he betrayed many of its leaders to the Austrians. The remainder, nevertheless, met in an Assembly at Bologna and formed a provisional government. But the French did nothing, while the pope, the duke, and Maria Luigia called in the Austrian army stationed in Lombardy. The revolution, the first to aim at uniting several Italian states under one ruler, collapsed. It was the last effort of the Carbonari, and a new phase of the Risorgimento emerged.

Its leader was Giuseppe Mazzini, a tall, thin, passionate young man from Genoa who could write with the force of an Old Testament prophet. Believing that the Carbonari had been too limited in their aim of constitutional monarchy, too ready to accept the existing Italian states as permanent, and too inclined to rely on France or Britain for support, Mazzini founded a new secret society, "La Giovine Italia" (Young Italy), whose purpose was to unite all the Italian states into one republic. The Italians were to do this alone, without foreign help, by putting aside all pettiness and regional jealousy. Becoming through moral regeneration a people ready to work and die to achieve a better world, they would make Italy a free, united republic.

From exile in Marseilles and later Geneva, Mazzini spread his ideas throughout Italy by a journal, *La Giovine Italia,* that was banned in every state. Yet copies were well distributed, traveling frequently in trunks with false bottoms or in crates of fish or pumice. Once through customs they passed from hand to hand, often circulating for years. Some articles proposed in detail how town uprisings might be organized; others described how guerilla bands could fight from the hills; another argued that a federation of states was more suitable for Italy than a republic. But as most of the journal was written by Mazzini, his views predominated, and they were presented with mystical authority.

As an active revolutionary, however, Mazzini soon proved incompetent. In 1834, he attempted to spark an uprising in the Kingdom of Sardinia by leading a small army from Switzerland into Piedmont. For months he and his men gathered in Swiss hotels, posing as tourists and imagining they were undetected. When the expedition finally crossed the border it was a complete failure. Not meeting any military opposition, it simply disintegrated; its only accomplishments were the temporary capture of a customs station, the burning of some customs uniforms, and the planting of a Tree of Liberty. But over

Mazzini, the republican revolutionary, in a photograph circulated by the police of monarchist Piedmont—Sardinia, c. 1857.

the years Mazzini's ideas, which he continued to propagate, had a powerful effect. Always he urged a united Italy as the only way to be free of foreign domination. Always, as a first step to unity, he urged Venetians, Romans, Neapolitans, and others to replace their traditional loyalties to towns or districts with a new loyalty—to the Italian nation. And always, he insisted, Rome must be the capital of that new nation. First there had been classical Rome, then medieval or Papal Rome; now there must be Italian Rome.

To these political and even religious ideas of Mazzini there was a literary counterpart. The poet Leopardi wrote verses of aching beauty about the ruin that was Italy and the cause of it that was Austria. Less direct but more influential because more widely read was Manzoni's novel, *I Promessi Sposi*, the story of a peasant marriage long prevented by evil men and circumstances. The novel's political and social significance, however, lay less in its story than in its language. When first published in 1827, its descriptive passages were in the current literary style, an eighteenth-century leftover that no one talked; and its dialogue was in the current slang of Milanese dialect that almost no one wrote. Then as the book sped through edition after edition, Manzoni constantly revised it to include more and more Italian words and constructions—essentially the Tuscan dialect—and where no words or constructions existed, he invented them. In the definitive edition of 1840 the language was entirely Italian, and for many the novel was also a primer and dictionary. *I Promessi Sposi* and the many lesser works it inspired in effect created a serviceable, modern language for an emerging nation.

And then in music there was Verdi. There were others before him, of course. Rossini's *William Tell* (1829) is charged with anti-Austrian feeling; and near Naples in 1844, a group of Mazzini's followers faced a firing squad while singing a patriotic chorus by Mercadante.[2] But with Verdi the nationalistic feeling was not incidental to one opera or even two but an integral part of his career.

His third opera, *Nabucco* (1842), and the first to make him famous, is a story of Nebuchadnezzar's pride, downfall, and subsequent acceptance of Jehovah, whose people he has taken captive. The music is rough, vigorous, exciting, and at times beautiful, but its chief glory is a long, slow chorus for the Israelites, captive in Babylon, yearning for their homeland: "Va, pensiero, sull'ale dorate [. . .]" (Go, thought, on golden wings).

All over Italy, as the opera passed from town to town, Italian patriots heard in that chorus their own emotions after failing so often to end their Austrian captivity.

> [. . .] *Oh, mia patria sì bella e perduta!*
> *Oh, membranza sì cara e fatal!* [. . .]

> [. . .] *Oh, my country so beautiful and lost!*
> *Oh, memory so dear and fatal!* [. . .]

At the opera's premiere at La Scala in Milan and at most later performances elsewhere, despite police prohibitions against repeats audiences demanded the chorus be sung again. The police disliked repeats for they were apt to become demonstrations against the Austrian officials in the boxes, but if the audience insisted, what could the conductor do? Generally he shrugged his shoulders and later pleaded that it seemed more dangerous to balk the audience than to satisfy it. In any event, why not repeat a chorus that was based on the Bible? The opera was difficult to censor because its text became offensive only by allusion.

Verdi followed *Nabucco* with *I Lombardi alla prima crociata* (1843) *(The Lombards on the First Crusade)*. The opera is based on a narrative poem of Tomasso Grossi in which a family feud in Milan, arising from the love of two brothers for the same woman, is finally resolved years later on a crusade to the Holy Land. At the premiere the audience identified itself with the Lombards and cast the Austrians as the Saracens defiling the Holy Land; it advanced the crusade into the future and greeted with frenzy a chorus calling the Lombards from despair to battle. The tenor cries, "La Santa Terra oggi nostra sarà" (The Holy Land today will be ours), to which the chorus—and audience—replied, "Si! . . . Guerra! Guerra!" (Yes! . . . War! War!). Pandemonium followed, and the police were unable to prevent a repeat.

Such scenes were not accidental. Verdi and his librettists deliberately wrote as close to sedition as the censors could be persuaded to allow. In *Attila* (1846), in which the audience was invited to equate the Habsburgs with the Huns, the electrifying lines were sung by a Roman general to Attila: "Avrai tu l'universo, Resti l' Italia a me" (You may have the universe, but leave Italy to me). The lines quickly became an anti-Austrian slogan; and if on police order they were dropped from a performance, then that, too, produced a demonstration in the theatre.[3]

The impact of such scenes at the time was very great partly because of the role of the opera house in the daily life of the towns. It was the principal center of recreation. Performances began generally at nine in the evening, and as the house was lit chiefly by chandeliers of candles, the house lights were not dimmed. Except at an opera's most exquisite or exciting passages, members of the audience constantly entered or left their boxes, waved and whispered to one another around the auditorium, conducted business in the halls and foyers, and made the evening as much a social as musical event. Even the wholly unmusical constantly went to the opera. In Milan *Nabucco* in its first full season played so often that more seats were sold to it than the city had inhabitants. And the same was true of Parma.

During the 1840s, after his success with *Nabucco*, Verdi composed an average of two operas a year, and most of them had at least one scene or chorus that struck a patriotic response. Even in *Macbeth* (1847), seemingly an unlikely opera for Italian patriotism, he inserted a chorus for Scottish exiles, "O patria oppressa" (O fatherland oppressed). At the performances in Venice the audiences took to throwing onto the stage bouquets of red and green, the Italian colors, which provoked demonstrations. When the police forbad red and green, the audience threw bouquets of yellow and black, the Austrian colors, for the pleasure of watching the singers refuse to pick them up.[4]

Nevertheless, Verdi's choice of *Macbeth* for an opera is an indication that he wanted to do more than compose patriotic potboilers. Shakespeare was almost unknown in Italy; *Macbeth* had never been performed in any theatre,[5] and very few Italians even had read it. For Verdi to have found his way to it is evidence of his instinctive good taste and wide reading.

The play was also an odd choice for an opera in its lack of love interest. There had been operas before without young lovers: Donizetti's *Lucrezia Borgia* was one, though even it had scenes of affection between a mother and son. In *Macbeth* there is only the disintegration of two adults destroyed by illegitimately held power. Though the subject was one with an obvious appeal for a Risorgimento audience, Verdi risked an easy success by frequently abandoning in his musical structure the traditional forms that audiences expected. Yet such was the appeal of Shakespeare combined with Verdi the opera had a popular success.[6]

Verdi's interest in statecraft, government, and the effect on men and women of the exercise of power is a recurring theme in his operas. It is prominent in *Nabucco, Ernani, Macbeth, Simon Boccanegra*, and *Don Carlos* and not far from the center of *I due Foscari, Giovanna d'Arco, Un ballo in maschera*, and *Otello*. Even in the triumphal scene of *Aida* it appears briefly in the clash between the priests and the king over the fate of the Ethiopian prisoners. The interest was lifelong and deep—Verdi's letters are full of it— and is perhaps a reason he had such success in putting political and patriotic ideas onto the stage. Certainly it is a reason that his operas seem to many to offer a wider range of experience than, say, those of Puccini.

The very lack of love interest in *Macbeth*, however, played to Verdi's strength. He plainly had no difficulty in putting his patriotic feelings onto the stage for all to share, but he seems for many years to have been shy about exhibiting his personal emotions. Not until *Un ballo in maschera* (1859), when he was forty-six, did he compose an extended love duet for passionate adults, and even after that he did not do it often. Typically before then, he would have a third person present, such as the hermit in the *I Lombardi* trio; or he would hasten almost ludicrously through the scene, as in *Giovanna d'Arco*; or, as in Act II of *La traviata*, the tenor would not respond because unaware of the reason for Violetta's great outburst. But most often the tenor-soprano love duet would be the most conventional music in the opera, as in *Rigoletto* or *Il trovatore*.

Why? The reason was not a failure of emotion within him; for as *Un ballo in maschera* demonstrated and *La traviata* and others hinted, he could write powerful music for love duets. And as his wife's letters to him suggest, his love was passionate. Rather, he was reticent. It is extraordinary that among the thousands of his letters that have survived, there is not one that can be called a love letter. He simply did not put such thoughts on paper or, for the most part, onto the stage. They were private. He is the opposite of those artists of today who cannot say "my country" without embarrassment yet will recount their love lives on television.

In this reticence there was a message for the audience: the fight to create a free and united Italy was more important than personal happiness. His operas are filled with lovers torn apart by the call of duty. Never for a moment did Verdi suggest that the choice presented was easy, but he left no doubt how it should be made.

For many in Italy the choice became real in 1848, sometimes called "the mad and holy year" because of the number of revolutions in Europe. Within the triangle of Paris, Warsaw, and Palermo, in almost every city of more than a hundred thousand the people suddenly demanded reforms and generally won them, sometimes peacefully, sometimes by force. Almost everywhere they asked for a free press and a constitution or, if one already existed, an extension of the franchise.

In Milan and in Venice, quite independently, the people rose and expelled the Austrian garrisons. Verdi, who was in Paris, wrote excitedly to his publisher in Milan of hearing "great news [. . .] but nothing for certain,"[7] and as soon as the first reports were confirmed he started for Italy. The Venetians in their freedom promptly proclaimed a republic, and from Milan Verdi wrote approvingly to his Venetian librettist Francesco Maria Piave that in "another few months Italy will be free, united, republican."[8] But in Milan, despite the urgings of republicans, the provisional government hesitated, hoping to persuade the king of Sardinia to support the city with his army. Even many who were not monarchists could see that the king's help was vital: the Austrian army had only withdrawn, not surrendered.

When that view began to prevail, with some kind of merger under the king increasingly likely, Verdi returned to Paris where he composed a patriotic hymn, *"Suona la tromba"* (Sound the Trumpet), which he sent to Mazzini: "Put it to any use you want; burn it if it doesn't seem good enough [. . .] May it soon, with the music of cannons, be sung on the plains of Lombardy."[9] Then he started to work on a patriotic opera, *La battaglia di Legnano*. The hymn had little success; the opera, more.

In January 1849, when Verdi went to Rome to conduct its premiere, the city was convulsed with excitement. The pope, who had been liberalizing his government, had suddenly been deposed as the political head of the Papal State and held prisoner by the most extreme republicans. Escaping, he and many conservatives had fled the city. Those leaders remaining, mostly republicans, announced that a Constitutent Assembly with representatives elected by direct and universal suffrage would meet on 5 February to select a new form of government for the Papal State. As the eyes of Catholics everywhere focused on the Eternal City, republicans from all the Italian states began to pour into it. Among them were Mazzini, the most famous revolutionary of the day; Giuseppe Garibaldi, who had just returned from South America where with his red-shirted Italian legion he had proved himself a brilliant military leader; and Verdi, the Risorgimento's outstanding artist, with a new opera to produce and conduct.

The premiere of *La battaglia di Legnano* was a "furore," which repeated at each performance. The opera tells the story of Italian cities of the Po valley uniting in 1176 to defeat the German invader, Frederick Barbarossa; and in addition to the usual call to place duty before happiness it also preaches the need for Italian unity. Historically, members of the Lombard League were men of medieval towns and cried "Verona" or "Milano," but throughout the opera Verdi has them cry "Italia," as he had done in *Attila*, and their loyalty is to the nation, not to the town.

Probably any opera that waved a flag and allowed the chorus to sing of "la patria" would have been popular, but *La battaglia* was also a musical success and even today is occasionally revived. At the opening performances Verdi was called again and again to the stage and cheered as a symbol of the patriotic movement. He did not enjoy the adulation and soon left Rome for Paris, once again missing an extraordinary historical episode.

As expected, the Constituent Assembly at Rome proclaimed the Papal State a republic with a constitution and its capital at Rome. In so doing the Assembly cut through the thorny problem of the pope's temporal power—his political power as head of the Papal State as opposed to his spiritual power as head of the Church—simply by voting it out of existence. In future, priests, cardinals, and the pope himself, if he chose to return to Rome, would be citizens like all other men, each with one vote, though the pope was also offered "all the guarantees necessary to secure his independence in the exercise of his spiritual power."

From the Kingdom of Naples where he was staying the pope responded with an appeal to the nearby Catholic countries, France, Spain, Austria, and Naples, to intervene with arms and restore him to power. Not only would he not negotiate any change in his temporal power but his previous reforms in his government he would now abrogate. At issue, roughly, was whether the Papal State could be merged in a unified Italian state, whether Rome could be an Italian as well as a Catholic city.

Austria was fighting the Milanesi, Venetians, and Sardinians in the Po valley, and France, eager to reestablish its influence in Italy, responded to the pope's call. Although at the time itself a republic, France sent an army to extinguish the Roman republic. The Romans put a band on the walls to play "La Marseillaise," but the French guns were not silenced by the irony. The campaign, while all of Europe watched, continued for ten weeks ending in a month-long siege of the city.

Despite a proclamation by the pope that "Rome, the principal seat of the Church, has now become, alas, a forest of roaring beasts, overflowing with men of every nation, apostates, or heretics, or leaders of communism and socialism," there was no Reign of Terror, no mass confiscation of property or persecution of priests. Five cardinals remained in the city throughout the siege, unmolested, and church services continued. Mazzini, with his sad, long face and dressed always in somber black, though the city's political leader, continued simple and democratic. He slept and worked in a small room in the Palazzo Quirinale, and anyone, official or not, could speak with him. At night he ate either in a cheap restaurant or had a supper of bread and raisins in his room. Sometimes when alone he would play his guitar.

Garibaldi, who commanded the city's defense, managed to hold out weeks longer than anyone had imagined possible, and by inspiring his volunteers to extraordinary feats of valor gave Rome a new glory. By contrast the French seemed militarily inept and, in their alliance with the pope, on an evil crusade to stamp out self-determination. In the coming years an increasing number of Catholics, within and outside of Italy, would agree that the capital of a unified Italian state had to be Rome.

For the moment, however, the movement for Italian unity and freedom ended in defeat and for many, death. Among these was a young aristocrat, Luciano Manara, whom Verdi knew well. They had met in Florence at the time of the premier of *Macbeth*, spent much time together, and thereafter corresponded. Just a year later Manara had led the fighting in Milan's uprising, the "Cinque Giornate," and then had formed a regiment of Milanesi to continue the fight against Austria. When Austria defeated the Milanesi and proclaimed Manara and his men outlaws, he led them to Rome. Although most were not republicans but monarchists, wanting to create a kingdom of northern Italy under the House of Savoy, at least at Rome they could fight for an independent Italy.

During the siege Manara was killed, still only twenty-four years old and leaving a wife and sons in Milan. A member of the regiment who was with him at his death later published an account of it that stirred still greater sympathy for the Italian cause.

After having partaken of the Sacrament, he did not speak for some time. Then once again he commended his sons to my care. "Bring them up," he said, "in love of religion, and of their country." He begged me to carry his remains into Lombardy, together with those of my brother. Seeing that I wept, he asked, "Does it grieve you so much that I die?" And when my suffocating sobs prevented my replying, he added in an undertone but with the holiest expression of resignation: "It grieves me also [. . .]" A short time before he died he took off a ring, which he held very dear, placed it himself on my finger, and then drawing me close to him, said, "Saluterò tuo fratello per te [. . .]" (I will greet your brother for you). [10]

It reads like an opera libretto. But in these years many Italians lived and died in just this exalted fashion, and Verdi wept for more than one as a personal friend. Years later he received from Manara's son a tiny statue of the hero, and when Verdi himself died, that statue still stood on his desk, in memory of Manara. [11]

With the fall of Rome in July 1849 to the pope and his French allies, and of Venice in August to the Austrians, the Italian revolutions of 1848 came to an end, leaving many in Italy to rage like Verdi: "Let us not talk of Rome! What would be the use! Force once again rules the world! And justice? What use is it against bayonets!!" [12] The only achievement, which at the time neither Verdi nor many others recognized, was in the Kingdom of Sardinia. There the House of Savoy, now led by twenty-nine-year-old Vittorio Emanuele II, had granted a constitution and, despite Austrian pressure, refused to retract it. Everywhere else Austria or its autocratic allies had regained control, and their governments became steadily more repressive, for they soon discovered that any concession led to demands for greater freedom and self-government. And the Risorgimento entered a new phase.

The leadership gradually passed from Mazzini to Vittorio Emanuele's prime minister, Camillo Cavour. His policy, as he developed it in the 1850s, reflected the feeling of many Italians after the failures of 1848 that Italy by itself could never expel Austria. The Austro-Hungarian empire, with its huge land mass, its population of millions, and great wealth, would always be able to field a larger and stronger army. An ally had to be found, and the only possibility of sufficient size and strength was France. But to persuade the French government to act, obviously certain concessions would have to be made.

One was clear and touched republicans. Plainly neither the king of Sardinia, nor his chief minister, nor Napoleon III, who recently had transformed France's Second Republic into its Second Empire, would risk war with Austria to create an Italian republic. Most republicans, including Garibaldi and Verdi, saw this and gradually throughout the decade abandoned a republic as the necessary form of government for a free and united Italy. A constitutional monarchy under Vittorio Emanuele would be acceptable *provided* the new Kingdom of Italy was truly independent and united all the Italian states including the Papal State, and with it, Rome.

There were many hesitations in the shifting loyalties. Cavour, a devious man by nature, became more so as a statesman because, in dealing with

France and Austria, he represented a weak state; and he kept his plans obscure. To republicans he often appeared to be aiming only at the expansion of the Kingdom of Sardinia in northern Italy, not at the unification of the entire peninsula. And it may have been so. It was clear that he was courting France, but not clear what concessions he was offering. With a French army supporting the pope at Rome, how could he persuade a French army to divest the pope of Rome? Napoleon III would never agree to it, for the Catholic party in France was one of the emperor's strongest supports. From exile in London Mazzini sent agitated warnings into Italy not to put any trust in Sardinian leadership and to rely as before on direct action. But most Italians, Verdi among them, were inclined to see what diplomacy could do.

What Verdi brought from the past to his work in this decade, chiefly *Rigoletto*, *La traviata*, and *Il trovatore*, was the quintessence of the Risorgimento, its quality of feeling and its point of view. These by now were deep in Verdi's soul—he was thirty-seven in 1850—and remained part of his character until he died. As with most men, his attitudes were formed in the years before forty.

The point of view is tragic and may be symbolized by Hector in *The Iliad*—Hector, knowing that he will be killed by Achilles, still fights to defend his city, and dies. This, Verdi's operas suggest, is man's lot in life, yet how noble. And this view of life, hopeless but magnificent, was dominant among those who were stirred by the Risorgimento. Again and again throughout the period Italians acted in a manner that seemed to say: We know our acts probably will achieve nothing except to cause us to die, yet we must do them if we are to be men. When Verdi was criticized for having too many deaths in *Il trovatore*, he replied, "But after all, death is all there is in life. What else is there?"[13]

He was not a fatalist in the sense of believing that nothing a man can do will affect his fate. He believed in individual action, but he was also enough of a realist, or perhaps pessimist, to know that action is often ineffective and almost always costly. Yet his operas are filled with individuals taking action against their immediate self-interest to respond to some nobler principle. Violetta in *La traviata* is one; Manrico in *Il trovatore*, another.

The quality of his feeling appears in the range and delicacy of his compassion, both matched at times by other artists and even by events of the Risorgimento. During Milan's Cinque Giornate, for example, the insurgents succeeded in capturing an Austrian barracks only when a cripple, Pasquale Sottocornola, hopped and skipped across the open street to put resin on the wooden doors and then risked his life again to ignite it with a torch of burning straw. Such courage and patriotism in a cripple seemed as remarkable to most Milanesi of 1848 as would the paternal love displayed by Rigoletto to audiences three years later. Art and events widened the scope of men's sympathies.

This perhaps was best stated by the Risorgimento poet Giuseppe Giusti in his short poem "Sant' Ambrogio" (1846). It is in the form of a letter from Giusti to "Your Excellency," an Austrian official in the government of Lombardy and consequently to patriotic Italians the enemy. Giusti tells of wandering one day into the church of Sant' Ambrogio in Milan where a large detachment of Austrian soldiers is attending mass. While the priest consecrates the bread and wine, a band near the altar softly plays a chorus from Verdi's *I Lombardi*, "O Signore, dal tetto natio," a chorus of longing for home in an opera whose theme is the reconciliation of two brothers. Giusti is deeply moved by the music, and under its influence his hatred of the soldiers begins to soften, only to harden again as the music ceases. Then a German song rises from the soldiers, a prayer, a lament, and in it Giusti hears "the bitter sweetness of songs learned in childhood" and sung again in days of sorrow and exile. In his heart sympathy overwhelms hate, and he recognizes the Austrians as brothers. Similarly Verdi, even in propaganda pieces such as *Attila* and *La battaglia di Legnano*, made of the enemy—Attila or Barbarossa—not a monster but a dignified warrior. At its best the Risorgimento, in its art and events, ennobled its participants.

By January 1859 it was evident that Cavour had reached some sort of understanding with Napoleon and that war with Austria was imminent. Verdi, in Rome in February for the premiere of *Un ballo in maschera*, once again became the symbol of patriotic aspiration. Excited Italians in all cities suddenly realized that his name was an acronym of "*Vittorio Emanuele Re D' Italia*" (Vittorio Emanuele King of Italy), and *Viva Verdi!* was scratched on walls and shouted in the streets. Wherever his operas were performed the audiences called endlessly for the composer, particularly if Austrians were present. And wherever Verdi himself was discovered, crowds often gathered spontaneously and broke into cheers.

Cavour meanwhile succeeded in bringing the French army into Italy, and aided by the Sardinian army greatly enlarged by volunteers it fought the Austrians to an armistice. The result after almost a year of negotiation was that Austria retained only Venice and its mainland province of Venetia; France received two small provinces from the Kingdom of Sardinia—Nice and Savoy; and the remainder of the Kingdom of Sardinia, by far the largest part, was allowed to unite with the former duchies of Parma, Modena, and Tuscany to form a new kingdom that in population and wealth dominated the peninsula. Verdi was one of the four delegates designated by the joint Assembly of Parma and Modena to inform Vittorio Emanuele that the people had voted for union.

The unification of Italy, or the expansion of Sardinia, I

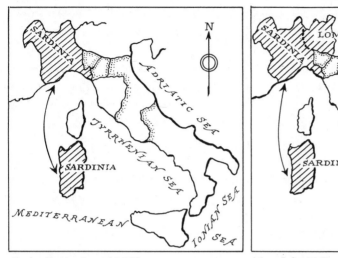

At the Beginning of 1859

After July 1859

The unification of Italy, or the expansion of Sardinia, II

After March 1860

After October 1860

The new Sardinian kingdom, however, stopped short of the major part of the Papal State and all of the Bourbon Kingdom of the Two Sicilies (Naples and Sicily). The fact infuriated Garibaldi: it was less than a united, free Italy, and not for any such half-loaf had he and so many others foresworn Mazzini's ideal of a republic. Embarking a thousand men, "I Mille," on two ships, Garibaldi one night steamed secretly out of Genoa and headed for Sicily. Escaping the gunboats Cavour sent to intercept them, he and The Thousand landed at Marsala and announced they would fight for "Italy and Vittorio Emanuele." To the astonishment of the world, within a month they had captured Palermo, the Sicilian capital, from 24,000 troops loyal to the Bourbon King of Naples but badly led. "Three cheers for Garibaldi," Verdi wrote to a friend. "By God, there truly is a man to kneel to!"[14]

But Garibaldi and his army, swelling day by day with volunteers, did not stop in Sicily. On three nights in August he and his men, evading patrols, crossed the Strait of Messina, and marching north through the mountains of the peninsula reached Naples early in September. Capturing it, again astounding the world, he successfully penned a Bourbon army of 50,000 between himself and the Papal border. At the rate volunteers rushed to join him it seemed possible that he might soon have soldiers enough to march on Rome, forcing the French army there to either attack him or withdraw. The situation lent itself to cartoons: Here was Garibaldi conquering half of Italy in Vittorio Emanuele's name, yet about to strike the king's best friend, Napoleon, in the eye.

Garibaldi's success and the dangers it threatened gave Cavour the chance to represent Vittorio Emanuele's government to Napoleon as the best hope for peace and order in Italy. With French connivance the Sardinian army took the two eastern provinces of the Papal State, leaving to the pope only Rome and its province, and joined Garibaldi in besieging the Neapolitan army near Gaeta. Of Garibaldi and the Sardinian generals Verdi exclaimed, "Those are composers! And what operas! What finales! To the sound of guns!"[15] By November 1860 all of Italy except the provinces of Venetia and Rome were ready to be joined in an independent Kingdom of Italy.

Garibaldi knew that the chief reason for the presence of the Sardinian army south of Rome was to prevent him from attacking the city, and this angered him deeply. He was also furious that Nizza (Nice), where he was born, had been ceded to France. Nevertheless he had said again and again that he would turn over to Vittorio Emanuele Sicily and Naples, half of Italy, and he did it, without conditions. Then, in the supreme gesture of the Risorgimento, the purity of which made him the world's most popular hero of the nineteenth century, he refused any reward for his services. He would not

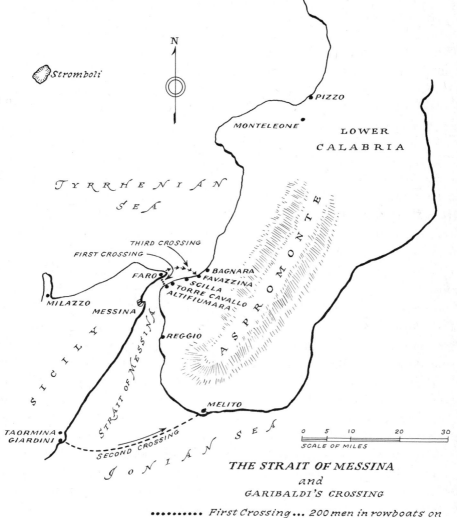

N

Stromboli

PIZZO

MONTELEONE

LOWER
CALABRIA

T Y R R H E N I A N
S E A

THIRD CROSSING

FIRST CROSSING

FARO

MILAZZO

MESSINA

SICILY

STRAIT OF MESSINA

BAGNARA
FAVAZZINA
SCILLA
TORRE CAVALLO
ALTIFIUMARA

A S P R O M O N T E

REGGIO

MELITO

TAORMINA
GIARDINI

SECOND CROSSING

I O N I A N   S E A

0   5   10   20   30
SCALE OF MILES

THE STRAIT OF MESSINA
and
GARIBALDI'S CROSSING

.... First Crossing... 200 men in rowboats on
night of 8–9 August.

– – – – – Second Crossing... 3,400 men in two
steamers under GARIBALDI and BIXIO
on night of 18–19 August.

→→→→→ Third Crossing... 1,500 men in rowboats
under COSENZ on night of 20–21 August.

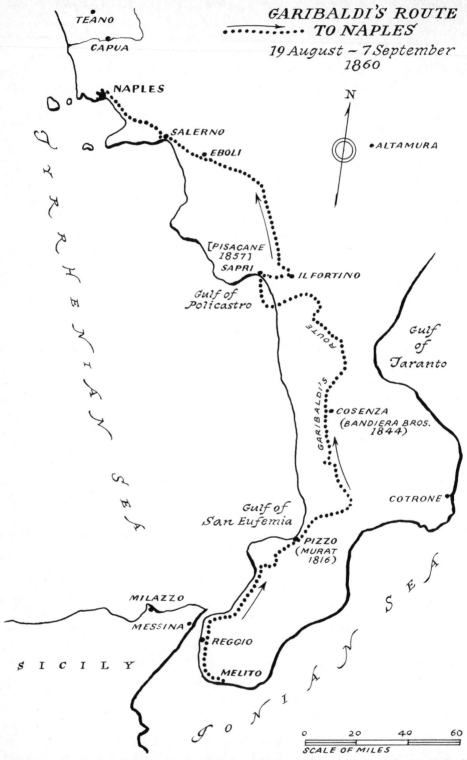

GARIBALDI'S ROUTE
·····> TO NAPLES
*19 August – 7 September
1860*

TEANO

CAPUA

NAPLES

N

•ALTAMURA

SALERNO

•EBOLI

[PISACANE
1857]
SAPRI   •IL FORTINO

*Gulf of
Policastro*

Gulf
of
Taranto

GARIBALDI'S ROUTE

COSENZA
(BANDIERA BROS.
1844)

COTRONE

*Gulf of
San Eufemia*

PIZZO
(MURAT
1816)

T Y R R H E N I A N   S E A

MILAZZO

MESSINA

REGGIO

MELITO

S   I   C   I   L   Y

I O N I A N   S E A

0   20   40   60
SCALE OF MILES

(The names and dates in parenthesis mark the defeats of others who in earlier years had
attempted to topple the Bourbon dynasty by a march north through the mountains.)

accept from the king a title, a castle, a steamer, or even a dowry for his daughter. What he had done, he had done for Italy.

The following year, on Cavour's personal insistence Verdi stood for election as a deputy from his district to the first national Parliament. Cavour was eager to have such a well-known Risorgimento figure in the government, and Verdi was elected easily. He conscientiously attended the meetings in Turin and in the voting always followed Cavour's lead, saying, "That way I can be absolutely certain of not making a mistake."[16] But after Cavour's sudden death in June 1861, a disaster for the new kingdom, Verdi's political activity declined, and though he dutifully finished out his term, he did not stand for reelection. His allegiance to Cavour had been personal, and he did not transfer it to any other of the king's ministers.

Indeed, like many republicans he seems to have offered his allegiance to the constitutional monarchy with his head but been unable to command it from his heart. Requested in 1862 to represent the new Kingdom of Italy at the London Exhibition he composed a cantata, the *Inno delle nazioni (Hymn of the Nations),* in the finale of which he intertwined "God Save the Queen," "La Marseillaise" and, to represent Italy, "Mameli's Hymn" (Fratelli d'Italia). His choice of anthems was startling, for "Partant pour la Syrie," not "La Marseillaise," was the national anthem of the French Empire, and "Mameli's Hymn" was simply a popular republican song particularly associated with the defense of the Roman Republic in 1849. Verdi himself seems to have had second thoughts about the fitness of his choice, for during his life he forbad any performance of the cantata in Italy. Today, when both France and Italy are republics, "La Marseillaise" and "Mameli's Hymn" are their national anthems.

In the decade of the 1860s the conflict over Rome steadily sharpened. In 1864, the pope issued an encyclical accompanied by a Syllabus of Errors that seemed to preclude any accommodation between the Papal and the Italian state. The Syllabus listed eighty propositions that the pope considered "the principal Errors of our times." Among them were freedom of conscience, religious tolerance, freedom of discussion and the press and, finally, the idea that "The Roman Pontiff can and should reconcile and harmonize himself with progress, liberalism and recent civilization." To many, Catholics and non-Catholics alike, the Syllabus seemed an incredibly reactionary attack on all that was most progressive in the nineteenth century. Two years later attention focused still more powerfully on the issue of Papal versus Italian Rome when the Kingdom of Italy, as its reward for supporting Prussia in the Austro-Prussian War, acquired Venice and mainland Venetia. Now only Rome and its province remained outside the Italian state.

Against the background of The Roman Question, as it was called increasingly, Verdi chose Schiller's play *Don Carlos* for an opera. The play deals with the conflict of church and state—but at the court of Spain under Philip II and the Inquisition; thus it combined topicality with the glamour of great days past. It also repeated in a new setting other Risorgimento themes that had constantly appeared in Verdi's work: the call to duty over happiness; the progressive prince of *Ernani*, the statecraft of *Boccanegra*; and as with Rigoletto and Violetta a character, Philip, often presented as unsympathetic, who could be portrayed with sympathy. And overriding all, perhaps, was the chance to affirm Verdi's own political views: freedom of conscience, discussion, and the press, and the necessity for the Church to accommodate itself to the more liberal doctrines of the Italian state.

At the opera's premiere in Paris on 11 March 1867, aside from any difficulty the audience may have had with its music, the opera's politics spoiled its reception. At the moment when the King tells the Grand Inquisitor "Tais-toi, prêtre" (Hold your tongue, priest), the Empress Eugénie, a leader of the Catholic party in France, turned her back on the stage. For some her gesture was a political command, and these successfully attached to the opera for many years the suggestion that it was anti-Catholic whereas at most it might be described as antipapal. But whatever the weight of the reasons, *Don Carlos* had only a moderate success until the next century, when following World War II it suddenly found enthusiastic audiences everywhere.

Verdi was fifty-three when he composed *Don Carlos*, and partly because of events and his increasing age it is the last of his operas on current political issues. Thereafter the Risorgimento themes appear in his work in forms more and more attenuated until they are absorbed almost entirely in pure art. This is often the way with artists, but few who start so topically can end so artistically. Or as Bernard Shaw said of him: "It is not often that a man's strength is so immense that he can remain an athlete after bartering half of it to old age for experience."[17]

In July 1870, while Verdi was composing *Aida*, two extraordinary events followed in quick succession. On 18 July, while the Church was meeting in Vatican Council I, the pope proclaimed the dogma of papal infallibility, and on the next day Napoleon III, egged on by Bismarck, declared war on Prussia. The new dogma irritated the governments of the great Catholic countries and cost the pope their support just when he needed it most, for Napoleon soon withdrew the few French troops remaining in Rome to fight the Prussians. Then all that stood between the Italian kingdom and its desired capital was the papal army of 13,000 men. After Napoleon's defeat at Sedan the Italian army began its advance, and on 20 September following a short bombardment, it entered the city in the name of Vittorio Emanuele II, king of

Italy. The pope, protesting, withdrew into the Vatican, and the Papal State, the oldest sovereignty in Europe, ceased to exist.

Only Ecuador protested the violation of the pope's territory. France, Austria, Spain, and Germany merely murmured that the pope's spiritual freedom must be preserved, and the Italian government promptly submitted to Parliament a bill that would guarantee it. Only after the passage of this Law of Guarantees, in May 1871, was the capital moved to Rome, and the Risorgimento came to as much of a formal end as such movements have.

In *Aida*, which had its premiere on 24 December 1871, all of Verdi's usual Risorgimento themes are present: the aria "o patria mia," the chorus calling for war, the antagonism between king and priests, and the oppressed people. But they are slightly distanced by the non-European setting, and time has begun its process of obscuring topical allusion to leave a drama more purely artistic. In one of the opera's most beautiful phrases Amonasro, after throwing Aida to the ground for refusing to put her duty to Ethiopia before her love for Radames, sings:

> *Pensa che un popolo vinto, straziato*
> *per te soltanto, per te soltanto risorger può [. . .]*

> *Think that a people conquered and tortured,*
> *through you alone, through you alone can rise [. . .]*

In the 1840s and 1850s during such a scene, with the very word *risorgere*, members of the audience would have thought: yes, yes, that is how it is. In the 1870s and 1880s the older members recalled, that is how it was.

Verdi's next work, the *Messa da Requiem*, was a formal farewell to the Risorgimento. Manzoni, the author of *I Promessi Sposi*, died at eighty-nine on 22 May 1873, and there was an outpouring of praise for him. There was criticism, too, chiefly in clerical newspapers, on the ground that he was a bad Catholic and had insulted the pope by accepting an honorary citizenship of Rome. Verdi, whose enthusiasm for Manzoni had grown steadily since first reading the novel at sixteen, was eager to honor him as one of the glories of Italy.

He did not attend the funeral but a week later visited the grave alone. Then through his publisher he proposed to the mayor of Milan that he write a Requiem Mass to honor Manzoni on the first anniversary of his death. Verdi offered to pay the expenses of preparing and printing the music, if the city would pay the cost of its performance on the anniversary date; thereafter the *Requiem* would belong to Verdi.

The performance took place as scheduled in the Church of San Marco and was a success in every way: international attention was focused on Manzoni; Milan was said by everyone to have done the right thing; and for the occasion Verdi had produced a masterpiece.

His Risorgimento themes are translated here into abstractions—pity, terror, conflict, joy, uncertainty—expressed in the liturgy of the Mass. Verdi himself was not a practicing Catholic: he would drive his wife to church but not accompany her inside. Like most Risorgimento figures he was an anti-cleric in that he opposed the organization of the Church, its financial and political power, and its priesthood. Of the love of God or even the existence of God he was, in his wife's words, "a very doubtful believer,"[18] and the *Requiem* reflects this. From the terrors of eternal death it offers no certain release. There is no vision of a kind God or promise of divine intercession—only dwindling power and continued uncertainty. Such apparently was Verdi's belief even in youth, and at the time of the *Requiem* it also reflected the increasing uncertainty felt by many as the doctrines of Darwin and the new sciences began to shake traditional beliefs. Thus the ancient text received a new, modern interpretation by an artist true to himself and his time.

Verdi was sixty when he composed the *Requiem*, and after its completion he gave every appearance of having retired. In 1880, he published a "Pater Noster" and an "Ave Maria" both on Italian texts reputedly by Dante;[19] the following year he staged a revision of *Boccanegra* with a powerful new scene once again attacking the medieval rivalry between cities that had betrayed Italy to foreign domination; and in 1884, he staged a shorter version of *Don Carlos* with several scenes rewritten and a new prelude to replace a large cut. Then, just when these short pieces and revisions had convinced the world that Verdi had indeed retired, he composed and produced two new masterworks, *Otello* in 1887 and *Falstaff* in 1893, at age eighty. For this extraordinary appendage to an already long career his wife, his publisher, and his librettist deserve much credit, for they conspired to keep him composing— but the will to work was also there.

In the past, Verdi had composed operas in which Risorgimento themes had played little or no part, but these, like *Luisa Miller*, *Stiffelio*, or *La traviata*, tended to be modest domestic dramas. *Falstaff*, a comedy, is in this line. Shakespeare's *Othello*, however, offered him a chance to incorporate just the kind of patriotic and martial spectacle that in the 1840s he invariably had seized. His different approach now shows how much he and the times had changed.

Italy in the last two decades of the century had moved steadily in directions of which Verdi disapproved. The government engaged in several tariff wars with France and in 1882 joined Germany and Austria in a Triple Alliance. To Verdi the policy was wrongheaded: France, not Germany, was Italy's natural ally. He also opposed Italian colonial ambition which he felt, like the pact with Germany, was a pursuit of empty prestige. Italy, with seventeen million illiterates and as many starving peasants, had no business in Ethiopia: "We are in the wrong, and we will pay for it."[20] And as in politics, so in art. German culture was increasingly admired, and the younger composers strove to imitate the symphonic and orchestral styles of Brahms and Wagner. Verdi, too, admired Wagner, but he felt Italian composers should follow Italian traditions: song not symphony. Though perhaps right in his ideas, in his feelings he was out of step with the times.

None of this, even indirectly, appears in *Otello,* and there are only a few of his old Risorgimento themes, now chiefly in abstract forms. In earlier days he might have composed an *Otello* in which Desdemona sings of Venice "O patria mia," or Otello rallies a Venetian army to drive the Moslems from Cyprus, or prisoners of either side lament their captivity. But now these earlier themes when present are only musical forms: a prayer for the soprano, a friendship duet for the tenor and baritone, or a chorus of victory. Along with Shakespeare's first act set in Venice Verdi dropped all the ephemera of politics and nationality to plumb the psychological truth of the human drama. The opera is art without topical allusion. Given an exceptional libretto and bringing to it the experience of a long, full life, he concentrated with more power than he had ever brought to an opera before on the two great mysteries of existence, love and death.

*   *   *   *   *   *

Like Molière and Bach, Verdi spoke for an age but also through his art created a body of work that transcends time and place. In his operas the political issues of the Risorgimento and the social attitudes underlying them are prominent—indeed, a good way to grasp the tone of the movement is through Verdi—yet the operas and the *Requiem* continue to speak to audiences who know nothing of the Risorgimento and whose problems are quite different. What, then, remains in his work if the ephemera of time and place are drained away?

First, the potential nobility of the human spirit. In his early and middle years Verdi saw men and women risking life and personal happiness to further an ideal, and in his operas he celebrated them, holding them up as models to be copied. In *La traviata* Verdi wept for Violetta, but he presents her decision in her circumstances as right. His operas, though with artistic restraint, are didactic: they urge us to be noble.

As a corollary, however, throughout his work sounds a constant note of melancholy. Life, he suggests, is hard, happiness fleeting, and death the only certainty. He never pretends in his call for generous, noble actions that these do not often end in suffering but offers them as the best response to death.

Though these themes, the potential nobility of mankind and the tragedy it often entails, were stimulated in Verdi by the events of the Risorgimento, they are universal, sensed by men and women everywhere. Though in different eras they may be more or less to the fore, they are never wholly absent from our experience of life. They are an important reason Verdi's operas, generations after his death, still find an audience.[21]

RELIGIOUS
ASPECTS

2

VERDI, MANZONI, AND THE *REQUIEM*

The connection between Verdi and Alessandro Manzoni proclaimed by Verdi with his *Messa da Requiem* seems in danger of becoming obscured. For many years, in the United States at least, the *Requiem*, which was occasioned by Manzoni's death on 22 May 1873, dedicated to his memory, and premiered on the first anniversary of his death, customarily was titled in programs and announcements "Verdi's *Manzoni Requiem*," and vocal and piano scores always carried a prominent notice of the dedication or even made of it a separate, handsome page. But today the scores reduce the dedication to a footnote, and the programs typically announce "Verdi's *Requiem*" with no mention of Manzoni.

The change apparently reflects a decline of interest outside Italy in Manzoni's works. Among Italians he reportedly continues to be the most widely read author after Dante; and in the universities of the world he still is studied as the leading Italian writer of the Romantic Age, one whose ideas on life, expressed in his only novel *I Promessi Sposi (The Betrothed)*, in translations and popular editions reached the masses of almost every country, even China. In this universal success with a single novel Manzoni resembles Cervantes, and for many years his characters—Renzo and Lucia, Don Abbondio, Fra Cristoforo, Don Rodrigo, the Cardinal, the Nun of Monza, and the Unnamed—were for millions of readers as real and meaningful as Don Quixote, Dulcinea, and Sancho Panza. But in the years since World War I popular interest in the novel, except in Italy, seems to have waned, perhaps because Manzoni's ideas and style have fallen out of fashion.

Verdi, if living, no doubt would regret the decline in readers, for long before he knew Manzoni personally, he revered him for his ideas; he probably also would insist that in all publications and at all performances of the *Requiem* its dedication be stated affirmatively, for he meant with his music to celebrate Manzoni. And for us today, I believe, the gradual obscuring of the connection between these two men, the greatest literary and musical figures of nineteenth-century Italy, is a loss. For the tie with Manzoni, I think, bears on the meaning of the *Requiem*: what Verdi intended to express in it and what audiences legitimately can conclude from it.

*   *   *   *   *   *

Verdi's first intense exposure to Manzoni's works, or so he implied in a letter, occurred when he was sixteen, or, since he was born in October 1813, sometime in 1829–30. The period is only two years after Manzoni, born in 1785 and twenty-eight years older than Verdi, confirmed his position as Italy's leading writer with the publication of *I Promessi Sposi*. Almost forty years later, but still before he had met Manzoni, Verdi wrote to a friend that the novel "was not only the greatest book of our epoch, but one of the greatest ever to emerge from a human brain. It is not only a book but a consolation for humanity. I was sixteen when I read it for the first time." He went on to say that his excitement in many books read in his youth had not survived rereading. "But for that book my enthusiasm has continued strong; or rather as I saw more of mankind, it grew stronger still. For that is one book that is *true*, true as the *truth*."[1]

Whether his enthusiasm for the novel led him to Manzoni's other works, or the reverse, is not known, but in what is probably the earliest of his letters to survive, dated conjecturally 1829–30, he asks a friend in Busseto to come quickly, for "I have just this minute finished a sketch of Manzoni's Ode."[2]

Inasmuch as Manzoni's second and only other Ode was not published until 1848, Verdi clearly had set the first, "Il Cinque Maggio" (The Fifth of May), written in a three-day blaze of inspiration upon learning of Napoleon's death in exile on 5 May 1821 (see Appendix A). Promptly translated into German by Goethe, it subsequently appeared in twenty-six other languages and generally was considered to be the best of the many poems inspired by the emperor's death. Verdi never published his setting of it and apparently in old age destroyed the manuscript, but as late as 1890 he acknowledged its existence in replying to a man who had enquired about unpublished works: "Some sixty years ago, before I went to Milan, I composed several choruses

Title page, Ricordi's (1876) four-hand piano score of the *Requiem*. Besides white and black, the colors are red, blue, and gold. Reproduced at about one-third full size.

from the tragedies of Manzoni and 'Il Cinque Maggio.' (They shall never see the light of day.)"[3]

Manzoni's two tragedies are the verse dramas *Il Conte di Carmagnola* (1820) and *Adelchi* (1822). Both have Italian subjects and exhibit Manzoni's interest in history and religion and his method of treating them dramatically. Carmagnola, a historical figure (1380?–1432), was a professional soldier, a *condottiere* who fought first for the Visconti of Milan and then for the Venetians. The latter, suspecting him of treason, tried and executed him. According to Manzoni, Carmagnola was innocent, and the crux of the play is Carmagnola's recognition that life in this world is full of injustice that cannot be resolved and the more meaningful life, therefore, is the life after death, with God.

The tragedy's single chorus, and perforce the one Verdi set, follows Carmagnola's posting of his soldiers for battle with the Milanesi. After describing the start of the battle—trumpets to the right, trumpets to the left, troops moving into line—Manzoni asks: Who are these men? Which the foreign invaders and which the defenders of their homeland? And he answers: Of the same land are they all; one language they speak, and foreigners call them brothers. To Italians of the nineteenth century the Risorgimento theme was clear: They must give up their regional animosities, recognize their common nationality, and unite against the real foreign invaders, the gutturaltongued Austrians. It was a theme to which Verdi responded strongly and which, twenty years later, was the basis of his opera *La battaglia di Legnano*.

Like Carmagnola, Adelchi is a historical figure characterized by Manzoni as a just man brought to death by injustices he cannot control. His father, Desiderio, was the last Lombard king in Italy (ruled 756–774) and his sister, Ermengarda, was Charlemagne's first wife. Evidently for political reasons Charlemagne repudiated her, and his contemporary biographer, Einhard, reports that the divorce stirred the only harsh words Charlemagne ever addressed to his mother, who disapproved. In the play, though Ermengarda loves Charlemagne, he sends her back to her family, and on the pope's invitation, invades Italy and topples the Lombard dynasty. As presented by Manzoni, Charlemagne is in no sense "great." He is simply a warrior-politician and one of the first of many foreigners called into Italy by the papacy to keep the people of the country weak and divided. Again the Risorgimento theme was clear. Further, in the play Charlemagne equates his invasion with God's will, raising still another of Manzoni's frequent themes, also relevant to the Risorgimento: the use of religion, by Desiderio, Charlemagne, and the pope, to mask political aims.

Though Ermengarda's role in the action is small—she merely suffers—

she is one of the more interesting, affecting characters. Urged by her father to seek revenge on Charlemagne, she replies: "My grief does not ask so much; I yearn only for oblivion; and the world willingly allows it to the wretched; it is enough; let my misfortune end in me. I was to be the pure emblem of friendship, of peace: but heaven did not wish it." Her philosophy of life, evolved through suffering, is to accept her lot and sustain it to the end without complaint and, if possible, without adding to the evils in the world. Manzoni's tenderness for her clearly carries approval.

The play has two choruses, the first occurring just as the balance of power in the Lombard kingdom shifts decisively to Charlemagne. For a moment the ordinary people of Italy come out of the shadows, as it were, and wonder aloud if the change in rulers will bring them a better life and greater freedom. And they conclude it will not: the new conqueror, like the old, has not their interests at heart. The second chorus, "Sparsa le trecce morbide," which appears in many anthologies of Italian poetry, concerns Ermengarda's death. Manzoni, speaking directly to her and to the audience, comments: "You, the descendant of the evil race of oppressors [i.e., the Lombards] . . . You were placed among the oppressed [i.e., the native Italians] by provident misfortune; die mourned and in tranquility; sink down to sleep with the oppressed; no one will disturb your blameless ashes." As we know from a reported conversation with Verdi in the last decade of his life, he always had felt drawn to Ermengarda and especially to this chorus.[4] It seems likely, therefore, that if as a youth he set only one of the two choruses in *Adelchi*, this was the one he chose.

The topics unfolded by Manzoni in his verse-dramas are vast, and he did not entirely succeed in dramatizing them. Though both tragedies have been staged, they are better read than played, and the choruses usually have been the parts most admired. Certainly in nineteenth-century Italy they were the parts best known, widely memorized, and frequently recited.

The Ode on Napoleon's death, "Il Cinque Maggio," shares many of the dramas' philosophic and theological themes. Though short (see Appendix A), it is in two parts: Napoleon's incredible, dynamic career; then the idleness of exile, his thoughts on his life, his increasing sense of its lack of meaning, his lonely death, and, after receiving the Church's last rites, his acceptance by God. It opens with a dramatic announcement: "Ei fu" (He was). With the title thus revealed to be a date of death, no name is needed, and the past definite tense, "fu," in place of the more usual perfect "Ei è morto" (he has died, or, is dead), adds to the initial shock. The world stands silent, astonished that the restless energy that had upset all of Europe, extinguishing and founding dynasties, promulgating and repealing laws, and forming divided peoples into new nations with new boundaries and new constitutions, finally has succumbed to time. Has stopped. Then in a series of tightly organized images Manzoni develops such questions as "Fu vera gloria?" (Was this true glory?) Was Napoleon part of God's plan for humanity? Would God receive Napoleon? His answers, crudely summarized, are No, No, and Yes. The last because for Manzoni, always, those who turn to God will be received.

It is easy to understand Verdi's refusal to publish his youthful settings of the choruses and the ode. However admirable his taste at sixteen in being drawn to Manzoni, whatever he composed must have been inadequate to the texts. But as his letters and reported remarks indicate, his enthusiasm for Manzoni was life-long. And for those familiar with "Il Cinque Maggio," which would include every educated Italian then and now, there is an echo of it late in Verdi's works. When he and Boito expressed another great warrior's judgment on his life, they had Otello exclaim in the past definite tense, "Oh! Gloria! Otello fu."*

Before leaving the ode and the choruses, note how Manzoni chose to present his themes in the tragedies, for he was to carry the method further in *I Promessi Sposi,* and his precepts evidently appealed to Verdi. He did not use a myth from which all of life but the theme in hand has been stripped, as did the Greeks and their chief imitators, the French classical dramatists; instead he set historical persons in real situations, and recounted their stories without regard for the supposedly Aristotelian unities of time and place. Indeed, in his essay on the Romantic movement (*Sul Romanticismo,* 1823), reacting against the strictures and principles laid down by French critics of the previous century, chiefly Voltaire, he specifically abjured the use of myths and observation of the unities. As he wrote to a friend, he sought "that mixture of great and trivial, of reasonable and crazy, which is seen in the great and small events of this world." For Manzoni the truth of life was not to be found in the distilled atmosphere of an archetypal myth but amid the hurly-burly of daily life, as rich and poor, great and small, strong and weak confronted one another in the piazza.

This was Shakespeare's method, and because of it he was canonized as the romantic movement's patron saint. In imitation of him, myths and the unities, with the strong sense of focus they could provide, were discarded in favor of a kaleidoscopic vision that could shift in place and time to any scene or person that seemed significant. According to contemporary critics, the style generated its own "organic" unity, superior to the others because less artificial, and though Italians in general did not adopt the new creed as fervently as did the Germans, in Italian literature Manzoni is one of its chief disciples, as is Verdi in Italian opera.

*See "*Otello,* Manzoni, and the Concept of 'La Gloria.' "

It is no surprise, therefore, that in choosing subjects for his twenty-six operas Verdi never seriously considered a myth. In 1853, writing to a librettist, he even warned against subjects like *Nabucco* and *Foscari*. "They offer extremely interesting dramatic situations, but they lack variety. They have but one burden to their song, elevated, if you like, but always the same. To be more explicit, Tasso's work may be better, but I prefer Ariosto a thousand times. For the same reason I prefer Shakespeare to all other dramatists, including the Greeks."[5] He sought variety in his librettos, and one reason he found Greek myths unsuitable was that "in Aeschylus one is never sure whether characters are men or gods. The only true character in Aeschylus is Clytemnestra."[6]

In *I Promessi Sposi*, on the other hand, the humanity of the characters spills from the pages. With the novel, far more than with his plays, Manzoni achieved his ideal of finding truth in a mixture of the great and small, the reasonable and crazy. There are, of course, scenes of great seriousness and, perhaps more unexpected, others of great comedy. Events range in size and significance from a European war to a village wedding; and characters, in rank, from prince and cardinal to peasant. Indeed, the novel's hero and heroine are both peasants, which in the previous century would have been inconceivable. Who would want to read of peasants?

One aspect of the novel worth noting, for it played a role in the Risorgimento, is its diction. To write a novel at all, but particularly to let peasants speak on the page, Manzoni had almost to invent a language, for in Italy in the 1820s every small region, almost every town, had its own dialect and literature published in that dialect. There was a stilted literary Italian used by poets and playwrights and spoken by a few pedants, but it lacked words. Poets, for example, constantly fashioned posies of roses and violets which, as the unpoetic never tired of remarking, do not bloom in the same season. Yet what were the poets to do? These were the only well-known flowers whose common names did not vary from town to town with the local dialect. There was no contemporary national language that every Italian shared. The most widely known dialect, at least in the archaic version used by Dante, Petrarch, and Boccaccio, was Tuscan, and Manzoni resolved to use it for subsequent editions of *I Promessi Sposi*. As the novel was reprinted, he rewrote much of it in Tuscan, discarding along the way many French and Milanese words and constructions and clarifying and modernizing many of the more obscure Tuscan idioms. The result, because Manzoni was a linguist as well as an artist, was a simple, straightforward, supple language of power and beauty, and over the years, as the book was read and reread by millions and became a primer in schools, it contributed greatly to the creation of a national language around which Italians of all regions could unite. For Italian musicians, however, the achievement had its disadvantage: so long as dialects continued numerous, competing, and divisive, music had as good a claim as any to be the common language around which Italians rallied. Indeed, the fact partially explains how Verdi, with *Nabucco* in 1842 and *I Lombardi* in 1843, could become a national figure in little more than a year.

The moment now has come to look more closely at the novel itself. And because it is no longer widely read, except in Italy, and because Verdi in his *Requiem* parts decisively from Manzoni's religious conclusions expressed in it, I will summarize it briefly.

The period is 1628–31, when the region of Lombardy, in the center of the Po valley, is held by the King of Spain under his title Duke of Milan. The royal duke's attention, however, is distracted by the Thirty Years War in Germany (1616–48)—Manzoni's historical detail throughout is accurate— and though Spanish officials and troops control the larger towns, local lords rule the countryside, many of them taking advantage of the anarchy to prey on the weak. And the novel begins with a spasm of fear as one of the weak, Don Abbondio, the parish priest of a mountain village overlooking Lake Como, suddenly comes face to face with two of the strong. As Don Abbondio turns the corner of the path to his village, he sees blocking his way two "bravoes," thugs, retainers of the local lord, Don Rodrigo.

With deliberate menace the bravoes inform the priest that their lord desires him to refuse on the morrow, or any other day, to unite in marriage the betrothed peasant couple, Renzo Tramaglino and Lucia Mondella. Don Abbondio, by nature uncourageous, assents at once, and the next day tells an astonished Renzo that despite the completed banns the wedding must be postponed. Though he tries to conceal the true reason, Renzo soon forces it from him, and later in the morning Renzo learns from a weeping Lucia that on the road one day she had met Don Rodrigo who, after leering at her, had made a bet with his cousin that he could possess her. On the advice of Lucia's mother, Agnese, Renzo seeks help from a lawyer in the nearby market town, but the attorney, on hearing that Don Rodrigo is involved, orders Renzo from his house. Then Fra Cristoforo, a Capuchin friar whom Lucia has consulted, goes to Don Rodrigo's castle to remonstrate with him. But under the lord's bullying he loses his temper and, by angrily prophesying that Don Rodrigo's day of judgment soon will come, strengthens the man's resolve to have Lucia. Agnese, meanwhile, has arranged a gathering at the priest's house where she hopes to trick him into solemnizing with his presence a statement by the couple before witnesses that they are married. But at the last second, in a scene of typical Italian buffoonery, Don Abbondio sees the trap, flees, locks himself in another room, and from its window shrieks to his neighbors for help. In the midst of the village uproar, as Lucia, Agnese, and Renzo hasten back to Lucia's cottage, a boy stops them with word from Fra Cristoforo that Don Rodrigo's bravoes are there, waiting to kidnap Lucia. So, on Cristoforo's suggestion and with his help they find a boat to take them across the lake. Their thoughts as they see their village and its familiar mountains disappearing—"Addio, monti sorgenti dall'acque . . ."—is one of the novel's most famous passages and for years was learned in school by every Italian. Once on the other side, following the friar's instructions, Renzo starts for a Capuchin monastery in Milan, and Agnese and Lucia go to one in Monza, from which they are sent on to a neighboring convent where they come under the protection of the nun Gertrude. Thus the betrothed are separated, and the wedding is further postponed.

Renzo soon worsens their situation by a bit of foolishness. Upon reaching Milan, he allows himself to be drawn into a riot over the price of bread

Manzoni in 1848. From a drawing done "in two rainy hours" by his stepson Stefano Stampa. Courtesy of Casa del Manzoni, Milan.

that ends in an assault on a bakery. A police agent, anxious for a scapegoat, arrests him, but Renzo, arousing the sympathy of the crowd, escapes, and as a fugitive from the law crosses the river Adda into Venetian territory. Going to Bergamo he locates his cousin Bortolo who finds work for him as a silk weaver.

Meanwhile Don Rodrigo, having discovered Lucia's sanctuary, visits one of the great lords of Lombardy, a nobleman of Milan. This lord is another of Rodrigo's kind, the most powerful in the region, and his castle, close to the Venetian border, is reputed to be a very workshop of crime. His family name, according to Manzoni, was so exalted that contemporary chroniclers dared not used it, referring to him only as "that man" or "that personage," and Manzoni continues the concealment, calling him the *"Innominato"* (the Unnamed). From this man Don Rodrigo requests help in kidnapping Lucia, and the deed, it turns out, can be accomplished easily because one of the Unnamed's bravoes has seduced the nun Gertrude and with her aid, or at least her knowledge, has murdered another nun who had discovered their liaison. Gertrude is therefore susceptible to pressure. One day Lucia is sent out of the convent on a fictitious errand, snatched from the street, and transported fainting to the Unnamed's castle.

But the great lord, like Napoleon in "Il Cinque Maggio," has reached an age where, looking back, he finds his life of violence increasingly meaningless and repugnant, and he is, though unclear about it, in the midst of a religious conversion. He is annoyed by Lucia's fear of him but impressed by her trust in God, and, on impulse, he calls on Cardinal Federigo Borromeo, Archbishop of Milan (1595–1631), who is making a tour of country parishes. The Cardinal, an active saint, recognizes the state of the Unnamed's soul, completes the man's conversion to Christianity, and urges him, as a first meaningful act, to send at once for Lucia. She in her prison, anticipating rape and perhaps death, has been praying and has promised the Virgin that if saved she will give up Renzo and live single and chaste. And on being saved she considers herself bound by her vow. The Cardinal, after listening to her story, arranges for her to live in Milan with a worthy couple and summons Don Abbondio to enquire why the village priest had failed to unite the betrothed in marriage. The scenes in which the Cardinal, on hearing of Don Rodrigo's threats, attempts to explain a priest's duties to Don Abbondio, who had joined the Church only to secure a comfortable haven in a perilous world, are among the most comic in the book. Never, perhaps, have two minds failing to find common ground been more hilariously displayed.

In the meantime a German army, descending from the Alps into Lombardy, has brought with it the plague. Renzo is infected but regains his health and leaves Bergamo for Milan to search for Lucia. There, in the *lazzaretto* where the sick are confined—the plague reduced the city's population from 250,000 to 64,000—he discovers Fra Cristoforo who is tending, among others, Don Rodrigo. Renzo starts to declare his hatred of the man, only to be rebuked angrily by the friar: Don Rodrigo is dying, it is a time for pardon. He takes Renzo into a cabin, points to the once proud lord, and Renzo, his pity stirred, forgives the man who had wronged him. Thus he becomes worthy of Lucia.

Renzo then finds Lucia, who also has had the plague but is recovering. Happiness is delayed, however, by her vow, from which Fra Cristoforo, upon hearing her account of its circumstance, releases her. Then she and Renzo return to their village where Don Abbondio, having convinced himself of Don Rodrigo's death, again publishes the banns and this time marries the betrothed. Immediately thereafter they sell all their property and with Agnese leave for Bergamo where Renzo can find work as a silk weaver and where, as the couple start their family life, they ponder the meaning of their experiences.

There are many aspects of the story that would seem to have an obvious appeal for Verdi. The protagonists, like himself, are from a small village. Even at sixteen, when he first read the book, he probably had met a priest like Don Abbondio, hiding from life in the Church, and another like Fra Cristoforo, who could lose his temper at a lord as well as at a peasant; and as a boy he surely must have had some experience of bullies. Then there is the history: Spanish rule in the Duchy of Milan, the manipulation of bread prices ending in riots, the clash of interests in the city, the plague; and all the religious figures of the period: nun, friar, village priest, and cardinal archbishop.

If critics are a measure, readers find in the novel quite different meanings: for some it is an attack on the Church—Don Abbondio and the nun Gertrude; for others, a justification of the Church—Fra Cristoforo and Cardinal Borromeo; for the economics-minded it is a treatise on price controls and subsidy—the bread riots in Milan and the rise of the silk industry in Venetia; and for still others, a Risorgimento allegory—Renzo and Lucia kept apart by foreign and unresponsive governments, class differences and conflicts, and the failures, ultimately moral, of individuals, all of which formed the fate of the Italian people under Austrian rule.

The novel also exhibits Manzoni's perennial theme: that society is riddled with injustice of all kinds and what matters, what determines a person's moral health and role, is his or her response to injustice. That point of view fits comfortably with Verdi's natural melancholy and constant call for nobility of soul. As he once wrote about *Il trovatore*, in a letter frequently quoted: "People say the opera is too sad and there are too many deaths in it. But after all, death is all there is in life. What else is there?"[7] So for Verdi what mattered is how one faces death: fighting for one's country perhaps, or, like Violetta, sacrificing love so that another, more innocent, may not be deprived of it.

Another theme of the novel that surely would have appealed to Verdi is Manzoni's insistence that men and women create many of their own problems by failing to use the reason God gave them—the nun Gertrude spinning a web of deceit and crime that entraps her, or Renzo stopping to watch the bread riot instead of continuing about his business. Verdi, asked to contribute to a fund to help his former librettist Temistocle Solera, who once again had fallen on hard times, replied that he would send only a small sum, for the man was in good health and it was "his own fault if he has not had a brilliant career."[8] But when another librettist, Francesco Maria Piave, was paralyzed by a stroke, Verdi contributed generously to his support until Piave died eight years later.

Yet on what Manzoni called "the juice of the whole tale," its moral, Verdi might have disagreed. In the book's final paragraphs Manzoni has Renzo and Lucia debate what they have learned, and they conclude "that trouble often comes to those who bring it on themselves, but that not even the most cautious and innocent behavior can ward it off; and that when it comes—whether or not by our own fault—confidence in God can lighten it and turn it to our improvement."

That "trust in God" would be too pat for Verdi. In 1879, when he was sixty-six and dictating an account of his life, he ended with a proverb: *Fidarsi è bene, ma non fidarsi è meglio* (To have faith is good, but not to rely on faith is better).[9] And we have the word of his wife, Giuseppina Strepponi, that he did not believe in God. A year before Manzoni's death in May 1873, she wrote to a friend with whom she discussed religious thoughts, "And yet this *brigand* [Verdi] permits himself to be, I will not say an atheist, but certainly very little of a believer. . . ." But, as Frank Walker points out, in the draft of her letter she had not softened the description but had written, "permits himself to be an atheist." Then she went on to say: "I exhaust myself in speaking to him of the marvels of the heavens, the earth, the sea etc. etc. Wasted breath! He laughs in my face and freezes me in the midst of my heightened speech and divine enthusiasm by saying, 'You're all mad,' and unfortunately he says it in good faith."[10]

Four months later, during the year he would begin to compose the *Manzoni Requiem*, she wrote to a friend in Milan: "Verdi is busy with his grotto and his garden. He is in fine health and splendid spirits. A happy man he is—and may God make him happy for many long years to come. There are virtuous natures that need to believe in God; others, equally perfect, are happy not believing in anything, and simply keeping strictly to all the precepts of an austere morality. Manzoni and Verdi: those two men make me think—to me they are a real subject for meditation. But my imperfection and my ignorance keep me from solving the knotty problem. Remember me to God and to Manzoni. I wish I might be in your shoes to talk of God with him!"[11]

Though Verdi had several friends in Milan who knew Manzoni well, he never asked for an introduction, and because Manzoni similarly respected another's privacy, the two presumably never would have met if Verdi's wife and his Milanese friend, Clarina Maffei, had not conspired to bring them together. Strepponi, in May 1867, going alone to Milan to shop, called upon Maffei, whom she did not know but often had heard Verdi mention. The two women became friends at once and decided to call on Manzoni. He lived around the corner from Maffei and, as an eighty-three-year-old widower without children at home, was under her eye. An unscheduled visit, therefore, was not unusual. A few days later, in a letter to Maffei, Strepponi described telling Verdi of the visit. He had come to the railway station with a carriage and on the drive home:

I told him . . . how you had received me, how (an extraordinary thing for you) you had gone out with me, how foolish I had been to wait so many years before making your acquaintance; and he kept on saying: "It doesn't surprise me; it doesn't surprise me; I know Clarina."

Wishing to push on as fast as possible, I said with affected indifference: "If you go to Milan I'll introduce you to Manzoni. He expects you, and I was there with her the other day."

Phew! The bombshell was so great and so unexpected that I didn't know whether I ought to open the carriage windows to give him air, or close them, fearing that in the paroxysm of surprise and joy he would jump out! He went red, he turned deadly pale, he perspired; he took off his hat and screwed it up in a way that reduced it almost to shapelessness. Furthermore (this is between ourselves) the most severe and savage Bear of Busseto had his eyes full of tears, and both of us, moved, convulsed, sat there for ten minutes in complete silence. Oh, the power of genius, of virtue and of friendship! Thank you, my good Clarina, at once in Verdi's name and my own. Since Sunday, in this solitude, your name and that of our Saint [Manzoni] are repeated at every moment, and with what accompaniment of praises and affectionate words I leave you to imagine.

Now Verdi is thinking of writing to Manzoni, and I laugh, because if I was so overcome, confused and foolish when you procured me that great honour of finding myself in *his* presence, it pleases me that those, too, who are much more than I am, feel also a bit of embarrassment, pull their whiskers and scratch their ears to find words worthy of saying to the mighty.

The more I think of it, the more I marvel, not at my gross foolishness, but at the incredible, and yet sincere and profound modesty . . . of whom?—of him who wrote the greatest book of modern times![12]

Like many Milanesi the two women constantly referred to Manzoni as a "saint," by which they seem to have meant—his life not showing any public good works or hint of a miracle—his apparent moral repose. Where others felt themselves to be in a turmoil of doubt on moral and religious issues, he seemed to have resolved them all and gained the inner strength and certainty that to others seemed so desirable. To many such persons Manzoni's life and works exhibited a spiritual quest. Though born and baptized a Catholic, he had in youth and early manhood wandered far from the Church into free-thinking; and then, in his twenty-sixth year, he had a direct experience of God, a conversion, in which his inclinations toward justice and virtue, until then drifting and ineffectual, suddenly found anchor in Catholic Christian belief. With *I Promessi Sposi* he successfully concluded the spiritual quest, having worked out his faith in a way that would support him the rest of his life. This was a possible reason he had not written another novel: he had no need.

In fact, he may not have been so inwardly certain as he appeared, for in very old age, at eighty-nine, he became obsessed with the sins of his youth and, though only those closest to him were aware of it, the old doubts returned. In the delirium of his final illness he feared to face God and repeatedly asked, "What will happen to me? What will happen to me?"

To the country as a whole, however, and probably also to Verdi, Strepponi, and even to Maffei, he died serene; and his death was a national event, the occasion for public eulogies, proclamations, renaming of streets, and in Milan an extraordinary funeral procession with his coffin attended by two princes of the House of Savoy, the president of the Italian Senate and Chamber, and the ministers for Education and Foreign Affairs. In all of this the Vatican remained notably silent, for to the Church the Risorgimento themes in Manzoni's works kept him suspect. In Milan, *L'Osservatore Cattolico* remarked on the "fine poison" in his works, observing that he was "never straight in his thoughts," and the head of the city's Jesuits commented, "He was a born revolutionary."

But it was, of course, just those themes in Manzoni's early works that had attracted Verdi as a youth and through which, in the novel particularly, Manzoni had dramatized his characters' humanity. Did Verdi also think of Manzoni as a saint? Either in the specifically Christian sense of one who is close to God and therefore sanctified, or in the more general sense of a good man whose goodness is informed by a belief in a God? The composer Ildebrando Pizzetti, in his Preface to the Facsimile Edition of the autograph score of the *Requiem*, concludes that Verdi did consider Manzoni a saint and in the first specifically Christian sense. For Pizzetti, the *Requiem* was not only a tribute from one artist to another but something more; "an act of sincere religious feeling . . . Manzoni was, for Verdi, a Saint, the only Saint that Verdi in his life had known. To whom if not to him could Verdi confide his religious aspirations, doubts and torments of soul. And I would say that in dedicating and offering the Mass to Manzoni, Verdi confessed to him. And in accordance with his own very jealous modesty, he confessed to him in music and Latin."

There is much with which to agree in that view, but I think Pizzetti pushes it too far. He seems to make of Verdi not only a man who was sensitive to religious feelings, either in himself or in others, but also one who subscribed to a particular belief, Christianity. And with that I disagree: the evidence, including the *Requiem* itself, is against it.

True, Verdi wrote to Maffei after his first visit with Manzoni: "What can I say? How to describe the extraordinary, indefinable sensation the presence of the saint, as you call him, produced in me. I would have gone down on my knees before him if we were allowed to worship men. They say it is wrong to do so, and it may be, although we raise up on altars many that have neither the talent nor the virtue of Manzoni and indeed are rascals."[13] But he did not adopt the word "saint" as a usual description of Manzoni, either to Maffei or to others. Following Manzoni's death, for example, in writing to Giulio Ricordi, he referred to Manzoni as "nostro Grande" (our Great One),[14] and in a letter to Maffei, as "the purest, holiest, highest of our glories"[15] and, in a later letter to her, as "Our Saint."[16] But the last, I suspect, is merely his adoption, in writing to her, of her phrase. For in his letter to the mayor of Milan about his proposal to honor Manzoni he does not mention any specific religious quality other than "virtue," and he three times avoids the word "saint" where it might have occurred naturally.

I do not deserve any thanks from you or the city authorities for the offer to write a funeral mass for the anniversary of Manzoni. It is an impulse, or better said, a heartfelt need that drives me to honor, as best I can, this Great Man [*questo Grande*, not *Santo*] whom I have valued so much as a writer and venerated as a man [*uomo*, not *santo*], a model of virtue and of patriotism. —When the work on the music is well along, I will not fail to tell you what we will need to make the performance worthy of our country and the man [*uomo*, not *santo*] whose death has deprived us all.[17]

In this letter which, considering the authorities to whom it was addressed, was almost a public statement of his feelings about Manzoni, I think Verdi chose his words with care: no reference to Christian belief, but "this Great Man whom I have valued so much as a writer and venerated as a man, a model of virtue and of patriotism."

*   *   *   *   *   *

In choosing a way to honor Manzoni, man and artist, Verdi need not have decided on a requiem mass. There were obvious alternatives. He might have returned to one of the tragedies, in whole or part, or made use of Manzoni's poetry. There were, for instance, the five *Inni Sacri (Sacred Hymns)*. Four of these recount events underlying the great festivals of the Church: "Il Natale" (Christmas), "La Passione" (Passiontide), "La Risurrezione" (Easter), and "Il Pentecoste" (Whitsuntide); the fifth, "In Nome di Maria," dedicated to the Madonna, tells of the Annunciation of the Virgin Birth to an obscure woman in Nazareth and of her rise to become the Queen of Heaven and the comfort of the poor and humble. Any of the five could have furnished the text for a dramatic cantata, and if Verdi had wished to cut and combine them, he might have created an Italian equivalent of Handel's *Messiah*.[18]

Yet he preferred the Latin mass to Manzoni's own words, and though he nowhere disclosed his reasons, I think they are clear. In 1817 Cherubini's *Requiem Mass in C minor*, commissioned by the French government, was performed in Saint Denis, Paris, on the twenty-fourth anniversary of the death of Louis XVI, and repeated there three years later for the funeral of the Duc de Berri, who had been assassinated. In 1837 Berlioz's *Grande Messe des Morts*, also commissioned by the government, was performed at Les Invalides as part of a public service to commemorate General Damrémont and the French soldiers who had died in the taking of Algiers. For Verdi, Paris was the capital of the music world, and there, by mid-nineteenth century, a requiem mass had become the notable way for a musician to mark a national bereavement. He could do no less for Manzoni.

Further, he already had part of a mass composed. Five years earlier, following Rossini's death, he had proposed that he and twelve other Italian composers each prepare a part of a requiem mass to be performed in the Church of San Petronio, Bologna, which Verdi considered to be Rossini's "true musical home."[19] The occasion would have marked the first anniversary of Rossini's death, and out of respect for their deceased colleague Verdi had suggested that the composers and performers underwrite the performance by contributing their fees and, if necessary, something more. He wanted no one who was "a stranger to the art" to have a hand in the musicians' homage.[20] The project failed. Though the composers completed their parts, the administrative committee proved inept and not every musician was as enthusiastic as Verdi; at the end of a year he was left with a chafed spirit and the music for the part of the mass assigned to him, the closing "Libera me." Four years passed, and on 22 May 1873 Manzoni died, the only other Italian Verdi ranked with Rossini as "a glory of Italy."[21] This time Verdi acted alone, and, in deciding how to honor Manzoni, probably more important to him than the draft of the "Libera me" was the thinking he had invested in the meaning of the mass. It was his habit in composing an opera to memorize the libretto first

Title page, first French edition (1874) of the *Requiem*. Colors, besides white and black, are beige, red, and gold. Reproduced at about two-thirds full size.

and then to rehearse it until he felt he had uncovered every nuance of meaning and had settled on his point of view. Evidently, for the mass as a whole, much of that work was done; for in 1871, to an acquaintance who had urged him to finish the "Rossini" mass on his own, he had replied that someday he might, "since with some greater development I would have the 'Requiem' [the introductory section] and 'Dies Irae' [succeeding section] completed, their recapitulation already having been written in the 'Libera.' "[22]

The fact that Verdi had begun the mass with Rossini in mind does not detract from its aptness as a form of homage to Manzoni. For in a significant respect a religious service was more appropriate to the latter. Rossini, though he had composed some sacred works and died within the Church, was not a noted believer, whereas Manzoni, as his life and writing made plain, constantly had turned to religion as a means to understanding life.

Also, the two projects were quite different in concept. The first, as the work of twelve composers, would have had little or no artistic unity and was to be performed only once, to make the first anniversary of Rossini's death a historic occasion. Thereafter the score was to be deposited in the archives of the Liceo Musicale, Bologna, where Rossini had studied and where it would remain as evidence to future generations of the honor in which he had been held. The "Manzoni" mass, on the other hand, as the work of a single composer would aim at artistic unity and be a work not for one occasion but for countless repetitions. From the start Verdi hoped it would be performed all over Europe, and for the most part not in churches but in concert halls. To follow immediately after the premiere in the Church of San Marco, Milan, he scheduled three performances at La Scala and then six at the Opéra-Comique in Paris. The next year, the mass having proved a masterpiece, he took it on tour, with himself conducting, for seven more performances in Paris, this time at the Théâtre-Italien, four performances in London at Albert Hall, and four in Vienna at the Hofoperntheater. With himself as composer and conductor his gesture to Manzoni was unmistakably personal—and extraordinarily effective. Verdi succeeded (and still does) in bringing Manzoni's name to the attention of millions.

The text of the requiem mass that Verdi undertook to set is a strange mixture of prayers and responses, some of them stretching back hundreds of years, but the collection never had been fixed, and over the centuries the mass, or burial rites that preceded it, had radically changed its tone. In the years of persecution under pagan emperors the Christians at Rome had buried their dead secretly in the catacombs beneath the city, and their prayers incised on the walls or tombs are essentially happy. Death for them was neither terrifying nor final, but an occasion for rejoicing, a passage to a better life that would be more true and meaningful because they were now with God.

When the persecutions ceased, under the policies of Emperor Constantine (288?–337), secret burial no longer was necessary, and there was a gradual shift to cemeteries. Now a priest always was present at a funeral or memorial services, and typically psalms and prayers were recited and sung. According to St. Jerome (c.347–420), Alec Robertson reports in his book *Requiem, Music of Mourning and Consolation,* the psalms most often chosen for singing were those with an "Alleluia" refrain, the Church's characteristic expression of joy.

Apparently, throughout its first millennium the Church slowly evolved a service for burial or memorial that continued to be essentially joyful in outlook, but by 1485, presumably in response to several centuries of increasing popular pressure, it had allowed into its prayer books as part of the service the thirteenth-century poem, "Dies Irae," which strongly emphasizes the Last Judgment as a day of terror. The poem, probably written by a Franciscan monk, was not originally intended for liturgical use, for in place of a communal voice it uses the first person singular, outspokenly so, and it also is quite *un*happy in its view of death and resurrection. For both these reasons— the sudden injection of an individual's voice and the emphasis on hell and damnation—the poem fits awkwardly into the service. Nevertheless, as hundreds of murals in Italian churches and burial grounds attest, its images and ideas were extremely popular; and probably also about the thirteenth century, or earlier, the predominant color at funerals and memorial services in Italy changed from white to black. But today, as Robertson points out, the Church would like to shift the color and emphasis back to that of the earlier period. In *The Liturgy Constitution* promulgated by Pope Paul VI at the second session of the Vatican Council (1963), a section on burial rites deprecated "the natural gloom of mourning that has tended to stifle at times the joyful hope of resurrection which belonged originally to the funeral rites of the Church" and expressed the hope that the white of Easter would replace the black of mourning, and a chant of *Alleluia,* the "Dies Irae." As a result, by Church decree, since 1969 the "Dies Irae" may be omitted from masses for the dead.

As this bit of history suggests, the requiem's text, by the time it reached the nineteenth century, was a jumble of responses and prayers—the soft whisperings of the "Requiem" and "Kyrie Eleison," the violent images of the "Dies Irae" and "Libera me," the pleadings of the "Domine Jesu" and "Agnus Dei," the shout of joy in the "Sanctus," and the serenity of the "Lux aeterna." Even excluding the closing "Libera me," which apparently was optional, the text was ambiguous enough to allow musicians, by emphasizing this or that part or individual lines, to create a mass that was primarily joyful or lamenting, majestic or simple, reflective or apocalyptic. Verdi, being a man of the theatre, chose to make it a drama.

In several respects his approach to the text was quite original. Though he was not the first musician lacking a personal belief in God to compose a requiem mass—Berlioz, for one, anticipated him—he was the first of any consequence to compose one primarily for concert halls and consequently without a role for an officiating priest. All the great funeral masses preceding his, notably those of Berlioz, Cherubini, and Mozart, were intended, at least at first, to be part of a church service, and between the sections of music the priest had lines to recite or intone and duties to perform. This was also how Verdi's mass had its premiere, in the Church of San Marco, Milan, at a service commemorating the first anniversary of Manzoni's death. Immediately thereafter, however, it moved to La Scala, where it was presented as a religious work literally and figuratively outside the Church. Plainly Verdi from the start had conceived it as a musical entity, with no role for a priest; and that concept, hardly noticed today, was then revolutionary, for it allowed him to treat the sung portions of the mass as an uninterrupted whole, greatly increasing the chance to make of them a continuous drama.

He also broke with tradition in deciding to use four soloists in addition to the usual chorus. Cherubini had no soloists, and Berlioz, only a tenor for part of the "Sanctus." But Berlioz had kept the voice impersonal, even authorizing its line to be sung by ten tenors in unison; and he seldom permitted it more than a phrase or two before the chorus responded, usually at great length. Mozart had four soloists but, as was customary at the time in church music, he employed them as a quartet. Though he gave each an occasional solo line, they remained quite unindividualized and never sang with or against the chorus. But Verdi used his four as true soloists, assigning to each long stretches of unbroken music, so that the singers become individuals: not merely a soprano or tenor voice, but *the* soprano, *the* tenor. Partly because of this he would be accused of introducing opera into the mass; certainly the soloists, like the omission of the priest, increased the drama.

Verdi used the same basic text as Berlioz, Cherubini, and Mozart, except that where they all ended with the "Lux aeterna" (sometimes treated as the closing section of the preceding "Agnus Dei"), he concluded with the optional "Libera me." Like the "Dies Irae," it had entered the mass about the fourteenth century, speaks in the first person singular, and projects violent images of the Last Judgment: "Free me, Lord, from eternal death on that terrifying day when the heavens and earth are shattered; when you will come to judge the age with fire. I tremble and am afraid at the judgment that will have come and the wrath to follow, when the heavens and earth are shattered."

Surely, to end in this vein, with a terrified reference to the Last Judgment and a plea for personal salvation, makes a very different mass from one that ends with the "Lux aeterna," requesting peace for others: "Let eternal light shine on them, Lord, with your saints in eternity, because you are kind. Give them eternal peace, Lord, and let perpetual light shine on them."

Verdi, however, changed the usual emphasis still more by the way he treated the preceding sections, and one way to grasp the extent of his changes, even before the powerful effects of his music are added, is to compare the text as he rearranged it with the more straightforward text set by Mozart. In Appendix B, Verdi's text is set out, with those lines he either repeated, inserted, or added to Mozart's text underlined; those words he emphasized by a musical climax or by frequent repetition are set in capital letters. Though such a schematic way of making the point cannot be exact, it does reveal how he stressed the line "Dies irae, dies illa," bringing it back again and again, and how, as if in answer to its threat and terror, he emphasized by repetitions of the phrases "Salva me" and "Libera me" the personal plea of an individual who after death faces judgment.

Grammatically that individual is the poet who wrote the "Dies Irae," though of course in writing the poem he meant to speak for us all, dead and living, because in his view of the Last Judgment all who ever have drawn breath, however briefly, must face their Creator and be judged. Thus, anyone reciting or singing the poem while alive is pleading for his own salvation on Judgment Day. Verdi, by emphasizing the poem and the pleas for personal salvation, shifts the focus of the mass from the dead—Give them peace, O Lord—to the living, who, in praying for the dead, become fearful for their own salvation. That shift is the stuff of drama: On that day of wrath, how will I fare?

Pizzetti, in his Preface to the Facsimile Edition of the score, points out that in Verdi's hands the mass becomes a musical account of the Last Judgment, arousing in us the same turbulence of emotion as does the *Last Judgment* of Michelangelo in the Sistine Chapel. Verdi's depiction, of course, attempts to reveal the essence of the emotions in a more general way than Michelangelo, who has visualized for us details of the event; but for Pizzetti there is, nevertheless, "a representation" that is almost a picture, and as an example he offers the beginning of the mass, from the opening notes of the *Requiem* section to the beginning of its second verse "Te decet hymnus."

In those first sixteen measures of A minor, with that "requiem" murmured by an invisible assembly across the slow undulation of a few basic chords, you sense at once the fear and sadness of the crowd before the mystery of death [. . . .] At the "lux perpetua" in A major, when for a moment the song flies free on that F sharp before it folds back upon itself, you sense the yearning of that crowd for consolation and for eternal peace [. . . .] I do not say that you ought to see a particular landscape and a specific crowd, but you *do see* at first a thick darkness and then a clear and gentle light—in the darkness, human beings bowed down by grief and fear; in the light, a stretching forth of their arms toward heaven, an invoking of mercy and pardon—so that the music, in sum, more than simply lyric expression, is the representation of sadness and hope [. . .][23]

The description is excellent, catching exactly the spirit and change of mood. And I like equally what he says of the joyful "Sanctus," the section in the drama of maximum confidence and hope: "the wide extensive sound of the voices, the pure diatonic fabric of the harmony, and the airy lightness of the orchestral texture create a representation of an immense celestial universe irradiated by the light of dawn. . . ."

But with his analysis of what follows the "Sanctus" I am less happy. His language becomes fuzzy, and he begins to ascribe to Verdi a Christian view of God, appropriate enough to Manzoni, but not to Verdi. He assumes that Verdi believes in a God who "is infinitely good and merciful" and that faced with eternal death Verdi expresses in his mass "timore, non paura" (awe, not fear) and gives voice "to cries of grief, but not to shouts of terror or horror."

That posits for the mass a more serene view of death, God, and judgment than I think is justified, but it is supported by several distinguished scholars. Alfred Einstein, in his *Mozart*, in comparing Mozart and Verdi's *Requiem*, states that both works display "the same trusting and childlike fearlessness before God," and goes on to say that in Mozart's mass "death is not a terrible vision but a friend." He concludes with the ringing assertion that along with Schubert "only one later composer was able to soar to the height of this conception: Giuseppe Verdi, in the *Requiem* for Alessandro Manzoni." And more recently Edward Downes, who has done a fine translation of a collection of Verdi's letters, in his program notes for a performance of the *Requiem* by the New York Philharmonic in 1980, advised the audience, "In the second half of the Mass the dominant mood changes gradually from grief and terror to confidence in the salvation to be granted by the Lord. This culminates in the grandiose fugue on the theme 'Libera me.' "

Culminates in confidence? Death a friend? These opinions, to my mind, ignore the fact that after the joy of the "Sanctus" and the serenity of the "Lux aeterna" the lines of the "Dies Irae" repeated in the "Libera me" return in all their fury; that the mass ends recapitulating music from the opening section of the "Requiem and Kyrie eleison," so that we are taken back to Pizzetti's scene of pleading—with the Lord's response still uncertain; and that the mass's final words, frequently repeated in the last bars, are "libera me," their individuality highlighted in shuddering tones by a solo soprano. For Verdi, the nonbeliever, there was no certainty such as for Manzoni.

Despite his admiration for Manzoni as an artist, a patriot, and a man of

Manzoni at age 85, the last photograph. Courtesy of Casa del Manzoni, Milan.

extraordinary rectitude, Verdi did not follow him into Christian belief. What that belief was like for Manzoni is illustrated by one of the crucial scenes of *I Promessi Sposi:* the conversion of the Innominato, which not only reflects, probably directly, Manzoni's feelings upon his own conversion, which he would never discuss, but also provides a context against which we can measure what we know of Verdi.

In the novel the great nobleman has Lucia in his custody and has promised to hand her over to Don Rodrigo for rape and possibly death, but he hesitates. He has begun to find his crimes repugnant, and he thinks back on his life:

Back, back he went, from year to year, from feud to feud, from murder to murder, from crime to crime: each reappeared to his new and aware mind, separated from the feelings that had made him will and do it, so that each reappeared in all its monstrousness which those earlier feelings had prevented him from seeing. They were his, all his: they were himself.

So far, no doubt, Verdi would agree. A man is the sum of his deeds and can be judged by them.

Then the Innominato, hearing church bells in the valley, on impulse visits the Cardinal, who, recognizing the state of the man's soul, tells him, "God has touched your heart, and wants to make you His."

"God! God! God!" cries the nobleman. "If only I could see Him! If only I could feel Him! Where is this God?"

So far again, perhaps, Verdi could agree, though to all of his wife's arguments about the existence of God he replied, "You're all mad!"[24] Still, in Pizzetti's "crowd" Verdi could be standing in that darkness, stretching his arms toward heaven, questioning.

But the response the Cardinal was able to draw from the Innominato, no one ever drew from Verdi: "God truly great! God truly good! I know myself now, I understand who I am; my crimes stand before me; I have a horror of myself; and yet! . . . and yet I feel a relief, a joy, yes, a joy such as I have never felt in all this loathsome life of mine!"

Manzoni had known that joy; it informed his life. For him, in the words of S. B. Chandler, "A right relationship with God produces true self-knowledge as a prelude to a right relationship with one's fellow men." Verdi had never known that joy. In all his letters he never mentions it, or anything like it, nor does it appear in any record of his conversation. For him, the premise that God exists was false, or at least unproven. Possibly he thought it an illusion. To those he knew best he sometimes expressed the truth as he saw it. When his friend and Clarina Maffei's lifetime companion, Carlo Tenca, died in 1883, a decade after the *Requiem*, Verdi wrote to her:

There are no words that can bring comfort to this sort of misfortune. And I will not say to you the one stupid word "courage": a word that has always aroused my anger when directed at me. It needs something quite different! You will find comfort only in the strength of your spirit and the firmness of your mind [. . . .]

   The years are beginning to be too heavy and I think . . . I think that life is a stupid thing and, worse still, useless. What do we do? What have we done? What shall we do? Summing it up, the answer is humiliating and very sad: NOTHING![25]

   At the time of the *Requiem*, however, he was not yet so gloomy, and in his wife's words he was "happy not believing in anything, and simply keeping strictly to all the precepts of an austere morality."[26] He was religious in the sense of giving thought to the mysteries of life and death and in acknowledging standards of good and evil beyond expediency. He was willing to contemplate the possibility of a God, but not convinced that one existed, or if by chance one did, that this God would receive kindly those who turned to him. Thus, though in a sense religious, he was not a Christian, and in his funeral mass for Manzoni he did not pretend a belief he did not have. His mass opens in A minor with the chorus's *sotto voce* "requiem" and at the seventeenth bar, to introduce the idea of "perpetual light," shifts to A major. In closing there is a corresponding shift from C minor to C major, a figurative ray of light in the darkness, though now the words do not shift. The solo soprano and chorus continue to the end to plead, "libera me." There is no happy resolution, no sunny Amen. Though the singers, and by extension the audience, are terrified by their sense of sin and their vision of a judgment, they are not sure that their appeal for mercy and salvation will be granted, or even heard.

   This theme of the nonbeliever's not knowing, or of the believer's failure to find a response in God, turns up in several of Verdi's works, though seldom so explicitly as here. Both *Giovanna d'Arco* and *I masnadieri* touch on it, but it can be seen more clearly, I think, in the aria "Tu puniscimi" from *Luisa Miller*. Luisa, blackmailed by threats to her father's life, is forced to write to her betrothed that she is about to flee with another man whom she loves more. In the midst of writing the letter she prays to the Lord, saying that in the past when she offended Him, if He punished her she was content. But now let Him not abandon her when she is being forced to save her father by her own dishonor. What is interesting about the aria is what Verdi, not his librettist, chose to emphasize: the single line "non lasciarmi in abbandono" (Do not leave me abandoned). Verdi repeats it so often that it becomes almost the entire aria, and he keeps on repeating it right to the end, where he has Luisa's phrases veer toward panic and hysteria. Evidently what struck his imagination in the situation was not the girl's spirit or self-pity but her terror in finding the God in whom she believed suddenly unresponsive.

   Similarly in 1896, when Verdi was thinking of composing a *Te Deum*, he wrote to Giovanni Tebaldini, a musicologist and composer, about the text:

I know some ancient *Te Deums* and have heard a few modern ones, and leaving aside the musical quality, I am not convinced by the way in which this canticle has been interpreted. It is usually sung on great, solemn, noisy feast days, or on the occasion of victories or coronations, etc. The opening words are therefore suitable: Heaven and Earth cry aloud . . . *"Sanctus Sanctus Deus Sabaoth"*; but toward the middle there is a change of colour and expression . . . *Tu ad liberandum* . . . it is Christ, born of the Virgin Mary, who opens the *Regnum coelorum* to man. Man believes in the *Judex venturus* . . . and invokes him . . . *Salvum fac* . . . and ends in a prayer: *Dignare in die isto* . . . moving, gloomy and sad to the point of terror! None of this has anything to do with victories and coronations.[27]

His analysis of the *Te Deum* might be summed up: Man starts in confidence, believes in the Judge who is to come, invokes him, pleads for salvation, loses confidence, and ends in prayer, moving, gloomy, and sad to the point of terror—because in the end God's response is uncertain. This view Verdi expressed musically in the work's key structure, associating the key of E flat major with heaven and salvation yet constantly disturbing it. As one scholar has summarized the ending: "The final E major itself is destabilized by emphasized C naturals, which appear where the text refers to human sin and eternal damnation. These C naturals tend to pull away from the tonic toward the subdominant, A minor, even in the final bars. Thus, Verdi's music in a very specific way articulates the domination of fear over hope."[28]

Two years after composing the *Te Deum* Verdi explained to Giuseppe Depanis and Toscanini, who were arranging for its Italian premiere in Turin, how the final bars should go. Depanis later wrote:

Toward the end of the choral *Te Deum*, a single soprano voice suddenly cries out for mercy. This solo of very few bars in a piece that is essentially choral arouses a certain surprise. To enhance its effect Verdi recommended that the singer be placed as far away as possible, hidden from the audience, almost a voice from beyond, a voice of awe and supplication. "It is the voice of humanity in fear of hell," he said to explain the idea more graphically, stressing in the French manner the ü of *umanità* and *paura*.[29]

Pizzetti, summarizing in his Preface his views of Verdi's religious ideas in the *Requiem*, suggests: "The *Messa da Requiem* expresses Verdi's awe when confronted with the mystery of Death and of the Eternal: but awe [*timore*], note, not fear [*paura*]: he has pages that we can call tremendous, but never terrifying; he has phrases of sadness and pain, and perhaps cries of grief, but never shouts of fear and horror. Even when Verdi thought of God and of eternity, or still more of death, I do not believe that he ever saw at his feet the abyss of hell [. . .]"

Verdi, I suspect, would shake his head over Pizzetti's desire to soften what may be the fate of many of us. In explaining his *Te Deum* Verdi saw hell as real, and to describe humanity's fear of it used the very word, *paura*, that Pizzetti denied to the *Requiem*. Verdi was logical. If for believers there is to be a judgment of some sort followed by a heaven for some, then there must be a hell for the others, a hell worth fearing. Similarly for nonbelievers, after death there may be nothing, or something. There is always, after all, the possibility that the nonbelievers are mistaken in their view, and then on the judgment day, so unexpected, where will they stand? To whom can they turn for support? Verdi had the courage to peer into the unknown, and to be afraid. The *Requiem* is his account of what he saw.

We know now, of course, that Manzoni, approaching death, had doubts about his reception by God, asking "What will happen to me?" and it is intriguing to think that perhaps Verdi knew of these doubts and designed the *Requiem* to reflect them. But I do not suggest it. Verdi was not present to hear the doubts expressed and, I am sure, was never told of them, or there would be references to them in his, Strepponi's, and Maffei's letters. His admiration for Manzoni was for the outward, visible life that had been part of Italian art and history for fifty years.

Today, if the decline of interest in Manzoni's work is a gauge, many persons find his ideas old-fashioned, in particular his Christian belief. Conversely, many seem to find Verdi's agnosticism and fear contemporary, which may be a reason why his requiem mass, in the years following World War II, has had so many more performances than those of more orthodox composers. Verdi himself, probably, would not view his ideas as being ahead of his time, or Manzoni's behind ours, seeing in them merely the proper expression of two quite different personalities. On this point, perhaps the wisest comment came from Verdi's wife:

They have all talked so much of the more, or less, religious spirit of this sacred music, of not having followed the style of Mozart, of Cherubini, etc. etc. I say that a man like Verdi must write like Verdi, that is according to how he feels and interprets the texts. And if the religions themselves have a beginning, a development, some modifications or transformations etc. according to the times and peoples, evidently the religious spirit and works that express it must carry the stamp of their time and (if you agree) of an individual personality. I'd have simply rejected a *Mass* by Verdi that had been modeled on A, B, or C!![30]

But not everyone was as perceptive as Strepponi, and even she was not consistent in her interpretation of the mass. When her friend Cesare Vigna wrote to her that the *Requiem* had been for him "a revelation" in the "word's genuine, biblical sense,"[31] she replied, equally enthusiastic and forgetting what she knew of Verdi's views, that it was "truly an emanation of the Divine

Spirit [. . .]" and "in order to discuss it worthily one must raise oneself nearer to the Throne of God [. . .]"[32]

Musical works, because less tangible and specific than those of other arts, are possibly more open to conflicting interpretation, and ever since the premiere of the *Requiem* some in the audience and some on the stage have heard in it and sung into it what they wished it to mean rather than what the composer intended. But Verdi intended something quite specific, for that was his way; he did not compose any major work just for sound and emotion, but for sound, emotion, and ideas. When Manzoni's works, particularly *I Promessi Sposi*, were widely read, his Christian belief was public knowledge, and by contrast Verdi's atheism, or at most his slight faith, was thrown into relief. Then, I suspect, it was more difficult to mistake his intent, for at every performance of the mass his name and Manzoni's were juxtaposed, in large type, forcing audiences and performers to think, if only for a moment, about the implications of the two names. But today, with the gradual obscuring of the connection between the two men and the decline of interest outside Italy in Manzoni's works, the vivid contrast of their religious views also is obscured, and performances that treat the *Requiem* as a mass that offers peace for the dead and assurance for the living seem increasingly common. Alas. Possibly a way to avoid that misinterpretation, for audiences and performers alike, is to keep bright in mind the contrast between Manzoni's view of death, judgment, and salvation and Verdi's. Both are known and need only be recalled for Verdi's statement with the mass to become clear.

LITERARY
ASPECTS

3

FRANZ WERFEL
AND THE
"VERDI RENAISSANCE"

There's a barrel-organ carolling across a golden street
  In the City as the sun sinks low;
And the music's not immortal. . . .

Verdi, Verdi, when you wrote Il Trovatore *did you dream*
  Of the City when the sun sinks low,
Of the organ and the monkey and the many-coloured stream
On the Piccadilly pavement, of the myriad eyes that seem
To be litten for a moment with a wild Italian gleam
As A che la morte *parodies the world's eternal theme*
  And pulses with the sunset-glow.

There's a barrel-organ carolling across a golden street
  In the City as the sun sinks low;
Though the music's only Verdi. . . .

—*Alfred Noyes, "The Barrel-Organ," 1902*

Today, when any one of Verdi's twenty-six operas (not counting revisions) is likely to be performed, and at least half are acknowledged to be excellent works, it is hard to imagine a time when only *Otello, Falstaff,* and possibly *Aida* were considered to be of any musical worth, and even *Rigoletto, Il trovatore*, and *La traviata* were left to provincial theatres and barrel organs as "only Verdi." As for such operas as *Macbeth, Simon Boccanegra, La forza del destino*, and *Don Carlos*, they existed only in the memory of the very old or on occasion in a program note as the source of a recitalist's aria.

The nadir of this eclipse was roughly 1900 to 1920, but the decline in esteem and popularity began earlier, about 1880, twenty-one years before Verdi died, and must have been hard for him to endure. No artist, however great his success in the past, enjoys going out of fashion, and though Verdi remained until his death in 1901 an immensely popular figure in Italy, he could see that *Otello* (1887), despite its triumph in every operatic capital of the world, did not reach the smaller theatres and popular audiences to the same extent as *Rigoletto, Trovatore*, and *Traviata*. And the same was even more true of *Falstaff* (1893), which for all its acclaim among musicians, early showed signs in its diminishing box-office receipts of becoming a connoisseur's opera, more admired than performed.[1] Verdi's dignity in the face of this decline was exemplary. In his letters there is not a word of personal complaint, of being deserted by the public, only much wise and sometimes angry talk of the general problems of Italian opera: poor administration in the theatres, low standards of performance, dwindling audiences, and overcomplication of the operatic form, to which he himself had contributed. His last two operas, and even their predecessor *Aida*, were beyond the capabilities of most small companies in what they required of spectacle, voice, and orchestral playing.

Behind these problems of the theatres and decreasing audiences lay a number of reasons, for some of which there were no easy solutions. In Europe the years 1870–1900 were a time of increasing industrialization during which material output jumped far ahead of demand, causing a decline in prices, profits, and investment yields, so that the period became known as "The Great Depression." In Italy the money for opera, whether contributed by state, city, or individual, decreased, while opera, because of more complicated and grander productions, grew more expensive. As a result, theatres in Venice, Bologna, Genoa, Florence, Rome, and Naples began to reduce their seasons or, in some cases, to close. Even La Scala in Milan, the country's richest and most industrial city, finally canceled its season for 1897–98 while the management struggled to adjust its finances.

Then, too, as the Risorgimento drew to an end with the country's unification largely achieved in 1860 and Rome proclaimed its capital in 1871, the position of the opera house at the center of Italian life began to crumble. Cities that had been seats of independent government—Turin, Milan, Venice, Parma, Florence, Naples, Palermo—now became provincial capitals, and their theatres, no longer supported by local courts and aristocracy, dwindled in importance. Only La Scala, and to some extent the Teatro Regio in Turin, the country's second industrial city, managed to retain a semblance of their former excellence and splendor.

With the country's unification and independence came a steady rise in literacy and a great increase in the use of Italian as the national language. Before then, when the mass of people had spoken a multitude of dialects and their leaders—the kings, dukes, popes and their courts—had spoken French, German, or Latin, music had a good claim to be the national language. People of all classes went to the opera, partly because in the opera house they felt themselves a community, a nation. With the gradual achievement of linguistic as well as political and social unity, the importance of music as a unifying force declined, and with it the importance of opera. About such developments there was nothing a musician could do.

Then, too, in the more limited world of music opera suffered from the rising interest in symphonic and chamber works, areas in which the Germans and Austrians were supreme. Even in Italy, where the art of sung drama had originated and flowered, a strong movement started about 1875 favoring instrumental over vocal music.[2] After the turn of the century the trend became virulent as a group of composers born in the 1880s, hence known as *La generazione dell' 80*, even went so far as to condemn vocal music and demand a ban on all those composers who had devoted themselves exclusively to opera.

Finally, in most of the larger opera houses Verdi and his works were eclipsed by the rising interest in Wagner. Though both men were born in the same year, 1813, Verdi had achieved international success with *Ernani* in the late 1840s, and cemented it with *Rigoletto, Trovatore*, and *Traviata* in the early 1850s. For Wagner recognition came more slowly and almost a generation later, starting in Germany with *Lohengrin* and *Tannhäuser* in the 1850s and becoming international only with the premiere of the *Ring* at the opening of Bayreuth in 1876. Then followed *Parsifal* in 1882, and the next year, with his fame still increasing, Wagner died. His life had not been easy, but in one respect, perhaps, it was easier than Verdi's: he died without having to face the possibility that he had lived too long and become, artistically speaking, a relic of the past.

As the world's educated musicians and music lovers turned their attention to Wagner and were overwhelmed by his music and theories, they seemed to lose any sense of what was admirable in Verdi. This was just as true in Italy as elsewhere. Looking back on this period from the vantage of 1968, Massimo Mila, one of Italy's outstanding critics, observed, "Italian cultural 'highbrows' of the time were ever more inclined to align themselves with the scornful opinions of Verdi's youthful works that dominated French and German musical circles. The delicate ears of D'Annunzio's Italy were wounded by the brutality of such swift and straightforward masterworks as *Rigoletto* and *Traviata*. . . . Today cultured Italians do not like to be reminded of this repudiation of Verdi's most popular works. When it is discussed, there is always someone who, as if to deny responsibility, feigns amazement: 'Verdi? But whoever doubted his greatness?' "[3]

The answer is, almost everyone whose opinion counted for anything. Not the ordinary public who continued to fill the opera house to hear the few works of Verdi that were presented, but the academicians, the newspaper critics, and the educated amateurs who from their positions on committees and boards of directors had some control over what was performed. The English scholar and critic, Francis Toye, also looking back, but from 1930, in particular pointed to "the amateurs of superior musical culture" who "appeared to think a liking for Verdi slightly incompatible with their reputation for good taste. There was no merit to be gained by professing admiration for a composer whose music could be enjoyed by anybody gifted with any musical receptivity whatever. Moreover, quite apart from snobbishness, conscious or unconscious, Verdi's shortcomings as a musician were calculated to antagonize such people, just as his virtues were not of a kind to attract them. About Verdi as a man they knew nothing and cared less." In England when Toye was young, 1900–14, *Traviata* and *Rigoletto* regularly were condemned for their "guitar-like orchestration," *Trovatore* was dismissed as "absurd," and *Aida* was said to be "flashy" or "empty."[4]

In the United States the attitude was much the same. The music world, including the conservatories, was dominated by visiting or immigrant Germans, and their interest focused almost entirely on German music, particularly on Wagner. At the Metropolitan in the years 1884–91 there were three seasons without any Verdi at all, and the few of his operas that were presented, including the first production in the house of *Aida*, were sung in German. The assistant conductor, young Walter Damrosch, later confessed that for the operas assigned to him, chiefly *Trovatore* and several by Meyerbeer, he had "a youthful intolerance" and knew little "of their traditions of tempi and nuance."[5] The only composer he cared to conduct was Wagner, and to satisfy fully his urge he founded his own company in 1895, opening in New York with twenty-one performances, all of Wagner, and then touring for five weeks with a repertory all of Wagner.

This passion for Wagner, and for German music generally, was at its strongest in the conservatories, where students were taught, and apparently believed, that German music was not only better than Italian musically, but also morally. In England, for example, Sir Hubert Parry of Oxford and the Royal College of Music, in his lectures collected as *Style in Musical Art*

(1911), had this to say of Italian musicians and their audiences in the previous century: "But the power of strenuous persistence in climbing up the steep ascent of art to higher things was not for them [the Italians], but for a race [the Germans] whose musical story is the very strongest contrast to theirs, and illustrates the persistent and patient and unweariable devotion to an ideal which was totally different throughout. . . . For though classical music was essentially the sphere of the Italians, even in that they had to give place to the Germans before they had approached the culmination of their own principles. They were easily pleased, and so they were easily passed in the race by those who required something of a higher order to satisfy their sense of responsibility."[6]

Naturally, the smugness and blindness were deepest at the very center of German operatic music of the time: Wahnfried, the Wagner household in Bayreuth. When Wagner's son Siegfried, thirty-four years old and on a visit in 1904 to a conservatory in Prague, was asked what the Wagner family thought of Verdi, he replied, "Such things are not discussed."[7] Some years later when the conductor Bruno Walter was visiting Wahnfried, he dared to mention Verdi to Wagner's widow and remarked on the astonishing development in the operas from *Ernani* to *Aida* and finally to *Falstaff*. "Development?" questioned Cosima. "I can see no difference between *Ernani* and *Falstaff*."[8]

Yet even in this darkest period there were those in every country who, like Walter, thought there was more to Verdi than just a few tunes fit for a barrel organ. In England there was the teacher, translator, and critic Edward J. Dent, one of whose pupils, Francis Toye, would write an important study of Verdi and his works. In Italy there was Toscanini, whose production of *Trovatore* at La Scala in 1902 was a revelation of what the opera could be; yet because at the time he, too, was fascinated by Wagner, and as a young conductor had little influence on general opinion, he struck a spark but did not ignite a fire. At the Metropolitan much the same could be said of Giulio Gatti-Casazza, the general manager from 1908 to 1935. Though in 1918 and 1920 he introduced to the house for the first time *Forza* and *Don Carlos*, not heard in New York since 1880 and 1887, he succeeded only with *Forza*, and *Don Carlos* was dismissed by most critics as a dismal failure: "the bungling libretto . . . the bubbling bosh of the romantic love episodes . . . this stodgy mess."[9]

Then in 1924 began a shift in taste, so sharp, so noticeable, that critics and journalists soon dubbed it "the Verdi Renaissance" and ascribed its impetus chiefly to the Austrian poet, playwright, and novelist Franz Werfel, best remembered today for his play *Jacobowsky and the Colonel* (1944) and his novels *The Forty Days of Musa Dagh* (1933), *Embezzled Heaven* (1940), and *The Song of Bernadette* (1941). But his first European success, widely translated, was *Verdi, a Novel of the Opera,* and to its publication in 1924 the critic Mila assigns "the official beginning" of the renaissance.[10] Werfel, however, promptly did more. Two years later, in conjunction with Paul Stefan, he published (in German) *Verdi, The Man in His Letters,* which included an autobiographical sketch of Verdi's youth published in 1881 as well as his Last Will, hand-written in 1900. The book was the first in a language other than Italian to present a selection of Verdi's writings in chronological order, enabling a reader to form an opinion of his character from his own words. In addition, Werfel included in his extended preface a biographical essay on Verdi that, despite some factual errors, remains today an extraordinarily vivid, spiritual portrait. And again, Werfel did more. Besides giving speeches and publishing articles on Verdi's artistry, when no one else of any stature was doing so, he prepared a German edition, really a version because it proposed a rearrangement of scenes, of *Forza,* which reportedly had not been heard in Germany since 1878. This "Werfel edition" was performed first at Altenberg in November 1925, and then, in a production conducted by Fritz Busch, at Dresden on 20 March 1926, a date which, because of this production's enormous success, is sometimes cited as the start of the renaissance. From Dresden the opera in its new version went at once to Vienna, then to Berlin, Hamburg, Basel, Prague, to the many smaller German houses, and subsequently, in translation, to Sweden, Hungary, Poland, Lithuania, Bulgaria, Slovenia, and Russia. Its progress stimulated an immediate demand for more of Verdi's operas, not only the old favorites but also the obscure and unfamiliar. Werfel made new German translations of *Boccanegra* and *Don Carlos;* the conductor Georg Gohler translated *Luisa Miller* and *Macbeth;* and others translated such hitherto forgotten works as *Nabucco, I due Foscari,* and *I masnadieri.* After the 1927–28 season in Germany, 135 opera houses reported 1,576 performances of Wagner and 1,513 of Verdi; at the Vienna Opera in 1930, of a total of 339 performances 49 were of Wagner and 46 of Verdi; and by the spring of 1933, when Busch left Dresden, he was offering seasons with ten Verdi operas in the repertory. A decade earlier such figures for Verdi would have been incredible.[11]

Clearly the revival burgeoned in part in reaction, not so much against Wagner, for his operas continued to be popular, as against the exclusivity of Wagnerism, the constant insistence by his admirers that his way was the only way. It was also in part a reaction against the complexity of opera orchestration developed by his disciples, such as Richard Strauss and Pfitzner; against the cerebralism of the atonality and serialism that Schönberg and Berg were introducing; and against the sensationalism of some Russian composers such as Prokofiev and even Stravinsky. Audiences and artists evidently were eager

GIUSEPPE VERDI

DIE MACHT DES SCHICKSALS ⑤ ⑤

OPER IN VIER AKTEN

DEM ITALIENISCHEN DES F. M. PIAVE
FREI NACHGEDICHTET
UND FÜR DIE DEUTSCHE OPERNBÜHNE
BEARBEITET

VON

FRANZ WERFEL

VOLLSTÄNDIGER KLAVIERAUSZUG
MIT TEXT . . . . R. M. 12.—

G. RICORDI & Co.
MAILAND - ROM - NEAPEL - PALERMO - PARIS
LONDON - LEIPZIG - BUENOS-AIRES - NEW YORK

Title page of Ricordi's vocal score *(La forza del destino)* "Werfel Edition," published in 1926 for German houses.

for melody, simplicity, clarity, and drama expressed in song, and because no contemporary composer of comparable genius was providing it, they turned back to Verdi.

It is fair to ask how significant in reality was Werfel in the renaissance. Journalists and critics often create figureheads around whom to group ideas or movements, but in this instance, even after the more general reasons are stated and subtracted, because of his books, speeches, and musical editions, the man remains important. In England the critic Neville Cardus concluded that *Verdi, A Novel of the Opera* "helped to put Verdi on the map,"[12] and in France, André Schaeffner cites as an important year in the renaissance, 1933, when the novel first was published in French.[13] In Italy, though Toscanini at La Scala in the years 1921–28 made Verdi his god and revitalized many of the operas, in Mila's opinion the greater influence in making Verdi once again intellectually respectable was Werfel.[14] Similarly Toye, in the preface to his *Giuseppe Verdi, His Life and Works* (1930), gives more weight to the German renaissance than to the Toscanini revivals, though the latter inspired him to begin his study. Yet it was the impact of the German performances, thousands of them in hundreds of theatres, that decided him "to write a long book instead of a comparatively short one."[15]

In the United States the renaissance started more slowly. The novel, translated and published in New York in 1925, did poorly, but the excitement in the German theatres and La Scala led Gatti-Casazza at the Metropolitan to give the house premiere of *Luisa Miller* in 1929 and the United States premiere of *Boccanegra* in 1931. Once again he had a half success; the first, despite Rosa Ponselle, failed, whereas *Boccanegra*, with Lawrence Tibbet, entered the repertory. Also in 1931, Toye's study of Verdi's life and works appeared in an American edition, but despite good reviews stirred little interest; similarly in 1942, an American edition of Werfel's collection of Verdi's letters, though well translated and expanded, had only moderate sales. Nevertheless, both books entered libraries, public and private, from which their influence could spread, and American studies of Verdi became more frequent and knowledgeable. Meanwhile, at the San Francisco Opera *Un ballo in maschera*, *Forza*, and *Otello* had their house premieres in 1931, 1933, and 1934, and continued in the repertory; at Chicago *Otello* joined *Rigoletto*, *Trovatore*, and *Traviata*. The second edition of Toye's book in 1946 aroused more general interest, and in 1950, the renaissance accelerated with Rudolf Bing's first new production of his regime at the Metropolitan, *Don Carlos*. Thereafter, almost in successive years, he presented new productions of thirteen more of the operas, including the Metropolitan premiere of *Macbeth* in 1959, for which two Germans, Carl Ebert and Caspar Neher, served as stage director and designer. And where did that production for the Met-

INHALT

Table of Contents of Ricordi's "Werfel Edition" *(La forza del destino)*. Werfel's proposals for reordering the numbers in Act III are made in footnotes.

ropolitan's first *Macbeth* originate? In the opera's premiere production in Britain, at Glyndebourne in 1938, where it was the joint work of Bing, then general manager of Glyndebourne, and of Ebert, Neher, and Fritz Busch, all four of whom had been young men in Germany at the start of the Verdi renaissance. In fact, Ebert, Neher, and Bing had staged a famous production of *Macbeth* in Berlin in 1931, and the following year, with Fritz Busch conducting, an even more famous one of *Un ballo in maschera*. Though the line of inspiration in every case and every country may not lead back to Germany and to Werfel, in most it does.

Werfel seems always to have liked Verdi's operas, and reportedly even as a boy he sang the arias with passion.[16] Though associated chiefly with Vienna, to which he moved after World War I, he was born in Prague in 1890, and grew up in the Jewish quarter with such fellow artists as Max Brod and Franz Kafka and in a cultural environment that was not Czech but German. Besides writing poetry that began to make a name for him in German circles, he played the piano, developed a tenor voice, and attended opera performances at Prague's German house, where among his friends he soon became notorious for "singing along" with the performers. There was hardly an opera he disliked except those of Wagner, which he professed to abhor, and those he liked best were from Verdi's so-called middle period, *Rigoletto* to *Don Carlos*. The final three, *Aida*, *Otello*, and *Falstaff*, he considered ponderous and inflated, and the low opinion generally held of his favorites irritated him greatly. Years later he told his secretary that he had "felt personally insulted whenever he heard that silly slogan 'organ-grinder's music,' " and that his desire to right the injustice and to engender in others his admiration for Verdi led him to fight for the composer in his own way: with literary weapons.[17]

A novel is an odd way to start an operatic revival, but then, *Verdi, A Novel of the Opera* is itself an unusual work. The idea of it, for example, lay in Werfel's mind for twelve years before he brought it to publication. In 1911, the tenth anniversary of Verdi's death, Werfel had attended a memorial performance in Prague of the *Requiem* (with Tetrazzini and Caruso) and had begun to ponder why between *Aida* in 1871 and *Otello* in 1887 Verdi had not produced a new opera. He had composed the *Requiem* (1874), a string quartet (1876), a "Pater Noster" and "Ave Maria" (1880), and revisions of *Boccanegra* (1881) and *Don Carlos* (1884), but not a new opera. Not in sixteen years. Why?

Today, of course, there are shelves of books and articles on such questions including several huge collections of Verdi's letters. But in 1911 none of these existed, and most of what was available, other than a few critical studies, were popular biographies, clichés dressed as the man, reverent, superficial, unsound. When Werfel, therefore, began to think seriously about his question, the only way an answer could be reached was intuitively. It is one reason, I suspect, why he developed the question as a novel; the documents needed for a conventional, biographical response were too sparse.

In 1913, however, the city of Milan as part of its centenary celebration of Verdi's birth published a 760-page collection of his letters entitled *I Copialettere (The Copybooks)*.[18] The first half of the volume contains a selection of copies and drafts of letters that Verdi had made in five school copybooks from the years 1844 to 1901, and the letters, at least as revealed by those selected, concern chiefly the composition and productions of his operas. The collection does not begin, however, until after the premiere of *Ernani*, the fifth of his twenty-six operas, and is weakened further by several gaps, notably from 1858 to 1867 and from 1875 to 1877. In the book's second half, the Appendix, as well as in an occasional footnote to the letters of the copybooks, the editors present an additional selection of letters from other sources, and these are somewhat more personal, though any remark that conceivably might wound someone still alive was cut. Werfel, when he came to write his novel, plainly knew this entire book almost by heart, so that all its facts and diction were aquiver in his mind. But because its letters chiefly concerned Verdi's public life, leaving concealed for the most part his private thoughts and emotions, the kind of psychological biography that Werfel was attempting still required an extraordinary leap of imagination.

The novel opens in the year 1882. Verdi is at the peak of his fame in Italy, but his inspiration is blocked. His most recent opera, *Aida*, is eleven years old, and he is unable to complete the new one, *King Lear*. He works at it daily, but without confidence, unsettled by the triumph of Wagner, whose music has penetrated everywhere, even into Italy. He does not blame Wagner—he is too honest for that—but he feels oppressed by him. On turning every corner, it seems, there is someone talking of Wagner, in every magazine an article on him, and in every theatre one of his operas. Wagner, he finds, is always on his mind, and he thinks of him as a rival, with anger and with admiration. Perhaps if he called on Wagner, who is in Venice, if he met the man, talked to him as one artist to another, was acknowledged by him as a fellow artist, the block would shatter and inspiration would return.

He goes to Venice, uncertain, proud, lonely, independent, and one night he goes to the Teatro La Fenice—the descriptions of Venice are excellent—where Wagner is conducting a program of his music in a private performance. Verdi, who knows the theatre well, lets himself in by a back entrance and reaches the foyer just as the concert ends. Standing on a step in a shadowed doorway, he sees Wagner coming toward him, surrounded by admirers.

The young men to whom Wagner's words and gestures were addressed were beside themselves. With the wild eyes of fanaticism, the relaxed lips of intoxication, the hissing breath of ecstasy, they drank in his words without understanding them. No, it was not the words they drank, but the mere sound of his voice. They drank in the life of this man, whose vitality was ten times greater in dimension and higher in power, it seemed, than that of any other man.[19]

Wagner stops near Verdi to answer an admirer's question, and for a brief moment, as he casts his eye upward, searching for the right word, the two composers look directly at each other.

Wagner beheld the face of a man whom he did not know, the face of a stranger over whom he had no power, a face firmly closed upon itself and seeking nothing of others. He saw pride and a solitary reserve in the glowing eyes, an effortless energy, which sought to borrow none from him, which stood apart and expressed itself without any secret desire to influence or master other men.

Verdi beheld an eye that was at first questioning, perplexed and searching. But soon the cloud vanished, and from that eye the inborn light flamed out, seeking love, seeking to attract: a stormy, strong, and yet feminine soul, imposing its will, uttering its dumb, self-inspired cry, "Be mine."[20]

Outside the theatre a huge, unnatural moon reigns over Venice, and Verdi calls a gondola. To its soft, rocking motion he thinks of what he has done and seems unable anymore to do:

I shall never write any more.—There must be a kink in my nature somewhere, that it all came to an end in my sixtieth year. Here I am in my seventieth now without four phrases to my credit since. Still, a man must live out his useless days to the last. Suppose I did write and produce a new opera? The press would make some good-natured comments upon "the worthy master of Saint Agatha" and it would go into the repertoire of all the barrel-organs. The sublime European critics would say as they have been saying about me since *Don Carlos* that I am a nice little pocket-Wagner. I nibble at his harmonies! I translate his sublime polyphony into my simple Busseto tongue! Ah, away with it![21]

But he cannot "away with it." A man cannot live with an art for sixty years and then abandon it, any more than he can walk out of his skin, or away from his shadow. The art is now part of him, and Verdi's failure of inspiration is with him daily, nagging. Where once he had only to pursue, seize, and perfect the melodies and drama that boiled in his imagination, now he has to toil, invent, and construct, and the great melodies by such means do not come to birth. "Even when he had tried to use the false invention he could not, it fell useless from his hand. And in such moments, when he remained powerless to bring to being the creations that he willed, when he could *create* nothing, he felt himself good for nothing."[22]

Verdi's personality is examined in a series of subplots and scenes with others than Wagner. There is a young German composer, scornful of the world, neglected by it and dying, who insists that his new system of music will change completely the art's structure and sound; an old, old aristocrat, living only for longevity and opera as it was before Verdi was born, who is as out of touch with the world as the young German composer; an Italian senator, a patriot who had fought with Garibaldi and Mazzini, whose open affection and emotionalism directly expressed embarrass Verdi; a disappointed Italian composer (a historical figure) driven mad with envy of Verdi; an unknown cripple who has the divine gift of Italian song but no way to share it with the world; and a prima donna who, in an otherwise shabby performance of *Forza*, brings her scenes to startling, absorbing life. And then, by chance, Verdi meets Wagner a second time.

They are in the Piazza San Marco, and Wagner, suddenly turning from his companions, walks alone toward Verdi.

A voice in Verdi's soul cried aloud, "Face him now, the moment of encounter has come! Now or never!"

Clearer, more definite, grew that face as it approached, as the compressed mouth, the conqueror's nose, the bright eyes revealed themselves.

He would, he would—but he could not. . . . And once more into these [Wagner's] eyes came the same pleading, demanding feminine look: "Why do you hate me so; why will you not bow down before the truth, the sole truth, that I am, and join in the universal chorus of praise?"[23]

But even though Wagner's shoe gently stubs Verdi's and he says "Excuse me!" Verdi can reply only "Pardon!" and the moment of encounter is missed.

Finally, on the last night of Carnival, in an act of self-reproach and renunciation, Verdi burns the manuscript of *Lear,* all of it—the vocal lines, the orchestration, the entire opera—telling himself it is "a failure, a hotchpotch, no good!"[24] After ten years of work he merely has constructed an opera, not created one; he has been more concerned for the graphic effects of his orchestration than for the flow of melody, and produced only stiff symmetrical phrases with the motifs of finger exercises. Thus he judges himself and his work.

Yet the peace he gains by destroying *Lear* soon passes, and once again restless and unhappy he concludes that for him the remainder of life must be only waiting for death, uncreative. For that he will go home. There is nothing more to keep him in Venice. On what he intends to be his last night in the city, in order to pass the evening neither alone nor with others, he goes to the Teatro Rossini, a second-string house where a small company is presenting

Forza. The music-making is miserable except for the soprano, and in her scenes Verdi is forced to acknowledge great art, not only hers but his. Later that night, with no *Lear* to work on, he opens the vocal score of *Tristan* to compare Wagner's work to his own. He is not familiar with the score, and is surprised to find the music drama so little different from his own operas. Though the vocal line seldom slips into aria, the orchestra more often does, and there are all the old forms of accompaniment, arpeggios, harmonized recitative, and staccato notes. The score, it is true, does not divide into numbers with a full close that might slow the drama, but then in *Aida* he, too, frequently had avoided the full close for just that reason; and the music drama is full of sequences, rising patterns, such as he, too, sometimes used. Altogether, he concludes, the artistry of *Forza* and *Aida* is no less than that of *Tristan,* and as a musician he need not blush before Wagner. With this realization a tremendous sympathy for the other composer sweeps through him. They are brothers. He will call on him in the morning.

After a night of rain the day is bright and fresh, and as Verdi steps into a gondola to go to the Palazzo Vendramin, the noon-hour bells ring their changes. But at the palazzo he learns he is too late; fifteen minutes earlier, Wagner died.

In the novel's closing scenes Verdi's artistic block begins to crumble, and one reason, he forces himself to acknowledge, is the shameful, animal joy of survival, of being able to add to his works when Wagner cannot. But whatever the reasons, he discovers with joy that his confidence is returning. Old melodies surge through his mind, and new ones begin to form around words and images as he begins again to tap his true creative sources. In one of these final scenes, comic yet touching, his friend the Senator has summoned the leading Venetian dignitaries to Verdi's hotel to honor the composer. Meeting in his suite, they discover that he has left an hour earlier for Milan. The Senator, moving to the center of the room, adopts "an oratorical attitude," much to everyone's relief because "they knew the efficacy of a speech in saving a situation in which there was nothing to be done."

The Senator begins to talk, and many readers have felt that in his words he spoke for Werfel.

Fire and self control! Who will measure the victory? Such is Giuseppe Verdi.

The romantic legend of today has created a false picture of the artist's nature: A Beethoven spitting on the wall, the Bohemian, debauched, inconsequent, irresponsible; the oversensitive, nervous, illogical imbecile! What art can be born of such natures? In one word, it is the idolizing of evil; the worship of perversity. . . . It is filled with a fanatical hatred. There is a spirit of evil in men today that impels them to seek each other's injury. In our Maestro there lived such strength as rendered all the allurements of corruption vain! . . . Now, I will tell you why Verdi is a god to me. There is no other man on earth so absolutely free from vanity. I know no living creature who has the power of judging himself so fearlessly and inexorably as he. . . . Had Verdi never written a note he would still have been great. But because he is so great, his melody runs in the veins of all mankind. . . . His choruses! To me they are not the trivial street singer's tunes. . . . No, the virtue and the simplicity of humanity are there out of which all that is good in life flows. Modern art attempts to render the banal complex so that its banality may not appear. But our Maestro has shown the simplicity of the mightiest and most complex things. He is the last of the great Folk-singers, the singer of humanity, a noble anachronism in this century.[25]

The city fathers, confused by the Senator's rhetoric, soon grow bored, and the Senator, perhaps himself confused, abruptly stops. As they leave the building, the crowd gathered outside, not knowing the purpose of the meeting, decides that it must have been to honor a well-known racing celebrity who is at the hotel, and with cheers it shouts the man's name.

Throughout the novel Verdi's artistic need and its resolution are impressively realized, and his personality, in the psychological sense, accurately portrayed. Though Werfel had the operas to study, and also the *Copialettere*, he relied for the most part on his instinctive understanding of Verdi, and the truth of his perception is a remarkable example of spiritual biography achieved primarily through artistic affinity. As history or conventional biography, of course, the novel is mostly false. Verdi did not go to Venice in 1882, never tried to meet Wagner, and was not oppressed by him in this fashion. In the years 1881 to 1883 he was not blocked artistically, for he revised *Boccanegra*, adding considerable new and excellent music, began work on *Otello*, and started revising *Don Carlos*, again adding marvelous new music. Yet, in its way, the "block" is a good symbol of the problem presented to Italian composers by the European triumph of Wagner and his theories: Would they remain true to their tradition of sung drama with the voice and melody predominant, or would they capitulate to Wagner's style? As Verdi in 1884, in a letter published in the *Copialettere*, put the question to a friend:

I have heard people speak well of the composer Puccini. I have seen a letter that speaks nothing but good of him. He follows the modern trends, which is natural, but he keeps close to melody which is neither new or old. But it seems that with him the orchestra predominates: no harm in that. Only in this one must be careful. Opera is opera; symphony is symphony; and I don't think it is a good idea to insert a symphonic piece into an opera just for the pleasure of allowing the orchestra to dance.

I say this by the way, with no importance to it, without even being sure I have made a true statement; but I am sure I have said something contrary to the modern trend. Each age has its own stamp.

History will decide later which age is good, which bad.[26]

The success of Werfel's novel in Europe, where it was both admired and extremely popular, is not surprising; it is the sort of conceptual tale, reminiscent of Thomas Mann's *Death in Venice*, that seems to appeal very much to Europeans, with a story about artistic creation that is less a plot than an argument by antitheses, masculine opposed to feminine, popular to elite, tradition to modernity, opera to music drama, and Verdi to Wagner. Equally, I think, its relative failure in the United States is unsurprising; for here we are not given much to discussions of art in these terms. Most reviewers criticized the novel's mixture of fact and fiction, though most, with none of the good biographies in English yet published, probably knew little about Verdi the man or artist except as revealed in the most popular of his operas. Nevertheless, the novel generally was said to fall "between the stools of critical biography and fiction."[27] One reviewer, however, Edward Goldbeck, touched on what was surely Werfel's chief aim: "Perhaps a little detail will best characterize the intensity of the impression which Verdi [as portrayed in the novel] produced on me. I thought quite spontaneously that I must use every opportunity to hear his music. Werfel never praises this music, never extols it at the expense of Wagner; he only shows Verdi's character, and the result is that I yearn to hear everything Verdi ever wrote."[28]

Even today, sixty years later, Werfel excites that desire in many people. In German-speaking countries his elegant, poetic translations of *Forza* and *Boccanegra* still are used, and his novel, periodically reissued, continues to be read. In English-speaking countries, on the other hand, the work of enduring importance—though I, for one, have found the novel unforgettable—is the collection of Verdi's letters first published in German in 1926 and translated for the American edition of 1942. Where the *Copialettere*, on which Werfel primarily based his collection, exists only in Italian and is a great hodgepodge of a book, difficult to read and use, Werfel's selection from it has a focus, *Verdi, The Man in His Letters*, which he brilliantly summarized in the "portrait" he provided as an introduction. The book is also improved by the letters Werfel and his coeditor Paul Stefan added to those of the *Copialettere*, such as Verdi's note to Giulio Ricordi reminding the publisher that the composer had the right to cancel the premiere of *Otello* even after the dress rehearsal, and another note to Ricordi about his disappointment in the rehearsals.[29] This strengthening of the selection was reinforced further in the American edition, well translated by Edward Downes, with the addition of more than sixty-five letters published for the first time in the 1930s. Reissued in 1970 and again in 1973 with a number of minor errors corrected, this American edition is still, after forty-five years, one of the better collections of Verdi's letters available in English and possibly the best introduction to Verdi the man.

Doubtless Verdi's music sometime again will go out of fashion, perhaps never to return to such full favor as it has enjoyed in the last fifty years. As he said, "Each age has its own stamp. History will decide." But for those who love his works the shadows can never be as deep as they were at the start of this century, for now all the operas are recorded, a critical edition of his works is under way, and his life and thought, through scholarly research, are far better known. A major artist of the nineteenth century has been resurrected and his greatness acknowledged. And for that we owe thanks to the writer who as a boy in Prague sang the arias so passionately and burned with a desire to avenge the slur, "organ-grinder's music."

4

VERDI'S IMITATION OF SHAKESPEARE: *LA FORZA DEL DESTINO*

Verdi's admiration of Shakespeare is too well known to need citation, and of course, in *Macbeth*, *Otello*, and *Falstaff* he fashioned three operas directly from Shakespeare. In addition to these, an argument can be made that *La forza del destino*, although based on a play by the Duke of Rivas, should be considered Verdi's fourth Shakespearean opera, and in some respects the most interesting because the most crucial. For in *Forza*, in the words of his letter of 20 October 1876 to Clarina Maffei, he tried "to invent reality" in Shakespeare's style rather than merely "to copy" a reality already invented by Shakespeare.[1] And just where he tried to invent the most, in the opera's structure, he failed the most, in his own eyes and in those of others. The wounds of that failure, it seems clear, influenced the choice and treatment of *Othello* and *The Merry Wives of Windsor* as the basic texts for *Otello* and *Falstaff*.

*   *   *   *   *   *

To begin with the general before moving toward the particular, *Forza*, consider what was the dominant critical tradition of Shakespeare on the Continent during the first half of the nineteenth century, the tradition within which Verdi read his Shakespeare and formed his ideas about Shakespearean drama.

The great men of this tradition are Lessing (1729–81), Goethe (1749–1832), and A. W. Schlegel (1767–1845). A fourth German, Gervinus (1805–71), continued the tradition into the second half of the century. But because he dealt more with Shakespeare's morality than structure, his work is not pertinent here, and I mention him only to point out that this German tradition of Shakespearean criticism was dominant on the Continent continuously throughout Verdi's life.

What Lessing and Goethe had begun with a crescendo of brilliant criticism, Schlegel brought to a climax with his lectures in Vienna in 1808 (published 1809–11).[2] Starting with Samuel Johnson's courageous but somewhat cautious defense of Shakespeare's mixing of the genres of tragedy and comedy and violating the unities of action, time and place,[3] the three Germans turned that defense into an all-out attack on the rules of French classical drama, particularly as represented and defended by Voltaire. In addition to the criticism, Schlegel, in the years 1825 to 1833, published, with contributions from others, verse translations of the complete plays. These translations, called a "work of genius," established Shakespeare as a leading dramatist in Germany, where for many years his plays were performed more frequently than in England.

For Schlegel, his disciples, colleagues, and admirers, Shakespeare, with his mixing of genres and disregard of the unities, created romantic drama, and with such success that it was self-validating. Or, in Lessing's words, "Every genius is a born critic. He has the proof of all rules within himself."[4]

Listen to what Schlegel says of romantic drama, while holding in mind Shakespeare's chronicle plays, particularly *Henry IV* Parts 1 and 2, *Henry V*, and such characters in the tragedies as the Porter in *Macbeth*, the Fool in *King Lear*, and Osric and the Gravediggers in *Hamlet*. Also bear in mind Verdi's *Forza*.

Schlegel said: "[Romantic drama] delights in indissoluble mixtures; all contrarieties: nature and art, poetry and prose, seriousness and mirth, recollection and anticipation, spirituality and sensuality, terrestrial and celestial, life and death, are by it blended together in the most intimate combinations."[5] This is not a defense of mixing genres—permitted in this or that special case—but a call to do it, to revel in it, mixing "poetry and prose, seriousness and mirth," all "in the most intimate combination."

Here is Schlegel again: "[Romantic drama] embraces at once the whole of the checkered drama of life with all its circumstances; and while it seems only to represent subjects brought accidentally together, it satisfies the unconscious requisitions of fancy, buries us in reflections on the inexpressible signification of the objects which we view blended by order, nearness and distance, light and color, into one harmonious whole; and thus lends, as it were, a soul to the prospect before us."[6]

That paragraph, I think, contains a good description of what Verdi attempted in *Forza:* to put onstage "the whole checkered drama of life with all its circumstances," and through his music and the singers' art to lend, as it were, "a soul to the prospect before us." Doubtless it is pure chance, but Verdi once, in discussing the opera, even used the word "soul"—*anima*. Writing to his friend Vincenzo Luccardi, 17 February 1863, after a performance of the opera at Rome, he lamented: "Certainly, in *La forza del destino* the artists need not know how to sing coloratura, but they must have some soul and understand the *words* and express them."[7]

Schlegel, having thundered against any prejudice or prohibition in mixing the genres, moved on to the unities of time, place, and action, which were, in fact, more invented and defended by the French classical dramatists and their supporting critics than by Aristotle and the Greeks.

Nevertheless, to begin with Aristotle: In his *Poetics*, discussing Sophoclean tragedy, he took as a rule of good structure a unity of action—in other words, a coherence of action. Each step in the drama should develop out of the last and bring the ultimate catastrophe one step closer. Think of how the drama proceeds and tightens in Sophocles's *Oedipus the King* as first Teiresias, then Kreon, Jocasta, the Messenger, and finally the Shepherd are brought on, ending with Oedipus looking up directly into the sun and screaming: "Light, Light, Light, Never again flood these eyes with your white radiance, oh gods, my eyes. All, all the oracles have proven true. . . ."[8] No doubt about it. The structure, through the unity of action, contributes greatly to the play's power.

About the unity of time Aristotle said very little and mostly parenthetically in comparing tragic and epic poetry. Tragedy, he said, "endeavors, as far as possible, to confine itself to a single revolution of the sun, or but slightly to exceed this limit."[9] Dramatists generally have taken this to mean about twenty-four hours, and Schlegel quotes Corneille as setting the limit at thirty.[10] There is argument, of course. Among Greek scholars the strict constructionists say that Aristotle, writing before Copernicus, meant twelve hours or even less. But I can sidestep that skirmish: for my purpose it is enough that dramatists generally have understood the rule to mean "twenty-four hours or thereabouts."[11] Unity of action and of time are therefore much the same, for if the artist abides by one, he is likely to achieve the other—though not necessarily a great or even good play.

About unity of place Aristotle said nothing, though most Greek dramatists observed it, being careful not to have the same, recognizable chorus appear first as people of Athens and then as people of Thebes.

In the seventeenth and eighteenth centuries French dramatists and critics, on the alleged authority of Aristotle, made rules of these unities and, using them as standards, judged Shakespeare to be a sometimes powerful poet with some grand conceptions, but in matters of structure, an ignorant barbarian. Compared with Corneille, Racine, or even Voltaire he was ranked low. It was this tradition that the Germans, as part of the Romantic Movement, turned right around. Schlegel, of course, did not propose that every playwright should always ignore the unities; he argued merely that the unities should not be the standards for judging a romantic dramatist's attempt to put upon the stage "the whole checkered drama of life with all its circumstances."

As Schlegel stated, "the dramatic and especially the tragic art of the ancients annihilates in some measure the external circumstances of space and time; while, by their changes, the romantic drama adorns its more varied pictures."[12] He proposed as the new standard of judgment a new kind of unity: organic. "Organical form . . . is innate; it unfolds itself from within, and acquires its determination contemporaneously with the perfect development of the germ. We everywhere discover such forms in nature. . . . In the fine arts, as well as in the domain of nature—the supreme artist, all genuine forms are organical, that is, determined by the quality of the work. In a word, the form is nothing but a significant exterior, the speaking physiognomy of each thing."[13]

At this point in his analysis Schlegel's usual clarity begins to desert him, and he does not succeed in defining organic unity or in explaining how a playwright achieves it. The Classicists are better than the Romantics at this sort of definition. Schlegel announces that romantic drama "satisfies the unconscious requisitions of fancy," but he never wholly uncovers these hidden rules. Still, to proceed.

Is it reasonable to suppose that Verdi as a young man was strongly influenced in his ideas about Shakespeare by this trend of German critical opinion? Seemingly against the possibility are certain facts: he was fluent neither in English nor German and was forced to read the plays in either Italian or French translations. He did not leave his tiny provincial town of Busseto until he was nineteen, when he went to Milan; he did not visit Vienna until thirty, or Paris and London until thirty-three. He did not see his first

Shakespearean play on the stage, *Macbeth,* until he reached London. Yet all of these disadvantages can be offset by remarkable opportunities for knowledge.

Busetto had (and still has) an excellent small library, and Verdi used it. He grew up in the Duchy of Parma at a time when it was ruled by Austrians and when not-too-distant Milan was the capital of the Habsburg Kingdom of Lombardo–Veneto. Until the revolutions of 1848 relations between the Milanesi and the Austrians were sometimes cordial, and even after 1848 for another eleven years Milan was ruled from Vienna. For the first half of the nineteenth century—Verdi's formative years—German culture was strong in the Po valley, particularly in its chief city.

As an example of that cultural tie, consider the following: Schlegel's lectures, published in German in Vienna, 1809–11, were translated into Italian by Giovanni Gherardini and published in Milan in 1817.[14] Thus for all of Verdi's reading life—he was born in 1813—the lectures were available to him in his own tongue. And here, recall for a moment the extraordinary range of his interest and reading. For example, Darwin published his *On the Origin of Species* in 1859. Verdi, in 1865, with no Italian translation yet in print, ordered a copy to be sent to him in either the French translation or the original English.[15] Remembering that Shakespeare was his favorite poet, it seems likely that at an early age he found his way to Schlegel's famous lectures.

Further, when he reached Milan he soon counted among his best friends two Shakespearean specialists, Giulio Carcano and Andrea Maffei. Carcano in 1850 offered Verdi a libretto based on *Hamlet*[16] and in later years, 1875–82, published in verse translation an edition of Shakespeare's complete plays. It is inconceivable that he could have been ignorant of Schlegel's criticism or did not discuss it with Verdi.

Maffei, who translated into Italian Schiller's plays and Milton's *Paradise Lost,* had been educated in Munich, was a Cavaliere of the Austrian Empire and well known for his German sympathies. With his wife Clarina, from whom he separated in 1846, he ran a salon where intellectuals gathered. He provided verses for Verdi's *Macbeth* and *Forza* as well as the libretto, based on Schiller, for *I masnadieri;* and in 1846, following his separation from his wife, he shared a vacation with Verdi at Recoaro, a spa near Vicenza, at a time when *Macbeth* and Shakespeare were much in Verdi's mind.

There is more. The first translation into Italian of Shakespeare's complete plays was published in prose by Carlo Rusconi in 1838,[17] and in the next twenty years his translation had two more printings, one a self-proclaimed "popular edition." Verdi for much of his life kept Rusconi's translation at his bedside (and later, also Carcano's verse translation),[18] and we know that in discussing *Otello* with Boito in 1886 Verdi preferred Rusconi's translation of a phrase over others.[19] Evidently he read Rusconi closely.

Now here is what is so nice. To fourteen of the thirty-seven plays Rusconi attached a *"nota"* at the close of his translation, and the *nota* was generally two or three pages of appropriate excerpt from the Gherardini translation of Schlegel's lectures.[20] For *Macbeth* there is a four-page *nota* taken from Schlegel's Lecture XXV,[21] and it sets out Schlegel's view of the play, which is, beyond dispute, Verdi's. Like Rusconi and most others at the time, Verdi was reading Shakespeare in the Schlegel tradition.

In saying that Verdi's view of *Macbeth* is Schlegel's "beyond dispute" I have assumed a conclusion. But to follow Verdi and Schlegel step by step through *Macbeth*—their approach to the witches, for example—would be too great a digression. Better to press on, hoping that by now it seems reasonable, at least, to assert that Verdi's ideas about dramatic structure were strongly influenced by Schlegel, particularly by Schlegel's view of romantic drama as exemplified by Shakespeare. Besides, for a further demonstration of that particular influence on Verdi there is the evidence of what he tried to do with the structure of *La forza del destino*.

There were, of course, many aspects of Shakespeare that appealed to Verdi—the poetry, the themes and characters of the plays. But in the fifteen years leading up to *Forza* two aspects that seem to have been often in mind were just those which Schlegel had found most important: the mixing of genres and the disregard of the unities.

Verdi, alas, has not left us an essay with his views on Shakespearean structure, so we must piece them together from observations here and there in his letters. I shall quote only two of the more important of these, with references to others in the footnotes: In his letter of 22 April 1853 to the librettist Antonio Somma, referring to their efforts to create a *King Lear*, Verdi stated: "To me, our opera nowadays sins in the direction of too great monotony, so much so that I should refuse to write on such subjects as 'Nabucco,' 'Foscari,' etc. They offer extremely interesting dramatic situations, but they lack variety. They have but one burden to their song; elevated, if you like, but always the same. To be more explicit, Tasso's work may be better, but I prefer Ariosto a thousand times. For the same reason I prefer Shakespeare to all other dramatists, including the Greeks."[22] So, what he liked in Shakespeare was the variety of dramatic situations within a single play.

In an earlier letter of 24 March 1849 to Salvatore Cammarano, in discussing the possibility of an opera on Guerrazzi's novel *L' assedio di Firenze* Verdi stated that he wished to blend the comic and tragic "a uso Shakespeare" (in Shakespeare's style) because such a mixture of genres, he said, "will serve to break up and cut the monotony of so many serious scenes."[23]

One way to achieve Shakespearean variety in a single opera therefore was to mix the comic and tragic genres. Verdi did this to some extent, and with great success, in *Un ballo in maschera*, the opera immediately preceding *Forza*. In *Ballo*, however, he observed the rules for unity of action and of time and, only slightly modified, of place. In *Forza* he would be far more daring, mixing the genres to a greater extent and abandoning the unities altogether.

Further, in this same letter to Cammarano, Verdi gives as an example of a scene containing within itself the kind of variety he sought, a military camp: "There is a grand scene in this style in Schiller's *Wallenstein:* soldiers, camp followers, gypsies, fortune tellers, even a monk, but you can put in all the rest, and you even can make a little dance for the gypsies. In short, make me a characteristic scene that will give a true picture of a military camp."[24] And, of course, thirteen years later that scene, including the monk (with Schiller's verses translated by Maffei) went into *Forza*.

The fact that *Forza* is the only one of Verdi's operas based on a play by a well-known playwright into which he inserted a whole scene by another well-known playwright is evidence, I think, that here he was trying to invent a reality—"a uso Shakespeare"—rather than merely using that of the Duke of Rivas. He also considerably changed the Rivas play by pushing three of the characters into greater prominence and much further toward comedy. On the casting of Preziosilla, Melitone, and Trabuco he wrote in a letter to Giulio Ricordi, 15 December 1868: "Their scenes are comedy, pure comedy. Therefore good diction and an easy stage manner."[25] The opera opens on a serious scene, thereafter roughly alternates the comic and the serious, and closes on a serious scene.

The comic, of course, was not to be just a joke thrown in but was to have some steady relation—organic unity—to the serious. Schlegel had noted Shakespeare's use of foils and written: "Shakespeare makes each of his principal characters the glass in which the others are reflected, and by like means enables us to discover what could not be immediately revealed to us."[26] Thus in *Twelfth Night* the "ideal follies" of the more serious characters are set off and reflected by the "naked absurdities" of the more comic.

In *Forza* Verdi used the comic and serious to contrast rather than to reflect the characters. He intended, clearly I think, for the comic characters to survive in life through their lack of pretense, sure identity, and sense of community. By contrast the serious characters, trapped in their aristocratic codes of honor and racial purity, are doomed first to be separated, then to be isolated from their fellows by false identities, and ultimately, in the opera's first version, all to die by violence. Verdi, imitating Shakespeare, mixed the genres for a purpose.

Just as Shakespeare ignored the unity of place in his chronicle plays and in many of his tragedies, moving Prince Hal, Falstaff, Lear, and others all over England and some of them even to France, so in *Forza* Verdi moved his characters from the city of Seville, to the countryside of Hornachuelos, across the sea to Italy, and back to Hornachuelos—though keeping the total number of scenes to eight. For as he had written to Somma, 29 June 1853, "The only thing that has prevented me from treating Shakespearean subjects more often has been precisely this necessity to change scenes at every moment. When I used to go to the theatre, it annoyed me greatly. I felt as if I were watching a magic lantern. In this the French are right: they plan their dramas so as to need only one scene for each act."[27]

That rule in application seemed to work well for Verdi. His *Rigoletto* and *La traviata*, based on French plays and structurally strong, each made do with four scenes. But *Forza* with twice the number was to prove structurally weak, particularly in its third act, which had three scenes.

Lastly, in *Forza* Verdi ignored the unities of time and action. According to the opera's production book, prepared by its librettist Piave: "About eighteen months pass between the first and second acts; several years between the second and third; more than five years between the third and fourth."[28] In all, the time spans about a decade. As a result the unity of action is wholly broken; between acts, a great deal happens.

Did Verdi succeed in creating a romantic drama in Shakespeare's style, one that developed the kind of organic unity about which Schlegel enthused? Verdi thought not, and after the premiere of *Forza* in 1862, for six years he restricted productions of the opera to those that he, or someone he trusted, could control. Nor, despite the opera's fine music, did he wholly succeed with the public with either the original or the revised "La Scala" version of 1869. Since the premieres of each there have been continual complaints that the opera is too long, that the comic and serious scenes do not cohere into any kind of unity—the word "organic" is often used by the critics—and that this lack of unity, in the end, exhausts the audience.[29] Producers, trying to improve the opera's reception, frequently cut scenes, rearrange their order, or even omit half an act.[30]

The most extraordinary of these producers' versions is one that Verdi either made himself or authorized in 1882 for performances in French-speaking theatres.[31] In its cuts, rearrangements, and additions it represents a major retreat from his Shakespearean model, almost an abandonment of the romantic ideal. He cuts out altogether Fra Melitone and all the comedy associated with him: the response to Leonora's arrival at the monastery, the sermon in the military camp, the dispensation of charity at the monastery, and the dialogue thereafter with Don Carlo. He cuts Trabuco's solo aria and much of his dialogue, again reducing the comedy; and he tightens the part of

Preziosilla. In the necessary rearrangements that follow, the opera's scenes are reduced from eight to six, with one cut from the third act and another from the fourth.

The chief addition to the score is a 142-bar Intermezzo introducing the final act, all of which now takes place at Leonora's grotto. All of the Intermezzo's music is associated with Leonora, and her aria, "Pace, pace, mio Dio!" opens the act, followed by the Alvaro/Carlo duet "Le minaccie, i fieri accenti." The men fight before the grotto, as in the original version, and throughout the duel Leonora's concealed, terrified presence is felt. And, following the "La Scala" revision, it is her death, not Alvaro's, that ends the opera. Far more than in previous versions Leonora dominates the entire last act.

Taken all together these changes remove any attempt at tragicomedy in Shakespeare's style and present only the story's serious side now treated as straightforward melodrama. Apparently Verdi felt that his efforts to present "the whole checkered drama of life with all its circumstances" had not succeeded, not even in the revised "La Scala" version, and in trying to correct the failure it was the Shakespearean structure that he changed.

It is fascinating to speculate whether Verdi *could* have succeeded in what he attempted in *Forza*. Was the failure simply in the libretto and music? Of the comic characters Melitone is well integrated into the drama and his music is delightful; Preziosilla and Trabuco are not, and to many ears their music is lengthy and boring. Or is it that Verdi's compositional style, based on metric verse, could not encompass the full variety of a Shakespearean drama? Recall his insistence in a letter to Cammarano, 28 February 1850, that the length and variety of *King Lear* required "a style wholly new"—"in una maniera del tutto nuova."[32] How large a break in style can a mature artist accomplish without sacrificing his individuality? But these are questions for another day.

Less speculative, I think, is how he got himself into what proved to be for him a cul-de-sac of operatic structure, and from which he steadily retreated. For among Verdi's operas *Forza* in its structure marks the closest imitation of Shakespeare he attempted.

The reason surely is that Verdi's experience of Shakespeare was literary, not theatrical; he read the plays, but seldom saw them performed. He tells us this himself in his letter to Léon Escudier, 28 April 1865, in which by way of protesting a critic's judgment that the revised version of *Macbeth* revealed a composer who neither understood nor felt Shakespeare, he wrote: "No, by God, no! He is one of my favorite poets. I have had him in my hands from earliest youth, and I read and reread him continually."[33]

The meaning of "in my hands" and "read and reread" has been clarified

Title page, French "third version" (1882) of *La forza del destino*.

by the research of William Weaver. In his article "Verdi the Playgoer"[34] he reveals that Shakespeare's *Macbeth* was not performed in Italy until 1858. Thus Verdi staged his first version of *Macbeth* in Florence in 1847 without ever having seen the play performed. Only later that year, when he went to London for the first time, did he see it acted; and that performance, in a language he did not understand, apparently was the first Shakespeare play he saw staged. He was thirty-three at the time and had composed eleven of his twenty-six operas.

As Weaver shows, this paucity of staged Shakespeare continued throughout Verdi's life. He certainly never sat through an uncut production of *Hamlet, King Lear,* or *Henry IV* Part 2, and he saw very few performances of the other plays, even with cuts. In Italy, Shakespeare was performed only rarely until close to the end of the nineteenth century. If Verdi had seen more of the plays in the theatre, he might have had more success with the structure of *Forza*.

*   *   *   *   *   *

Finally, there is the question of how Verdi's experience with the structure of *La forza del destino* affected his choice and treatment of Shakespearean plays for the basis of his last two operas, *Otello* and *Falstaff*.

Critics and biographers sometimes write of the joining of Verdi and Shakespeare, so carefully brought about by Strepponi, Ricordi, and Boito, as if it were a match made in heaven, a euphoric juncture of artists of a kindred spirit. That seems too simple. At the end of his life Verdi returned to Shakespeare. Yes. But after his experience with *Forza* he came with a wary eye, rejecting just what Schlegel and other nineteenth-century critics declared to be the essence of Shakespeare and of romantic drama in general: the mixing of genres and disregard of the unities.

Romantic drama with its structural principle of organic unity had delighted Verdi, and he had used a number of its plays for his operas. He also, however, had admired Scribe's well-made plays and once even had used a libretto based on Voltaire's *Alzire*. Like many artists of Mediterranean culture he was not overwhelmed by the Romantic Movement and never wholly abandoned the precepts of classical culture. When in old age he returned to Shakespeare, after a lifetime of operatic composition, he came as a classicist in matters of structure, as an anti-Shakespearean.

For years critics had commented that *Othello* was the least Shakespearean in structure of the tragedies. Samuel Johnson, for one, had remarked, "Had the scene opened in Cyprus, and the preceding incidents been occasionally related, there had been little wanting to a drama of the most exact and scrupulous regularity."[35] To represent a mixing of genres there is only

LA FORCE DU DESTIN

OPÉRA EN 4 ACTES.

Personnages.	Voix.	Personnages.	Voix.
Dona Léonore	Soprano.	Don Alvar	Ténor.
Préciosilla	M. Sop: ou Contr:	Don Carlo	Baryton.
Le Père Guardi	Basse.	Le Marquis	2e. Basse.

Laura — Un Alcade — Trabuco — Un Esclave — Un Soldat.

Pour toute la Musique, la Mise en Scène, le droit de représentations,
s'adresser à M.rs CHOUDENS, PÈRE et FILS, Éditeurs-Propriétaires de LA FORCE DU DESTIN.

CATALOGUE DES MORCEAUX.

A.C. 5554.   Paris, Imp. Fouquet, rue du Delta 26.   Bandou Gr

Table of Contents, French "third version" (1882) of *La forza del destino*. Note the absence of Fra Melitone in the *Personnages*, and compare the order of the numbers, particularly in acts III and IV, with the "Werfel Edition."

Othello's Clown, a role smaller than the Fool in *Lear* or the First Gravedigger in *Hamlet* and not so distinctive as the Porter in *Macbeth*. Once in Cyprus, the unity of place is fixed; the span of time becomes twenty-four hours or thereabouts: evening, morning, afternoon, and evening; and the action is unbroken and inexorable.

As if on Johnson's hint, Verdi and Boito took the play and made of it a classical drama of "scrupulous regularity." Out went the Clown; out, also, went the entire Venetian first act, with its hints of comedy, its father-daughter confrontation (usually a great stimulus to Verdi), and all its breaks in continuity of time, action, and place. Whatever was added was kept within the classical framework. With regard to structure the barbarian Shakespeare was not treated as an equal; he was tamed.

Consider, too, *The Merry Wives of Windsor*. In its structure it is the most untypical of all Shakespeare's plays, for it is the only one to observe the unities of time and action, and it goes farther than most in observing the unity of place, never departing from Windsor and its environs. As pure farce, without any sustained serious scene or character, it does not mix genres. Though Boito deepened the character of Falstaff by introducing speeches for him from other plays, he tightened rather than loosened the play's classical structure, reducing the changes of scene from seventeen to five, and making the timing more evident and certain: Act I, morning; Act II, afternoon; and Act III, evening and midnight. Although *Falstaff* is unquestionably an opera based on Shakespeare, in its structure it is very *un*Shakespearean.

In conclusion, therefore, if the essay's hypothesis may be extended to include Verdi's *Macbeth* by implication—to avoid repetitious argument—it will pose for consideration two paradoxes, the second following from the first as a corollary.

The first is that in structure—note the limitation—the most Shakespearean of Verdi's operas is not *Macbeth*, *Otello*, or *Falstaff*, but *La forza del destino*.

And the corollary? That because of his experience with the structure of *Forza*, Verdi returned in old age to Shakespeare, looking not for what he loved best in him or was most typical, say, *King Lear*, but for what was most useful, which proved to be, paradoxically, the plays of his favorite poet that were the least typical.[36]

5

POSA IN
DON CARLOS:
THE FLAWED HERO

A movement is stirring among Schiller scholars. In the last quarter century some have suggested that for the past 175 years scholars and audiences alike have misinterpreted his plays, particularly the historical dramas such as *Don Carlos, Mary Stuart,* and *William Tell.* The mistake, it seems, was born of political bias, whether liberal or conservative, which led everyone to see as the primary theme in all these works the opposition of great political ideas: freedom versus tyranny, liberalism versus absolutism, Protestantism versus Catholicism. To the contrary, say those supporting the new perception, Schiller was more concerned to expose the moral ambiguity of most political action and to show how it affected character. Thus *Don Carlos,* they argue, is not predominantly a clash of ideas, but of personalities, which are as much formed by the actions taken during the drama as the actions are expressions of pre-existing personalities.

This new perception, admirably summarized by Lesley Sharpe in *Schiller and the Historical Character* (1982), ultimately may shift our interpretation of Verdi's *Don Carlos,* based on Schiller. The change, if it comes about, will be a modification, not a reversal, but it will alter our view of the opera's chief theme as well as of several characters, especially the Marquis of Posa. To many persons, however, the new ideas may seem faintly familiar, for in the deliberate ambiguity of the play, carefully preserved in the opera, they have been there right along, dimly perceived but not articulated for us by critics. They were overlooked in the past because of the prejudices of the past, just as the new view, if it takes hold, will owe much to the tone and events of contemporary life.

Of Verdi's operas only *Don Carlos* has the depth and breadth in its story and characters to shift the ground of its pertinence in this fashion. Perceptions of *Rigoletto* or *La traviata*, for example, probably have changed very little in 130 years; we interpret the characters and their actions much as audiences have done for generations. But *Don Carlos*, in its extraordinary relevance to the year of its premiere, 1867, and in its equally extraordinary ability to adapt its significance to other times and circumstances, is in conception the greatest of Verdi's operas.

Note, however, the superlative's limitation to conception, for somehow, despite all Verdi's efforts and revisions, a proper balance or proportion among the parts of *Don Carlos* evaded him, just as it had in the opera immediately preceding, *La forza del destino*. Those that follow, *Aida*, *Otello*, and *Falstaff*, are all marvels of proportion, but in them Verdi attempted less. For size and scope of canvas, number of leading roles, subtlety and complication of the characters' emotions, and importance of political themes, there is no opera in all of Verdi like *Don Carlos*. And it may indeed contain more meaning than critics or performers yet have mined from it.

Before applying this new perception to *Don Carlos*, play and opera, consider how it has uncovered meaning in another of Schiller's historical dramas, *Mary Stuart*, in which he invented so imaginatively a confrontation between Mary, Queen of Scots and her jailer, Elizabeth I of England. Mary starts the play imprisoned, ineptly fosters a conspiracy, at the famous meeting refuses to be humiliated by Elizabeth, and goes to her execution. According to the traditional view, the play's paramount theme is the rise of a new concept of national monarchy, supported by Protestants, over the older divine right of kings, associated with Catholics; Mary, the legitimate daughter of kings and a queen by divine right, is defeated by Elizabeth who, in the eyes of Mary and her advocates, is both a bastard and a usurper. At the play's end Elizabeth is secure on her throne, triumphant. But for scholars of the new perception such a reading is too simple. Elizabeth, as well as Mary, has suffered a tragedy, perhaps equally severe. Whereas Mary, faced with what amounts to judicial murder, gains dignity and discovers in the prospect of death a release and freedom, Elizabeth, although surviving in the world of politics, by her equivocal actions has begun to injure those who served her and finds herself increasingly isolated in her success, even imprisoned.

This ambiguity of character and event is yet more apparent in *William Tell*, a play that from 1804 until about 1920, when its rhetoric about freedom began to sound old-fashioned, was performed regularly in Germany and became a national pageant in Switzerland, presented annually in many towns. Though today performances are less frequent, most people still are sure that they know Tell's story and assume that Schiller's play, its chief source, portrays the Swiss bowman as an ideal man, noble in spirit, liberal in thought, and prepared to sacrifice his life to establish freedom in his country—like Posa in *Don Carlos*. Yet whatever Tell may have been in real life, if he had one, in the play he is an equivocal figure; and people often are unaware of it because for years many productions of the play, particularly those in Switzerland, cut out entire Schiller's most important scene. Similarly, nineteenth-century critics tended to ignore the scene or to conclude that it was misconceived, or badly written, and therefore properly omitted. For critics of the new tradition, not unexpectedly, it is crucial.

According to Schiller: In 1307 Tell, a Swiss of the Canton of Uri, because of his skill with the crossbow, is a natural leader of his people and

Schiller

enemy of Gessler, the lieutenant of the Habsburg duke who as Holy Roman Emperor rules the Canton. One day Gessler puts his hat atop a pole, ordering all the Swiss, as a sign of obedience to the Emperor, to bow before it. Tell refuses, and Gessler requires him to shoot an apple from his son's head or to forfeit his own. Not for a moment does Gessler believe that Tell will risk the shot nor probably does he mean to decapitate Tell if the latter refuses the attempt. He hopes, by forcing Tell to plead, lament, and back down in public, to destroy his image among the people as a leader. Throughout the play Schiller is much concerned with the relation of image to reality. Tell shoots, and hits the apple. His spirit, however, has been seared by the event, and he seeks revenge, acting more as an outraged father than as a patriot. So one day, from cliffs overlooking a sunken road, from ambush and without warning, he shoots Gessler; and the act, if staged as Schiller directed, is a nasty assassination. Nevertheless, Tell's countrymen, who have been plotting a revolt, refuse to see the killing as a murder, hail Tell as their savior, and take his crossbow in order to enshrine it as a relic of their fight for freedom. In the final scene as they cheer him outside his cottage, he is, though still alive, losing his humanity and becoming a legend. Thus his character is formed by the event, rather than the event expressing his character.*

As for the scene that frequently is cut: it occurs shortly after the murder of Gessler, when the legend of Tell the Hero is beginning to form. Tell, after several days of hiding, returns to his home, where he finds a man asking for food and shelter. He is Duke John of Swabia, who a few days earlier murdered his uncle, the Habsburg Emperor, and he seeks help from Tell because, he explains, their actions were alike. The tyrannical Emperor had affronted family feeling by stealing his nephew's inheritance, and John, in killing him and forcing the election of a new emperor of the Holy Roman Empire, can claim to have done more for Swiss freedom than Tell in killing a minor lieutenant. But Tell cannot see the similarities:

> TELL: Can you confuse the blood guilt of ambition
> With what a father did in self defense?
> Did you defend beloved heads of children?
> Did you protect the hearth's pure sanctity? Did you
> Ward off the worst and utmost from your own?
> I lift my stainless hands aloft to Heaven
> And curse you and your deed. I have avenged

*Verdi and his companion, Emanuele Muzio, on their way to Paris in May 1847, their first trip outside Italy, as fervent anti-Austrians stopped to visit Tell's cottage and to see the glen where he had killed Gessler. L. G. Garibaldi, *Verdi, nelle lettere di E. Muzio* etc., 322.

The sacredness of Nature, which you have
Disgraced—We share no common ground—*You* murdered,
While *I* defended what was dearest to me.[1]

There is not a word about freedom for the fatherland, and throughout the play that motive more often is ascribed to Tell by others than claimed by him. But even granting a touch of patriotism, he sounds smug, sanctimonious, and a little stupid, in the sense of not fully understanding what he has done, or why. Small wonder the Swiss for years cut the scene; but with it the play is more interesting. Schiller clearly wanted us to ponder not only how, if circumstances are favorable, we can get away with murder, but also how in politics our acts frequently are morally ambiguous. Tell, at best, is a flawed hero.

In the light of such interpretations of *Mary Stuart* and *William Tell,* consider now *Don Carlos.* The traditional view of the play holds that it presents in stark opposition the extremes of liberty and tyranny, liberal and absolutist theories of government, church and state, and incipient Protestantism and full-blown Catholicism. The critic George Steiner, writing of Schiller in *The Death of Tragedy* (1961), stated, "In the Marquis of Posa (the true hero of the play) he dramatised his vision of the ideal man: noble, liberal, immensely alive, yet prepared to sacrifice his life to the romantic ideals of freedom and masculine friendship."[2] This interpretation, originating in the early nineteenth century, has been continuous and powerful, and the Verdi scholar Julian Budden accepts it without question, for both play and opera, when he writes in his *Operas of Verdi* (1981), "The lesson that Schiller is concerned to drive home is that *between liberalism and absolutism no compromise is possible*" [Budden's italics].[3]

The opera, despite cuts and additions by Verdi and his two librettists, Joseph Méry and Camille Du Locle, is remarkably true to the spirit of the play, and in the summary below it is the opera's story that is told, with digressions from the play noted where necessary. Some of the minor scenes are omitted or curtailed in order to focus on the events involving Posa. He is the mainspring of the action, and significantly Verdi in all his revisions never, not even tentatively, cut from the opera one of Posa's scenes, though every other of the six leading characters at one time or another lost at least one. Nevertheless, in the opera's first act, which Verdi and his librettists added to explain much that in the play becomes clear by reference, Posa does not appear.

To end a war with France Philip II of Spain sent his ambassadors to Fontainebleau to arrange a marriage between his son and heir, Don Carlos, and Elisabeth Valois, a French princess. Late in the engagement, for dynastic reasons, Philip himself married Elisabeth. Unfortunately, Carlos and Elisabeth had met briefly in the forest of Fontainebleau and fallen in love (Act I of the opera's original five-act version), and so after her marriage with the father life at the Spanish court is not easy. Though Elisabeth's behavior is impeccable, Philip suspects that Carlos still reigns in her heart, and Carlos suffers the agonies of frustrated love.

Father and son, opposed at this human level, are also opposed in matters of state, as kings and heirs apparent almost always are. In Spain's Netherlands, chiefly the provinces of Brabant and Flanders, the people and their leaders are demanding greater freedom in political and religious affairs, and Philip's policy is one of repression, fire and sword. Carlos favors conciliation, but he is kept idle at court by his father and denied any post or power with which to implement his ideas. More frustration.

Into this crucible of trouble comes the Marquis of Posa, a childhood friend of Carlos and a believer in such nineteenth-century doctrines as a free church in a free state, freedom of the press, and a limited monarchy. Both Schiller and Verdi were quite aware that Posa was an anachronism at Philip's court, an utter impossibility. Verdi, in writing to his publisher, described him as "an imaginary being who could never have existed under Philip's reign," and he evidently viewed the libretto and its underlying play, which he found "splendid in form and in its highminded concepts,"[4] as a highly theatrical dream, wholly *un*historical in its events and personalities but in their relationships psychologically true.

The opening of the opera's second act (first in the four-act revision) offers a particularly dreamlike sequence and takes place before the tomb of Emperor Charles V in the Convent of St. Just, north of Madrid. The Emperor, Philip's father, had abdicated his throne and retired to the convent to end his days, which is historically correct; and at the period of the drama, 1568, he was thought by many, despite the tomb, to be still alive.

From the shadows of the tomb a monk emerges and sings of the vanity of the world, and Carlos, coming in, is terrified by the monk's vocal and physical resemblance to his grandfather. Before he can collect himself, the monk disappears, and Posa enters. He recently has returned from Flanders and at once urges Carlos to request of the king an appointment to the provinces so that Carlos may temper, even reverse, the king's policy. Carlos looks glum and, under questioning, confesses that he can think only of Elisabeth, whom he continues to love. Posa, aghast, advises him to sublimate the impossible love in service to the people of Flanders. Carlos agrees, and the two, in a friendship duet, sing ecstatically of living and dying together to advance the cause of Liberty.

Posa's next action, which follows immediately, is to seek out the queen. He finds her in a garden with her ladies-in-waiting and asks her to grant Carlos an interview. Elisabeth is loath, believing it better that she and Carlos never meet alone, but Posa presses, and in the end she consents. Carlos appears—there is much dreamlike telescoping of time in both play and opera—and the ladies-in-waiting, guided by Posa, withdraw. Carlos, kneeling before her, murmurs that his position at court is intolerable and requests that she ask the king on his behalf for the appointment to Flanders; and she, addressing him in the terms of their royal, public relationship—"Mon fils" (my son)—promises to speak for him. But under the impact of her presence he cannot contain his emotion and begins to talk of love, moving quickly from nostalgia to passion. She tries to stop him and succeeds finally by exclaiming: "Then murder, murder the king and, stained with his blood, come to lead your mother to the altar." Carlos, horrified, rushes out cursing the false relationship in which he is trapped, "Ah fils maudit, fils maudit" (Ah damned son, damned son).

The king enters and, angered at finding the queen unattended, summons the court and in its presence dismisses the lady-in-waiting on duty. His action, so brusque and disrespectful to the queen, displays to everyone the unhappiness in the marriage. Here, I think, the new perception of Schiller's primary aims would begin to diverge from the traditional view of Posa as the ideal man. Though Philip is the one who dismisses the lady-in-waiting, who created the situation that led to the event? Was it not Posa, with his insistence that the queen grant Carlos an interview? Would not common sense and, even more, common decency have suggested that the queen and Carlos, given the danger of their love, be kept apart? And having made the mistake, is Posa now not on notice of just how swift and savage are the emotional undercurrents in the royal family?

Next the king and Posa, after the others have retired, have a dialogue in which Posa reports the results of the king's policy in Flanders. He is outspoken: blood runs in the streets, and there is a silence on the land, the silence of the grave; if Philip does not change his policy, he will be known in history as another Nero. Passionate and idealistic, Posa ends with the cry, "Bring happiness to the world. Give it liberty!"

Philip at first is offended, then charmed. He is used to hearing only sycophants, and here, however misguided, is an honest man. He calls Posa "a strange dreamer," one out of touch with the real world, and warns him to beware of the Grand Inquisitor. For in this Age of Inquisition he need not explain that the Church does not favor the tolerance of other faiths that Posa advocates in his cry for liberty. He goes on to say that he wants Posa as a friend, a confidant—clearly this is a very dreamlike unhistorical story!—

and tells him of his fears that Elisabeth and Carlos are in love. Posa must observe them: "I put my heart into your loyal hands." And as Philip goes off, he warns again of the Grand Inquisitor.

At this point, with Posa now the king's confidant and Carlos prepared to sacrifice his love for service in Flanders, another character begins to meddle, the Princess Eboli, one of the richest, best born, and most beautiful ladies at court. She is also a woman of monstrous vanity and a sexual schemer, and about her character neither Schiller nor Verdi had any doubt. When Verdi's librettist suggested to him that they make Eboli a mite less odious, Verdi refused, insisting, "Eboli is not and cannot be anything but a *coquine!*"[5] Or, in English, "a slut." As she soon reveals, she has been sleeping with Philip and hopes to sleep with Carlos: first, the king; then the prince.

In a scene later cut by Verdi to shorten the opera, Eboli sends Carlos a note, presumably in disguised handwriting, asking him to meet her in the garden at midnight. Carlos, thinking only of Elisabeth, assumes the note is from her, and in the play we are shown Eboli using the queen's page to deliver the note. In the opera, in the scene that was cut but sometimes is performed, the deception is buttressed by having the queen, who is tiring of an outdoor festivity, give her mantilla, necklace, and mask to Eboli, so that the princess may take the queen's place in the royal box and preserve for the populace the illusion of the royal presence. After Eboli has put on the clothing and penned the note to Carlos, she waits eagerly through the opera's ballet, usually cut, for midnight. Thus, when we arrive at the scene that we still do see and hear, we find Carlos in the garden at the appointed hour awaiting Elisabeth, and when a woman appears wearing the queen's mantilla, jewels, and mask, he proclaims his love. When she responds, equally passionate, and removes her veil, he gasps, "Ce n'est pas la Reine!" (It is *not* the Queen!). And Eboli, scorned, has his secret.

Posa comes in, and when he realizes what has been revealed, and to whom, in a flash of violence he tries to kill Eboli, but Carlos stops him. She goes off vowing vengeance, and all too clearly she will hasten to the king and report a scandal about Carlos and the queen. Equally certain, in view of the already bad relations between father and son, her tale-bearing will result in Carlos's activities being watched, his apartment searched, and his letters opened. Posa suggests, therefore, that if Carlos has any incriminating letters, perhaps from persons in Flanders, he give them for safekeeping to him, Posa, who as the king's confidant will be above suspicion. Carlos takes a packet from his doublet but hesitates, murmuring that Posa is indeed the king's confidant. Then resolutely he hands it over, and the scene ends with a vocal and orchestral reprise of their friendship duet—noble, enthusiastic, assured.

Again, consider Posa's action. Is he wise? Is he honorable? In using the king's trust to conceal letters that presumably are treasonable, does he not betray the king? It may be said that his relationship with Carlos is friendship, and with Philip, patronage; and so Carlos rightly is first in his thoughts and actions. But it also can be argued that he is very careless of where his political ideals lead him, allowing his passions, shockingly displayed in the spasm of violence against Eboli, to plunge him ever deeper into morally ambiguous actions. However he may think of himself, he is more controlled by events than in control of them.

The next scene, an *auto-da-fé* at which several heretics are burned, is the opera's great production number, and not in the play. Verdi inserted it to provide a scene of spectacle, and one small miracle of it is that in the midst of its parade the plot does advance. Before the entire court, people of Madrid, and priests of the Inquisition, Carlos leads in a band of Flemish deputies, asking an audience for them with the king and for himself the post of viceroy to the Netherlands. When Philip refuses both, calling him "a madman," Carlos draws his sword, crying out that he will be the savior of Flanders, the role, remember, that Posa continually has urged him to assume. The king orders his guards to disarm the prince, and when they hesitate, he seizes a guard's sword and himself advances on Carlos. At that instant Posa comes forward, takes Carlos's sword and, while the orchestra sadly recalls their friendship theme, hands it to the king. Though the action may be done with the best of motives, the music describes it as a betrayal of Carlos.

Following this grand scene Philip sits alone in his study, musing on Eboli's stories. He knows now that the queen does not love him, has never loved him. Even in death, wrapped in his robes of state, he must sleep alone in the tombs of the Escorial. Despite his royal power he cannot read the hearts of men, or of a woman. Verdi, even more emphatically than Schiller, by stressing Philip's love for Elisabeth, stirs sympathy for him.

The Grand Inquisitor, old and blind, is led in. The king seeks reassurance. He has had Carlos arrested for treason, and if he orders his son's execution, will the Church absolve him? Yes, replies the priest. And can the Church help him to stifle his parental love? All such feelings must be silenced to exalt the faith, says the priest.

Then the Inquisitor takes the offense. The king has a friend, Posa, who is guilty of heresy. Philip protests: In Posa he has at last a friend whom he can trust. But, asks the Inquisitor, how can the king have a friend, for to have a friend is to have an equal? "Tais-toi, prêtre" (Be silent, priest), cries Philip. (It was at this moment at the opera's premiere that Eugénie, the French empress, turned her back on the stage; discussed below.) The Inquisitor demands Posa for trial. Philip refuses, and the Inquisitor leaves in anger, with Posa's fate undecided, unless perhaps it is indicated in Philip's final, bitter remark, "Thus the crown must always bow before the altar."

Elisabeth enters asking for justice: her jewel box has been stolen. The king points to it on a table and, because it contains a miniature of Carlos, accuses her of adultery. She faints, and he calls for attendants. Posa and Eboli rush in, and a quartet develops in which Philip feels remorse, realizing that he has been misled about the queen's fidelity; Posa sees that the king's jealousy of Carlos has been pushed to a point where he probably will have the prince executed on grounds of treason; Eboli, beginning to comprehend the results of her sexual intrigue, grieves; and the queen, reviving, laments that in Spain she is a stranger, without friends. The two men depart, and Eboli confesses to the queen that it was she who stole the jewel box and nurtured Philip's suspicions, and all because she had been spurned by Carlos. Elisabeth forgives her. But Eboli has more to confess. Where the queen is innocent of adultery, she is guilty, with the king. "You may choose between exile and a cloister," says Elisabeth, leaving, and Eboli launches into her great aria "O don fatal," in which she curses her beauty and vanity. At its end she resolves, in the day of freedom left to her, to save Carlos's life.

He is in prison, and Posa, who has assumed full responsibility for the incriminating letters, comes to say farewell. The letters, he reports, have been discovered, and doubtless a dossier against him as the leader of the Flemish rebels soon will be presented to the king. His arrest perhaps already has been ordered, and his death will follow quickly. Even as he speaks, a priest guides one of the Inquisitor's musketeers to the cell's gate and points to Posa. The soldier fires, and Posa falls dying, eloquently urging Carlos "to save Flanders," or, to continue on the very course that thus far has led the prince to disaster.

Moments later Philip and his courtiers enter, and the king, having decided to ignore the Inquisitor and to pardon his son, attempts to return to Carlos the sword taken from him at the *auto-da-fé*. He is astonished to be rebuffed and, apparently not yet knowing of the evidence collected against Posa, is genuinely upset to find the latter dead. "Who will give me back this man?" he cries, as Carlos berates him for the murder. But the sounds of a riot overwhelm them, and almost immediately a mob, roused by Eboli, surges into the prison demanding the prince's release and threatening the king. In the confusion Carlos escapes. The Grand Inquisitor enters, ordering the people to kneel to the king, which they do, more obedient to church than state.

In the play Posa is murdered by order of the king; in the opera, though the point easily is missed, by order of the Grand Inquisitor. Schiller, with a long scene in which Carlos turns angrily on his father, emphasized the clash

Posa dying, shot by the Grand Inquisitor's agents, who are stealing away. Front page of No. 19 of a French edition (1867) of twenty-one individual numbers from the opera.

between generations; Verdi, for reasons to be explained, the conflict between church and state.

The final act, played in a single scene, takes place at the Convent of St. Just where Elisabeth and Carlos plan to meet before the tomb of Emperor Charles V. She arrives first, and in an aria to the deceased emperor, who she feels will understand her suffering, discloses that she has promised Posa to watch over Carlos and to aid him in escaping to Flanders. It is an exquisite aria, full of lament for happiness left behind in France, but it reveals, as the subsequent duet with Carlos confirms, that even from beyond the grave Posa is manipulating their lives to achieve his political end. Under Posa's urging the queen has abandoned her position of emotional and political loyalty to the king and now actively is assisting Carlos in treason. He enters, and they sing of Posa's sacrifice, of Carlos's mission in Flanders, and of their own eventual reunion in heaven. Farewell, they sigh, and forever.

"Yes, forever!" cries Philip, approaching with the Grand Inquisitor and guards, and taking the queen roughly by the arm, he offers Carlos to the Grand Inquisitor. In Schiller, that is the ending: Carlos turned over to the Inquisition, which will execute him for heresy. In Verdi, Carlos draws his sword, starts to defend himself, and then a monk bearing Emperor Charles V's crown and mantle emerges from the shadow of the tomb and leads Carlos out of sight behind it. What does the brief episode mean? Is the monk truly the emperor? Is he a symbol of death? No one, not even Verdi, was happy with the ending, but possibly the best way to view it is as a closing of the dream.

It is true that in the end Posa gives his life to save Carlos and to further the cause of liberty, and the fact must weigh heavily in his favor. But there is much to be put on the scale against him. Recall his actions: He returns to the Spanish court after a time abroad; he finds a king and queen in a troubled marriage; and even after hearing from the prince that the trouble's origin is the smothered love of the prince and queen, he urges on both a private meeting. He—what word should be used to describe his behavior?—treats the king less than honestly in offering to use the king's trust in him to conceal the prince's treasonable letters; in public, at the *auto-da-fé*, he does not speak out for the cause of liberty but humiliates the prince, who does; and in persuading the queen to aid the prince in escaping to the Netherlands he leads her to participate in treason. The results of his actions are death for the prince, probable death or imprisonment for the queen,[6] and, perhaps most tragic, a lifetime of frozen solitude for the king. For Philip never again will trust another human. Posa's record, in terms of human relations, is appalling.

Yet unlike Iago he cannot be called a "villain," for his ideals are noble and he does not intend anyone's destruction. Can he be said to "betray" the trust he receives from each member of the royal family? Possibly that word is too strong. But certainly he is foolish in the extreme and becomes, in pursuing his political aims, a ruthless manipulator of persons; some might even say that by his actions he sullies the shining cause of liberty. Yet however one may view him, he cannot be taken, in Steiner's words, as Schiller's "vision of the ideal man."

The revisionists in Schiller scholarship, as summarized by Sharpe, have concluded: "Schiller's works were flagrantly misused in the nineteenth century by those who wished to proclaim liberal, political ideals or to call for national unity, and *Don Carlos* and *William Tell* were particularly useful for this purpose."[7] Their arguments and their new perception of Schiller's meaning in his historical dramas are, in my opinion, quite convincing, especially as they do not require any corrections or additions to the texts. The plays are there and need only to be read without the preconceptions handed down over the years.

Questions then arise for those concerned with the opera *Don Carlos*. Have we, critics and audiences alike, for more than a century misinterpreted what Verdi wrote? Did he, while composing, accept without question the prevailing nineteenth-century view of the play? Do his changes in turning the play into an opera offer any clues to his meaning in 1867, or to how we might interpret the opera today?

*   *   *   *   *   *

In some respects Schiller's *Don Carlos* is a strange choice for an opera. It is a huge, sprawling drama that in its definitive version, cut to 5,370 lines, is still almost twice as long as the average Shakespeare play. Its translator, Charles E. Passage, states bluntly, "The play as it stands is much too long," adding, among a list of other obvious flaws, "its plot is snarled with intricacies, and its motivations are not always clear."[8] In addition, its history is askew. Not only is Posa an anachronism in the period, but Don Carlos, in fact, was physically and mentally deformed, suffering probably from some sort of brain injury, and he and Elisabeth never were betrothed and never involved in any kind of romantic attachment.

None of this was secret in 1865, when Verdi began to reread the play. Schiller had written the greater part of it in the years 1783–88, publishing sections of it as he progressed, and thereafter had added, cut, and published—at one time it had swollen to 6,282 lines—until the final edition in 1805. In its various versions, as well as in numerous parodies, it had been performed, read, and discussed throughout Europe, and its virtues and defects were known.

The virtues were considerable, and perhaps the greatest is grandeur. Though the play is drawn on a vast scale, the characters are not distanced by it; Schiller, and then Verdi, manage to clothe them with enough humanity so that we can discover in their outsized emotions our own more modest feelings. And one of the most complicated of these, because so ambiguous, is stirred by the clash of legitimate authority with the usurper: not just in political action but also in the generational conflict between father and son. Because in our own lives we know both sides of the latter, Schiller and Verdi are able to arouse in us an ambivalent response to its presentation; and that ambivalent response once aroused, they then can attach it to the problems of state and religion, so that we feel that we share in the complexities of history.[9]

The Paris Opéra as early as 1850 had proposed the play to Verdi, but he had turned it down, apparently more out of pique with the Opéra's administration than any dissatisfaction with the play.[10] Then fifteen years later, in the summer of 1865, the Opéra again approached him. Its director, Emile Perrin, sent an agent to Busseto, suggesting an opera either on Cleopatra or *Don Carlos*, and Verdi inclined to the latter,[11] probably for the same reasons that had led Perrin to recommend it. Though old, the play suddenly, because of a series of events in Europe, had become topical. There was a confrontation developing between church and state that for grandeur and resonance rivaled that between Philip and the Grand Inquisitor. The pope and the king of Italy were headed for a collision likely to unseat one or the other and, in the clash, possibly to topple the emperor of France. For Verdi, the chance to discuss the issues of the day at several centuries remove, amid the glamour of Spain in its Golden Century, to put a drama full of double meanings on the stage of what was then the leading opera house of Europe, must have been intriguing.

The series of events in the contemporary confrontation were of such magnitude and excitement that they were known almost everywhere, even among those who ordinarily did not follow politics or who could not read. Because the Roman Catholic Church was involved, each crisis reverberated around the world, and each was yet another episode in the history of the Risorgimento, the movement among Italians for independence and unity.

By the end of October 1860 the Risorgimento's leaders had succeeded in uniting all but two of the peninsula's former small states (see maps in "Verdi and the Risorgimento") into a single Kingdom of Italy under Vittorio Emanuele II of the House of Savoy. The exceptions were Venice and its mainland province, still held by the Austrians, and Rome and its province known as the Patrimony of St. Peter, ruled by the pope. This new Kingdom of Italy, with its capital in Turin, its Constitution, Senate, and Chamber of Deputies, was a tremendous achievement, but to Italian patriots, so long as it lacked Venice and Rome, it was incomplete. And of the missing parts the one that posed the more difficult problem, and made *Don Carlos* topical, was Rome.

The question was: Who was to rule in Rome, Vittorio Emanuele or the pope? Was the city to be the capital of the Italian kingdom or of a papal state? Or, if an agreement could be reached, of both? As the liberal slogan then was: A free church in a free state. The question stirred deep emotions in Catholics everywhere, but its resolution, as most persons recognized, ultimately would depend on Italians and upon two uneasy alliances in which they were involved. The oldest was between the two groups of patriots, monarchists and republicans, and it had roots in the popular revolts of 1848 that had swept aside the governments of most Italian states. The provisional governments set up had been republican, and in the Papal State the pope, as head of state, though not as head of church, had been dethroned and a Roman Republic proclaimed, led by Mazzini and Garibaldi. Its chief cultural event had been the premiere of Verdi's *La battaglia di Legnano*, with Verdi himself, an ardent republican, conducting. But none of the 1848 republics had been able to survive. The French government of the day, responding to pressure from the French Catholic party, had reestablished the pope on his temporal throne in Rome, and the Austrians had restored themselves or their puppets to their states: the duchies of Parma, Modena, and Tuscany, and the kingdom of Lombardo–Veneto. The only Italian state with an independent Italian ruler was Piedmont–Sardinia, under Vittorio Emanuele.

In the next ten years patriots of all persuasions began to realize that the one hope of uniting even a part of Italy lay in defeating the powerful Austrian armies stationed in the Po valley, and such a victory was conceivable only if a French army entered Italy to fight alongside the monarchist Piemontesi under Vittorio Emanuele and the republican volunteers under Garibaldi. The French government, however, was now a monarchy under Emperor Napoleon III, and he had no interest in establishing republics; and therefore, in order to attain a French alliance most Italian republicans, including Verdi, agreed in their hearts to support Vittorio Emanuele *provided* he and his minister, Cavour, united all of Italy and made Rome its capital. The agreement was not formally signed by representatives of the parties, but its terms were discussed openly and understood, so that when in 1860, following a war with Austria, the new Kingdom of Italy emerged without Venice and Rome, and with its capital still in Turin, many republicans, Verdi as well as Garibaldi, felt betrayed. Verdi wrote in the greatest anger to a friend: "What a result! So much blood for nothing! So many poor young people cheated! And Garibaldi, who sacrificed his long-held, deep convictions in order to support the king, has not achieved what he hoped. It's enough to drive one mad!"[12]

But what could Cavour and Vittorio Emanuele do? Napoleon III, after the bloody battle of Solferino, refused to continue the war against Austria, so Venice and its mainland remained Austrian; and in Rome, at the pope's request, there was again a French army. Whatever may have been Napoleon's personal feelings about the papal government, widely condemned as corrupt and ignorant, he was not going to withdraw that garrison and allow the pope to be deposed as head of state, for to do so would rock his own throne by offending the strong Catholic party in France. Thus, with foreign troops—mercenaries, sneered the Italian patriots—the pope kept his temporal power at Rome and the Patrimony of St. Peter.

The situation clearly was unstable. Some republicans, among them Verdi, were inclined to follow Cavour's policy of wait-and-see; others, like Garibaldi, wanted action. Earlier, in the making of the Italian kingdom in 1860 Garibaldi had acted alone, when no one else would, with startling results. To insure the inclusion of the Bourbon Kingdom of the Two Sicilies (Palermo and Naples) in the new Kingdom of Italy, he had gone to Sicily with 1,000 volunteers and had overthrown the unpopular Bourbon dynasty and conquered for Vittorio Emanuele all of Italy south of Rome. His daring, skill, and adamant refusal to accept any reward for himself had delighted the world. For many, not only Italians, he embodied their concept of the ideal man: noble, free-thinking, immensely alive, yet prepared to sacrifice his life for his country's unity and independence.

But then Cavour had died, two years had passed, and Venice and Rome still remained outside the Kingdom of Italy. So in mid-summer 1862 Garibaldi, apparently with Vittorio Emanuele's secret approval, organized a similar campaign to seize Rome. "Roma o morte" (Rome or death) was his battle cry, and from balconies overlooking the cities' piazzas he proclaimed it in speech after speech to cheering, frenzied crowds. As before, he started in Sicily with a corps of volunteers, crossed the Strait of Messina, and started north through Calabria, concealing himself in the mountains (see maps in "Verdi and the Risorgimento"). But this time, because his objective was Rome, not Naples, the world's reaction was different. The governments of Europe, as well as the pope, protested so vigorously that Vittorio Emanuele's government, losing its nerve, sent an army to stop him. On 29 August 1862, on Aspromonte, there was a brief skirmish in which Garibaldi ordered his troops not to fire on their fellow Italians, while sharpshooters in the government's force managed to hit him twice, in the thigh and ankle. Thus, in shame and bloodshed, ended the march on Rome. It revealed for all to see how inept was Vittorio Emanuele's government, how close to civil war were Italians of opposing political parties, and what a festering sore was the pope's temporal power at the heart of the Italian peninsula. The search for a cure became known as "the Roman Question."

In the summer of 1864, as part of an agreement with France, the Italian government moved its capital from Turin to Florence, ostensibly renouncing forever the possibility of Rome, and agreeing to protect the Papal State from attack by anyone. With that guarantee to placate the Catholic party in France, Napoleon withdrew most of the French army from Rome. But no one believed that the Roman Question had been solved.

Soon after, in December 1864, Pope Pius IX compounded the difficulty of a solution by issuing, in preparation for a Holy Year in 1865, a Syllabus of Errors, so that the Church's bishops "may have before their eyes all the errors and pernicious doctrines which he has reprobated and condemned." The Syllabus, which circulated throughout Europe and Catholic countries everywhere, caused a sensation, for although the pope's temporal government had a reputation for being backward, few of his supporters outside of Rome were prepared for him to list as doctrinal errors the premises on which many of the liberal states of the day were founded. Eighty propositions were stated and condemned, among them Bible societies, pantheism, communism, and such concepts as freedom of conscience and religious toleration (No. 77), freedom of discussion and the press (No. 79), and finally (No. 80), the idea that "The Roman Pontiff can and should reconcile and harmonize himself with progress, liberalism and recent civilization."[13]

Seven months later, in July 1865, when all of Europe was discussing the confrontation between the pope and liberalism in its various forms, Emile Perrin of the Opéra sent Léon Escudier, Verdi's French publisher, to Busseto with a libretto for an opera *Cleopatra* and a scenario for an opera on *Don Carlos*. Verdi replied:

Cleopatra is not a subject for me. *Don Carlos*, a magnificent drama, possibly a little lacking in spectacle. Otherwise it's an excellent idea to make Charles V appear; likewise the scene at Fontainebleau [Act I of the original five-act version]. I should like as in Schiller a little scene between Philip and the Inquisitor, the latter blind and very old (Escudier will tell you why by word of mouth). I should also like a scene between Philip and Posa.[14]

Other plays were discussed, but in the coming months Verdi's interest focused on *Don Carlos*. Alas, neither he nor Escudier recorded the reasons for the Grand Inquisitor to be old and blind (he is both in the play), so we cannot be sure of Verdi's intent, but starting with Sophocles's *Oedipus at Colonus*, and perhaps before, age and blindness often have been symbols of inner certainty. Unfortunately, much about the writing of this libretto is obscure, for in late autumn Verdi went to Paris where he could discuss it face to face with his two poets, Joseph Méry and Camille Du Locle; and evidently the talks went well, for by the year's end he had signed a contract for the opera and had begun work on the music. By early December 1866 he had completed the scoring, and the premiere was set for March 1867.

Meanwhile in the summer of 1866, in a seven-week war, the Italian kingdom again fought the Austrian Empire for Venice, this time as an ally of Prussia, and came near to defeat. The Prussians, however, won so decisively on their front that Austria ceded Venice to France as the latter's reward for staying neutral, and Napoleon III, following the wishes of the Venetians as declared in a plebiscite, ceded the city and its mainland province to Italy. Except for a successful campaign in the Alps led by Garibaldi, for Italians the war lacked any touch of glory, and many were ashamed of how Venice had been won—through France. Verdi felt so angry and humiliated as an Italian that he tried, and failed, to cancel his contract with the Opéra.[15] Nevertheless, with Venice joined to the Italian kingdom a major objective had been achieved and a source of friction removed. Now, with only Rome and its province lacking, the pressure to seize these increased, and as the confrontation between the Papal and Italian governments sharpened, its reverberations everywhere echoed louder.

Of all Verdi's operas *Don Carlos* was the most finely tuned to the politics of its day. Not even *La battaglia di Legnano* (1849), with its premiere at Rome in the heady days of Mazzini and Garibaldi's Roman Republic, had touched so surely so many questions of the moment; and that opera had not been produced at the Opéra in Paris, the capital of Europe. What the world saw at the premiere of *Don Carlos*, on 11 March 1867, was an intensely human drama in which the figures also clearly represented current, conflicting policies: Posa and the King, freedom against so-called law and order; Posa and the Inquisitor, the clash between liberalism, both Protestant and Catholic, and papal conservatism; Philip and the Inquisitor, the constant strife between church and state. In European politics of the period the issues not only were capable of unseating governments in Italy, France, and the Papal State but also of causing schism in the Church, which occurred in Germany in 1870 with the still existing split between the Vatican and the "Old Catholics."

In the opera, as everyone perceived, only the Inquisitor in any sense "won," but in history, as everyone knew, he ultimately "lost." The seven northern provinces of the Netherlands in 1581 succeeded finally in breaking away from Catholic Spain and in their freedom entered on an era of startling artistic and commercial success. The same, said the liberals of 1867, would be true for Rome and its province if its people could free themselves from a government of priests. Similarly, the Church would be freer to devote itself to spiritual affairs if it would rid itself of the need to provide a secular govern-ment. On the other side, strong arguments were made that for the Church to be free of interference by the State it must have its own city, territory, and government: Rome, the Patrimony of St. Peter, and the bureaucracy of the temporal Papal State.

In Paris the state's censors, on examining the libretto, questioned as too severe the portrayal of the Grand Inquisitor in his scene with the King. "Taken as a satire on religious absolutism," they remarked, "this scene might find complete favour in the classic land of reform [Britain];[16] but will it be the same for us, who have not the same reasons for applauding it?"[17] In the end they allowed the text, but events proved their apprehension justified.

The Empress Eugénie, a leader of the conservative Catholic party in France, attended the premiere performance, found the portrayal offensive, and, as all of Paris soon heard, partway through the scene turned her back on the stage.[18] Her gesture attached to the opera, which certainly in terms of the day was anti-Papal, the more general charge that it was anti-Catholic, which it arguably was not. Nevertheless, to its problems of length and casting was now added one of politics, and at the Opéra it had only a season's run, forty-three performances, and then was dropped until 1963.[19] Perhaps, too, politics prompted the immediate production in Protestant London, where the opera succeeded, while helping to delay, until 1933, its premiere in Catholic Vienna. Indeed, the repercussions lasted still longer: when Rudolf Bing pre-sented *Don Carlos* at the Metropolitan, as the first production of his regime, 6 November 1950, there were pickets outside the house, protesting that the opera was anti-Catholic.

The Protestant and Catholic liberals of 1867, however, as much as Catholic conservatives, stressed the opera's politics. For them, Posa was the hero. Posa was for liberty, and in the end liberty would triumph. Philip's absolutism, which owed so much to the Grand Inquisitor, ultimately would give way. That was history. Then in 1870 came the Franco-Prussian War, and Napoleon III recalled the last French troops from Rome. As France began to lose the war, Vittorio Emanuele's government advised the other European governments of its intent to take over the pope's temporal power and of its plans to insure his spiritual freedom. No European government protested; most at the time were angry at the pope for his recent declaration of papal infallibility. On 20 September, therefore, Vittorio Emanuele's troops marched into Rome, ostensibly to prevent popular uprisings, and Pius IX retreated into the Vatican Palace, announcing to the world that he was a prisoner. The episode, though lacking glamour, was the culmination of the Risorgimento, the final step in the independence and unification of Italy.

In the worlds of literature and music the event, for most persons, jus-

Posa dead, with Don Carlo wrongfully accusing his father of murder and Eboli at the door to effect Carlo's escape. Front wrapper of Ricordi's two-hand piano score (1867). Because this score was intended for the Italian public, the Prince's name lacks its final "s."

tified the liberal interpretation of *Don Carlos,* which quickly became the only one. But now, a hundred years later, Schiller scholars have begun to question it, offering another that seems to me richer and deeper. Impressed as I am by their conclusions about the play, I have begun to think that the opera, too, has been impoverished over the years by discussions and performances that have ignored the ambiguity in Posa's character and actions. It is a facet of the play that I believe Verdi instinctively admired and intended to preserve in the opera.

The best evidence of this would be some document in which he stated in detail, as he once did about Eboli, his intentions for Posa; but alas, as his letter about the Grand Inquisitor's age and blindness suggests, he often passed on such observations by word of mouth, or left them unexpressed, to be revealed in the opera. Still, it is not unreasonable, I think, to infer that what scholars can see in Schiller, Verdi, who read Schiller closely, also could see; and I will sketch a circumstantial argument.

Verdi surely was interested in the kind of political drama that fascinated Schiller, for he set to music more of Schiller's plays than of any other dramatist: four complete plays and even a fifth, if one includes the introductory play to the Wallenstein trilogy that became a scene in *La forza del destino.* Of Shakespeare's plays, on the other hand, he set only three, and of Victor Hugo's, two. But in addition to *Don Carlos* many other of his operas have scenes—particularly *Ernani, La battaglia di Legnano,* and *Simon Boccanegra,* and to a lesser extent, *Nabucco, I due Foscari, Macbeth,* and *Un ballo in maschera*—in which he attempted to portray in music acts of statesmanship.

He also cared deeply for the sort of ambiguity that appealed to Schiller and responded to it in other playwrights. To cite four operas not based on Schiller——*Rigoletto* (Hugo): about which he wrote, "That is just what seemed so wonderful to me, to portray this ridiculous, terribly deformed creature, who is inwardly filled with passion and love."[20]——*Il trovatore* (Gutiérrez): about whose character Azucena he wrote, "It is necessary to conserve to the very end this woman's two great passions: her love for Manrico [her foster son] and her wild thirst to avenge her mother."[21] Why? Because the thirst for vengeance leads directly to the beloved son's execution. Also in *Trovatore* is another character torn by ambivalence: Manrico, who first abandons his mother to rescue his fiancée, then his fiancée to rescue his mother.——*La traviata* (Dumas *fils*): in which society's image of a "fallen woman" and her true nobility conflict.——And *Les Vêpres Siciliennes* (Scribe): in which the political revolutionary Procida, though he sings beautifully of liberty and the fatherland, is a monomaniac and a bully with whom, at the opera's end, it is almost impossible to sympathize.

About the political figures of 1867, how did Verdi feel? Did he see in them this kind of ambiguity? Take Garibaldi. In 1860 when Garibaldi, determined to unite all of Italy under Vittorio Emanuele, took 1,000 volunteers, landed in Sicily, and defeating much larger Bourbon armies captured the island, Verdi wrote, "By God, there really is a man to kneel to!"[22] Months later when Garibaldi, his army swollen with volunteers, crossed the Strait and marching north captured Naples, Verdi wrote, "What operas! What finales! To the sound of guns!"[23] And finally, when Garibaldi, refusing anything for himself turned over all he had won to the new kingdom of Italy, he was described by Verdi's wife, who seems always to have shared her husband's political views, as "the purest and greatest hero since the world was created."[24] But two years later, after Garibaldi's campaign to make Rome the kingdom's capital had ended in the fiasco of Aspromonte, she wrote: "As for the simple Garibaldi, he has dropped far in the opinion of right-thinking persons."[25] In 1860, he was a hero; in 1862, though pursuing the same goal of Italian unity by the same method, he was not.[26]

Then there is Posa's role in the opera, on which I would like to add two points. First, Verdi cast Posa as a baritone, a voice category he usually reserved for villains, or at least, ambiguous figures. And second, he carefully preserved a characteristic of Schiller's Posa that is typical of his own villainous baritones: a tendency to violence. In the garden at midnight when Posa realizes that Eboli has learned that Carlos loves the queen, his immediate thought is to silence Eboli by killing her. He draws his dagger, raises his arm to strike, and is stopped by Carlos, who is genuinely shocked. The action is swift, and the music beneath less distinctive than what precedes and follows, so that the scene, unless clearly staged, often passes without the point made. Some baritones even are too lazy to draw their daggers.

A moment, however, in which the music unmistakably comments on the ambiguity of Posa's role in the drama occurs during the *auto-da-fé*, in a scene that Verdi in a letter called "the climax" and "the heart of the drama,"[27] and about which he has left explicit instructions.

At the end of the third act, when the King steps forward to arrest his son, after the [King's] words, "Disarm him," there are three fortissimo bars for the orchestra of extreme violence, especially the final note A, which is accented by the bass drum and percussion. Then, after the words [of Posa] "Give me the sword," I would like a very long silence. And then when the clarinets [two, playing in thirds] reprise the theme of the friendship duet [during which Posa takes the sword from Carlos and presents it to the King], I would like a very soft, veiled sound, almost as if ifstage, quiet, smooth, without accent. You surely see what I mean. Needless to add, the brief exclamations of the singers should be *senza voce* [hushed, without the usual resonance]. If I linger on this point it is because I think it is important. I may not have done well by the scene, but it is a good one, you know, and makes a great impression, if well performed.[28]

Verdi did not exaggerate; the scene is one of the opera's most memorable. The friendship theme now sounds mocking, partly for the reasons stated by Verdi and partly, I think, because he also directs that it be taken at a slower pace. He drains the ardor from it, leaving irony, uncertainty, and the suggestion of betrayal. Posa's action in the confrontation between father and son may offer the best resolution to it, but he cannot escape responsibility for creating the situation, for urging Carlos to oppose his father. Verdi must have noticed in the play the ambiguity in Posa that now seems so clear to students of Schiller, because with this scene he not only preserved it but enlarged on it, for the action has no counterpart in Schiller. Yet here it is, entirely the creation of Verdi and his librettists and placed at the very heart of the drama where it sits not like a pearl, distinct from its surroundings that remain in health, but like a cancer spreading its corruption throughout the whole body. Posa is not the opera's hero as we have been led to believe; he is too deeply, tragically flawed. He is what is ultimately far more interesting: a man whose enthusiasm for a noble ideal gradually misleads him into actions of such moral ambiguity that he injures all his friends and causes one to die. This interpretation, I think, is not only truer to Verdi's intent but also better reveals the opera's richness.

*   *   *   *   *   *

As a coda, let me return to the idea that *Don Carlos* has the depth and breadth in its story and characters to shift the ground of its relevance for us. This already has happened once. From the opera's premiere in 1867 to about 1900, when it had all but disappeared from the repertory, Posa, as the illustrated jackets to the published scores suggest, was its hero. Then with the opera's rediscovery in the 1930s his theme of Liberty apparently began to pall. Even such a great and sympathetic Verdi scholar as Francis Toye could write at the start of this period of revival, "Posa often comes perilously near being a bore."[29] Ten years later, as the revival gathered momentum, Dyneley Hussey, another English scholar, suggested that "Philip is so remarkable a creation that he comes near to being the real hero of the opera."[30] Audiences in the years following seemed to acquiesce in these opinions. Ignoring the ambiguity in Posa's character, they flattened him into a one-dimensional figure, far less engaging than Philip. Articulating this opinion, Andrew Porter wrote in 1979, "The characters most fully felt are Philip, a lonely monarch, loving but unlovable and unloved, upright and honorable in action according to his own terrible lights, and the gentle, pure, dignified Elizabeth, whose lineaments Verdi traced with a tender and delicate hand. These are two full-scale tragic portraits."[31] Even the neurotic, weak Carlos came to seem more developed than Posa. Yet in the future, if performers, stage directors, and critics will restore Posa's ambiguity—and they need not change a note of music, only alter their own and the audience's perception of him—he may regain our interest.

We go to performances of *Don Carlos*, revel in the music, and are impressed by the range and psychological truth of the characters. In them we see, or should see, ourselves and the issues of our day, for that was Verdi's intent: he wanted the audiences of 1867 to see in the opera the European issues and events of that year, not of the opera's period, 1560. Something of ourselves we surely can find in the tangle of emotions among the royal family and Eboli, for these being chiefly human—love, loyalty, adultery, and generational conflict—are always with us. Of the political issues, the question of repression versus liberty is constantly renewed, and during the 1960s and early 1970s many persons heard in Posa's denunciation of Philip's "fire and sword" in the Netherlands a condemnation of the United States' policy in Vietnam.[32] Of the religious issues, the continual struggle between church and state at the moment is muted in most Christian societies though not entirely in some Communist and Islamic countries; and, as recent events in Iran have shown, a Grand Inquisitor employing church-sponsored terrorism against his own people is not yet caricature. Still, in Western countries, of all the opera's characters the one possibly most prevalent today, most typical of our society, is Posa, the political enthusiast who, in pursuing his aims, gradually falls into ambiguities, even to the point of sacrificing his friends and countrymen. Thus, in the coming years it may be that the character most likely to increase in fascination for us will be Posa. Not as before, simply as hero, but now, reflecting the peculiar complications and confusions of our time, as a vulnerable, fallible, modern man.[33]

6

OTELLO, MANZONI,
AND THE CONCEPT
OF "LA GLORIA"

It is hard enough in one's own language to be sure of the connotations of a word and harder still when the language is foreign. In American-English is a "film" the same as a "movie"? For many persons, apparently not; or not quite. For them a film is indeed a movie, but more artistic than the typical Hollywood product and almost invariably produced elsewhere. With such uncertainty on two homely terms, how likely are we to understand the nineteenth-century Italian concept of "la gloria" that Verdi and Boito made central to the character of Otello?

In English "la gloria" translates into "glory," and if "la gloria" is at the core of the operatic Otello, one might expect to find its English equivalent associated frequently by Shakespeare with his Othello. Yet Shakespeare not only never used the word in connection with Othello, he never used it in the play, not once. The closest he came to it is the adjective "glorious," used twice to describe war.[1] In Act II, scene 3, Iago states that he would have preferred to lose his legs "in action glorious" than to have seen Cassio drunk and brawling; and in Act III, scene 3, Othello, on the suspicion of Desdemona's infidelity, cries farewell to a catalog of qualities and virtues among which are "Pride, pomp, and circumstance of glorious war!" But in that line the arresting words are "pomp, and circumstance."

In the opera, on the other hand, "la gloria" is given prime musical and dramatic emphasis in Otello's first entrance as he cries:

Esultate! L'orgoglio musulmano
Sepolto è in mar, nostra e del ciel è gloria!
Dopo l'armi lo vinse l'uragano.

Rejoice! The Mussulman's pride
Is buried in the sea; ours and heaven's is the glory!
After our weapons the hurricane finished him.

Unquestionably the glory here is military, and this aspect of it is reinforced on Otello's second entrance, to quell the fight between Cassio and Montano. He is their General, and also, in person, a commanding presence, and this impression is further strengthened by Desdemona's first words to him when they are alone, "Mio superbo guerrier!" (My proud warrior!) But as their love duet proceeds, Otello broadens this concept by recalling how her attention to his accounts of his life had nurtured his love for her.

Scendean sulle mie tenebre la gloria,
Il paradiso e gli astri a benedir.

There descended on my darkness glory,
Paradise, and the stars to give their blessing.

For Otello, "la gloria" means more than the heroism of war. In the lines preceding the above, Desdemona had spoken of the dangers he had passed, the sorrows of his life in exile, and a period of slavery in Africa. For him the term includes freedom won and a homeland obtained, a civil as well as military life with dignity and honor. And perhaps even something more—"There descended on my darkness glory, paradise [. . .]"—perhaps an inner peace, a sense of balance achieved.

Later, in the quartet of Act II, when Iago has succeeded in arousing Otello's jealousy, Otello reveals three deep insecurities that Desdemona's love, he thought, had put to rest: his age, his color, and his lack of polish. Now, with the possibility that she loves another, these insecurities revive and hasten his readiness to think she might betray him. When, moments later, he has convinced himself of her adultery, he bids farewell to his "gloria" and includes in the concept—indeed he lists them first—his "sacred memories" and "sublime enchantments of thought"; only after these come the excitements of war. The loss is of more than merely military glory.

Ora e per sempre addio, sante memorie,
Addio sublimi incanti del pensier!
[. . .]
Della gloria d'Otello è questo il fin;
È questo il fin, è questo il fin.

Now and forever farewell sacred memories
[. . .]
Of the glory of Otello this is the end.

In nineteenth-century Italy, as in most Latin countries, the concept of "la gloria," the connotations it aroused, owed much to Napoleon. The term *"la gloire"* was often on his lips, and one of his most famous maxims was: "J' avais le goût de la fondation et non celui de la propriété. Ma propriété à moi était dans la gloire et la célébrité." (I had a taste for creation, but not for possession. My property was glory and celebrity.)

Napoleon at the beginning of the century had set a new style for glory, the self-made man of humble origin who could surpass in brilliance the best of the old aristocracy. And the brilliance was not only in military ventures but in law, religion, and culture. To the Latin peoples—particularly to the Italians who liked to recall that Corsica had been part of Genoa until 1768 and that Napoleon's family, therefore, was Italian—he was almost as much associated with legal advances, the Code Napoléon, and with religious reformation, the Concordats with the Papacy, as with military campaigns. In his meteoric rise he personified the breakdown of old social barriers, the principle of careers open to anyone with talent, and in the range of his talents, new possibilities of achievement. Probably no one in modern times has left a more profound impression on the imagination of posterity.

Shakespeare, of course, knew nothing of Napoleon, but Verdi and Boito could see in Shakespeare's Othello many of Napoleon's qualities and also how the nineteenth-century concept of "la gloria," which owed so much to Napoleon, could attach to the operatic Otello. In this they perhaps were inspired, certainly aided, by a famous poem, "Il Cinque Maggio" (The Fifth of May), by Alessandro Manzoni, the same Manzoni to whom Verdi dedicated his *Messa da Requiem*.

The poem is an ode on Napoleon, inspired by word of his death on 5 May 1821, and it quickly became the most widely read of all such poems and was translated into every European language (see Appendix A).[2] Verdi as a young man set it to music, though he never would allow the composition to be published.[3]

Manzoni begins with an effect that Verdi and Boito would repeat and amplify in Otello's death scene. Without naming Napoleon he starts with a two-word sentence, "Ei fu" (He was). The lack of any proper name is surprising, and commanding, but more surprising still is the past definite tense *fu* rather than the perfect *è morto* (is dead, or has died). In Italian the past definite, in a way that we can only approximate in English, at once moves the event and person into remote history, as if Napoleon were, say, Charlemagne. All the furies of contemporary politics are thus drained away, leaving only the man's essence. Of Napoleon's deeds and personality Manzoni asks, with a phrase that has sunk deep into Italian literature and thought, "Fu vera gloria?" (Was it true glory?). He implies it was not, with still another phrase that has become almost a maxim, "La gloria che passò" (the glory that faded). But he leaves a more definite answer for future generations and moves on to a subject not raised by either Shakespeare or Verdi: their protagonist's relation to God.[4]

Throughout the opera Verdi and Boito are notably careful not to squander the connotations of "gloria," and they use the word only rarely—in this essay I discuss every appearance of it—conserving it always for dramatic moments. In Act III, scene 2, for example, when all the Cypriots, the Venetian military staff, their wives and retainers gather to receive the ambassadors from Venice, one might expect a chorus of "Gloria a Venezia." But no. The offstage shouts are all "Eviva" or "Viva," and even the symbol of Venice, the Lion of St. Mark, is greeted "Eviva."

After Otello has thrown Desdemona to the ground and all except he and Iago have departed, he swoons, and from offstage, over rapid trumpet calls, come choral shouts of "Eviva! Eviva Otello!" And then in unison, with light accompaniment so that the words can be clearly heard, there is one great shout, "Gloria al Leon di Venezia!" followed at once by Iago pointing to Otello's motionless body, "Ecco il Leone!" (Behold the Lion!) Otello's glory is not true glory.

In the fourth act the word occurs only twice but each time at a crucial moment. The act divides in two parts, roughly equal, the first dominated by Desdemona, the second by Otello. In the first, Desdemona, having a premonition of her death, sings to her companion, Emilia, a sad song that she recalls from childhood. The song is in Shakespeare but comes earlier in the play, is less developed, and, of course, has no hint of "la gloria."

The song in the opera tells of a young woman who, abandoned by her lover, sees only death for herself. Desdemona constantly breaks its continuity with remarks to Emilia—"Hurry, Otello soon will be here" and "Put away this ring"—and in the third and final stanza she interrupts herself to say: The story used to end with this simple refrain,

> *Egli era nato per la sua gloria,*
> *Io per amarlo e per morir.*
>
> *He was born for his glory,*
> *I to love him and to die.*

There is nothing essentially martial in "la gloria" here; it is simply what one makes of life. Presumably the girl of the song died, but what happened to the young man is not disclosed.

Desdemona, of course, was singing about herself, and now in the second half of the act Verdi and Boito show us what happened to the young man who left the girl to follow his "gloria." Thus the song expands to become the opera.

Otello, believing Iago's lies, has killed Desdemona and, as her innocence is revealed, Iago flees. Otello seizes a sword, and when it is demanded of him, replies wearily: "Let no one fear me, though seeing me armed. This is the end of my road." Then with a great cry he exclaims, "Oh! Gloria! Otello fu."

For Italian ears, or for any with some familiarity with the connotations of Manzoni's "gloria," Otello with the word laments the loss of far more than his military splendor. He includes in it all those defeats and triumphs that made him a civilized man, a force for good for himself and for others. And his use of the past definite tense, so reminiscent of Manzoni's ode, is here far more shocking. For where Manzoni had used it to speak of a man already dead, though only recently, Otello speaks of a man who is still alive. Or rather, though living, already is dead. Thus Verdi and Boito, by a subtle use of grammar and a literary echo, were able to infuse Otello's brief outcry with deep emotion and meaning.[5]

CULINARY
ASPECTS

7

VERDI, FOOD, AND COOKS

Most of us who admire Verdi greatly are, I suspect, subject to fits of silliness about him. I have one of his discarded top hats, very battered to be sure, but still authentically his, and from time to time I put it on, hoping that some of his wisdom, talent, and capacity for work will rub off the interior band and stick with me. Others, too, have been so afflicted. When Mascagni visited Milan, after beginning to reap the riches of *Cavalleria Rusticana,* he often would stay at the Hotel de Milan, asking for "l'appartamento di Verdi" and agreeing to move if the great man gave notice of arriving; and move he did one night, about 3:00 A.M., so the suite could be made ready.[1] Even Arnaldo Bonaventura, a distinguished librarian and musicologist, a modest, mature man, admitted shyly that once while at the spa of Montecatini he had followed Verdi at a distance without speaking to him. Instead, "on that morning, just to say that in one respect I too had acted like Giuseppe Verdi, I drank what he drank: two glasses of water at the 'Regina' [bathhouse] and four at the 'Tettucio.' "[2]

To those who collect Verdi's autograph letters these offer a similar excitement, perhaps even more concentrated. The page on which the heel of Verdi's hand has rested, on which his eyes have focused as he scrawled his thoughts, retains the essence of him as he was in that brief moment of anger, humor, concern, or exasperation. No one, I think, can resist smiling at this two-sentence letter he wrote to Giovanni Maloberti, a man who often did errands for him in Piacenza: "Be assured I am not angry. I only wished to tell you not to send me any such pictures, and try in general to give me some room to breathe . . . because frankly you never leave me in peace and I have many things to do and sometimes I cannot even read your letters."[3]

Most persons, however, do not own an autograph letter, and a more universal way of associating with Verdi is to share his enjoyment of food. His pleasure in eating is a side of him not much noted by austere scholars and critics, but the more fleshly of us—gourmets, gourmands, and gluttons— find it delightful. I first came across a dish that Verdi liked in reading T. R. Ybarra's biography, *Verdi, Miracle Man of Opera* (1955). Ybarra's book, written in a popular, breathless style, was not much admired by critics and soon disappeared, but it was vivid, reasonably accurate, and had a short scene of Verdi going to market in Cremona.[4] After finishing his chores he enters the Albergo del Sole, sits at his usual table, and orders his favorite dish. "And, remember, plenty of butter," he calls after the waiter, who promises, "Sí, maestro." What did Verdi order? Veal cutlet *alla milanese*. I never have been able to find Ybarra's source for the scene, but as he usually was careful I am inclined to trust him, and the Baedeker *Handbook for Travellers to Northern Italy*, 1882, lists the Albergo del Sole in Cremona, rating it "mediocre." To this day, I find, if I am dining out with friends and one of us orders a cutlet *alla milanese*, I will remark, unable to conceive of any who do not care, "It was a favorite of Verdi."

Cremona, like Parma, Modena, and other cities in the Po valley, is still today, and was even more so in Verdi's time, an agricultural center where many of the local dishes are slathered in butter and cream, and yet, it should be recorded, the local population seems less inclined toward overweight than its counterpart in the industrial cities. Verdi, as his photographs reveal, never lost his figure; but his wife, Giuseppina Strepponi, as she herself ruefully admitted, at times developed an embarrassing "embonpoint."[5]

Whether or not Verdi frequented Cremona's Albergo del Sole and ate *cotoletto alla milanese* cooked in butter, there is no doubt that he rated highly the town's *torroni*, crisp almond biscuits very like a nougat, which he sometimes sent to friends as Christmas and New Year's presents.[6] He also admired its *mostarda di frutta*, a fruit preserve or relish flavored with mustard oil,[7] and in March 1868, having passed through Cremona on his way to Genoa, he wrote to his friend Opprandino Arrivabene:

I returned late last night from S. Agata and I found here your letter of the 8th. I am wracking my brain to think what there may be that is good and beautiful in Cremona. . . .

The *torroni*, the *mostarda*, and the *Torrazzo* [reputedly the tallest medieval tower in Italy]. Good Heavens! You don't expect me to send you the *Torrazzo* in a letter! Do me a favor; write me what you would like from Cremona. I will return on the 20th to S. Agata [via Cremona]; write me here at once, so that you may have at once what you desire. [. . .][8]

Three days later he wrote again about the "marvelous biscuits of Cremona" and talked of going to the bakeshops to buy some.[9] But his efforts came to naught. "I was the other day in Cremona, and I searched in many shops for your biscuits without being able to find them. Don't collapse in despair, however, because I have put my henchmen at every corner of the street, and if they see even a single biscuit passing by, it will be taken by assault and sent to [you in] Florence."[10]

To accompany the *torroni,* as still another letter suggests, Verdi preferred a white wine from Asti, not dry but sweet and bubbly, today's *Asti spumante.*[11] In general his taste in wine seems to have been that of the average late-nineteenth-century man of means. In his cellar at Sant' Agata he kept for special occasions French bordeaux and champagnes as well as the best Chianti, his favorite among Italian red wines. Strepponi in 1875, reporting on his health to the soprano Teresa Stolz, wrote: "Verdi is very well; he eats, runs about in the garden, sleeps and . . . drinks Chianti, nothing but Chianti, Chianti!"[12]

In these years Chianti was probably the best Italian wine, particularly that developed by the Baron Bettino Ricasoli on his estate at Brolio, near Siena. He gradually refined a mixture of three grapes: sangiovese at 70 percent, malvasia at 15, and canaiolo at 15, and at the Great Exhibition of 1855, in Paris, he won an award for it. Nevertheless, of the many Chianti vineyards Verdi preferred a small one, Pomino, not in the *classico* district, the hills running north from Siena to Greve, but in the foothills of the Apennines to the east of Florence, the area around Pontassieve. Today Pomino is a relatively cheap, rough wine—but a century ago it may have been excellent. Blights and subsequent replanting of vines, often of quite different stock, have changed the quality of many labels. But whatever the wine's merits in Verdi's day, he liked it, kept a standing order for it with Fratelli Conti, his wine dealer in Florence, and was tenacious in pursuit of it. Once he wrote to Signor Conti: "I received the Pomino but have found *six* bottles that are not full, others two-thirds. They are not broken; they carry the seal; but the wine is missing. Nevertheless, I am sending the amount due, and you, if you believe me, will consider making good on the wine that is missing." And he included a money order for 135 *lire.*[13]

For ordinary days at Sant' Agata he presumably drank the local wines of his region of the Po valley, most of them doubtless from his own vineyards. These local wines were then, and still are, mostly red and often *frizzante,* slightly bubbly, such as today's Lambrusco. In Ybarra's scene at the Albergo del Sole, for instance, Verdi ordered with the veal cutlet "a rough country wine," which almost surely was red and sparkling.

His interest in the preparation of food as an art developed only gradually, and one of the earliest stories to touch on it, revealing a taste for salted ham, dates from about 1845, a period when his first wife and children were dead and he had not yet begun to live with Giuseppina Strepponi, whom he later would marry. As a widower visiting his former in-laws in Busseto, he sometimes would drive alone to San Secondo to dine with a family of friends and enjoy the town's specialty, shoulder of ham. Others would be invited, and after dinner there would be music-making, often with selections from his works. On one occasion, however, while everyone was still at table, eating, his host's daughter seated herself at the piano and began to play arias from his operas. Apparently music, even his own, spoiled Verdi's enjoyment of food, and according to Dr. Michele Vitali, who was present, Verdi suffered patiently until he could no longer, and then, with an expression equally of embarrassment and annoyance, he rose suddenly and cried, "Stop, stop playing that music and close the piano!"[14]

In the decade following *Rigoletto, Il trovatore,* and *La traviata,* when he was assured of greater leisure and means to savor food, this interest begins to appear in his letters. Perhaps, too, by then his farms at Sant' Agata were beginning to produce foods and wines of quality and so enhanced his interest.[15] But he certainly had learned how to cook much earlier, probably as a child, and Melchiorre Delfico's cartoon of him (opposite), in which Verdi and his friend Baron Giovanni Genovesi reportedly are preparing rice and maccheroni, was sketched in Naples probably in 1858. Delfico and Genovesi were among Verdi's small circle of Neapolitan friends who entertained one another constantly, and the cartoon is, I believe, the earliest reference to Verdi as a cook for an occasion.[16]

One of his specialties evidently was rice, for Strepponi mentions it in two letters, the first from Turin to his former father-in-law Antonio Barezzi. Verdi had been elected a member of the Chamber of Deputies for the first Parliament of the newly formed Kingdom of Italy, and she had accompanied him to the opening.

Last night Verdi went to the Teatro Regio, in a reserved stall, hoping to remain incognito. But at the end of the second act of *La favorita* he was recognized and they began to shout "Viva Verdi," and everyone, from the boxes to the pit, stood up to salute the Great Composer from Le Roncole. If only they knew how well he composes *risotto alla milanese,* God knows what ovations would have showered on his shoulders![17]

Her second encomium occurs in a letter to a theatrical agent in St. Petersburg, where she and Verdi expected to spend the winter of 1861–62 while he completed and produced *La forza del destino*. The agent, Mauro Corticelli, represented the actress Adelaide Ristori, who was playing in Rus-

Verdi and his friend the Baron Giovanni Genovesi cooking maccheroni and rice. Caricature by Melchiorre Delfico, c. 1858.

sia; and Strepponi, asking Corticelli to provision Verdi's apartment with rice, maccheroni, cheese, salumi, and some French wines,[18] added: "Incidently, before I forget, if La Ristori expects *to outshine, to predominate* with her *tagliatelle,* Verdi plans to eclipse her with his *risotto,* which truly he knows how to prepare divinely."[19] Presumably this was *risotto alla milanese,* and probably in 1861 the term meant much the same as now: at its most basic, rice cooked with chicken broth and flavored with saffron, with butter and grated Parmigiano cheese stirred in toward the end of cooking, and more butter and cheese served with it. But its first variation (more likely to be served) adds white wine and beef marrow. Thereafter, all sorts of elaborations are possible: Marsala substituted for white wine; the addition of chicken, duck, game, mushrooms, truffles, goose or chicken livers, peas, chopped *prosciutto,* or almost anything the cook wishes. Verdi no doubt suited the recipe to the occasion, depending on what was fresh and available.

Plainly, however, he had more than one dish in his repertory, for when he gave a shoulder of ham to a friend, he was apt to advise exactly how to cook it. For example, he wrote to Teresa Stolz:

With this letter you will receive by rail a case containing two shoulders of ham, San Secondo style, which we are sending, one for you and one for the Ricordi family. Pick the one you want. Mind you, to cook this kind of shoulder well, you must:

1. Soak it in tepid water for about twelve hours to remove the salt.

2. Cover it afterwards in cold water and boil over a slow fire, so it won't blow up, for about three hours and a half, perhaps four for the larger one. To see if it's done, prick the shoulder with a *curedents* [French toothpick], if it enters easily, the shoulder is done.

3. Let it cool in its own broth and serve. Take special care in the cooking: if it's hard, it's not good, if it's overcooked it becomes dry and chewy.[. . .][20]

Ham in all cuts is a specialty of the Po valley, particularly around Parma, the area in which Verdi lived, and to many connoisseurs *prosciutto di Parma* and the rival but less well-known *prosciutto di San Daniele* (north of Venice) are, at their best, the most delicious hams in the world. Parma ham has several famous subdivisions: *culatello di Zibello*, a rump cut; Verdi's *spalla di San Secondo*, a shoulder cut; and *salame di Felino*, a sausage made from pure lean pork with no more than 20 percent of fat, flavored with white wine from Felino, whole peppercorns, and a little garlic.

There apparently is no record of Verdi cooking fish, although on market day in Busseto fresh fish is plentiful; but he evidently liked it, for his Venetian friend Cesare Vigna frequently sent him gifts of Adriatic delicacies,[21] and in Genoa, where Verdi and Strepponi kept an apartment for the winter months from 1866 until his death in 1901, he knew enough about fish to shop for it. One time, so the story goes, he was recognized by the fish-seller at the market, who remarked that he used to sing the King in *Aida*. Verdi supposedly replied, "I'll bet that you earn more from this basket [of fish] than from that crown." And the man ruefully agreed. Though to which of Verdi's possible meanings he was responding—bad voice, poor pay, or both—is not clear.[22]

In Genoa, Verdi's favorite restaurant was the Concordia, opposite the Palazzo Rosso on the Via Nuova (today the Via Garibaldi). Baedeker, 1882, described it as "handsomely fitted up and cool, music frequently in the evening." Verdi, however, most likely seldom heard the music, for he dined always at six, his hour for dinner on the farm at Sant' Agata. His wine usually was a Chianti, and if any remained in the bottle, he would write his name on a slip of paper, insert the paper in the bottle's neck, and drink the leftover the next evening. Among the waiters he was popular, for he was generous with his tips.

In addition to dining at the restaurant with Strepponi, he often ate there with the conductor Angelo Mariani or with Giuseppe De Amicis, an engineer with a large part in the building of the new section of Genoa, a project that greatly interested Verdi. Because of the evenings with Mariani, however, the Concordia has a certain fame in the history of *Aida,* for it was there one evening in the spring of 1871 that the great conductor reportedly told Verdi that he would not go to Cairo to conduct the opera's premiere. Instead, as it turned out, he went to Bologna to conduct *Lohengrin,* the first production of a Wagner opera in Italy. According to their waiter at the Concordia, the two men parted with Verdi saying angrily, "Anyone who breaks his word is not a man, but a boy."[23]

The cuisine at the Ristorante della Concordia was predominantly French, as the term "restaurant" implies, for in the nineteenth century an Italian restaurant, even the best, still called itself a *trattoria*. But in the years Verdi spent the winters in Genoa, according to his friend Ferdinando Resasco, he developed a liking for the local dishes, particularly *gnocchi* seasoned with basil and *ravioli genovese,* the stuffing for which, according to the twentieth-century gourmet Elizabeth David, should be made in the following proportions: four *scarole* (small Batavian endives), a bunch of borage, one pound of lean veal, one-half pound of calf's udder, half a calf's brain or a lamb's brain, a sweetbread, butter, four whole eggs and two yolks, a handful each of bread crumbs and grated Parmigiano cheese, and seasoning.

He also, by Resasco's report, enjoyed Genoa's *cappon magro,* which is not a lean chicken, but an immense mound of crustaceans, mollusks, fish, and vegetables served with a green sauce made of oil, lemon juice, parsley, capers, garlic, salt and pepper, with emphasis on the parsley.[24]

Another Genoese specialty he learned from a fellow composer, Serafino Amedeo De Ferrari, a native of Genoa and a frequent dinner guest. De Ferrari composed a number of successful operas, chiefly *Pipelè* (1855) and *Il menestrello* (1859),[25] and was at that time the head of Genoa's Institute of Music, but he and Verdi seem to have talked little of music and much of food. One night their conversation turned to snails, which De Ferrari extolled as a great delicacy, though Strepponi insisted that snails would make "a horrible, nauseating dish."

"Certainly, to be tasty," conceded De Ferrari, "snails must be cooked as I know how." And growing expansive, he recited a string of notable families whom he had converted to the dish by preparing a sample for them.

Verdi, taking up the challenge, cried, "Accepted for tomorrow!" And De Ferrari agreed.

The next day he came with a long white apron and chef's hat, *un berretto bianco,* and disappeared into the kitchen. At the appointed hour the snails were served. Verdi pronounced them delicious; Strepponi's opinion seems not to have been recorded, and De Ferrari is said to have grumbled at the cost of the animals which, apparently by agreement, had fallen on him. But he reaped a big reward, for he dined out on the story all over Genoa, saying, "The dish was one of the most beautiful of my compositions, and the one most authoritatively acclaimed."[26]

For daily eating at home, of course, Verdi and Strepponi relied on a cook, and there was sometimes trouble over these. Strepponi preferred women for the job, finding them less wasteful, lazy, and demanding than men.[27] Verdi, however, wanted more than an average cook, and he searched constantly for an artist, a *berretto bianco*. Coming back to Sant' Agata in June 1875, after conducting the *Requiem* on tour in Paris, London, and Vienna, he wrote to his friend Maloberti in Piacenza:

After Vienna I returned immediately here, and will not go to Venice.

Don't talk to me of pictures or furniture. I tell you again that I don't want any, and I would like you to stop writing to me about them.

I have need of something else—more material, if you like, but more necessary. I need a Cook; but I want one that's honest and capable, very capable. As for terms, we can come to an agreement easily enough. Would there be one at Piacenza? Mind now, I want him good and not a boaster.[28]

To find the right man he was prepared to go still further afield, and he wrote to a friend in Reggio Emilia, "Tell me whether at Reggio one could find a good cook. But I don't want one who knows how to make, well or poorly, three or four home-cooked dishes: I really want a cook, a real cook. I'll pay him what he is worth, but, I repeat, let him be a cook."[29]

At least one of the men hired soon proved to have some nonculinary faults. One day when Strepponi went into the kitchen, this Napoleon of the stove refused to acknowledge her presence, and when she reprimanded him he replied that "an officer on duty was not obliged to salute." Similarly, when Verdi expressed dissatisfaction with him he dismissed the censure by saying, "Anyway, how much do you think your four notes are worth?" Fired, he got another position, and upon discovering that having been Verdi's cook brought him honor, he wrote Strepponi a letter withdrawing his remark about the "four notes."[30]

Of course, sometimes difficulties arose because of Verdi's habits. When composing he could be oblivious of time, and there is the story, supposedly true, of his working on the final act of *Traviata* while the dinner hour came and went. Strepponi, caught between the cook's rising irritation and the certainty of Verdi's if interrupted, stood before his closed door, hesitating to knock. Hearing the strains of "Addio, del passato" and overcome by its beauty, or perhaps by the domestic tension, she began to weep. Fortunately

Verdi, pleased with his music, soon stopped work, opened the door, and embracing the weeping lady said in a matter-of-fact tone, "Ed ora andiamo a pranzo" (And now, let's go to dinner).[31] Though music lovers would judge the dinner well spoiled in return for the aria, the cook might not.

But however the fault in the Verdi household should be distributed, no *berretto bianco* ever seems to have lasted long. In May 1887, Verdi once again was writing to a friend in Piacenza, Signor Castignani:

I thank you for concerning yourself about the cook.

Ceresini has been over to my place twice, and I absolutely <u>renounce</u> him.

There remain the other two.

I will be in Piacenza Tuesday morning the 17th. Please send me at the hotel first one and then the other of the two cooks. The first at eleven o'clock, the other at twelve, and we shall see what can be arranged.[32]

Yet if the cooks seldom were satisfactory, food and cooking as an art plainly gave Verdi great pleasure and at least in one instance, allegedly, inspiration. According to Stefano Sivelli, an instrumentalist who grew up in Parma and who later at Cairo played in the orchestra at the premiere of *Aida* (1871), he one day in 1869 or 1870 was in a shop in Parma that sold earthenware goods when Verdi and Strepponi entered and began to examine the bowls. While they were debating which to buy, in the street outside a man named Paita, who sold cooked pears, began to call his wares in the Parmigiano dialect: "Boiènt i pèr còtt. Boièèèn!" (Hot cooked pears. Ho-o-ot!). It was no more than a street cry to a rhythmic refrain in a singsong voice, but as the man came closer—"Boiènt i pèr còtt. Boièèèn!"—it caught Verdi's ear. He listened for a moment, then hastened into the street. Drawing a small notebook from his waistcoat pocket he listened again, scribbled a few lines, and reentered the shop smiling.

Sivelli thought no more of it until a year or so later when he was in Cairo for the premiere of *Aida*. At rehearsal, as the orchestra for the first time played the opening chorus of priests and priestesses in Act III, he suddenly heard in the priestesses' soft refrain a familiar theme, the cry of a fruit

peddler in Parma offering hot cooked pears. "From that moment on," said Sivelli, "Paita was for me no longer the good old man from whom as a boy, I used to buy tasty fruit; he had become nothing less than an unknown collaborator of Giuseppe Verdi."[33]

We today cannot hope for any such glory as the old fruit peddler achieved—Collaborator! Still, like Mascagni and Bonaventura, we can, from time to time, partake of Verdi's activities and pleasures, sharing with him on occasion his enjoyment of such dishes as *risotto alla milanese, ravioli alla genovese,* or *spalletta di San Secondo.* And when in his last opera, *Falstaff,* we hear the fat knight, fresh from his dunking in the Thames, ask for a glass of hot wine, and hear, as he takes his first sip, the famous trill, starting in the flutes and progressing gradually into every instrument of the orchestra, we can be sure that Verdi himself once had known the joys of a glass of mulled wine.

> FALSTAFF: Good. To drink some sweet wine
> And unbutton oneself in the sun:
> Lovely thing! Good wine
> Dispels the grim nonsense
> Of dejection, kindles
> The eye and the thought; from the lip
> It rises to the brain and there wakens
> The little smith
> Of trills; a black cricket
> That hums within the tipsy man,
> Every fiber of the heart trills;
> The gay air, at the trill,
> Flashes, and a trilling
> Madness unbalances the merry
> Globe! And the trill
> Invades the world!!![34]

Verdi engrossed in reading. Caricature by Melchiorre Delfico.

MUSICAL
ASPECTS

8

TWO UNPUBLISHED EARLY WORKS: "LA MADRE E LA PATRIA" AND "MARCIA FUNEBRE"

Verdi's first published work was a collection of six songs entitled *Sei romanze*, which appeared sometime in 1838, when he was twenty-four or, if after his birthday in early October,[1] twenty-five. The songs anticipated by a year his first opera, *Oberto*, and perhaps only because of his steadily increasing fame had several editions, in France and Germany as well as Italy. But of the many unpublished works of all kinds that preceded these songs—we know the titles or specific character of at least thirty of the hundreds—we have had until now only two, and for that small number Verdi himself is responsible.

Few composers have been as resolved as he to rid the world of his early, unpublished works, and even with his operas he would do nothing in later years to advance those that he felt were unworthy. Asked one time about the quality of *Alzira* (1845), he replied, "Quella è proprio brutta" (That one is downright ugly),[2] and when La Scala planned a revival of *Oberto* for 17 November 1889, to mark the fiftieth anniversary of the opera's premiere, he tried privately to stop it. "Can you believe," he wrote to Arrigo Boito, "that today's public, with tastes so different from that of fifty years ago, ever would have the patience to sit through the two long acts of *Oberto*! Either they would be bored to death in polite silence (always a humiliating affair) or they would demonstrate their disapproval!"[3]

But La Scala went ahead, and Verdi, who had refused to leave his farm for the occasion, received congratulatory messages from the king, the prime minister, and thousands of ordinary people who sincerely believed that he was their country's greatest glory.

No doubt in Verdi's attitude there was a streak of irritation: he always hated personal publicity, being put on exhibition; he wanted attention for the work. There was also, however, modesty: his judgment of *Oberto* was fair. Even for its day it was old-fashioned and poorly constructed, and by 1889, two years after *Otello*, its only interest was that Verdi had composed it. Then, too, there was a sense of artistic responsibility: If La Scala must have an occasion, why not one based on a good opera? To involve the king, the prime minister, and the country's music lovers in celebrating *Oberto* was ridiculous.

These feelings of irritation, modesty, and responsibility attached even more strongly to the early unpublished works. In 1893, the owner of an autograph manuscript asked Verdi to authenticate it. The work was a setting, 184 bars for voice and orchestra with alternative accompaniment for solo organ, of the Eucharistic hymn "Tantum Ergo," sometimes sung in the Catholic Church at the Benediction. The title page of the score, not in Verdi's hand, stated that it "was composed in November 1836 and first performed on New Year's Day 1837 in the Church of San Bartolomeo, Busseto, by Luigi Macchiarelli, to whom the composer presented the autograph score as a gift in recognition of their friendship." Verdi wrote underneath, "I admit, alas, to having set to music, some sixty years ago, this *Tantum Ergo*!!! I advise the owner of this unhappy composition to throw it on the fire. These notes have not the slightest musical value or shadow of religious feeling."[4] The owner declined the advice, and today the autograph score is displayed in the museum at La Scala.

Only one other positively identified work exists that seems to date from these early years, 1825–38, when Verdi was growing up in Busseto, studying in Milan (1832–35), and then returning to Busseto to hold the post of *maestro di musica*. It is an operatic scene, "Io la vidi," scored for two male voices and orchestra. Its text, by Calisto Bassi, was written originally for an opera, *Il solitario ed Eliosa,* by Stefano Pavesi, and used again for another opera, *Il solitario,* by Giuseppe Persiani, presented at La Scala in 1829. At that time Vincenzo Lavigna, who three years later would become Verdi's tutor in Milan, was *maestro al cembalo* in the La Scala orchestra, and this fact has led several scholars to suppose that Verdi's manuscript score was an exercise in composition set by Lavigna.[5] That, however, is conjecture; to date, the only clues to the year of composition are those of musical style.

Verdi in his own hand entitled the work "Aria," but it is a full operatic scene of 183 bars, well structured and paced. No category of voice is specified for either of the two vocal lines, but clearly the melodic line should be sung by a tenor, and the other, less important and lower in range, by a lower, contrasting voice. There are many deletions and alterations in the vocal and orchestral lines, but the work is complete and has been performed. Verdi neither signed nor dated it, and nothing is known of its early history. Most scholars today seem willing to accept the date suggested by the present owner, the Pierpont Morgan Library, New York: "circa 1835." This would make it the earliest known fully scored work by Verdi to survive. To my ears the aria sounds as sophisticated as much of *Oberto* (1839), so I would date it later, circa 1837 or 1838. But who can be sure?[6]

Where are all those works that were composed, performed, and praised locally during Verdi's early years in Busseto? In 1828 there was an overture to precede a performance of Rossini's *Barbiere di Siviglia,* and some time after, a cantata in eight movements for baritone and orchestra, *I deliri di Saul,* and another for baritone, *Le lamentazioni di Geremia,* which Antonio Barezzi, Verdi's patron in Busseto and father of his first wife, described as "Che portentoso lavoro!" (What an astonishing work!). Still later, perhaps, were the settings of the choruses in Manzoni's dramas and the ode on the death of Napoleon. In addition, throughout these years Busseto had a Philharmonic Society, with Barezzi as president, and some of its handwritten programs for 1834 and 1838 have survived, showing most of every concert devoted to Verdi: vocal pieces, overtures, instrumental concertos, themes and variations.[7] Possibly the most tantalizing of all these missing works is a sinfonietta, *La capricciosa,* which was played as late as 1868 at the opening of the Teatro Verdi in Busseto, and which the *Gazzetta di Parma,* reporting the event, declared to be "a charming piece, composed by Verdi at the age of twelve."[8]

In 1853 Verdi stated, replying to a man who had written seeking information for a Catalog of Works:

From my thirteenth to my eighteenth year (the age at which I went to Milan to study counterpoint) I wrote an assortment of pieces: marches for brass band by the hundred, perhaps as many little *sinfonie,* that were used in church, in the theatre or at concerts, five or six concertos and sets of variations for pianoforte, which I played myself at concerts, many serenades, cantatas (arias, duets, very many trios) and various pieces of church music, of which I remember only a *Stabat Mater.* In the three years I was at Milan, I wrote very few original compositions: two *sinfonie,* that were performed at Milan at a private concert in the Contrada degli Orefici, I can't remember any more in which house, a cantata that was performed at the house of Count Renato Borromeo, and various pieces, most of them comic, which my master [Vincenzo Lavigna] made me do as exercises and which were not even scored. Back again in my home town, I began to write marches, *sinfonie,* vocal pieces, etc., a complete Mass, a complete set of Vespers, three or four settings of *Tantum Ergo* and other church music that I don't recall. Among the vocal pieces there were choruses from the tragedies of Manzoni, for three voices, and "Il Cinque Maggio" for solo voice.

All that is lost, and a good job too, except for some *sinfonie* that are still played here, but which I have never heard again, and the Hymns of Manzoni, which I have kept.[9]

In declaring all the works "lost" Verdi bent the truth, for many of them not only survived but were carefully kept, and he knew where. Indeed, only the previous year one of his houseguests, Léon Escudier, had seen them. In August 1852, Escudier, Verdi's French publisher, had come to Sant' Agata to deliver to him, on behalf of the French government and people, the Chevalier's Cross of the Legion of Honor, and as Escudier ten years later recalled:

I arrived as Verdi was about to start dinner. Another man was there, with a frank, open, likable face, a magnificent presence and almost twice Verdi's age; his simple manners, gentle and affectionate way of speaking, his broad shoulders impressed me; he seemed a true patriarch. He was Verdi's father-in-law. His name is Antonio [Barezzi]. We soon made acquaintance, and a quarter-hour later I was calling him familiarly Papa Antonio.

Now, to Papa Antonio, Verdi is a demigod; and in saying demi, I am stating only a half-truth. He cannot talk of Verdi without tears coming into his eyes. He lives in Busseto, and he is the town's natural keeper and archivist. He shows you with a pride that makes the composer smile and shrug his shoulders the room in which Verdi wrote *I due Foscari* [in Barezzi's house; still standing]. There, if you have won his confidence, if he sees in you a great enough admiration for Verdi, he shows you a mound of manuscripts that he guards like the apples of his eyes. These are the composer's first efforts.

"Look," he said, "at this pile of accumulated notes, these are the first melodic pearls harvested from the mind of my dear Verdi. At thirteen, he already was writing quintets and symphonies, without anyone teaching him the rules of composition; not only did he score for the different instruments of the orchestra, but he wrote them out the most astonishing facility. One can still examine these first attempts today, and one will not find the least fault in harmony. Five children, whom I myself trained, played at a village soirée the quintets of the maestro in embryo, and on hearing them, one recognized instantly the genius burning in that young imagination. Also at this age he composed, in his instinctive way, a grand overture whose manuscript is here. A military band that used to come to Busseto on feast days, played it publicly, and it caused such surprise, that everyone refused to believe that Verdi had composed it. He wrote a second. All doubt disappeared. Since then these overtures have continued in the band's repertory and even today appear on its programs."

How many times would Verdi have liked to stuff these old papers into the fire, with only a heartrending look from Papa Antonio to stop the auto-da-fé. I saw there a number of pieces of religious music, and I recalled that the first studies of the author of *Rigoletto* and *La traviata* were made on the organ of the neighboring church. These are the archives, or rather the *sancta sanctorum* of Papa Antonio. He has the key to that room and trusts it to no one.[10]

Plainly, while Barezzi lived, the man to whom Verdi, as he once wrote, felt he owed everything, "tutto, tutto, tutto,"[11] the collection was safe. But Verdi was the younger man and prepared to wait.

In July 1867 Barezzi, in his eightieth year, died, and possibly Verdi thought that because of Barezzi's love for him, the collection would be left to him, or that he might be given a chance to buy it from the heirs. But another event had intervened. In 1854 Barezzi, a widower, had married his house-keeper, Maddalena Fagnoni, and perhaps because he feared what Verdi would do with the manuscripts he apparently left them all to her. No doubt he had told her many times of their sentimental value and great artistic interest, and perhaps, too, he had mentioned their financial value, though that seems never to have been of concern to anyone in this story. So once again Verdi settled down to wait, but because Fagnoni was eleven years younger than he, the odds for success now shifted against him.

Nevertheless, he survived her, and on her death in 1895 he seems to have obtained the collection, or what was left of it,[12] though whether by gift or purchase from the heirs is uncertain. Equally unclear is whether he destroyed some of the manuscripts at once. Possibly he burned those that interested him least, saving only a few, among them surely his settings of Manzoni's cho-ruses and the ode. In any event, upon leaving for Milan in December 1900, when his age and health suggested that he might never return to Sant' Agata, he rehearsed his cousin, whom he had adopted as a daughter, in her promise that upon news of his death she would burn the two boxes of polished wood with all their contents. And this she did, with a fire in the corner of the garden. Did she believe what Verdi so often had told her, that the contents were of no importance to the world? I doubt it.[13]

If it seems incredible, considering Verdi's fame in Italy after *Nabucco* (1842), that of his hundreds of early unpublished works only the "Tantum Ergo" and the aria "Io la vidi" have survived, the explanation may lie in the small size of Busseto throughout the nineteenth century. Probably its popu-lation never exceeded 2,000 persons, never more than 500 families.[14] Imag-ine, then, the impact on it of Barezzi and Verdi working successively for more than sixty years to discover and own every scrap of music that Verdi had composed as a youth. True, Barezzi collected to preserve, and Verdi, to destroy. But who, possessing an autograph manuscript, could refuse it to either man, one the town's acknowledged archivist, and the other the composer—who reportedly was willing, if he could not obtain what he wanted by persuasion, to pay a high price? Is it any wonder that between them they swept the town clean?[15]

For a number of years, 1959–76, scholars thought that the sketch of part of a third work had survived, and it was added to many catalogs of Verdi's works. Entitled "Gesù morì," the sketch was of three duets, with sections of two more, for a traditional Good Friday service. The autograph manuscript was discovered in the Library of Congress by two scholars, Hans F. Redlich and Frank Walker, who jointly published an article on it.[16] Seventeen years later another scholar, David Stivender, after examining the manuscript, wrote a reply, concluding that Verdi's signature was "obviously a forgery," pointing out that the music was no more than "a sketchy copy" of Bellini's setting of the identical texts, and throwing strong doubt on the possibility that even the copying was done by Verdi. All in all, Stivender's arguments seem persuasive, and he closed his article with the stern remark: "Since it was Verdi's wish that not one of his early compositions should survive, there is a certain satisfaction in the fact that 'Gesù morì' can no longer be attributed to him."[17]

Against that background of apparent mistake and disapproval I come forward with what I believe are two short works in Verdi's hand that, from their simple style, probably date from the early Busseto years, perhaps as early as 1832. How they escaped destruction I do not know.

The two works are on a single, small sheet of paper, one on each side, and both are reproduced here in photographs of exact size. One is an aria, or because of its simplicity perhaps better described as a song; it is entitled "La madre e la patria" (Mother and the Fatherland, or possibly more suitably simple, My Mother and My Country). The other is a "Marcia funebre" (Funeral March), and its title includes the direction *"che segue all' ultimo rec.vo"* (which follows the final recitative).

Note where Verdi signed the sheet, high in the right-hand corner of the side with "La madre e la patria"; and where he dated it, Sera 20 Novembre (Evening 20 November), at the bottom of the reverse side with the "Marcia funebre." Because of these positions, and because the "Marcia funebre" is to follow some final recitative, I suggest that the vocal piece is on the front side of the sheet, or recto, and the march on the back, or verso. Whether this positioning also implies some relation between the two works is more problematic.

As can be seen in the photograph, "La madre e la patria" is a complete vocal piece to a patriotic text, reprinted below (as far as it has been possible to decipher it) and very literally translated. The music, at a designated tempo

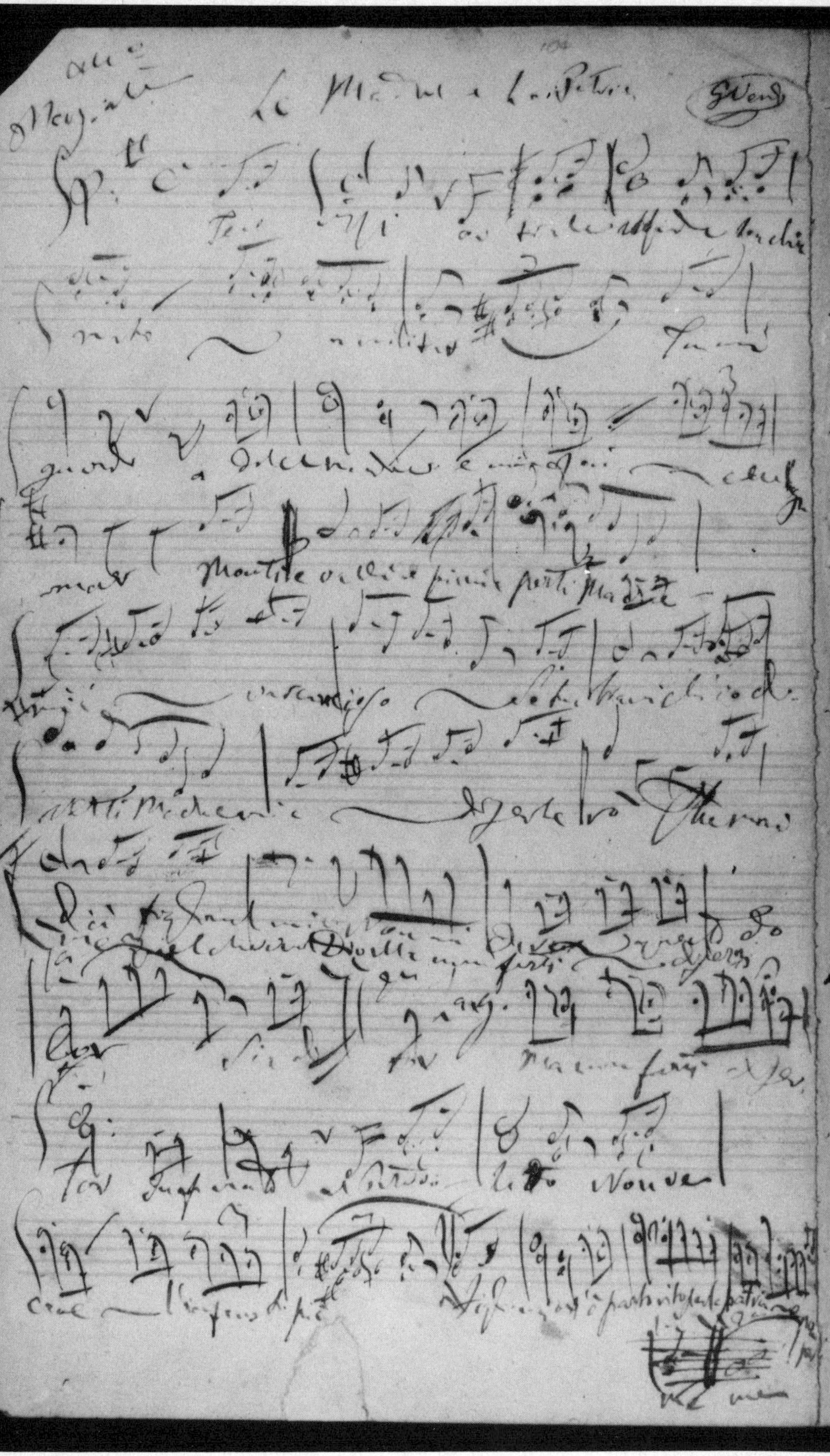

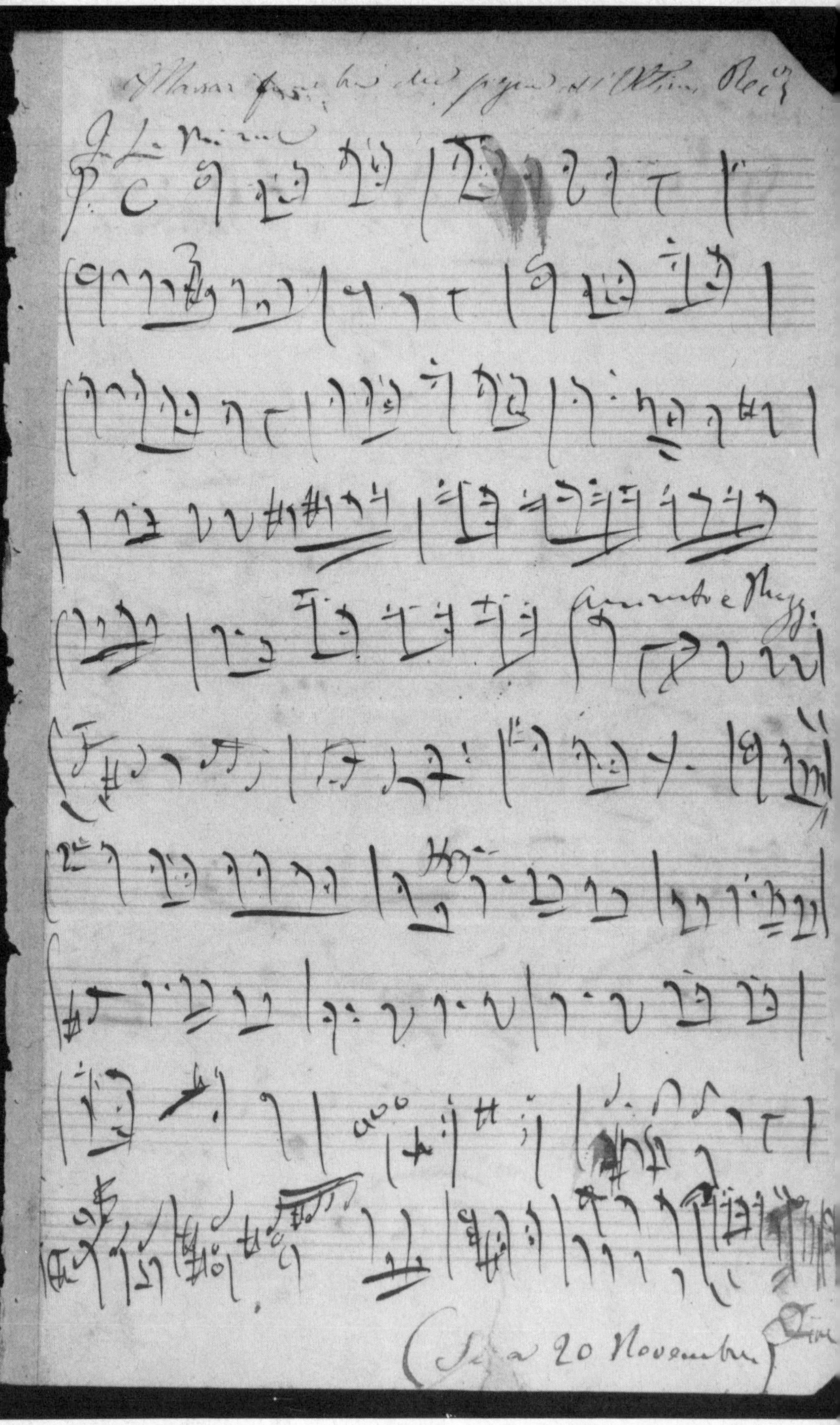
20 Novembre

of *allegro marziale*, consists of only the vocal line, written on a single stave with occasional two-part harmony, usually in thirds; it is in G major and runs to thirty bars, of which two four-bar sections are marked for repeats (the first of them to a different text). The text's meaning and the music's style suggest a solo piece, probably for tenor.

The "Marcia funebre" is a complete thirty-two-bar movement in A minor, written on a single stave with occasional harmonic indications, in a style and rhythm similar to "La madre e la patria." The title, with its direction that it is to follow some final recitative, indicates clearly that it was part of some longer work.

The text and music for both pieces is hard to read, and in my Acknowledgments I have named all those who worked on them. To the best of our multiple efforts the text of "La madre e la patria" reads as follows:

Teco vissi, or tra le squadre	*With you I have lived, but now with the troops*
Son chiamato a militar.	*I am called to the colors.*
Tu mi guardi, o dolce madre,	*You gaze at me, oh sweet mother,*
E non fai che lagrimar.	*And you do nothing but weep.*
Monti e valli e piani aperti,	*Mountains and valleys and open fields,*
Madre mia, varcare io so;	*Mother mine, I know how to roam!*
Se tu brami che io diserti,	*If you wish that I desert,*
Madre mia, disterò.	*Mother mine, I will desert.*
Che mai dici, Figluol mio,	*What ever are you saying, my son,*
Non mi dir questo dolor;	*Do not tell me this grief;*
Sia di me quel che vuol Dio,	*Let befall me what God wishes,*
Ma non farti disertor.	*But do not become a deserter.*
Infrangendo al giusto rito	*Shattering the honored custom*
Non recare l'infausto pie;	*Do not take this unhappy step;*
Figlio mio, t'o partorito	*My Son, I gave birth to you*
Per la patria e non per me.	*For the country and not for me.*

The thirteenth line, first of the last verse, has proved the most difficult, and no one yet has produced a reading that satisfies anyone else. Seemingly, the line begins with the syllable "In" or "Im," and ends, in order to make the rhyme, ". . . ito"; and in its center there is "al." Little is missing, yet it remains a puzzle.

Similarly, no one thus far has been able to identify the poem or its author, but it is most unlikely that Verdi himself wrote it, for that would be wholly out of character. Though he contributed to many of his texts by constant revision and suggestions to his librettists, he always stopped short of a finished literary work. Besides, the poem in its simplicity, drama, and patriotism is a typical early Risorgimento ballad. Anyone might have written it, possibly one of Verdi's friends in Busseto.[18]

What Verdi's setting might sound like if rewritten in modern notation and given a simple but appropriate harmonic underpinning is indicated in the two transcriptions prepared by Marvin Tartak, a musician and musicologist with experience in this sort of detective work and specializing in this period of Italian music. What appears in the treble clef of the two transcriptions is exactly what Verdi wrote; the bass clef, as indicated by the enclosing brackets, is Tartak's addition.

Before taking up the question of authenticity, let me give the history of the two works, so far as I know it. The sheet was advertised for sale by the English dealer Richard Macnutt in his Catalog No. 104, issued in 1972, and I bought it. Then, as eager purchasers do, I asked about its previous owners, only to be reminded by Macnutt that sellers or donors seldom give such information: they have their reasons. The Pierpont Morgan Library, for example, on purchasing "Io la vidi" from Macnutt in 1969, received from him an excellent analysis of the manuscript but no history. Such restricted knowledge is usual.[19]

Obviously, Macnutt and I think both works are authentic; equally clearly our opinions are disqualified for interest. My experts (see Acknowledgments), though they no doubt have their opinions, properly have limited their conclusions to deciphering the song's text. The authenticity of the two works must be decided, as in the case of "Gesù morì," by scholars working over a long period of years. Here, however, are some of Tartak's feelings about the words and music after living and working with them daily for almost a year.

Both of these pieces are written in treble clef only, often in two-part counterpoint (usually parallel thirds), occasionally with added lower parts to fill out the harmony. Both are complete, each filling out a page, even to the point, as in the song, of adding extra staff lines to make the music fit the space. In order to be so inclusive repeat signs are used in both pieces, with first and second endings.

The musical notation is often very hasty; occasional mistakes are immediately corrected. This handwriting does not look like any of Verdi's other manuscripts of the earliest period extant ("Io la vidi" aria of 1832–1835 or "Tantum Ergo" for tenor, c. 1836); these works are much cleaner and careful in their appearance. However, the words of the song and the composer's signature on the same page seem to be more closely in Verdi's handwriting.

The authenticity of the signature, of course, ultimately has little bearing on whether Verdi composed this music, but in itself it raises some interesting questions. Verdi, in writing his name, always included the final ring-around that is shown in six examples in this chapter, including the "forgery" on "Gesù morì." Sometimes it is said that a pattern exists in the way Verdi drew the grand final flourish, clockwise or counterclockwise. But after examining sixty of his signatures, nineteen of them in photographs and forty-one in autographs, I could not detect any pattern consistent enough to constitute a test. From the drag of the pen and flow of ink the majority seemed to go clockwise, but there were some that went counterclockwise and many in which I was left in doubt.

On a related point, however, I did reach a conclusion. Franz Werfel in his "A Portrait of Giuseppe Verdi" that introduces his collection of Verdi's letters put forward the theory that Verdi subconsciously encircled his name in order "to protect" his inner, creative self from "the shameless presumptions of a perpetually exigent world."[20] It is an interesting idea, and possibly true. Then Werfel added that as Verdi aged he drew the loop tighter, "leaving a smaller and smaller opening for the admittance of the world." And here, fresh from examining signatures, I disagree. The loop is drawn looser and looser, perhaps reflecting a changing attitude toward the world. His character, too, apparently changed gradually, growing more genial. His librettist for *Aida*, Antonio Ghislanzoni, found Verdi in 1868 a far less prickly person than in 1846, for with success had come confidence: "Verdi [. . .] may be said to have proceeded through a career of triumphs and discarded after each a part of that hard and rough exterior, which characterized him in his younger years."[21] Perhaps, therefore, an early work, if signed close to the time of its composition, should have a cramped, close signature. But all this is conjecture.

Here are Tartak's feelings as a scholar about "La madre e la patria" and the "Marcia funebre":

Can these pieces be forgeries? One can't be certain, but in my opinion it is unlikely. The purpose of forgery is to invent something which can pass for the real thing. These examples have so many questionable moments—the way notes are drawn, the messy appearance of the mistakes and their corrections—one must conclude the forger was remarkably unsuccessful. The fact that it doesn't immediately look like Verdi probably speaks *for* the composer as the author.

These pieces seem to be copies designed previously to fit on single pages. They are not incomplete sketches, nor are they compositional fragments in progress, à la Beethoven drawings. Most of the errors in rhythm or pitch really seem to be copying problems, not creative calculations. True, they lack a bass line; they can't be published as they appear, nor even performed as finished works. Yet, the entire idea is given; bass lines can be deduced from the given music.

Because these seem to be copies, one can allow a margin of uncertainty for the handwriting; it could be Verdi, copying in haste. Because there is little of this early period to compare with, one cannot be sure; the copyist of the music could be somebody else.

LA MADRE E LA PATRIA

Teco vissi or tra le squadre son chia-mato, son chiamato a mili-

-tar Tu mi guardi o dolce madre e mi fai, e mi fai che lagri-

-mar. Mon-ti e val-li e piani a-per-ti, Madre mia, madre mia varcare io

so, varcare io so; Se tu bra- mi che io di- ser-ti Madre mia, madre mia, diserter-

-ò. Che mai di- ci Figliuol mi- o; Non mi dire, non mi dire questo do-

-lor;   Sia di me   quel che vuol Dio, Ma   non   farti, non farti diser-

-tor. Ma non farti di-   ser-   tor. (In- fran- gen- do il giu- sto ri- to Non re-

-care, non recar l'infausto   pie;)   Figlio   mio t'o par-   ti-

-ri-   to per la patrià per la pátria e non per   me.   Figlio   mio t'o par- ti-

-ri-   to per la   patria per la patria e non per   me.

Marcia funebre che segue all' ultimo rec.vo

In La Minore

Animato e ?

(Sera 20 Novembre)

FINE

Assuming for the moment that Verdi wrote these two works, what is interesting in them? The song's text would have an obvious appeal for him, and its simplicity suggests that it probably preceded by a number of years the patriotic choruses that stretch from *Nabucco* to *La battaglia di Legnano*. Yet notice that even the song, despite its brevity, is not an account of an event by an outsider, but a drama: the young man speaks, his mother replies, and because of what she says he leaves her to fight for his country.

I have wondered whether the funeral march is the final chapter of the same story. Does the reference to recitative in its title mean that the two works were to be connected by a passage over shifting chords in which the singer states briefly that the young man fought, was wounded, and died? The funeral march then would follow as a requiem for the patriot. In short, a tiny dramatic cantata. Such a theory would explain why the two works are on a single sheet, why Verdi signed them on what appears to be the sheet's front side, or recto,[22] and why he wrote the word *"Fine"* (End) only below the march on the back sheet, or verso. Also, as is usual with musicians, he put the date, Sera 20 Novembre, at the close of the two pieces, apparently treating them as one.

How the sheet with the two works escaped Verdi and Barezzi, I have no idea. Presumably someone in Busseto very early got possession of it and thereafter kept it in a private collection. The margins of the sheet are cropped close to the music, as if to conform it to the size of a book or to prepare it for framing; but again, Who knows? Only two opinions can be certain: Verdi would be displeased the works have surfaced, and Papa Antonio, delighted.

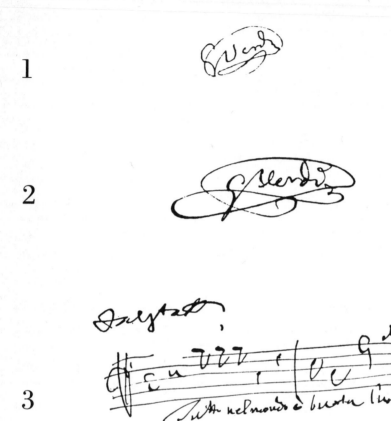

Signatures: 1. The "forgery" on "Gesù morì" (supposedly composed in the 1830s); 2. From the title page of the autograph score of *Falstaff* (1893); 3. From a card written in 1898, with the opening bars of the fugue that closes *Falstaff*.

A comparison of these signatures with others reproduced in this chapter—on "La madre e la patria" (circa 1832–35), the letter to [Léon] Escudier (1848)[a], and the autograph sketch of an aria for *La battaglia di Legnano* (circa 1848)[b]—reveals that Verdi seldom made his *V* as rounded at its bottom as in the "Gesù morì" signature and never drew the final flourish so deeply through the top loop of *G*. These are two reasons the "Gesù morì" signature[c] seems a forgery.

Car[issi]mo Gautier

Se il Sig.[r] Gravrand in vece di partire stasera per Bruxelles potesse aspettare fino a domani io potrei darle la musica dei balletti perché senza fallo domattina prima delle 12 ore io avrò a Parigi colla partitura terminata — Procurate di vedere il Sig.[r] Gravrand ed in ogni modo scrivetemi un bigliettino per la piccola posta

Add[i]o

G. Verdi

Besides offering at full-size a typical example of Verdi's handwriting and signature, this previously unpublished letter also is interesting in its reference to ballet music, now lost, that he composed for a performance of *Nabucco* in Brussels in 1848. The letter's date can be determined and its significance clarified if read in conjunction with another hitherto unpublished letter, also transcribed and translated in Appendix C.

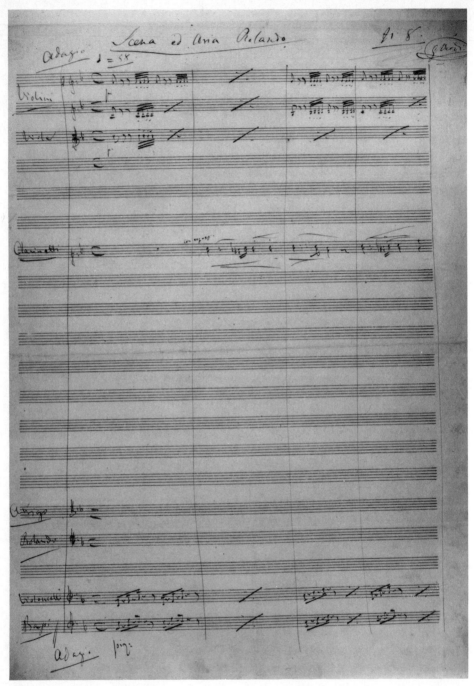

Autograph sketch, previously unpublished, for the start of Scene 8 in *La battaglia di Legnano*. Note how Verdi put the lower strings at the bottom of the page and the vocal line just above them. The reproduction is about quarter-size.

9

THE
CURSE IN
RIGOLETTO

The use of a recurring theme in a musical work to signify the return of a person or idea has a long history. Indeed, it is such an instinctive form of drama that its roots probably lie in the first appearance, whether in song or ritual, of a refrain. In opera it can be found in one of the earliest, Monteverdi's *Orfeo* (1607), and ever since, particularly in opera, it has flourished. Wagner, as all the world knows, developed in the four operas of the *Ring* his system of themes or motifs that return in different manifestations as the drama unfolds, and Verdi, though the fact is not so well recognized, created a technique almost as revolutionary in his handling of the curse in *Rigoletto* (1851).

By the mid-nineteenth century, as Joseph Kerman has shown in his essay "Verdi's Use of Recurring Themes,"[1] Italian composers were employing these in several ways. The most common was, in Kerman's phrase, as an "identifying theme," which at its simplest, as in Verdi's *Nabucco*, represents groups of people, the Babylonian army or the Hebrew priests. In *I Lombardi*, for instance, the Christians and the Moslems each have a melody, and an offstage battle is represented by the two melodies alternating, then contending, with that of the Christians emerging triumphant. Or sometimes a theme can represent a person, such as the short, rather rigid phrase for Lucrezia in *I due Foscari* or the longer, more supple melody for Aida. A theme also can signify an idea. In *Un ballo in maschera* the broken, staccato phrases for Sam and Tom also represent their conspiracy against the king, and in *La forza del destino* the pounding, rushing melody of the overture epitomizes the irreversible fate of the title. Verdi's use of themes in this fashion, throughout his long career, remained relatively simple.

Composers also frequently employed "recalling themes," and these usually were introduced late in the opera to impress on the audience how the situation associated with the melody's first appearance now was changed. Typically, the melody reappeared in dreams or mad scenes, as in the final act of *Lucia di Lammermoor* (1835), when Lucia in her madness recalls the man she loves, but did not marry, with music from their love scene in Act I. Perhaps the greatest of such recollections is Verdi's "bacio" or "kiss" theme in *Otello* (1887), which because of its beauty and position in the opera's final bars not only summarizes the preceding four acts but also provides their catharsis. Characteristically, Verdi, though relying on an old technique, revitalized it by using it to perfection.

Among recalling themes Kerman distinguishes two sorts, literal and imaginative, and though at times, as in *Otello*, the two seem to overlap, the distinction is valid. In *Ernani*, for example, the theme's return in Act IV as Silva quotes Ernani's pledge is almost an exact repetition of Ernani making the pledge in Act II: the two men are again face to face, and the music is the same. But in *Rigoletto*, only seven years later, the recollection is treated quite differently. Rigoletto recalls Monterone's curse without Monterone onstage and in music which, though related to the curse, is not the same. Even more surprising, the recollection occurs not toward the end of the opera but at the opening of Act I, scene 2. In fact, the music of the curse delivered in the opening scene and by its repetition, sometimes varied, in every scene thereafter, forms the musical core of the opera. As a result, *Rigoletto* differs not only in structure from its Verdian predecessors but also in humanity. In *Ernani*, however passionately the characters may protest their feelings, they are at best only fitfully human. Because their story resides essentially in the events in which they are involved, we tend to remain outside them, seeing them almost as costumed voices: the tenor, the bass, the soprano. In *Rigoletto*, on the other hand, because the jester's feelings and his response to them are the heart of the story, from which the focus seldom shifts, we tend to enter into his spirit, to see the events wholly from his point of view and, finally, to understand him. No one talks of Rigoletto as "the baritone." In him Verdi created a psychological study that still seems remarkably modern.

How Verdi achieved this sudden advance in subject matter and technique is interesting in itself and, surprisingly, often not well understood. There are many of us, I suspect, who have heard the opera ten times or more, and yet are not fully aware of the extent to which Verdi bedded into its musical structure the curse's theme. Frequently we sense its presence without penetrating its disguise—which no doubt is what Verdi intended. But he would not be angry, I think, if I try to reveal a little of his magic, tracing through the opera the musical theme in most of its variations, and, in so doing, attempting to define more precisely what also often is only partially grasped: the exact nature of the curse.

But first a word about sources, for in examining Verdi's approach to *Rigoletto* and the curse, we have more material available than for most of his operas. Because he and his librettist, Francesco Maria Piave, were in different parts of Italy when they began to discuss the libretto to be drawn from Victor Hugo's play *Le roi s'amuse*, their thoughts were set down in letters. And later, because the censors in Venice objected to "the revolting immorality and obscene triviality of the libretto entitled *La maledizione*,"[2] the opera's proposed title, Verdi was forced to reiterate many of his ideas, again in letters, not only to Piave, who represented him before the censors, but also to the management of the Teatro La Fenice, which was to stage the opera's premiere. Nevertheless, there are two gaps in the correspondence, occurring when Piave visited Verdi in Busseto. The shorter, a week over New Year's Day, 1851, probably is not important; but the other, four weeks in midsummer, may well be crucial, for it was then that the libretto was fashioned. Though we know much, we cannot follow every turn of their thinking.

With regard to the music, we have, in addition to the published score, Verdi's preliminary sketch for the entire opera, lacking only the opening prelude and part of the final duet. The prelude, as was Verdi's custom, almost certainly was the last music to be composed, probably not until the fortnight before the premiere on 11 March 1851. Similar sketches for all the operas from *Luisa Miller* through *Falstaff* are reported to be in the possession of his heirs, but thus far only this one has been released.[3] The existence of the others, however, strongly suggests that such a preliminary sketch was always an important step in composing an opera, and the one we have for *Rigoletto* is a fascinating document, revealing in part how Verdi conceived and revised a work in the course of composition.

It consists of twenty-eight large sheets of thick paper with printed musical staves on both sides.[4] On these fifty-six pages Verdi inscribed the vocal lines with text, sometimes adding brief indications of accompaniment and orchestration. Many details are lacking, such as clefs, key signatures, tempos, and dynamic markings as well as most repeats and second stanzas of arias. In several instances, where we know from letters that Verdi was unhappy with Piave's verses, the vocal line is indicated but the text is omitted, suggesting that despite his remarks to the contrary, he sometimes composed without specific words. The whole gives the appearance of having been written swiftly and, except for an occasional correction, without hesitation. Obviously by the time he was able to set down a continuous vocal line for the opera he must have done a great deal of work on the libretto, letting its drama, rhythms, and nuances sink deep into his subconscious, and this is borne out by the correspondence. By early June 1850, he and Piave had settled on *Le roi s'amuse* as the opera for Venice in the winter of 1851;[5] by mid-August, as he wrote to the opera house management, he had fixed in his mind the musical concept and color of the opera;[6] and in mid-October, after much discussion back and forth, Piave mailed to him the final lines of a libretto they were calling *La maledizione*. But even then Verdi had not composed any music for it, or so he wrote to Piave; he always preferred, he said, to delay actual composition until the libretto was finished and polished.[7] But also, he only recently had returned from eleven days in Bologna, where he had produced a revival of *Macbeth*, and he was in the midst of orchestrating another opera, *Stiffelio*, for its premiere at Trieste on 16 November.

By late November he was back in Busseto and began at once on *La maledizione*. His letters reveal that he wrote the sketch from late November to late January 1851, and toward the end of this period, because of the censors, the opera's title was changed to *Rigoletto*. Some time earlier, again because of the censors, the characters' names had been changed. Thus, in Act I of the sketch the Duke of Mantua is still the King of France and his jester, not yet Rigoletto, is Triboulet; by Act II they have their present titles and names, though on one page Verdi almost forgot, started to write "Triboulet" and had to scratch it out. Work on the sketch, therefore, stretched over seven or eight weeks, and surely there must have been some experimentation with the music before it was put to paper. Nevertheless, the sketch probably is as close as we can come to his original inspiration.

Roughly ten years after the opera's premiere a friend asked Verdi, "When you are composing one of your stupendous pieces of music, how does the idea for it present itself to your mind? Do you work out the main theme first and then add an accompaniment, whether it shall be for flutes or violins and so forth?" Verdi interrupted, "No, no, no. The idea comes complete, and above all I feel the color of which you speak, whether it shall be for flutes, violins and so forth. My difficulty is in writing down the musical thought quickly enough to capture it in its integrity just as it comes into my mind."[8] The sketch for *Rigoletto* suggests that this flood of inspiration, suddenly released after months of work on the libretto—discussing it, brooding on it, memorizing it—encompassed not only individual arias and scenes but the opera as a whole. Though Verdi polished and revised, and even completely rewrote one number, the entire opera, dramatically and musically, is in the sketch.

Finally, before starting to analyze his treatment of the curse, let me add that after the premiere of *Rigoletto* Verdi never changed a note. The opera was an immediate success, and he saw no reason to revise any part of it. So, happily, we do not have to deal with subsequent versions.

*　　　*　　　*　　　*　　　*　　　*

In deriving a libretto from Hugo's play Verdi and Piave were directed by Hugo himself to the importance of the curse. The play had been closed by the French government on the ground of immorality after a single performance, 22 November 1832, and was not permitted to reopen;[9] but Hugo, reveling in the scandal, wrote a Preface to the published text in which, with his usual rhetoric, he analyzed the morality of the play's thesis:

Triboulet [Rigoletto] is deformed, Triboulet is diseased, Triboulet is a court jester—a triple misery that leads to evil. Triboulet hates the King [the Duke of Mantua] because he is the King, hates the nobles because they are the nobles, his fellow men because they have no humps on their backs. His sole occupation is setting the nobles against the King, breaking the weak and strong alike. He debases the King, corrupts him, brutalizes him [. . .] continually showing him which [noble's] wife to seduce, sister to kidnap, daughter to dishonor. The King in Triboulet's hands is merely an all-powerful puppet who shatters the lives of those the jester leads before him.

One day, in the midst of a court festival, at the very moment Triboulet is urging the King to abduct the wife of M. de Cossé [Ceprano], M. de Saint-Vallier [Monterone] steps before the King and boldly reproaches him for the dishonor of Diane de Poitiers. This father, from whom the King has taken his daughter, is mocked and insulted by Triboulet. The father raises his arm and curses the jester. From this act springs the whole story. The real subject of the drama is *the curse of Saint-Vallier* [Hugo's emphasis] [. . .]

Triboulet has a daughter [. . . .] He hides her from all eyes, in a deserted quarter of the city, in an isolated house [. . . .] He raises his child to be innocent, trusting, modest. His greatest fear is that she will fall into evil, since, being evil himself, he knows what suffering it causes. Well then! The old man's curse will strike Triboulet through the only person in the world he loves, his daughter. This same King whom Triboulet urges to the practice of rape will ravish Triboulet's daughter. The jester will be struck by Providence exactly in the same manner as was M. de Saint-Vallier.

Then Triboulet, his daughter assaulted and dishonored, will lay a trap for the King by which to avenge her; but it is she who will fall into it. Thus he has two pupils—the King and his daughter; the King, whom he has trained to vice, and his daughter, whom he has raised to virtue. One will destroy the other. He intends Mme. de Cossé to be abducted for the King; it is his daughter who is kidnapped. He means to kill the King, and so avenge his child; it is his daughter whom he kills. Punishment does not stop halfway; the curse of the father of Diane is accomplished on the father of Blanche [Gilda].[10]

Hugo's defense notwithstanding, the play is a parade of nastiness, which is advanced by unlikely coincidence and redeemed, if at all, by a few scenes of tremendous emotion. The opera, though adding to the play's improbabilities, otherwise improves on it by lessening the display of vice, increasing the number and intensity of the powerful scenes, and strengthening the structure of the final act. It even enlarges on the theme of the curse, which is where Verdi and Piave began their discussions. In one of his early letters to Piave, 3 June 1850, Verdi, closely following Hugo, wrote: "The whole subject is in that curse which [. . .] seems to me to be moral and great in the loftiest sense of the word. Take care that La Vallier [Monterone] must not appear (as in the play) more than twice and must speak very few, emphatic words. I repeat: the whole subject lies in that curse."[11]

What sort of music, then, does Verdi give to the curse? And how, despite the distraction of events, does he keep it to the fore? Let us start with the opera's first scene, which is the same as the play's: an outraged father—Saint-Vallier in the play and original libretto, Monterone in the opera—forces his way into a court ball, insisting that he will speak to the Duke.

MONTERONE *(offstage)*: Let me speak.
DUKE: No!
MONTERONE *(entering)*: I wish it.
ALL: Monterone!
MONTERONE *(looking at the Duke, with noble pride)*:
    Yes. Monterone.
    My voice like thunder
    Will reach you everywhere.

Before he can continue, Rigoletto comes forward, imitating his voice and requesting the Duke's permission to reply.

In Verdi's final version Monterone in this entrance has twenty-six notes to sing and twenty-five are middle C or an octave below. The bars shown (Ex. 1, page 176) are typical, and the corresponding bars of the sketch (Ex. 2) are almost identical. In polishing, however, Verdi tightened the rhythms slightly,

making its dotted quality, typically (te-DEE, te-DEE), more pronounced; further, by eliminating the rise to E above middle C, he emphasized the tonal quality of the C and its octave.

He made a similar change later in the scene when Monterone delivers the curse. Actually, as in the play, Monterone delivers the curse twice. First, in a relatively gentle outburst, he damns the Duke and Rigoletto jointly, "Ah, may you both be cursed," and the two men, though startled, are unimpressed. But then, turning on the jester alone, he grows far more threatening and, unknowing, touches on the one fear that can unnerve Rigoletto, the possibility of harm to the beloved daughter concealed from the court. At full voice Monterone thunders, "And you, serpent, who mock a father's grief, be accursed!" (Sii maledetto!).

Verdi, in revising the musical line of "Sii maledetto!", included in the final version a middle C (Ex. 3), where there had been none in the sketch (Ex. 4), and gave it weight by assigning to it the first, snarling syllable of "mal-edetto." In addition, by indicating with an "eyebrow" that the singer was to hold that note, accenting it still more, he introduced into the phrase the equivalent of a dotted rhythm. In performance this new tonality and rhythm for the curse are very marked because the crucial first three notes, "Sii ma - le . . . ," are sung unaccompanied whereas the final two, ". . . det - to!", are obscured by the full orchestra crashing in *double-forte*.[12]

Now compare this with Rigoletto's entrance, which precedes Monte-rone's. He appears onstage usually (neither the score nor the libretto indicates exactly when) a moment or two before the Duke, who has been flirting with the Countess Ceprano, leads her away from the ball into another room. Rig-oletto's first words, to the unhappy Count Ceprano, are a sexual jeer, a reference to a cuckold's horns, "What have you on your head, Signor Cepra-no?"[13] Then, after a few more remarks ending with a laugh at Ceprano's agony, he goes off, having sung in all seventy-eight notes, of which fifty-eight are on middle C and many in Monterone's dotted rhythm. The final twenty-four are all on middle C, and because the orchestra is silent the note's tonality is driven home hard. Thus the predominant tonality and rhythm of Rigoletto's entrance has prepared us to pick up more quickly the identical stress in Monterone's.

Rigoletto is offstage only a few minutes, but during that time the court-iers, who hate him, hear from one of their number, Marullo, that he has discovered something important about the jester: he has a mistress. In fact she is Rigoletto's daughter Gilda, but the courtiers, if they knew, would not care: any beloved makes vulnerable the one who loves.

Rigoletto returns with the Duke, still before Monterone appears, and with his opening phrase suggests that the Duke, for the night's sexual fun, kidnap the Countess Ceprano. The suggestion is sung entirely on middle C and, by Verdi's direction, against a much reduced accompaniment. There-after a large ensemble develops in which the Duke stops Ceprano from attack-ing Rigoletto, and the courtiers agree among themselves to meet in the morn-ing with Ceprano to plan revenge on the jester. Note that, as in the play, they start their action before Monterone delivers his curse, and though they may be considered by the superstitious, including Rigoletto, to be agents of the curse, they in fact plot and act independently of it. Meanwhile, dancers sweep to center stage, everyone sings of the evening's pleasures, and then Monterone enters, silencing all with his barrage of middle Cs in dotted rhythms.

Though today many opera companies cast Monterone as a bass, Verdi in the month before the premiere requested for the role "the best baritone" on the Fenice roster.[14] He wanted Monterone's timbre of voice to resemble Rigoletto's. And from the way he planned their initial entrances, each with so many middle Cs and dotted rhythms, I believe that he conceived the two men, so alike in their love for their daughters, so dissimilar in their characters and relationship to the Duke, as musically related because dramatically bound to each other. Rigoletto, who has instructed the Duke in sexual vice and abuse of power, cannot escape judgment forever, and Monterone alone at court has the courage and character to denounce him publicly.[15] At this court one day they will collide. The curse is inevitable.

The concept of two men bound to each other by circumstances and personalities that must result in a curse and therefore, even before its declaration, sharing in its distinctive tonality and rhythm seems to me artistically valid because psychologically true. The idea evidently was in Verdi's mind when he began the sketch, but we can see in his revisions from sketch to final version how he sharpened it, conforming the particularity of the curse to the more general relationship of the two men. As Act I, scene 2 opens, Rigoletto has left the ball at court and started for home. In the street, as the curtain rises, he murmurs to himself, "Quel vecchio maledivami" (That old man cursed me). In the sketch this starts on middle C but moves up the scale to F and then drops to octave F (Ex. 5); in the final version it is delivered entirely on middle C and in the curse's dotted rhythm (Ex. 6). Dramatically this change makes his musing more introverted; musically it relates the phrase more closely to the Cs and dotted rhythms of the two entrances.

The same is true when Rigoletto, after dismissing the assassin Sparafucile, ruminates again, "Quel vecchio maledivami." The sketch, as before, starts on middle C and rises to F before dropping the octave (Ex. 7), though in this case the original rhythm is dotted. In his revision, however, Verdi repeats exactly the middle Cs and dotted rhythms of the final version's first setting (Ex. 5).

Similarly a few moments later: when Rigoletto reiterates the thought before dismissing belief in the curse as "Folly!", the sketch ends on a rise to D flat followed by an octave drop, straying briefly from middle C (Ex. 8). But in the final version the vocal line, as in the two previous statements, is entirely on middle C, with the dotted rhythm varied only slightly (Ex. 9). The accompanying instrumentation, however, is just as before: clarinets, bassoons, violas, cellos, and double basses. Thus, in the opera's final version

Rigoletto within a brief period thrice repeats the thought to almost identical music, always on middle C, always to the same orchestral sound, always in dotted rhythm.

Then, toward the end of the scene when Rigoletto, returning home, is about to meet the courtiers who are gathered to abduct Gilda, he muses, "Ah by that old man I was cursed." And again Verdi has revised the sketch, which was entirely on E flat and its octave (Ex. 10), to be sung entirely on middle C and in a dotted rhythm (Ex. 11). Again, at the close of the scene he has made an almost identical change in Rigoletto's cry on discovering the abduction, "Ah! la maledizione!" In the sketch it is primarily on E flat and the rhythm is not dotted (Ex. 12); in the final version, primarily on middle C, and dotted (Ex. 13). Thus in Act I, scene 2, as in Hugo's Act II, the opening and closing words as well as three interior repetitions have been closely related and give the scene a clear structure.

No musical phrase is repeated so insistently in the opera as the setting of "Quel vecchio maledivami"; it is the essential statement of Monterone's curse, musically at its most succinct and dramatically as it exists as a fear in Rigoletto's mind. For though Rigoletto and Monterone in my view are tied by the curse, sharing its tonality and rhythm, this is Rigoletto's story, not Monterone's, and so Verdi, following Hugo, insisted that Monterone appear onstage only twice and briefly. All that precedes Rigoletto's repetitions of "Quel vecchio maledivami"—Monterone's declaration of the curse as well as his and Rigoletto's entrance—merely foreshadows the gathering darkness of the second scene. There, as Rigoletto goes home to Gilda, the thought rises in his mind that the curse, because of its origin, will strike him through his beloved daughter.

Rigoletto fears Monterone, but rationalists in the audience would advise him that he would do better to fear the courtiers. The division in opinion reflects the fact that the curse in this act operates in two ways: through the mysterious channel of superstition, Monterone; and through straightforward thuggery, the courtiers. This dualism is implicit, I think, in both the play and opera, each written by a nineteenth-century free-thinker who did not believe in curses and therefore would take some trouble to make their fulfillment onstage seem as reasonable as possible.

Before leaving this first act we should consider briefly the opera's prelude, which leads neatly into it. We have every reason to believe that Verdi composed the prelude last, when he was surest of what he was doing, and he built it out of an orchestral statement of "Quel vecchio maledivami," opening with a solo trombone on middle C (Ex. 14) joined by a solo trumpet on the octave above. This motif he repeated in various chordal positions, adding instruments, extending it into an oft-repeated note in dotted rhythm, carrying it swiftly to a double-forte climax that dissolves in a chain of weeping figures, and finally bringing it to rest in the thirty-fifth bar with the full orchestra playing a single, loud dotted rhythm on middle C and its octaves. The prelude, short and dramatically apt, builds a strong sense of menace, and, for those familiar with the words sung to the motif, it presents the fear that develops in Rigoletto's mind along with his special relationship to Monterone: "That old man cursed me."

*   *   *   *   *   *

Thus far there is general agreement, if not in every detail, at least for the most part. Audiences instinctively grasp the emphasis on the theme of the curse, dramatically and musically, and many scholars have written of it. But as Act II progresses, audiences, though continuing to recognize the power of the curse in the drama, perhaps have greater difficulty detecting its presence in the music. Scholars, too, seem to feel that the musical motif becomes more elusive in this act, and some even say it disappears altogether. With the latter I wholly disagree. Verdi did not stress the motif so strongly in Act I only to abandon it in Act II.

The act opens at court with the Duke alone, wondering what has happened to Gilda. In the previous scene, by bribing Rigoletto's housekeeper and disguised as a student he had been admitted to the courtyard of Gilda's house, had protested his love for her, but had been forced to leave by the sound of someone approaching. Later, when he had returned to the house, the courtyard door was open, the house empty, the girl gone. Now, as he regrets her disappearance, the courtiers enter, telling him that they have abducted the girl and locked her in his bedroom. He goes in to rape her. In all of this there is no reference to the curse's motif, and properly so. In this scene the Duke dominates events, and it is part of the drama that he is unaffected by the curse.

While the courtiers stand outside the bedroom door, snickering, Rigoletto approaches, announced by an orchestral tune to which, once onstage, he will sing a wordless refrain, "la rà, la rà, la rà" (Ex. 15). Though the notes move up and down the scale, they repeat constantly the dotted rhythm of the curse's motif, and because the accent of "la rà" falls steadily on the second syllable, the rhythm is stressed strongly—more so than if Verdi had used the more familiar, more evenly accented "la la."[16] Such a refrain usually connotes happiness, or at least absent-mindedness, but here, because of these accents, what it reveals beneath Rigoletto's attempt at nonchalance is fear. While he fences verbally with the courtiers, trying to discover Gilda's whereabouts without disclosing what he seeks, he returns three times to "la rà, la rà," so that it becomes a cornerstone of the musical structure, opening the scene and recurring throughout. This seems artistically right. With Gilda kidnapped, Rigoletto is obsessed with the curse.

Another structural device for the scene, slighter but also related to the curse, appears with the first words sung. The orchestra has begun the "la rà" refrain, and the courtier Marullo, looking down the hall, sees Rigoletto coming. He remarks, "Povero Rigoletto" (Poor Rigoletto), and of the seven notes, one for each syllable, five are middle C (Ex. 16). Verdi gave an identical musical setting to a subsequent aside of Rigoletto, "Ove l'avran nascosta?" (Where have they hidden her?), and in both cases he added the words and music after the sketch was completed. The idea for them may have originated in his setting of a third line that *is* in the sketch, "Ah, voi dormiste!" (Ah, you slept!). This is Rigoletto's sarcastic observation on Marullo's lie that he spent the night in bed. Of this line's five syllables, in both sketch and final version, four are set on middle C in dotted rhythm, and because of the two similar lines that Verdi added for the final version, the note and dotted rhythm now are anticipated twice. Like "la rà," the thrice-repeated phrase contributes to the scene's musical structure.

When Rigoletto discovers that Gilda is in the bedroom he runs toward the door but is blocked by the courtiers. Turning furiously on them, he begins his famous denunciation, "Cortigiani, vil razza dannata" (Courtiers! vile, damned race), and toward its end his vocal line has settled on middle C. As he throws himself again at the door and once more is blocked by the courtiers, he cries out, "That door, assassins, murderers, open that door for me! Open the door!" Twenty-six of his twenty-seven notes, all but the penultimate E flat, are middle C, and as he falls back exhausted and weeping, an additional fourteen of sixteen. At the very moment, therefore, in which Monterone's curse is being fulfilled, the persistent pounding of its musical motif is with us. In performance, of course, with the drama before us no one counts the notes, or even thinks of them, but the sound and rhythm of the curse are at work on our sensibilities.

Then, when Gilda runs from the Duke's room with her clothes in disarray, Rigoletto puts his arm around her, turns to the courtiers, and "in an imperious fashion" orders them from the room, "Ite di qua, voi tutti" (Get out of here, all of you), adding that the Duke is to keep away, for "I am here." This command is delivered on thirty-one notes of which twenty-nine are on middle C or its octave and many of the phrases are organized in the curse's dotted rhythm.

At this point I should confess that in the above scenes I have begun to part company with several distinguished scholars. Martin Chusid, editor of the critical edition of the opera and author of many essays on it, has an idea that I believe is true, though I disagree with his argument to support it. He writes, "Once Gilda has been deflowered, Rigoletto no longer fears the curse. Witness the fact that there are no references to the curse—prior to Gilda's death—after Act I."[17] Yet here I am arguing that references to the curse, through its musical motif, abound in Act II. Still, my disagreement with Chusid may be largely semantic, for his next sentence is: "Furthermore, as was noted earlier, in Act II he [Rigoletto] identifies closely enough with Monterone to adopt the latter's outspoken manner of speech and music." Possibly my idea that the two men share the curse, are bound to each other by it, is only another way of suggesting that Rigoletto "adopts" Monterone's manner in Act II. But I think not. As I have tried to show, the two men share the curse's motif, and therefore the manner, from the start, even before the declaration of the curse.

Like Chusid, David Kimbell, another noted scholar, believes that "once catastrophe has struck, the menace [of the curse] is no longer a dramatically efficacious thing, and the motif is simply abandoned. It does not even recur at the end of the opera, when the curse has been horribly fulfilled."[18] If this were true, it would seem to me a flaw in the opera's structure. Both men, in my opinion, take too narrow a view of the curse in the drama and of its motif in the music, failing to recognize the extent to which, as Verdi conceived them, they are capable of change. Just as the musical motif can appear in many different forms, similarly in the drama, as events unfold, the basic curse can change its dominant aspect. At the start, before its formal declaration, it is merely a cloud over Rigoletto, the tension between him and Monterone and between him and the courtiers. After Monterone's "Sii maledetto!" it becomes the obsessive fear in Rigoletto's mind. Later when that fear, because of Gilda's abduction and rape, is removed, it turns into something different, as we shall see. Yet always underneath, in some guise, are those repeated middle Cs with their rhythm frequently dotted.

Rigoletto, after dismissing the courtiers, embraces Gilda and listens quietly while she tells of how she had seen a young student in church, had exchanged glances with him and begun to love him, had talked with him for the first time yesterday, and of how later she had been abducted. Rigoletto, at the end of her account, sings quietly to himself in what serves as a link to their duet of lament. Like the previous connecting passage, Rigoletto's dismissal of the courtiers, which had led to Gilda's narrative, this second short passage, "Solo per me l'infamia" (Only for me the infamy), leading to the duet, begins on middle Cs with dotted rhythms (Ex. 17). Thus the motif, continually recurring, provides the scene with a musical structure.

Father and daughter comfort each other, "Piangi" (Weep), and as they fall silent, Monterone, on his way to prison and between guards, appears at the back of the room. He glares at the portrait of the Duke and, on his characteristic note (twenty-eight of the thirty-five on middle C) and in his usual rhythm, grieves that his curse has proved vain: "since no thunderbolt or sword has struck, the Duke will continue to live happily." He does not see Rigoletto and makes no reference to him, but after he is led out by the guards, Rigoletto cries after him, "No, old man, you are wrong. You will have an avenger."

With this line Hugo ended the act, but Verdi continues with a duet, one of the most startling and memorable in the opera and one that brings down the curtain on a scene of much greater emotional violence. Verdi, using the line merely as a link to the duet, has Rigoletto sing it entirely on Monterone's middle C and its octave and in his dotted rhythm, so that the two men, as before, apparently are intended to sound related, two facets of the one curse. Then turning to the portrait, Rigoletto swears, over Gilda's protests, that he, the jester, will strike down the Duke "like a thunderbolt hurled by God."

The music for this *vendetta* duet seems to me to fit Verdi's use of the curse as a recurring theme. But the majority of critics, I suspect, would deny any recollection here. A few, if pressed, might say that if such exists it is not intentional, merely a product of the general suffusion of dotted rhythms throughout the opera. Yet, though I am not unaware of the danger of discovering a recurring theme in every bar, I have come to believe that Verdi consciously based this duet on the curse's motif.

Its vocal line is in the sketch but without text, and we know from Verdi's letter to Piave, 20 January 1851, that he disliked the verses that Piave had sent but was not particular about their replacements so long as they were "espansivo" (unreserved, passionate) and in a particular meter, "decasillabi," that has ten syllables to a line with strong accents on the third, sixth, and ninth.[19] It seems, therefore, that in this instance he composed the music before the words were fixed, which was not his habit. But here, I think, he was ready to do this because he knew exactly what the music was to be: a swift, closing duet for Rigoletto and Gilda based on the curse motif, a duet capable of increasing tempo as it went along and capable, finally, of bringing down the curtain while stirring the audience to the greatest possible excitement. The traditional method of doing this in mid-nineteenth-century Italian opera was with a cabaletta, and Verdi wrote to Piave that he wanted to compose a "cabaletta *sfarzosa*," a gorgeous cabaletta (his emphasis).[20] Typically this musical form is a marching rhythm combined with some sort of triple rhythm that will give the regular beat a strong sense of propulsion. The idea dates back to Greek drama, in which the chorus made its entrance, always a stirring moment as the massed voices burst into song, to a meter of "marching anapaests," a steady walking rhythm in which the bars had three syllables each with the accent, as in the Italian "decasillabi," falling on the third, sixth, ninth, etc., one–two–THREE, one–two–THREE. Or, expressed in a line of English verse: "And the mark of the Duchy was violence, the basest that ever was known."

To achieve a similar powerful rhythm Verdi, I believe, took the curse's motif—before knowing the duet's final wording—and turned it into a phrase in which he substituted for the shorter of the two notes in the usual dotted rhythm, a triplet. Compare the final two bars of his typical "Quel vecchio maledivami" (Ex. 5) with the rhythmic figure of the cabaletta (Ex. 19) which is ONE, one–two–three–ONE, one–two–three–ONE. Or, in a line of English verse, "See, over the Duke, there is the threat of retrib–u–tion." With the recognition that beneath the cabaletta is the curse's motif, the musical structure of the final two-thirds of this act, in which Rigoletto is continually onstage, becomes clear. It opens with the motif in "la rà, la rà," has many connecting passages based on middle Cs and dotted rhythms, and closes with a duet based on the motif in a new rhythm.

Rigoletto's passionate address to the portrait, stimulated by Monterone's reappearance, also is important dramatically, for with it the nature of the curse begins to change, not in its basis but in its operation. In the play this is only implied; in the opera, because of the cabaletta, it becomes more specific. Facing the Duke's portrait, Rigoletto declares in music that steadily accelerates its tempo, almost to a frenzy:

> *Yes, vengeance, terrible vengeance*
> *Is my soul's one desire.*
> *The hour of punishment approaches,*
> *And when it sounds, you die.*
> *Like a thunderbolt hurled by God,*
> *The jester will strike you down.*

When well sung and conducted, the power of the piece, with its extraordinary focus of emotion, is overwhelming. Rigoletto's passion and purpose, however, are excessive, a case of a man going too far, of hubris. Who is Rigoletto, having trained the Duke to vice, to punish him for it? Who is Rigoletto, the most evil man at the court, to proclaim himself the agent of God? Even Gilda, who knows nothing of her father's wickedness, protests. Speaking partly out of her love for the Duke, which still survives, but partly also out of recognition that her father has lost all self-control, is becoming hysterical, and is in danger of blasphemy with his self-comparison to God, she urges him to forgive the Duke "and from heaven a voice of forgiveness will come for us, too." But Rigoletto in his new-found righteousness sweeps aside all restraint.

There is only vengeance. To a monstrous crime he cannot imagine any response except another, still more monstrous. In his eagerness for murder he becomes as obsessed with it as he ever was with fear for Gilda. Out of the fire of his tremendous but sordid passion the curse revives, in a new aspect.

Some persons, among whom will be Rigoletto, see in the tragic events to come merely a continuation of the curse as originally delivered by Monterone. Others, myself included, think that Monterone's curse was limited to the idea that Rigoletto should know the sufferings of a parent—specifically, if possible, the grief of a father in the dishonor of a daughter. With Gilda's abduction and rape Rigoletto experiences that suffering, and the penalty for his mockery of Monterone has been paid. Similarly, with his public humiliation before the courtiers his account with them is settled. In the opera's final act, therefore, if the curse is to be, in Verdi's words, "moral and great in the loftiest sense of the word," it must become more than an old man's anger, and so the nemesis that pursues Rigoletto, even unto Gilda's death, must be either a new curse or the old one in a new aspect. In my opinion it is the latter. The fundamental reason for the curse always was Rigoletto's evil life at court, which finally stirred the courtiers to act and Monterone to curse. With Rigoletto's plan to murder the Duke the old curse revives, but now on a larger scale, as a revulsion of Nature or Providence against Rigoletto for his continued resort to crime and arrogance in equating himself with Justice. From Gilda's abduction and rape he has learned nothing; he must be punished again, and harder.

*   *   *   *   *   *

Verdi and Piave's structure for the opera's final act is an improvement on Acts IV and V of the play. They advance events more swiftly; through music they can and do make better use of Hugo's storm; and at the end, where Hugo introduced irrelevant characters, they eliminate these, keeping the focus sharply on Rigoletto. They also rewrite Hugo's last line in a way that has implications for how we are to view Rigoletto at the opera's end, but I will get to that later.

After the extraordinary energy of the duet that closed the preceding act, the curtain rises on a quiet passage, scored only for strings and alternating with the hushed voices of Rigoletto and Gilda. Thirty days have passed, and now he has brought her to the street outside the inn of the assassin Sparafucile, hoping that the sight of the Duke in assignation with Sparafucile's sister Maddalena will convince her that the Duke is not worthy of her love. In the string passages and in the unaccompanied remarks of the voices there are a few dotted rhythms and even several on middle C, but they are so brief that Verdi perhaps did not intend them to have meaning. For the most part he treats the events of this act, the results of the curse in its new, enlarged aspect, as less directly tied to Monterone, and so there are fewer references.

Rigoletto and Gilda are outside the inn, and through a crack in the wall they watch and listen as the Duke, disguised as a cavalry officer, sings "La donna è mobile" and then, when Maddalena enters, attempts to seduce her with talk of love. The quartet follows, with the Duke charming, Maddalena laughing, Gilda despairing, and Rigoletto murmuring grimly of vengeance. At its end, he sends Gilda home to disguise herself as a man and depart for Verona, where she is to wait for him. Then with Sparafucile, who comes out of the inn, he negotiates his contract: twenty *scudi* for the murder of the cavalry officer. And because he wishes for himself the pleasure of throwing the corpse into the river, he will return for it at midnight. Asked for his own and the officer's name, as in the play he replies: "Elgi è *Delitto, Punizion* son io" (He is Crime; I am Punishment). This pretentious statement of what is in fact a coward's crime[21] is delivered in dotted rhythms with an octave drop. Not on middle C, to be sure, but on D (Ex. 20).[22] A recurring theme, however, need not always be identical; it can be effective in any form that an audience recognizes and, logically, in a opera's final act as passions rise, so does the pitch. Thus, to my ear the reference to the curse seems clear, and Rigoletto's presumptuous answer is typical of his new, inflated view of himself. It is followed immediately by the first flash of lightning in a gathering storm, a warning that Nature and the Heavens have begun to take a part in his activities.

Is it reasonable to ascribe a special significance to the storm? The answer, I think, depends on distinguishing the different aims of religious and political censors of the day, for though the police in Venice and Milan spoke as agents of the state, they also represented the Church. In Milan in 1843, for example, the chief source of pressure for changes in *I Lombardi* had been the archbishop, who had wanted a scene of baptism to be cut. His point was simple: baptism was a sacrament, and to portray it on the stage was sacrilegious. His demand became a public issue, and though he ultimately lost on the baptism he won other changes.

Eight years later in Venice with *Rigoletto*, though the facts are more obscure, the source of the objections can be deduced from the correspondence and from the changes made in the libretto. The political censors objected to having Rigoletto attempt to murder the Duke, and with reason: assassination then was a threat to monarchs. Indeed, in 1854 the Duke of Parma, Verdi's sovereign, would be stabbed to death on a street in Parma; in 1857, in Naples, an attempt would be made on the life of the king of the Two Sicilies; and in 1858, in Paris, on Napoleon III of France.

The Church's representatives, on the other hand, presumably objected to the portrayal of their Lord as responsible, through the operation of a curse, for an innocent girl's abduction, rape, and death. That was blasphemy. Consider, for example, how *Rigoletto* was performed in the summer of 1852 at Sinigaglia, in the Papal State, where the Church's views were law. The title was changed to *Viscardello;* the locale was shifted to Boston, England, with the Duke now of Nottingham; Gilda, at the opera's end, survived; and along the way every line with the word "curse" was rewritten to excise it. Monterone's "Sii maledetto" became "Trema, s' hai figli!" (Tremble, if you have children!); Viscardello, on discovering Gilda's abduction, in place of "Ah! la maledizione!" cries "Ah! me, me, disperato!" (Ah, I, I am in despair!); and in the final bars, as Gilda revives, he thanks Heaven for Its mercy, "Ah! Clemenza del Cielo!" It seems likely, therefore, that in Venice the change of title from *La maledizione* to *Rigoletto* was made to meet religious objections.[23]

Such changes in these years were not restricted to Italy or even to Catholic countries. In 1846, in Protestant England *Nabucco* could not be presented onstage because of its biblical background, so its story was rewritten and its title changed to *Nino, Re d'Assyria*. In the mid-nineteenth century European composers and playwrights had to be careful of how they portrayed religious concepts, institutions, and festivals.

Against that background, I believe, any hints of role for God in the story must be taken as seriously intended, and they are there. In the play, Hugo from time to time uses the word "Providence" (Divine Will) and makes much, for a playwright, of the nonverbal storm. Verdi continues these hints with frequent references to Heaven or God, or in such phrases as "a thunderbolt hurled by God," and carries them farther by giving such power to the storm that for a time it dominates the stage with greater force than Monterone ever could muster. It becomes almost another character in the drama and as such possibly should be taken as a symbol of outraged Nature or Divine Will.

Rigoletto, having made his contract with Sparafucile, goes off, and Gilda, disobeying him, returns in man's clothing and at the crack in the tavern wall overhears Maddalena urging her brother to spare the attractive young officer. Sparafucile refuses: he has a bargain. But as the storm increases its intensity, he begins to weaken, finally half-consenting: if another man comes to the inn before midnight, he can die in the officer's place. During a lull in the rain and lightning a distant clock strikes 11:30, five long beats and two short, all on middle C.[24] Though that note sometimes is used for clocks or bells,[25] here it also heralds the curse's fulfillment. The storm blows up again, more furiously, and Gilda knocks at the door. "Who's there?" cries Sparafucile, and she replies, with the orchestra silent except for an ominous rumble in the cellos, "Have pity on a beggar; shelter for the night." Though all her notes are on an E, not middle C or its octave, they are in a variation of the curse's dotted rhythm (Ex. 21). Thus even Gilda, with her foolish, wasted heroism, lends herself to the operation of the curse. Lightning, rain, and thunder flare again. Sparafucile and Maddalena make their preparations, open the door, and as the storm reaches its greatest fury, Gilda goes to her death, praying, "God! Forgive them."

At this point Hugo brought down the curtain on his Act IV, braking the momentum of the action. But what could he do? He had to advance his plot from eleven-thirty to midnight and with no events he wished to portray, he opted for an intermission. Verdi and Piave, on the other hand, had the advantage of an orchestra. They plunged the stage into darkness but kept the musical storm raging. It thus not only covers a passage of time (roughly thirty minutes reduced to five) and is a typical device of the romantic sensibility, a storm in heaven to reflect a crime on earth, but by its very prominence, in effect taking over the stage, it proclaims Nature and the Heavens' disapproval of Rigoletto.

It is not exaggeration to say that the storm "takes over the stage." Verdi apparently meant it to do just that. At its start its thunder is represented by a bass drum backstage, "interna," and only as Gilda enters the inn does Verdi add bass drum and cymbals in the orchestra. But as soon as the "storm intermezzo" begins, he directs that a thunder machine onstage, "sul palco-scenico," continually sound for the first twenty measures, ceasing only as the storm begins to lessen.[26] This "onstage" effect, which he perhaps expected to achieve by rolling the thunder machine to center stage in the first measure of darkness, is often omitted or diluted, but I suspect that Verdi might not be displeased if some modern stage director "zapped" the inn with light and sound to indicate supernatural involvement.

As the storm abates, Rigoletto returns. He is full of himself: "The moment of vengeance comes at last. . . . Oh, how truly great I feel myself now!" Midnight strikes: six strokes on middle C. He knocks at the inn door, and Sparafucile brings out a sack with a body in it. Beneath the fading storm Rigoletto preens: "Look at me now, O world! This is the jester, and this the mighty prince." But as he prepares to dump the corpse in the river, he hears in the distance the Duke singing. Ripping open the sack, by the last faint bolt of lightning he discovers Gilda.

"What murderer struck you?" he gasps, and she replies that she dies for the Duke; she loves him.

"Oh, terrible God!" cries Rigoletto. "She was hit by the arrow of my own just revenge." His own just revenge. Even now he does not comprehend what has happened or why.

He and Gilda sing the opera's concluding duet, she promising to pray for him in heaven and he begging her not to die, not to leave him. As Julian Budden has pointed out, though the idea of the duet may be conventional, its orchestration continually grows more imaginative and "Gilda's final four bars contain a harmonic side-slip worthy of the Requiem."[27] Certainly in an opera house, in context, it effectively conveys a sense of Rigoletto's desolation. His final despairing cry, "Ah! la maledizione!" is not sung on middle C but on the higher, more strident, more hysterical F flat. Its rhythm, however, is dotted (Ex. 22) and recalls the curse.

In closing the play Hugo had Triboulet cry, "J'ai tué mon enfant. J'ai tué mon enfant" (I have killed my child), and the line carries slightly different implications for how we leave Triboulet/Rigoletto as the curtain falls. Hugo, in his final scene, introduced bystanders and a doctor who pronounced Blanche dead. But collecting the crowd, summoning the doctor, and allowing him time to examine Blanche took a number of minutes, during which Triboulet could begin to appreciate the true cause of the curse and see that it lay within himself. In the opera, no. In the seconds immediately following Gilda's death, for Rigoletto the cause is still outside him, someone else's fault. Possibly his failure to understand what has happened increases the pathos.

*   *   *   *   *   *

An account of *Rigoletto* that concentrates exclusively on the curse will leave an unbalanced view of the opera, for its success, of course, depends on the contrast between foul and fair, between the evil Rigoletto does at court and his love for his daughter. As Verdi wrote to the management of the Teatro La Fenice, "That is just what seemed so wonderful to me: to portray this ridiculous, terribly deformed creature, who is inwardly filled with passion and love."[28] And, ultimately, it is not the evil but the love, the relationship between father and daughter, that provides the spark of life, and of tragedy.

Nevertheless, what gives the opera its unity and focus is the recurring theme of the curse. Verdi never again used a theme in quite this mosaic fashion: a phrase, a rhythm, and a repetition of a single pitch. Evidently he heard in the libretto something unique, and in searching for a way to express it developed a special technique. Of such care and imagination was a masterwork born, and it says much for his artistic integrity that he did not use his new, successful technique for the next opera, and the next. Rather, he gave to each its own distinct quality. He was that sort of artist.

Ex. 1 Act I, Scene 1

Si, Mon—te—ron, la vo—ce mia qual tuo—no

Ex. 2 (Sketch)

Si, Saint Val—lier la vo — ce mia qual tuo—no

Ex. 3 Act I, Scene 1

sii ma—le— det—to!

Ex. 4 (Sketch)

sii ma—le—det—to

Ex. 5 (Sketch)

Quel Vec chio ma—le—di va—mi

Ex. 6 Act I, Scene 2

Quel vec—chio ma—le—di — va—mi

Ex. 19., Act II

Sì, ven-det-ta, tre men da ven det-ta

Ex. 20. Act III

E-gli è De-lit-to Pu-ni-zion son i — o

Ex. 21. Act III

Pie —tà d'un men-di-co; a— sil per la

Ex. 22.
Act III

Ah! la ma-le-di-zio- - - —ne!

10

THE ESSENCE OF
IL TROVATORE

Every Verdi opera has both general qualities that are part of his individuality as a composer and singular qualities of melody, rhythm, and orchestration that create the particular opera's unique world of sound. Though *Il trovatore* and *La traviata* are unmistakably by the same composer, the difference in their musical worlds is equally apparent. No one fails to hear it.

Verdi seldom talked of the general qualities of his music and never gave them any generic name, but one among them that audiences always have admired and critics have declared characteristic is the forward movement of his melodic line. The quality is quite distinctive. At their best his arias, duets, and choruses—whether in *Trovatore* or *Traviata*—seem to surge ahead, giving the operas, if well performed, an exhilarating pace.

To an opera's special qualities, however, he did give a name, calling them collectively the opera's *"tinta"* or *"colorito"* (tint, coloring),[1] and he included in the meaning of those words sight as well as sound—settings, costumes, and stage movements as well as types of melody, rhythm, and orchestration.[2] The prevailing *tinta* of *Traviata*, for example, is subdued, subtle, and introverted. All of the scenes, for the only time in Verdi, are set indoors, and the characters are given few physical movements. Indeed, for a remarkable number of scenes one or all characters are seated—by Verdi's direction even at Violetta's party,[3] and for most of the final act the soprano is either on a chaise longue or in bed. Accordingly, much of the music is conversational or introspective; many of the arias move stepwise on the scale, by a tone or half-tone; and their rhythms are often in gentle, triple time. The opera's focus, meanwhile, remains almost exclusively on the chief character, and the air of sickness surrounding her, a thinness of tone, is established in the first notes of the prelude and often repeated.

In *Trovatore*, on the other hand, the *tinta* is more extroverted and some-times even harsh and violent. Many of the scenes are set outdoors, and there is much physical movement: duels, rescues, gypsy and military life. The music, without reticence, externalizes the characters' feelings; most of the arias move boldly up and down the scale; and their rhythms frequently are heavily accented and in vigorous, double time. The opera's focus shifts con-stantly from one character to another, and in the brief introduction the full orchestra, playing a descending scale of arpeggios in unison, at once estab-lishes the opera's assertive tone.

Verdi several times stated that all of an opera's qualities, general and special, came to him in a single vision. "I have put this first act in the drawer," he wrote to a librettist, "because I do not want to start work without the complete libretto. I usually do this, and I find it works better because when I have a general idea of the entire poem, the notes come of their own accord."[4] And to a friend who asked, he replied: "The concept comes to me complete, and especially I feel the coloring of which you speak, whether it should be a flute or violin. The difficulty then is to note down the musical concept fast enough to preserve the integrity with which it came to mind."[5]

Though he sometimes destroyed sketches and revisions of a work after it was produced, many of his first inspirations, his initial sketches for the operas from *Luisa Miller* through *Falstaff*, reportedly still exist, preserved by his heirs. One such sketch, for *Rigoletto*, the opera immediately preceding *Trovatore*, has been published in facsimile and consists of fifty-six pages of music notepaper on which Verdi has written out most of the opera's vocal line with text. (See pp. 159 for a fuller description.) Despite the lack of many details, such as key signatures, the sketch is of the opera almost complete, from start to finish.[6]

For any opera, however, a great deal of work was necessary before such a vision could be received. Of *Trovatore* there is a legend, too often repeated as true, that Verdi composed it in forty days. Alas, no. He proposed the opera to his librettist, Salvatore Cammarano, in January 1850, three years before the premiere on 19 January 1853, and by April 1851 the two were discussing the libretto in detail.[7] In these years Verdi's method of work, to the extent that he could force librettists, impresarios, and censors to conform, was to complete the libretto, memorize it, walk around his farm brooding on it until the musical concept of the whole fell into place, and then, usually in the last forty days before the premiere, struggle to get the notes onto paper in time for rehearsals. He might get out of a carriage, hurry to a hotel desk, and write out the "Miserere." But, as the friend reporting the scene remarked, "Who can say how long that page grew in his mind?"[8]

Of course, the stronger the vision, the better the opera; and though paradoxical, the greater the integrity of the whole, the greater the variation in detail that can fit comfortably into it. With *Trovatore*, evidently, the vision was remarkably strong, for not only is the opera's assertive *tinta* unusually pronounced, but so also is Verdi's general quality of forward movement. Indeed, in this opera the two reinforce each other, so that most persons, I suspect, would describe as the opera's prime characteristic its aggressive or breathless pace.

In any vocal work Verdi could achieve a feeling of propulsion in several ways. Easiest, of course, was simply to increase the tempo. But if an aria or scene was constructed of stanzas, he also could begin to shorten the stanzas, thus hastening the climaxes; within a stanza he could shorten the verses, usually from eleven to seven syllables, thus compressing the musical phrases; or he could begin to accelerate the movement in the melody's bass line or in its harmonic changes.[9] Perhaps of greatest importance, however, is the shape he seems instinctively, at least during the first half of his career, to have given his melodies.

In this respect he and Puccini, taking the latter also in his earlier years, seem quite different. In Verdi's melodies, through, say, *Traviata* (1853), typically an aria's *tessitura*, or average level of pitch, starts low, gradually rises, and ends high. Also, within an aria the individual phrases tend to press upward and the memorable phrase comes toward the end rather than the beginning. Conversely, Puccini, through, say, *Madama Butterfly* (1904), creates melodies in which the average level of pitch starts relatively high, sinks as the individual phrases curve downward, and then struggles up to end not very much higher than it began. And the memorable phrase comes early, often right at the start. With increasing experience both men, particularly Verdi, varied the style of their melodies to a greater extent, and in *Aida*, for example, part of Amneris's vocal profile is a melodic line that tends to move downward.[10] Nevertheless, in their earlier operas there is a notable difference in the shape of their melodies.

Compare Leonora's aria "Tacea la notte" in *Trovatore*, Act I, scene 2, with Butterfly's "Un bel dì." In each the soprano, awaiting the man she loves, talks of him to her lady-in-waiting. Verdi gives Leonora two stanzas and a short coda. In the first half of the first stanza Leonora, starting low, rises only to E flat; in the second half, to B flat above; and after repeating this pattern in the second stanza, to high D flat in the final bar of the coda—steadily upward, for the most part step by step, pulling up the average level of pitch.

And the aria's most memorable phrase, itself rising, does not appear until the start of the second half of each stanza (Ex. 1, page 191). Puccini, on the other hand, shapes "Un bel dì" as essentially a descending scale (Ex. 2), and except for the final leap up to B flat the aria begins within a half-tone of its highest note. And its most striking phrase, repeated at the climax, opens the aria.

Or consider how Leonora and Mimi (La Bohème) die. Leonora's short line rises mostly by half-tones more than an octave, from G to A flat; then, on a single note, drops the octave, exhausted (Ex. 3). Mimi, like Butterfly, starts relatively high and sings another long, slow descending scale (Ex. 4) before a brief outburst of high notes. Again, the definitive phrase of Puccini's aria occurs toward the beginning, whereas in Verdi's line it is in the middle, in the tension of the slow, swelling rise and the sudden, exhausted drop. Verdi's heroine, typically, seems to die struggling to live; Puccini's seems more resigned.

Or contrast Leonora's aria in Act IV, scene 1, "D' amor sull'ali rose," with Manon Lescaut's "In quelle trine morbide," from Puccini's opera. In Verdi's aria the pitch starts low, circling around an F, only three notes above middle C (Ex. 5), gradually rises to the climactic words "le pene, le pene del mio cor" (the pain in my heart), which come toward the end and are floated amid the highest notes, B flat, C and D flat. Whereas Puccini's melody begins (Ex. 6) on an E flat, ten notes above middle C, and then in a long phrase sinks down to an E flat, only two above. Then it climbs back and, starting slightly higher with the same opening phrase, the memorable one of the aria, again moves down an octave. For the ending it climbs very quickly, compared to Verdi's, to the high note, B flat, from which it almost at once falls away. The aria's emphasis, roughly speaking, is distributed equally, beginning, middle, and end, whereas with Verdi the weight is emphatically toward the end.[11]

The sense of forward movement Verdi's melodic style gives to the music is especially important in Trovatore, for in each of the opera's first three scenes Verdi had to begin with a long, narrative aria. The first, lasting roughly ten minutes and filling the entire scene, is an account by Ferrando, captain of the guard, of how a gypsy woman many years ago was burned at the stake for allegedly casting a spell on the old Count di Luna's second son, a baby. Her daughter, in revenge, stole the child and, rekindling the flames, burned it—or so, from the charred remains, most persons supposed. The old Count, however, died believing that his son somehow had survived and charged the elder brother, the present Count di Luna, to search for him.

In the next scene Leonora, in "Tacea la notte," tells how an unknown knight in black armor won a jousting tournament and later courted her with serenades. "If I cannot live for him, then I will die for him," she concludes prophetically. Finally, in the gypsy camp Azucena describes to Manrico, who is Leonora's knight in black armor, how she saw her mother burned, stole the old Count's child, and in her delirium threw onto the rekindled embers not the stolen baby but her own—thus revealing to the audience, though she promptly denies it to Manrico, that he is not her son but the present Count's brother. Not only are there three narrative arias, but two of them, though from different points of view, tell the same story!

The first of these three scenes Verdi and his librettist, Salvatore Cammarano, turned into a ghostly occasion. Ferrando, asked by the guards to tell the story of the present Count's lost brother, begins slowly, relatively low in pitch, and in two stanzas with lines of eleven syllables reaches the moment where the baby's skeleton, "half burned, still smoking," was discovered at the foot of the stake. But then the stanzas become less regular, the lines shorten to seven syllables, and the chorus interjects more frequently. The men would like to catch the daughter and send her to her mother in hell, "all' inferno." "In hell?" exclaims Ferrando. The evil mother is still an earthly presence, often appearing at night as a raven or an owl. A soldier who had struck her later died of fright when an owl flew into his room, stared at him with gleaming eyes, and, as midnight sounded, started for him. At that moment, onstage, the midnight bell clangs loudly, and the men, much startled, jump up excitedly, cursing the witch.

Verdi worked all his musical effects toward that clanging bell, to make of it the scene's single, scary climax, only bars before the curtain falls. Though in the scene's first half he allowed the pitch to rise, he then lowered it while beginning to shorten the stanzas and lines and to increase the choral interjections; thereafter he began to accelerate the tempo and again to raise the pitch. As the bell clangs—he warned the impresario in charge of the premiere that the scene "needs a big bell to sound a full peal of midnight"[12]—the pitch reaches its highest, the tempo its fastest, and the chorus its loudest. By creating a strong feeling of propulsion toward this moment he hoped to carry the audience through an otherwise static scene.

He also did more, for in this first scene and its brief introduction he worked hard to establish a few of the opera's special qualities, its *tinta*. The Introduction, for example, begins with three soft, swelling rolls on the tympani and bass drum followed by the orchestra in unison playing a *double-forte* downward scale of rising and falling arpeggios and ending in a rhythmic figure set off by a trill (Ex. 7). These arpeggios, increasingly broken up, and the rhythmic figure repeat several times as the scene begins, and in variation they form the melodic base of Ferrando's story of the gypsy women. As he sings of Azucena and her mother, the audience instinctively begins to link the rather simple, brash music with the gypsies, and later examples of it, such as the "Anvil Chorus," confirm the association. (In Exs. 8 through 14 the arpeggio variations are marked "x" and the rhythmic figures "y.")

In the second scene Verdi introduces Leonora, the lady at court, and distinguishes her musically from the gypsies by a vocal line more suavely lyrical and dominated usually by soaring phrases. In addition to Exs. 1, 3, and 5, listen to how in the finale to Act II, scene 2 she greets Manrico, whom she thought dead, and how in Act IV, scene 1 she offers herself to the Count di Luna in exchange for Manrico's life.

The conflicting pull on Manrico of Leonora and Azucena and of their different worlds is brought to issue musically in Act III, scene 2. Safe in his castle and about to marry Leonora, Manrico sings in her style, in a smooth, long-lined *adagio*, "Ah sì, ben mio." It is almost an art song. Then, receiving word that Azucena has been captured and is about to be burned at the stake, he bursts into the rough and ready "Di quella pira," constructed like Azucena's "Stride la vampa" with a note thrice repeated and followed by a gypsy rhythmic figure (Exs. 13 and 14). The success of "Di quella pira" is not only that of a fast, exciting aria following a slow one. With it Manrico moves from the upper-class world of Leonora to the lower of Azucena. No words are necessary. The drama—Manrico's choice at that moment between the two women[13]—is presented in the music.

Over the years many commentators, without distinguishing between general and special qualities, have sought to describe in a word the unique character of *Trovatore*, and Abramo Basevi, one of the earliest, still seems the most successful: his word was *insistenza*, or insistence.[14] Some of what he meant lies in the propulsion of the arias and scenes, but even more is embedded in the opera's *tinta*, in the initial repeated notes and rhythmic figures of much of Azucena and Manrico's music.

This *insistenza* appears in various forms throughout the opera. There is the famous, opening phrase of the "Anvil Chorus" (Ex. 15) that begins with the same note four times repeated and heavily accented, and the style of which is adopted by Azucena in "Stride la vampa" (Ex. 13) and Manrico in "Di quella pira" (Ex. 14). There is the repetitive figure underlying the "Mi-

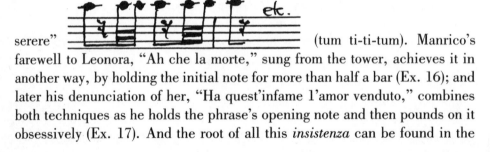

serere" (tum ti-ti-tum). Manrico's farewell to Leonora, "Ah che la morte," sung from the tower, achieves it in another way, by holding the initial note for more than half a bar (Ex. 16); and later his denunciation of her, "Ha quest'infame l'amor venduto," combines both techniques as he holds the phrase's opening note and then pounds on it obsessively (Ex. 17). And the root of all this *insistenza* can be found in the opera's introduction, where Verdi has marked every note of the downward scale of rising and falling arpeggios to be punched out (Ex. 7).

In performance, of course, any careful division of general and special qualities, however useful for analysis, becomes largely illusory as they all, through the integrity of the original musical concept, merge, overlap, momentarily grow or decrease in importance, or perhaps through the weakness of the artists fail to achieve their intended effect. Nevertheless, the distinction is real. The insistence that Basevi noted and the melodic and rhythmic style that Verdi gave to his gypsies are part of the *tinta* of *Trovatore* and peculiar to it. On the other hand, the shape of his melodies and his efforts to infuse the opera's structure with a strong forward movement are general characteristics of all his operas of this period. Indeed, these general qualities, reflecting apparently his spontaneous response to any theatrical work, played an important part in transforming Italian romantic opera, as composed by Bellini and Donizetti, into a swifter-paced, more sensational style perhaps best called melodrama.

This change occurred gradually in the quarter century 1840 to 1865, and Verdi, because he was the period's most successful composer, had the chief role. A good way to grasp his influence is to compare the libretto he sought for *Trovatore* (1853) with the one Donizetti accepted for *Lucia di Lammermoor* (1835), for the same man, Salvatore Cammarano, served as librettist for both. The first draft of *Trovatore* that Cammarano submitted to Verdi was laid out along the lines of *Lucia*, particularly in the grand finale that closes the second act of each opera. But Verdi asked for changes in the draft, and a comparison of the ultimate structure of this finale in the two operas will not only illustrate further the general quality of pace that Verdi sought, but also clarify the shift in operatic style.

In Italian romantic opera at its height, of which *Lucia* is an example, the basic unit of structure was the "number," typically a double aria of two contrasting halves, the first slow and lyrical, the "cantabile," and the second faster and more showy, the "cabaletta." Sometimes to finish off the cabaletta there would be a third part, short and very fast, the "stretta." These double arias, usually introduced and connected by several bars of recitative, could be for one, two, or more soloists and might include the chorus. But they were units, complete in themselves, excerptible, and titled in vocal and orchestral scores "No. 1," "No. 2," etc. Further, as an important part of the marketing of an opera, they were sold to the public as separate pieces both for voice and piano and in piano, flute, and violin transcriptions. During the rehearsals of *Trovatore* Verdi might write expansively to a friend, "I want subjects that are *new, great, beautiful, varied, bold*—bold to the last degree—with *new forms*, etc., etc. [. . .]"[15] But the institution of Italian opera—singers, impresarios, publishers, and public—were against change, and any composer who attempted too much too fast would be shut out. As Verdi's contemporary, the composer Giovanni Pacini, observed: "Everyone followed the same school, the same fashions, and in consequence were all imitators of the great luminary [Rossini]. But, good heavens, what else could one do, since there was no other way of making a living."[16]

With that necessity always before the librettist, his primary job was to tell a story in such a way that it fell into a succession of numbers, usually from ten to twenty, which allowed the voices to be introduced, alternated, combined, and displayed. Many stories did not lend themselves to this kind of structure, but even among those that did the system imposed a uniformity. From one opera to the next scenes were apt to repeat: a prison scene, a wedding scene, a mad scene, or, more abstractly, a cantabile of sorrow (the soprano believes the tenor has died) followed by a cabaletta of joy (she is told in the intervening recitative that he is alive).

Verdi, a generation younger than Rossini, seems instinctively to have disliked this system of numbers. One reason was that by 1840, when Verdi was starting his career, the style was obvious and growing stale. Another was that the numbers, by coming to a full musical stop and allowing a break for applause, brought the drama to a stop. Though Verdi accepted the system as basic to Italian opera, he constantly tried to improve on it, and at the rehearsals of his fifth opera, *Ernani* (1844), he won his first major fight on form, waged against a soprano who wanted to conclude the opera with a solo aria for her in place of his more dramatically suitable trio.[17] Seven years later, in thinking about the libretto for *Trovatore,* he wrote to Cammarano:

If in opera there were neither cavatinas [solo arias], duets, trios, choruses, finales, et cetera, and the whole work consisted, let's say, of a single number, I should find that all the more right and proper. For this reason I would say that if you could avoid beginning with an opening chorus (all operas begin with a chorus!) and start straightaway with the troubadour's song and run the first two acts into one, it would be a good thing because these separate numbers, with changes of scene in between, seem to be designed for the concert hall rather than the stage.[18]

Though at the time of writing Verdi imagined *Trovatore* beginning with what is now the second scene, he ultimately had his way about the opening chorus, for what is now the first scene, Ferrando's account of the two gypsies and the burned child, has none. But *Lucia,* composed eighteen years earlier, opens with a chorus of the heroine's family retainers out hunting, after which their leaders, with her brother in command, discuss her meetings with a stranger, and the opera's drama begins. The preceding chorus has added nothing to it, for neither hunting nor the huntsmen have any role in the plot or even in setting the atmosphere. The musical number merely lengthens the scene; Verdi, in composing *Trovatore*, constantly sought ways to keep the opera short. As he wrote to a friend about Cammarano's work: "Only let him remember the demands of the public, which wants brevity."[19]

Traditionally in an opera constructed of numbers, the crucial scene in the story, toward which all that precedes should build and all that follows should fall away, the keystone in a musical arch of gathering tension and release, was the "central finale." This was not the end of the opera but its climax. In *Lucia* this scene is the confrontation of the lovers Edgardo and Lucia only seconds after she has been tricked into signing a contract to marry Arturo, whom she does not love. Musically, it is the famous sextet, the cantabile, in a tempo of *larghetto;* then Edgardo's cursing of Lucia, the cabaletta, starting *allegro* and increasing to *vivace;* followed by his expulsion from the hall, the stretta, at a still faster tempo. In both the cantabile and the cabaletta, to give them added weight, the chorus periodically joins, and it sings continuously throughout the stretta.

With the conclusion of this central finale, the action all but stops, and the remainder of the opera consists of three scenes that are essentially tableaux. The first, a scene of pride and anger in which Lucia's brother challenges Edgardo to a duel "at dawn," frequently is cut; then follows a double aria to exhibit Lucia in her fatal madness, and one to show Edgardo in his despair which, after he learns of Lucia's death, culminates in suicide. In both, the choral support is considerably more subdued than in the central finale, the tempo of the cabaletta considerably less swift and agitated, and the concluding stretta is omitted. The story now is retrospection, not action, the characters looking back rather than forward.

The scene in *Trovatore* that Cammarano made the opera's central finale occurs at the conclusion of Act II, scene 2. Here the Count di Luna, the baritone, waits with his soldiers outside the convent where Leonora, believing her knight in black armor dead, is about to retire for life. The Count plans to kidnap her but is prevented by Manrico, who, arriving at the last possible moment with his men, carries her off for himself. Verdi did not want his characters standing around singing, in the manner of the central finale of *Lucia*, when his drama seemed clearly to require that the tenor swoop in, snatch up the soprano, and depart. If the *Lucia* pattern had been followed, as Cammarano at first outlined, then just as the Count was about to seize Leonora, Manrico would burst upon the scene alone, without retainers, and there would follow a slow cantabile corresponding to the *Lucia* sextet, in which the three principals, Leonora's lady-in-waiting, the Count's captain, Ferrando, and the chorus of attending nuns and the Count's soldiers would express their private thoughts: hope, defiance, anger, horror, and martial confidence.

Then, as Manrico's men arrive and begin to outnumber the Count's smaller party, the cabaletta would start, and toward its end as it sped into the stretta, Manrico would make off with Leonora.[20]

The pattern was too leisurely for Verdi. After fussing with Cammarano, who died in the midst of the correspondence, Verdi set what Cammarano had intended to be the slow cantabile at a faster tempo, *andante mosso* rather than *largo*; he reduced what should have been the cabaletta to a few swift exclamations between the principals, to be sung *allegro vivo* over choral interjections; and he cut the stretta altogether. As he explained to Cesare De Sanctis, who had served as his liaison with Cammarano, he had not set the first part of the finale's double aria as a *largo* or *adagio*, "as is usual," but at a faster tempo because "a largo would have been impossible. For this reason I have decided to suppress the stretta especially since it isn't necessary to the drama and perhaps Cammarano only wrote it for the sake of tradition." Then, after quoting the lines he had set for the principals over chorus at *allegro vivo*, he added: "This strikes me as more novel in form, perhaps more effective, and above all shorter (and that's no flaw, especially in this libretto which is a bit long)."[21] And he closed the finale in a most unusual fashion by giving Leonora a single reprise of her soaring cantabile phrase at its *andante mosso* tempo, followed by a single *allegro* sentence of exclamation by everyone else. There is no lingering. About as quickly as the audience's eye can record Leonora's departure with Manrico, the curtain falls.

For some, Verdi's handling of the scene may be musically disappointing, ending too soon; for others it is dramatically effective. Verdi's way is not necessarily better than Donizetti's, he merely stressed different values.

Those that Verdi preferred seem rooted in his instinctive feelings about drama in general and, equally important, in how he received and worked up his musical ideas to express any one value in particular. In *Trovatore* he sought pace and was prepared to adjust structure to obtain it, and through *tinta* he sought unity. Twenty years later he felt just as strongly about what he was trying to achieve, and with regard to some performances of *Aida* he wrote to his publisher, Giulio Ricordi, with underlining for emphasis: "I don't care about singers who know how to be applauded for a solo. . . . The whole is what matters, even a modest whole. In that way, both art and the opera gain. Otherwise, go back to *cavatina* [number] operas."[22] And five months later, again to Ricordi: "When a piece or even an entire section stands out too much, that is harmful to the *whole*. It is no longer a drama, but a concert. Let the artist have his piece, if the drama calls for it; but he must be more or less consistent throughout and contribute to the totality of the musical structure."[23]

For Verdi, *Trovatore* was never a singers' opera, as singers and critics often claim, but a drama.[24]

Ex. 13 Act II, Scene 1: Azucena

Stri-de la vam — — pa! la — — fol-la in-do — — mi-ta

Ex. 14 Act III, Scene 2: Manrico

Di quel-la pi — — ra L'or-ren-do fo — — co

Ex. 15 Act II, Scene 1: Gipsies' Anvil Chorus

Chi del gi-ta — no i' gior-ni ab-bel-la?

Ex. 16 Act IV, Scene 1: Manrico

Ah! che la mor-te ognor — a

Ex. 17 Act IV, Scene 2: Manrico

Ha — quest'in-fa-me l'a-mor ven-du — to

11

THE ORCHESTRATION
OF *LA TRAVIATA*

One of Bernard Shaw's more unfortunate remarks was that Verdi used an orchestra like a "big guitar." Though the phrase was not original with Shaw,[1] by his music criticism he made it common, and though his wording sometimes varied, its gist was always the same: Verdi, in typical Italian fashion, was lazy and unimaginative in his scoring, too easily satisfied with a rum-tum accompaniment. Finally, in an article following Verdi's death and summarizing his career, Shaw wrote: "As to the orchestra, until Boito came, it was for the most part nothing but the big guitar, with the whole wind playing the tune in unison or in thirds or sixths with the singer."[2] Alas, the phrase is catchy and, because associated with Shaw, often quoted. It is nonsense.

Let me leave for another day a marshaling of evidence that Arrigo Boito, the librettist of Verdi's last two operas, *Otello* and *Falstaff*, had no influence on the development of Verdi's orchestration, which progressed quite consistently on its own, and focus instead on the second part of the charge: that before Boito, Verdi's orchestration "was for the most part nothing but the big guitar." Possibly I can demonstrate the falsity of that judgment by displaying the truth of its opposite: that Verdi's scoring for an opera was often remarkably sensitive and restrained while also dramatically effective. To that end I propose to review some examples of his orchestration drawn from *La traviata*, an opera pre-Boito by more than twenty-five years, and one so familiar that the rhythms, notes, and timbres of its orchestral accompaniment, though silent on the page, may in description echo in memory.

For another reason, too, *Traviata* seems a good choice. Of all Verdi's operas it is the most direct and intimate, the closest to a chamber opera; and to support its conversational tone Verdi used only a relatively small, classical orchestra that even for its day was conservative. Six years earlier, for example, he had employed an orchestra considerably more exotic for *Macbeth*. In *Traviata*, however, except for the choruses for gypsies, matadors, and Carnival crowd (offstage), which call for a triangle, castanets, tambourines, and picadors' lances to thump on the floor, the instruments needed are only the most usual. Though Verdi did not specify the number of strings, a typical Italian opera house of that period would provide 14 first violins, 10 second violins, 6 violas, 3 violincellos, and 8 double basses.[3] In the wind section, Verdi asked for pairs of flutes, oboes, clarinets, and bassoons, with the second flute doubling on the piccolo (but note, no English horn, bass clarinet, or double bassoon); in the brass, four horns, two trumpets, three trombones, and a bass trombone (cimbasso), which is more trombones than in a classical orchestra for symphony, but not for opera; and finally, a harp, which is limited to a single scene. With such an orchestra the strings, however tinged by brass or wind, will predominate and, if scored unimaginatively, indeed may produce a coarse, monotonous strumming.

Then, too, the types of melodies Verdi composed for *La traviata* would seem likely to lend themselves to a guitarlike accompaniment. The majority are in triple time, some form of waltz, for which the obvious, simple accompaniment is the traditional "oom-pah-pah." There are, of course, the two big choral waltz numbers, "Libiamo, libiamo ne' lieti calici [. . .]" (Act I) and "Alfredo, Alfredo di questo core [. . .]" (Act II, scene 2 finale). But still more important are the many arias and duets that in some form of triple time move up and down the scale by small intervals. Verdi uses this melodic style to express the characters' inner thoughts, of which there are a great many, for *Traviata* is the most introspective of his operas. To hear its essence, sing to yourself these lines:

"Un dì felice eterea [. . .] Di quell'amor [. . .]" (Act I)

"Ah fors'è lue. . . .   A quell'amor. . . ."
"De' miei bollenti spiriti [. . .]" (Act II, scene 1)

"*Non sapete quale affetto [. . .]*"
"*Dite alla giovine [. . .]*"
"*Morrò! morrò! la mia memoria [. . .]*"
"*Amami, Alfredo, amami quant'io t'amo [. . .]*"
"*Di Provenza il mar, il suol [. . .]*"
"*Addio, del passato [. . .]*" *(Act III)*
"*Parigi, o cara, noi lasceremo [. . .]*"

Surely, if Shaw's charge is justified, the evidence to support it will reveal itself beneath these vocal lines and in this opera that is so unexceptional in setting and soft-spoken in tone. Of course some might argue, citing Berlioz, that such an accompaniment is not inappropriate, for Berlioz, in his *Treatise on Instrumentation,* says of the guitar that it "is an instrument suitable for accompanying the voice and for taking part in instrumental compositions of intimate character."[4] And I intend, in what may seem an unreasonable fashion but is not, to argue both ways: that when appropriate Verdi used the orchestra like a guitar, yet when his orchestration is taken altogether it is too varied and skillful to be characterized pejoratively as "the big guitar." Though in the end I may not succeed in wholly discrediting Shaw's famous charge, at least in the effort I can draw attention to the sensitivity of much of Verdi's scoring.

*   *   *   *   *   *

The prelude to *Traviata* is only forty-nine bars, yet in its three parts it presents a miniature of Violetta that neatly suggests her personality and fate. In the first sixteen bars, with a thin, etiolated sound that will pervade the final act, there is a proclamation of her illness; then, with a broad theme warmly scored, her personality emerges, sentimental and capable of love; and finally, in a skittering descant to the broad theme repeated, as if in explication of it, are the charm and frivolity that soon will be broken by illness and love.

All the themes of this first prelude reappear in the opera, sometimes significantly changed, but the opening seven bars, Violetta's illness, Verdi repeats exactly at the start of the prelude to Act III, before elaborating on them. The best description I know of this music depicting illness was written by Boito in a letter to the French critic Camille Bellaigue, who evidently somewhere had referred to it as *sottile* (thin, slender, subtle).

I applaud the word "*sottile*" applied to the last-act prelude of *La traviata*. *Sottile*, in the sense of the Latin words *gracilis* and *exilis*, is exactly the right epithet to characterize those very moving bars. Perhaps without knowing it you have chanced upon an Italian expression. To describe someone who dies of consumption we say: *muore di mal sottile*.

The prelude seems to say this with sounds, with elevated, sad, frail sounds, almost without body, ethereal, sick, with death imminent. Who would have thought that music had the power to depict the scene of a room completely closed to the dawn, in winter, where an invalid awakens? That silence! that calm, painful silence created by sounds!

The soul of a dying woman tied to her body by the thinnest ["sottilissimo"] thread of breath! repeating before her death a final memory of love![5]

In both preludes Verdi achieves his effect by scoring for sixteen violins *divisi* dividing them in fours to play the four shifting lines of the successive chords. The sound reminds many operagoers of Wagner's prelude to the opening act of *Lohengrin*, but Verdi in 1852–53, when composing *Traviata*, had not heard a note of Wagner; nor was the idea of divided strings new to Italian opera. Verdi had used them beneath Giselda's prayer in *I Lombardi*, in the conspirators' scene in *Ernani*, and, imitating Rossini's ensemble of five solo cellos that open the overture to *William Tell*, had scored individual lines for six cellos to accompany Zaccaria's prayer in *Nabucco*.

To contrast with the prelude, dominated by strings, as the curtain rises on the party at Violetta's house, Verdi has the tune and accompaniment carried for the first seventeen bars by brass and wind alone. The sound is raucous, deliberately so, but when the voices enter he brings in the strings again, allowing brass and wind to be silent. At times, it is true, the accompaniment duplicates the vocal line, but seldom for long, and throughout the party, which occupies two-thirds of the act, Verdi successfully avoids any feeling of orchestral monotony. He does this mainly by varying loud and soft and by alternating the timbres of strings, brass, and wind. In addition, using a technique that Rossini had developed in his comedies, he often supports the voices with a melody in the orchestra that no one sings. When Gastone, for example, presents Alfredo to Violetta, he has one tune, and the accompaniment, another, played on strings; and, *pace* Shaw, neither is duplicated by wind instruments (Ex. 1). In the "Libiamo," of course, there are measures where the solo voice is accompanied by winds in unison with it, and the choral refrains are joined not only by every person onstage but by almost every instrument in the pit. But then, for a drinking song that would be sung even in a spoken play, a certain ordinariness seems in order.

Verdi also varies the party's sound by having an onstage band play behind the scenes for the dancing, and it is against this band's distanced, somewhat brassy waltz that Alfredo begins his declaration of love. As he grows more intense and reaches "Un dì felice," the backstage band stops, and the strings in the pit orchestra pick up. One of the aria's early phrases, I must admit, is matched by a flute and clarinet, though only for two bars. Then at the start of the most expansive phrase, "Di quell'amor," amid the strings and woodwind Verdi softly brings in the horns for two chords to reenforce

Ex. 1: The melody is carried by the first violins and the violincellos.

Alfredo's call to romance (Ex. 2); and later, over the repeated word "misterioso," a solo horn gently sounds on a single, long-held note to hint at the mystery of love. It is a simple touch, yet skillfully done.

Again in this passage: As Alfredo begins to talk of true love, "Di quell' amor," Verdi directs that the string instruments are to be plucked—*pizzicato*—rather than stroked with the bow (Ex. 2). This increases the guitar quality of the sound and is in the tradition of such operatic serenades as "Deh, vieni alla finestra" in *Don Giovanni,* which is sung to a mandolin, a plucked instrument. Frequently in *La traviata,* when Alfredo or Violetta sing quietly of love, their string accompaniment is plucked, creating a special sound for their statements.

Because strings are the predominant instruments in this opera, to appreciate it fully one should try to hear the different quality of sound as the strings are bowed or plucked, as their groups play in unison, in reduced numbers, or *divisi,* and as their notes are played *legato* (smoothly tied) or *staccato* (detached). Yet, despite Verdi's plain intent to exploit the variety of string

Ex. 2: The horns, *Corni*, reinforcing the call to romance while the strings, in the tradition of serenades, are plucked, *pizzicato*.

effects, two of the most common are missing. He was not yet scoring for string harmonics, and the first occasion would not occur until *Un ballo in maschera*, six years later; and he nowhere directed the strings to play with mutes, *con sordine*, though he had used mutes for the solo cello and double bass that carry the tune beneath the first meeting of Sparafucile and Rigoletto and for the first violins beneath the close of "Ai nostri monti" in *Trovatore*. Perhaps he felt that mutes, which both reduce an instrument's power and muffle its tone, slightly distance the sound, whereas in *Traviata* he sought the immediacy, the intensity of the full tone, however quietly sounded.

In her reply to Alfredo's offer of love, Violetta urges him to forget her; his love will not, cannot be returned. Her vocal line, which is related closely to the skittering descant of the prelude, is accompanied, just as Shaw protested it too often was, by a flute and clarinet in unison with her. Yet the scoring is not unimaginative. In the prelude the descant is played by violins alone, and Violetta's grace and frivolity seem warm and attractive; here, the flute and clarinet tinge her line with a cooler sound, making her appear more arch, even hard. But that is appropriate: her heart has not yet responded to Alfredo.

After he leaves, having won permission to return the next day, the party ends, the guests depart in a noisy chorus with many instruments duplicating the tune, and Violetta is left onstage alone. While she wonders if perhaps Alfredo could be her true love, "Ah fors'è lui," the lower winds, particularly the clarinet, color her thoughts without repeating her line. But as she decides against him in "Sempre libera," her tune is doubled by all the winds, with trills added by the piccolo, some phrases supported by the two trumpets, and the rhythmic pulse strengthened by the four horns. Now, definitely, she is shrill and harsh. Before the new timbre can begin to sound too crude, however, Verdi cuts it off to allow Alfredo's voice, singing of true love, to float through the window, accompanied only by the harp. The sudden change in sound is arresting, and though the instrument is usual for an offstage troubadour, its effect is seldom so well prepared, or so little diluted: for in this opera, only in this scene and for this purpose does Verdi use the harp. Throughout all that follows, therefore, the moment's aural impact remains pristine.

*   *   *   *   *   *

The second act, with Violetta and Alfredo now living together outside of Paris, brings us promptly to a curiosity of the score: the accompaniment of Alfredo's aria, "De' miei bollenti spiriti." The curtain rises and Alfredo, who has been hunting, enters the room, puts down his gun, and soliloquizes on his happiness with Violetta. After a few lines of recitative he launches into a short, passionate aria that Verdi scores for strings with some soft horns and an occasional duplication of the vocal line in the winds. Now, as in Alfredo's call to romance in the previous act, he intends the accompaniment to approximate a guitar.

In the score he orders the cellos and double basses to bow the on-beat notes of the accompaniment's repeating figure, and the violins and violas to pluck those on the off-beat (Ex. 3). This reverses the directions usually given by composers for this common figure, which, if played fast in the more familiar style, would sound "plink-ta-ta-ta," but here should sound "ta-plink-plink-plink." The difference in performance is marked, yet most conductors, both in the opera house and in recordings, refuse to follow Verdi's instructions. Among these are Toscanini, Giulini, and Pritchard. Monteux, on the other hand, in his recording has the orchestra play as directed.[6]

Why in this instance so many conductors feel they know better than Verdi is not clear. Even scholars are divided on the question. Spike Hughes feels that bowing allows the accompaniment to flow "smoothly and urgently" and doubts that Verdi intended the notes to be played *pizzicato*. The direction, he suggests, was added to the score "by some conductor."[7] Julian Budden, however, insists that the autograph score leaves no room for doubt and prefers the music played as written.[8] As Monteux and his instrumentalists

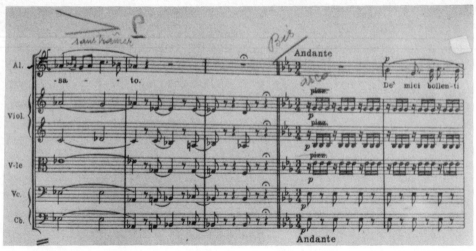

Ex. 3: This copy of the score was used by a French conductor who wrote in some pointers for himself and changed Verdi's direction to the violins and violas from *"pizzicato"* (plucked) to *"arco"* (bowed).

demonstrate, there is no reason not to follow Verdi's directions: a questionable practice merely has become a bad tradition. To my mind Verdi plainly wished this intimate moment to share the sound of Alfredo's declaration of love in the previous act, and he also wished to contrast the tenor's line, smoothly rising and falling, with the nervous accompaniment: the serenity of love against its agitation. When played as directed the accompaniment seems to froth, effectively setting apart the aria from its preceding recitative and giving it, for this act, a unique sound.

As for those conductors who ignore Verdi's directions, he would have had words for them. Writing one time to Giulio Ricordi about conductors' changes, he exploded: "No. I want a single creator, and I would count myself happy if the conductors would perform simply and exactly what is written." And again to Ricordi: "I hardly think we need to have conductors and singers discover new effects; and for my part I vow that no one has ever, ever, ever even succeeded in bringing out all the effects that I intended . . . No one!! Never, never . . . neither singers nor conductors!!"[9]

In Violetta's duet with Alfredo's father, Germont *père*, there are many vocal phrases duplicated by the winds, but as with the party music of the first act Verdi constantly varies the sound, not only with timbres but with tiny orchestral melodies. Consider, for example, the scene in which Violetta realizes the extent of the sacrifice Germont is asking.

"You don't mean," she protests, "I should renounce Alfredo for ever?"

"It is necessary."

"Ah, no! Never! Never!"

Verdi directs that the exchange be followed by a "long pause" which, if the soprano has the courage for silence and the skill to maintain tension by physical posture, can be very effective.[10]

"You don't understand," she begins, "the kind of love . . ." (Non sapete quale affetto). Beneath her broken phrases Verdi scores the strings percussively, little hammer blows that quickly grow louder, harsher, and as she repeats her thoughts and musical phrases, beneath them the clarinets and bassoons sound a downward chromatic scale that suggests defeat. Then, in summary, she cries, "The sentence is so merciless" (il supplizio è sì spietato), "I would rather die" (preferirò morir). The first half of this crucial line she delivers and repeats on a single note matched by a flute, an oboe, and the first violins. Not, however, as Shaw complains, by *all* the winds: Underneath, Verdi has an arched phrase for a clarinet, a bassoon, violas, and cellos that rises and falls chromatically, ending with a strong rhythmic twist that propels her voice onward. Almost no conductor misses this, and no audience either, as we are catapulted into the second half of the line, "I would rather die" (Ex. 4).

Here the musical phrasing shifts to the vocal line as Violetta gasps "preferirò morir," and the winds duplicate her phrases as she rises to a B flat, not high for her role, and holds the note for two full measures. Beneath it Verdi keeps the momentum going with a rising scale punched out by the bassoons, three trombones, bass trombone, cellos, and double basses. This is heavy artillery, and if only the conductor will stress the scale's five rising notes, which in the score Verdi accented, the passage will be exciting. Then very briefly Violetta and the orchestra alternate phrases until she insists one last time, with the orchestra silent, that she would rather die, after which it puts a full stop to her line with a single chord delivered like the slam of a door.

"It is a heavy sacrifice," begins Germont smoothly, moving the drama into its next scene. But before leaving this one, consider how much of its passion and forward movement lie in the orchestra. Long before Boito joined him, Verdi was using it for more than "rum-tum" accompaniment.

There are many other small scenes of Act II that might be used as examples of Verdi's imaginative orchestration, but I will limit myself to two, of which the first is important because it is related to another bit of orchestration in Act III. After Germont has left, Violetta undertakes to write a note to Alfredo that will end their liaison. Until this moment Verdi often has accompanied Violetta's vocal line with clarinets, so that to some extent the instrument's sound has become associated with her. Now, as she silently searches for words that will deceive Alfredo as to the depth of her love, Verdi

Ex. 4: The rhythmic twist is in the clarinet, bassoon, violas, and violincellos. This passage, as it now stands, was rewritten by Verdi after the fiasco of the opera's first season and is possibly the most important change he made. Note the accents on the rising and falling orchestral arch beneath the voice held to one pitch. If observed they give the vocal line great momentum.

scores a mournful, weary tune for solo clarinet that seems to emerge from her soul. The tune, in a minor key, is scarcely more than a phrase, four bars, repeated once with slight embellishment, and it starts with a rising interval of a sixth which it cannot sustain and from which it sadly falls away, ending a fifth below where it started. On the repeat it tries again, and fails again. It is her spirit, noble but broken, just as the related passage in the third act is her fate. But more of that later.

The other passage in Act II I want to mention is Violetta's cry of pain as she parts from Alfredo, though he, of course, is unaware that she is leaving him. Her music is the broad theme of the first-act prelude that figuratively represented her personality, warm and loving, but here very differently scored. As she fights to hold back her tears, she faces Alfredo and blurts out, full force, "Amami, Alfredo" (Love me, Alfredo), and Verdi supports her with the strings, horns, oboes, tympani, and bass drum, all of them (except the bass drum, which has no definite pitch) merely trembling on the chief notes of the harmony while the voice alone has the phrase. In the prelude the tune had been carried by all the first violins, violas, and cellos, but here, as Violetta reiterates the musical phrase to the words "amami quant'io t'amo" (love me as much as I love you), Verdi once again gives the melody only to the voice while keeping the accompaniment trembling beneath it. But then, when she repeats her cry, deploying her last reserve of strength, he starts the phrase a third higher, adds the other winds to duplicate her line, and emphasizes it and her gallantry further with a solo trumpet. It is her most heroic moment, and she deserves the trumpet's sound.

Yet the trumpet in its singleness represents extraordinary restraint: for Verdi has left silent the second trumpet, all three trombones, and the bass trombone. We have the word of a contemporary critic, Abramo Basevi, writing in 1859, that for this moment "other composers of the period would have brought on the cannons."[11] But Verdi, while sparing of the brass, "brought on the cannon" in a form that Basevi did not mention. To underpin Violetta's outcry he scored for the only time in the opera a roll on the bass drum, swelling and decreasing its volume as it follows her voice for sixteen bars. A bass drum roll, perhaps just because it has no definite pitch, for most persons is profoundly moving, even disturbing, as if the depths themselves were stirred.[12] And once again, by reserving a special effect to a single scene, Verdi has used the orchestra to help him create a moment that is unique.

*   *   *   *   *   *

The prelude to Act III, as Boito has described, is an evocation of a sickroom, a pervasive silence and at its center a woman dying. Starting with the same seven bars that open the opera, slowly shifting chords scored for sixteen violins *divisi,* Verdi now expands on their theme for another thirty-three bars, rising only once to *forte* and, except for an occasional supporting chord on a few winds and a horn, using only the strings. That he is able, at his chosen slow pace, to avoid the double danger of slackening tension and monotony is extraordinary; and he succeeds in part by his melody, which after the first seven bars is played entirely on the first violins, and in part by the constantly shifting sound of the string accompaniment.

The particular virtue of the prelude's melody, aside from its beauty, lies in the way each successive phrase appears to emerge from the one immediately preceding, so that until the last two are repeated in order to bring the prelude to a close, the melodic line seems to consist of a single arc that rises slowly to a climax at the highest, loudest note, which is placed just two thirds of the way through the thirty-three bars, the classic point for a climax—two thirds rising, one third falling away. Throughout the arc there is not a moment when the melody seems to lose its forward motion until near the end it begins to falter, deliberately so, with the two repeated phrases.

In maintaining this momentum it is assisted by the continuous, subtle changes in the sound of the string accompaniment. As the melody starts with the first violins bowed, the other stringed instruments all are plucked. After eleven bars Verdi changes this sound by directing that the accompaniment be bowed, though in two bars he returns the cellos, only the cellos, to plucking. Four bars later the cellos and double basses start to bow a relatively long arched phrase beneath short rising trills on the first violins (Ex. 5). As the melody above, shifting into quarter notes, steps chromatically up, up to the climax, beneath it the arched phrase curves downward. This divergence of lines is called "contrary motion," and for some deep, mysterious reason it always is more stirring to a listener than "parallel motion"; hence the climax is reinforced. Then, as the prelude begins to close, a melodic phrase for the first time repeats, over plucked strings; then another phrase, made by grace notes to sound slightly tweaked, repeats over bowed strings; and at the end, on a long trill, the first violins reduce their number to four, then to two, then die away on the thinnest thread of sound. Of course, counting the bars is of no importance, but alerting one's ears to the ever-changing quality of the string sound, full or dwindling, plucked or bowed, with grace notes or trills, in long phrases or short, is essential in order to grasp the prelude's full beauty.

Though many persons are inclined not to believe it, Verdi intended the prelude to be played from its first note with the curtain up and the audience gazing at Violetta asleep on the bed, with her maid Annina dozing on a chair. Raising the curtain slowly during the prelude, as sometimes is done, distracts the audience's attention from the music, and raising it afterward gives the act an awkward beginning; for Violetta and Annina's first two exchanges—"Annina, are you asleep? . . . I need a glass of water."—take place with the orchestra silent.

The truth is, though in 1910 when Boito wrote to Bellaigue it already was obscured, Verdi did not compose a prelude to the opera's final act. What is now generally called the prelude is merely the opening bars of what he entitled "Scena ed Aria" (Scene and Aria) and conceived as a single unit stretching from the first note, past Violetta's reading of Germont's letter, to the last note of accompaniment to her aria, "Addio, del passato." The structure throughout is very like that of the sleepwalking scene he had composed six years earlier for Lady Macbeth. Both start with a long orchestral introduction, bring on the voices in a hushed dialogue in which, unaccompanied, they alternate with orchestral phrases repeated from the introduction, then slowly build toward the climax of the aria, and thereafter fade away.[13]

In *Traviata* the scene and aria consume almost half the act, and throughout this long period the orchestral sound remains chiefly strings alone, sometimes plucked, sometimes bowed, and contrasted, as the voices enter, with

Ex. 5: Act III "Prelude." The short arched phrase in the violincellos (Vc.) and double basses (Cb.) begins on the third beat of the first measure and rises steadily to the first beat of the fourth measure, after which it turns down, "contrary motion," as the first violins continue to rise to the prelude's climax.

bars of silence—which Verdi did not want spoiled by the soprano coughing: "There should be no cough in the last act of *La traviata*," he wrote emphatically.[14] Only when Violetta is left alone to read her letter does the sound become more continuous, building toward the scene's climax, the aria, for which Verdi increases the number of woodwinds. When the overall scene is conceived and performed as a single unit it gains pacing and seems short; treated as a succession of miniscenes—a prelude, a recitative, a letter-reading, and an aria—it becomes patchy and can seem long. To unattuned ears it can even become, in its subdued, subtle scoring, slightly boring.[15]

Two orchestral points in the aria, "Addio, del passato," should be mentioned, and the first reflects the advance of Violetta's fate during the three acts. Her vocal line at the start of the aria, over a string accompaniment reinforced from time to time by winds, is essentially a descending scale that she shares with a solo instrument that alternates phrases with her. In the earlier acts the instrument for this purpose was the clarinet; here it is the oboe, whose sound is more plaintive and pinched, more suitable for one nearer to death.

The second is the orchestration of the aria's climax. In its first part Violetta has sung of the passing of her joys; in the second, of the failure, since Alfredo does not return, of his love for her. Then leaving the predominant key of A minor for A major, though the new theme is to be played *leggiero* (lightly), she addresses God directly: "Ah, della traviata . . . Ah, smile on the wish of the *'traviata'* " (the one gone astray, the lost sheep), "forgive her, and gather her to you." For this Verdi adds winds, while directing all the instruments to play *pianissimo,* though the addition, of course, will increase the volume of sound. The curiosity and perhaps effectiveness of the scoring is that the first and second violins, reduced to eight each and playing pulsating chords, are scored for notes toward the top of their normal range while the cellos and double basses, playing the same chords, are scored toward the bottom of theirs, leaving between the groups more than two and a third octaves. To some ears the effect may sound ugly, but to others it suggests the gaping jaws of death that Violetta soon must enter.[16]

With the chorus of Carnival revelers whose offstage voices shatter the sickroom's silence, and even more with Alfredo's arrival, Verdi changes the sound entirely, bringing in the full orchestra and raising the volume for the first time in the act to full strength. But soon, narrowing the focus again to Violetta for her duet with Alfredo, "Parigi, o cara," in which the two plan to leave Paris, he returns to a string accompaniment, starting and continuing it plucked while each sings a verse, and then, for the broader, closing section, shifting to bowing. The street noises and excitement of Alfredo's arrival are the illusion of life; the reality is Violetta's imminent death.

That she will die is expressed musically in the moments following her effort to clothe herself in order to visit the church and give thanks to God for Alfredo's return. Unable to stand, she repeats Alfredo's order to Annina to go for the doctor. "Yes. Tell him . . . tell him that Alfredo has returned . . . that I want to live again." Her line, delivered on a fast descending scale, is cut off brutally by all the brass except trumpets blasting and holding, *"con tutta forza,"* the single note G. It is the only moment in the opera that the brass as a group sound alone, and the harsh sound is unmistakably a warning of death (Ex. 6).

Violetta knows what she hears. Turning to Alfredo, she acknowledges, "If you, coming back, cannot save me, then it is not given to anyone to save me." Rising angrily, she protests her death in the cabaletta, the fast aria sequel to her preceding slow one, the duet "Parigi, o cara."

The cabaletta as a musical form was by the 1850s already in disrepute for being, typically, an effect without cause, but Verdi constantly assured his librettists that he was prepared to compose one provided some new action or understanding had intervened between the slow and fast arias to justify the

Ex. 6: Act III, The Deathknell Note. "Digli . . . che vivere ancor vogl' io . . ." (Tell him . . .
that I want to live again).

latter's excitement.[17] Here the new event has occurred, and Verdi has the
cabaletta in the same form as the slower duet, two verses sung individually by
Alfredo and Violetta and then a long final section sung together. "Gran Dio!
Morir sì giovine . . . ," she cries. "Great God! To die so young. . . ." And
except for supporting chords on the winds the accompaniment, as for most of
her music in this act, is by strings alone. Twice during the duet's early part,
though many conductors make little of it, the horns repeat the summons of
death.

My last example of Verdi's orchestration is Violetta's final delirium in which she imagines that her strength is returning and she will live. The melody over which she recites as much as sings her delusion is, as everyone knows, the music of Alfredo's call to love in the first act, "Di quell'amor." To ensure that our memories of the theme and its connotations will be strong, Verdi already has repeated it in this act as the accompaniment to Violetta's reading of Germont's letter with his promise that Alfredo will return to her.

In the first act the melody, sung offstage by Alfredo, is accompanied by harp alone. In this act, in the letter-reading Verdi shifted the orchestration to the instruments associated with Violetta, the strings. Beneath her voice, while she half recites the letter, two violins carry the tune while one violin, two violas, and two cellos accompany—in all seven instruments. How does Verdi accompany the tune when she is dying? Two violins carry it, while six more and two violas accompany. Three more instruments than before, but notice: there are no cellos. Without their lower tones the sound is greatly thinned. For fifteen measures, two thirds of the sequence, as Violetta expresses her surprise and agitation in the seeming miracle, Verdi keeps the bleached sound constant; then, as her voice rises, he adds winds until on her cry of joy, over the full orchestra, she falls dead. Her collapse is an event we take in with our eyes, and the sight deafens our ears. The musically memorable part of this final delirium, as Verdi knew it would be, is the first two thirds, where that call to love is spun out over the last, fraying thread of life.

We cannot pretend surprise that Violetta dies. Verdi has led us to this moment from the very start of the opera with some remarkably effective music. Most of it, of course, is in the vocal lines, but some is in the orchestration. While we watch the drama onstage and listen to the voices, we are manipulated by the subtle changes in orchestral sound. To say repeatedly, as did a critic who shall be nameless, that "until Boito came" Verdi's orchestration for the most part was "nothing but the big guitar" was a blunder that, because catchy and quoted, became a crime against truth. In *Traviata*, composed twenty-six years before Boito's advent, Verdi demonstrated that his orchestration, though without the consistency of refinement he later would achieve, was even then frequently delicate, imaginative, and dramatically appropriate. It shows him well on the way to becoming a master.

12

VERDI'S
SECOND
"AVE MARIA," 1880

In all, Verdi four times composed settings of the "Ave Maria," once using the fundamental Latin text, and thrice, expanded Italian versions of it. In his final setting, with the Latin text, he wrote for a chorus of four-part mixed voices, unaccompanied; in each of the previous three, for a single soprano with small orchestra. Of these four settings the first, third, and fourth are well known, occurring in his operas *I Lombardi* (1843) and *Otello* (1887) and as one of his *Quattro Pezzi Sacri (Four Sacred Works)* (1898). But the second, an independent work of considerable merit, despite a premiere at La Scala in 1880 and prompt worldwide distribution by his publisher, Ricordi, gradually disappeared from the recital repertory. Indeed, in thirty years of pursuing Verdi's uncommon works in halls of all kinds I have never heard a performance of it; and to my knowledge has not been recorded with orchestra in an even longer time. It has become, with several of his songs and the "popular hymn" for use in the revolutions of 1848, one of his most obscure works.

Such was not always its fate. Yet because of its nature, a ninety-eight-bar solo for soprano with organ or piano frequently substituted for the string ensemble that Verdi scored, it more often was performed in churches or recital halls, which do not keep records, than in opera houses, which do; and accordingly its history is sparse. In England, however, scholars of different periods writing on Verdi indirectly record the retreat to limbo. Frederick J.

Crowest, one of Verdi's earliest English biographers, in 1897 described the piece as "cherished," a word that implies "in use" or "on display," for an heirloom that is cherished will be in the parlor, not in the cellar.[1] Thirty-three years later and fifty after the work's premiere, Francis Toye wrote, "In view of the graceful writing for the voice and the effective harmony of the accompaniment, its infrequent performance is rather surprising."[2] By 1930, therefore, it apparently was more remembered than encountered; and by 1940, with World War II begun, it evidently had vanished, for Dyneley Hussey sourly observed: "It is surprising that it has not occurred to some enterprising soprano to sing this quite beautiful air on the concert platform. But then, perhaps it would be more surprising if the kind of soprano who could sing it well showed enterprise."[3]

The English are not alone in blaming sopranos for the neglect of this "Ave Maria." When I recently asked an Italian in a position of some cultural responsibility why no soprano had thought of reviving it, he replied, "Sopranos don't think; they buy furs."[4] And certainly many singers, men and women, in selecting Verdi for recitals are remarkably unadventurous, probably because unaware.[5] But there are other reasons too, for the disappearance of this "Ave Maria," and some of these have their roots in movements and events not directly concerned with its music.

*   *   *   *   *   *

Exactly when in the late 1870s Verdi began to compose the "Ave Maria" and its more familiar companion piece, a "Pater Noster," is not known. One of the earliest references to either occurs in his correspondence with Ferdinand Hiller, a German musician whom he found congenial. In the spring of 1877, Hiller had invited Verdi to conduct a performance of his *Requiem* at the Cologne Festival, and Verdi had gone, been pleased with the chorus (though not with the soloists), and charmed by Hiller.[6] Thereafter the two exchanged letters frequently, and on 31 July 1879 Verdi wrote:

Imagine my surprise on returning from Genoa and finding on my desk a new work by you! And my surprise doubled on seeing that it was the *De Profundis* in Dante's translation. The joke is that last winter I thought of setting that psalm to music, but fortunately changed my mind and decided to compose as a piece for five-part voices the *Pater Noster*, which also is translated by Dante and can be found in his Minor Works from which you selected the *De Profundis*.[7]

Plainly Verdi had been reading Dante, whose works he kept with those of Schiller and Shakespeare on the top shelf of the small bookcase by his bed.

His love of the poet was lifelong. One of his earliest surviving letters, written in 1835 to his tutor in Milan, Vincenzo Lavigna, opens with a quotation from the *Inferno*, Canto VI, "Nuovi tormenti e nuovi tormentati" (New torments and new tormented): "Just when I thought I soon would be free of all my troubles and have an honorable, decent living, I find myself once more plunged into the depths where I can see nothing but darkness [. . .]"[8] And sixty-one years later, in 1896, he wrote to a friend, "Ah, yes: Dante is simply the greatest of all! Homer, the Greek tragedians, Shakespeare, the biblical writers are great, often sublime, but they are neither so universal nor so exhaustive [. . .]"[9] Presumably about this same year, he expressed his admiration musically by composing a work that later had its premiere as the third of his *Quattro Pezzi Sacri* (1898), the "Laudi alla Vergine Maria" (Praise to the Virgin Mary), with a text from the *Paradiso*, Canto XXXIII.

Then, too, there is this "Pater Noster" and, though he does not mention it in the letter to Hiller, the "Ave Maria," both texts taken from a 250-line poem "La professione di fede" (The Profession of Faith) or, as it was more popularly known, "Credo di Dante" (Dante's Credo). The titles that Verdi gave his two works, which his publisher, Ricordi, thus far has repeated in all editions, are "Ave Maria, volgarizzata da Dante" (i.e., the prayer translated from Latin into the popular dialect, Italian, by Dante) and "Pater Noster, volgarizzato da Dante." Alas, not long after Verdi's death in 1901, scholars concluded that the "professione di fede," though in Dante's favorite verse form, *terza rima*, was written not by him but by the very minor though not uninteresting poet, Antonio de' Beccari da Ferrara.

Not much is known about this new Verdi "collaborator" who, after 550 years, was awarded one of Dante's most popular minor works. He has left a collection of about 150 poems, many of them sonnets, and in them he reveals that in 1315, only six years before Dante died, he was born in Ferrara, where his father, Tura, was a butcher; hence the name Antonio de' Beccari (Antonio of the Butchers [guild]). The father sacrificed much to give his son an education, and Antonio in his poems speaks of him often and always with gratitude. But despite the education, Antonio grew up dissolute and soon was famous for his gambling and brawling—but also for his poetry, and apparently for much of his life he was a populist poet in the tradition that a century later in France would produce François Villon. In 1340 Antonio was at Modena and, fearing the plague, which was virulent, vowed to the Virgin to give up his dissipated life and make a series of pilgrimages. When the plague slackened, so did the good intentions; and in March 1343 at Bologna he seriously injured another poet in a brawl, was outlawed, and fled. For a time he disappeared from view, though during this period he seems to have married and fathered children. After some years he returned to Bologna, though still proscribed, and through the intervention of the powerful de' Pepoli family managed to have the ban against him rescinded. Thereafter he moved frequently from town to town—Forlì, Ravenna, Venice, Padua, Florence, Siena—living by his wits, writing poetry, and returning finally to Bologna in 1358. The following year his movements again become obscure; but eventually his death is mentioned in a letter by Petrarch, and he is thought to have died about 1373.

Throughout Antonio's life his hero was Dante, and he never missed an opportunity to celebrate the poet. His devotion, arising from an art shared however unequally, is appealing, and apparently about 1350, in genuine homage expressed by deliberate imitation, he wrote the "Profession of Faith." So successful was he in adopting Dante's style that, intentionally or not, he fooled almost everyone, and the poem was copied by monks and other scribes into their manuscripts of Dante's works, so that by the time printing became common there existed a century-old belief that the poem was Dante's. This continued, with only a rare challenge, until the second decade of the present century when scholars, applying ever more rigorous tests to the language of the text and the history of the manuscripts, decided that its author was Antonio.[10]

Would we, I wonder, admire Verdi's *Otello* as much as we do if the underlying play turned out to be not by Shakespeare but by John of Birmingham, the Butcher's Son? I doubt it; the cachet of Shakespeare or of Dante counts for something. And should we, singers, writers, publishers, continue to use the titles with Dante's name? I think not. Verdi scholarship has been remarkably slow to reflect the change in attribution, and even the careful *New Grove Dictionary of Music and Musicians* (1980) still reports the text of the "Ave Maria" as by Dante and of the "Pater Noster" as "attributed to Dante." And I know of no book or article on Verdi that mentions Antonio da Ferraro. How, then, should we refer to the works' titles? I suggest that in place of the "volgarizzata(o) da Dante" we substitute the year of the works' common premiere: "Ave Maria, 1880" and "Pater Noster, 1880."[11]

Though Verdi was mistaken about Dante's connection with the two prayers (as was also Hiller about the psalm "De Profundis"), his letter to Hiller refutes, or at least greatly limits, an observation frequently made of this "Ave Maria": that it is "a study" for the "Ave Maria" in *Otello*. The remark suggests that the prayer of 1880 is merely a sketch or "tryout" for the other, which followed in seven years. But in no ordinary sense can this be true, for Verdi did not begin to discuss the possibility of an opera on Shakespeare's play until June 1879, did not receive the first draft of its complete libretto from Arrigo Boito until mid-November, and then did not start composing the music for almost another five years. Meanwhile, sometime in the winter before his letter to Hiller of 31 July 1879, and before the first discussion of *Otello*, he had completed the "Pater Noster" and probably the "Ave Maria." Strengthening this presumption is Verdi's letter to Giulio Ricordi, 7 January 1880, in which he states that the two works were composed "a long time ago."[12] Chronologically, therefore, this second setting seems clearly to have originated not in an enthusiasm for Shakespeare, but for Dante. Musically, too, though it shares some qualities with the operatic settings, enough so that the three may be said to be related, it differs radically from them in its structure, and so is distinct. In sum, not a study, but a finished unique work.

All three of Verdi's Italian versions of the "Ave Maria" have texts that, in addition to translating the prayer, add to it, just as individuals throughout the centuries have done when reciting it privately and in the vernacular. The fundamental Latin text, however, reads:

Ave, Maria, gratia plena,	*Hail, Mary, full of grace,*
Dominus tecum;	*the Lord is with thee;*
benedicta tu in mulieribus,	*blessed art thou among women,*
et benedictus	*and blessed*
fructus ventris tui Jesus.	*is the fruit of thy womb, Jesus.*
Sancta Maria, Mater Dei,	*Holy Mary, Mother of God,*
ora pro nobis peccatoribus	*pray for us sinners*
nunc et in hora mortis nostrae.	*now and in the hour of our death.*
Amen!	*Amen!*

The text is based on the greetings to Mary of the angel Gabriel (Luke 1:28) and of Elizabeth to Mary (Luke 1:42), and the opening five lines, used as a devotional prayer, apparently originated in the eleventh century and became common in the twelfth; the closing four, perhaps aided by the "Professione di fede," came into frequent use only in the sixteenth century, when the Church officially recognized the Latin prayer by including the entire text in the Roman Breviary of 1568. Generally speaking, Italian versions translate the opening lines without additions, and then at the plea, "pray for us sinners," begin to elaborate with specific requests and references. Thus, in the "Ave Maria" for *Otello* Verdi and Boito individualize the prayer by having Desdemona petition Mary to pray not for the hungry or homeless, categories of persons, but for one "who kneels in adoration to you," the "sinner," the "innocent," the one who is "weak and oppressed," all descriptions of herself; then, because she would never pray without asking grace for Otello, she pleads for one who is "mighty—yet himself unhappy"; and finally, again for herself, for one who bows her head to an "evil fate," a description later echoed by Otello who, having killed her, refers to her as one who was born under an "evil star." Of Verdi's three Italian settings of the prayer, this is the most specific in its pleas, the most tied to a context.

In contrast, consider the text of a second setting, the one supposedly written by Dante but actually by Antonio da Ferrara. Its pleas and its sinners, like those of the "Ave Maria" in *I Lombardi*, are kept impersonal by the use of plural pronouns.

Ave regina Vergine Maria	*Hail Queen, Virgin Mary,*
Piena di grazia: Iddio è sempre	*Full of grace: God is always*
teco;	*with thee;*
Sopra ogni donna benedetta	*More than any woman may*
sia.	*thou be blessed.*
E 'l frutto del tuo ventre, il qual	*And the fruit of thy womb, to*
io preco	*whom I pray,*
Che ci guardi dal mal, Cristo	*May he guard us from evil, Je-*
Gesù,	*sus Christ,*
Sia benedetto, e noi tiri con	*May he be blessed, and draw*
seco.	*us to him.*
Vergine benedetta, sempre tu	*Blessed Virgin, do thou always*
Ora per noi a Dio, che ci per-	*Pray for us to God, who may*
doni,	*pardon us,*
E diaci grazia a viver si quag-	*And give us grace to exist here*
giù,	*below,*
Che 'l Paradiso al nostro fin ci	*So that at our end he may grant*
doni.	*us Paradise.*
[Ave Maria, ave Maria, ôra per	*[Hail Mary, hail Mary, pray*
noi	*for us*
A Dio, ôra per noi, ôra per	*To God, pray for us, pray for*
noi.]	*us.]*

The final two lines, in brackets, were added by Verdi, presumably to give the work four balanced verses and to allow it a fading close.

It is interesting that all three Verdi settings of the "Ave Maria" in Italian are for solo soprano. There is no intrinsic reason why the prayer could not be sung by a man, or a men's choir, but Verdi evidently heard it with a feminine quality. Also, in all these settings he treats the first half of the prayer more impersonally than the second, using the lines that correspond to the first five of the Latin text almost as an introduction to those that follow. Thus there is a greeting, "Ave Maria," at a low level of intensity, followed by the petition "pray for us" at a rising level. Finally, in all the settings Verdi heard the prayer accompanied by a special string sound.

In *I Lombardi*, an early opera with relatively rough orchestration, the prayer in Act I, scene 2 is effective partly because of the unexpected delicacy of its accompaniment. He scored for eight violins *divisi*, in pairs, to play four lines; two violas to play one line; and a single double bass, clarinet, and flute. The two woodwinds with rising arpeggios softly punctuate the vocal line, which is supported continuously except for a few bars, by the strings. These, except for the double bass, play *con sordine* (with mutes) throughout, and over an occasional *pizzicato* on the bass, sustain long, unbroken phrases with dynamics limited to *pianissimo*, *poco crescendo*, and *morendo*. The over-all impression is of a woman in prayer starting somewhat formally, warming into intimacy and direct expression, and then allowing the strings to bring her thoughts to a quiet, instrumental close.

In both the "Ave Maria, 1880" and that of *Otello*, Verdi excluded the woodwinds and scored for strings alone. In *Otello* he does not limit the number of strings or divide them until the final bars; but he drops the double bass, replacing it with cellos. All play with mutes, and the effect, when the prayer's petition is reached, is of a large string ensemble playing as a quartet and weaving a soft four-part counterpoint to the vocal line. For the "Ave Maria, 1880," in his autograph score he asked for 6 first violins, 6 second violins, 4 violas, 4 cellos, and 2 additional cellos *"abbassati (mezzo tono) la 4ª corda"* (with the fourth string lowered a half-tone) to allow a low note to sound with full, open-string resonance. Further, knowing that the premiere was to be at La Scala, with possible subsequent performances in other large halls, he added, "Eseguendosi in vasto locale si potranno raddoppiare gl' istromenti" (Performing in large spaces the instruments should be doubled).[13] In fact, for the La Scala premiere they were nearly quadrupled: 24 first violins, 20 second violins, 16 violas, and 16 cellos divided into three groups, one group with the fourth string lowered a half-tone.[14]

The premiere took place on the afternoon of 18 April 1880 as part of a predominantly choral and vocal concert presented by the Orchestral Society of La Scala. The forces gathered for the occasion were enormous and distinguished: an orchestra of 130, a chorus of 300, and as their leader Franco Faccio, then the outstanding conductor in Italy.[15] The diverse program included the "Ave Maria" and the premiere of the "Pater Noster" as a five-part chorus for unaccompanied mixed voices; in addition, there were works by Bazzini, Palestrina, Monteviti, Cherubini, Lotti, Stradella, and Rossini. Some, like the "Pater Noster," were unaccompanied; others, like Rossini's "Inflammatus" from the *Stabat Mater*, were for soloist, chorus, and full orchestra. Teresina Ponchielli Brambina was the soloist for the "Inflammatus" and Teresina Singer, for the "Ave Maria."

Verdi was present and, according to his letters to friends the next day, he was pleased with the execution of his two works.[16] He probably enjoyed less, if in usual character, an event of the morning in which he was made the focus of a ceremony at the opera house: La Scala's president, surrounded by musical dignitaries and rich patrons, presented him with a parchment recording the administration's decision to erect in the house, by subscription, the statue of Verdi that now stands there. Possibly he enjoyed more the evening's event, a serenade beneath his window at the Hotel Milan by La Scala's musicians. [17]

The next morning, reviews of the concert appeared, and Filippo Filippi, perhaps the most influential of the critics, wrote in *La perseveranza*: "The *Ave Maria* is a piece altogether modern, a work tender, noble, passionate at times, in which Verdi's personality is more pronounced [than in the *Pater Noster*]. He wrote it in the key of B that he likes, and it reminds one a little of the *romanza* in *Forza del destino* [Leonora's first act aria] with the orchestral technique of the *Messa da Requiem*. The tiny prelude with mutes is a gem; and then the voice enters with a melody in the minor [the prayer's greeting] that expands later into the major [the petition] with passion [. . .]"[18]

As in the two operatic settings the strings are muted, and this time, because the prayer is an independent work without context, there is a "tiny prelude" of twenty-one bars, which is indeed beautiful. Further, Verdi repeats the prelude's opening as the soprano enters, shifting the melody only gradually from the strings to her voice; and the transition is smooth. In contrast, in *I Lombardi* (1843) it is a mite abrupt. The soprano simply announces in a four-bar statement that she will pray, kneels, and begins. In *Otello* (1887), on the other hand, Verdi achieves the feeling of a prelude, but not as he did in the 1880 prayer. In *Otello* there is only a six-bar introduction for the strings; then Desdemona's voice enters, and she quietly recites the entire greeting on a single low note over slowly shifting harmonies. Only with the petition does her melody rise and the strings begin their counterpoint. Thus the greeting has become the prelude.

The difference in musical structure of the "Ave Maria, 1880" continues into the shape of its vocal line: its rise and fall is more evenly balanced. In both the operatic prayers the vocal climax, the highest note—B flat in *I Lombardi*, A flat in *Otello*—is almost the last note sung, whereas in the 1880 work the high note, G sharp, comes close to the opening of the petition, on the first word of "pray for us." In neither operatic version is there a change of key; but in the 1880 version, passing from the greeting to the petition Verdi shifts from B minor to B major, and then for the two lines he added at the end, "Ave Maria, ôra per noi a Dio, ôra per noi, ôra per noi," back to the minor. And he reinforces the feeling of a return by repeating beneath the lines several phrases of the prelude. Then, when the voice stops he continues these for another eight bars in what is the longest postlude of the three prayers. Thus the structure of the 1880 work, which any listener will feel, is essentially A–

B–A, whereas that of the two operatic prayers is closer to A–B.

After their premieres the "Ave Maria" and "Pater Noster" were heard again the following week, on 25 April, when the Orchestral Society repeated the concert with a few changes elsewhere in the program. But by then Verdi had left for Genoa; he was eager to rest. In March he had gone to Paris to conduct the first performance of *Aida* at the Opéra, where it was destined to become his most popular work after *Rigoletto,* and then in April to Milan for the premieres of the two prayers at La Scala. It was his practice to do what he could to launch his works to their best advantage and then leave them to their fate. As suggested earlier, for the "Ave Maria" this ultimately would prove harsh. Yet the controlling factors, it seems, lay not in the music itself but in Ricordi's method of publishing and distributing it and in a change of ideas within the Roman Church on what constitutes religious music.

*   *   *   *   *   *

In the same month as the premieres Ricordi issued a score of the five-part, unaccompanied "Pater Noster" and a piano-vocal score of the "Ave Maria," both of them astonishingly sumptuous. The "Ave Maria" in particular, with a front wrapper of multiple colors and initial letters garlanded and decorated with figures as if painted by a medieval scribe, is gorgeous. The color, however, does not stop with the wrapper; inside, the title, Verdi's name, and every capital letter of the text are printed in red with many also decorated. In later printings, not surprisingly, the decorations and colors gradually disappeared, to the point where the edition now available is conversely drab; and copies of the original, if they can be found, are highly prized.

In Italy, in 1880, perhaps it is not surprising that a new work by Verdi, especially one with the potential popularity of an Ave Maria, should receive such splendid treatment. He was, by then, the country's outstanding artist as well as an important figure in its political history, so that anything he published would be of enormous interest. More startling, I think, is the expense to which the work's American publisher, Wm. A. Pond & Co., was prepared to go. Pond's cover is reproduced here at roughly a third of its size and only in black and white. Its actual colors were white, red, blue, and gold, with the Virgin's image and Verdi's name printed on beds of gold and every letter of the title gold-outlined. The music is engraved, not lithographed, and the back cover is free of advertising. In United States music publishing of any period such color and care are extraordinary.

Following the original editions for both works Ricordi promptly issued others with text translations into English, French, German, and Spanish. For the "Pater Noster" the firm published editions with piano or harmonium accompaniments for use in rehearsal, and for the "Ave Maria," in addition to

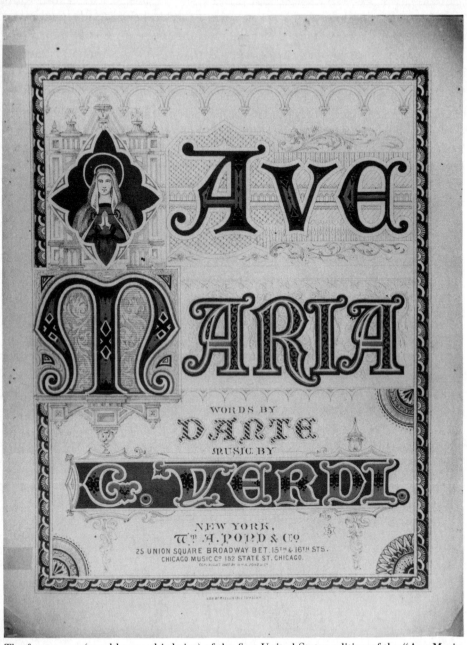

The front cover (roughly one-third size) of the first United States edition of the "Ave Maria, 1880," in white, red, blue, and gold. The words allegedly by Dante are translated by F. W. Rosier. The engraver was Hounslow, N.Y., plate number 10154.

the piano-vocal score, another with violin and harmonium accompaniment. [19] But despite the promotion both works apparently soon ran into the economic difficulty that still plagues them, particularly the "Ave Maria." Today any Ricordi edition of the "Pater Noster," an unaccompanied chorus, will give the purchaser exactly what Verdi wrote: along with the rehearsal accompaniment the five vocal lines are on the page, complete. But for the "Ave Maria," whether published by Ricordi or Pond, the purchaser receives only a piano-vocal score in which the string ensemble that Verdi heard in his ear has been replaced by a piano reduction. To obtain the string accompaniment, a singer, impresario, or choirmaster must, just as with an opera, rent the parts from Ricordi and return them after the contracted number of performances. But the bother and expense that are worthwhile for an opera, with many repetitions in a season, may not seem so for a five-and-a-half-minute solo, scheduled probably for a single performance.

One of the first to complain was Hiller. He had performed both works at his Cologne Festival in May 1881, with Marcella Sembrich as the soloist for the "Ave Maria," and neither piece had gone as well as he had hoped. He wanted to do them again but, as he wrote to Verdi:

It is unfortunate that Ricordi only *rents* all this music. In Germany we are used to buying all the great works and playing them often, at least as often as possible. But our concert managers will be disgusted when they must pay as rent for a single performance what they usually pay to buy. And it is too bad, for it is necessary to hear good music frequently in order to understand it completely. [20]

Hiller went on to talk of other matters and apparently never returned to the point, and Verdi, for his part, seems never to have responded to it. Perhaps by mid-summer 1881 nothing could be done; or perhaps initial rentals were sufficient to lull any fears. But the danger for the works was obvious: concert managers would not schedule them, or not more than once, and individual choirmasters or artists would tend either to ignore them or—as many in all periods have done—to violate copyright. With the "Pater Noster" an energetic choirmaster could buy a single copy and then himself make as many more of the five vocal lines as needed—not an arduous job in a choir, where there are many helping hands. But with the "Ave Maria" this was not possible, for the string accompaniment was not there to be copied, only the piano reduction that produced not at all the same sound. Imagine Desdemona's "Ave Maria" sung to an organ or piano. No one who knows it with strings would listen for a moment. Yet, as the years passed, this increasingly was the fate of the "Ave Maria, 1880," to be performed with the wrong accompaniment and, consequently, to sound less beautiful than it is.

It seems strange that neither Verdi nor Giulio Ricordi considered an alternative method of publication, one already at hand. Ricordi offered for sale in full-score editions Verdi's songs, composed for voice and piano, and the *String Quartet* (1876). The firm reserved "all its rights" in the works, notably that of public performance, but a purchaser received the work complete and could hear it performed in private—and despite the copyright, often no doubt in public—just as Verdi composed it. In the days before recordings such performances greatly helped to establish a work. Verdi's *String Quartet*, for example, was much played by amateurs, and at any public performance probably a sizable part of the audience had a good idea of how it should sound.

But the possibility of issuing the "Ave Maria" as if it were a song to be bought, rather than an opera to be rented, seems never to have entered Verdi's mind. It was he who ordered the piano reduction of the string accompaniment,[21] and when Ricordi sent him the proof sheets he examined them carefully, suggesting that an accent be placed on "ôra" to show that it was a verb, and requesting that the piano reduction "be revised to bring out certain notes for the first cellos 'more distinctly.' "[22] He was attentive; but his mind, I think, was elsewhere, focused on an aspect of the piece that has more to do with cultural history than with the music itself.

Unexpectedly, the major part of Verdi's letter in which he corrects the proofs of the "Ave Maria" is not devoted to it but to a joke that he starts in the text and continues in a lengthy postscript:

The Stabat of Pergolesi is a masterpiece (that is well established) although it is in some places weak and without character; but it belongs to the category of boring. That would not matter if this composition were by some old German who has come into fashion [. . .]

P. S. Among the less boring old things, there is a Motet by Vittoria . . . really beautiful, sublime: well performed without the coloring added by the French masters, this could have a very great effect. If then one could substitute the name of Vittoria with that of Back [deliberately misspelled] you would have a fanatic success! And the name of Bach would not be dishonoured, because He, the giant, the colossus, the indefinable one, could never write for voices like that! What an awful thing to say: But I've said it!

I cannot now tell you which Motet it is, but if you like I will let you know.[23]

Ricordi, of course, asked Verdi to identify the motet, and Verdi promised to look it up; but alas, the identification apparently was relayed in a conversation in Paris when Ricordi joined him there for the premiere of *Aida* at the Opéra. Meanwhile, however, Verdi had suggested in another letter that Pergolesi's *Stabat Mater*, if performed under the name of Bach, would be greeted with cheers.[24] Plainly, by mid-winter 1880 Bach had become a symbol for Verdi of the vogue for German music that was sweeping Italy, and his jokes hardly concealed his strong feelings about it. These were both personal and cultural; and in combination, I believe, they almost overwhelmed the "Pater Noster" and the "Ave Maria." Personally, Verdi at this time felt oppressed by being constantly and unfavorably compared by critics to Wagner (see "Franz Werfel and the 'Verdi Renaissance' "). Since *Aida* (1871), though he had completed the *Requiem* (1874) and the *String Quartet* (1876), he had not composed an opera, and to the distress of his admirers there was no talk of any. He seemed to have retired. When in the winter of 1878 his friend Clarina Maffei wrote, urging him to compose, he replied: "Why should I? What would I succeed in doing? What would I gain? The results would be quite wretched. I would have it said of me all over again that I didn't know how to write and that I have become a follower of Wagner. Some glory! After a career of nearly forty years to end up as an imitator!"[25] This was apparently about the time that he turned consciously back to Italian artists, restudying Dante and Palestrina, and composing somewhat in the latter's style, the "Pater Noster."

More generally, the enthusiasm for German music distressed him because, as he wrote to Giulio Ricordi the following month:

We are all aiding, without wishing, in the destruction of our theatre. Perhaps I myself, you, etc. etc. are among the wreckers. And if I might say something that may sound foolish, I would say that the first cause was the Italian Quartet Societies; a more recent one, the success of the performances (not the works) given by the Orchestral Society of La Scala in Paris [. . .] Why the devil if we are living in Italy must we do German art? [. . .] Art is universal—no one believes that more than I; but those who practice it are individuals; and since the Germans have different artistic methods than we, their art in essence is different. We cannot, should not, compose like the Germans; nor they, like us. Let them assimilate our qualities, as Haydn and Mozart did in their time, though remaining always symphonically inclined; and let Rossini assimilate some formal elements from Mozart, while remaining always melodically inclined. That's good. But for us to renounce our art because of fashion, frenzy for novelty, or affectation of science, to give up our art, our instinct, certainty, spontaneity, natural feelings, and clarity, is absurd and stupid.[26]

In April of the following year, just twelve months before the premieres of the "Ave Maria" and the "Pater Noster," the Orchestral Society of La Scala asked Verdi to be its honorary president, and he replied:

As you rightly say, I am by nature averse to this sort of undertaking, and all the more so in the present *chaos* of ideas, into which trends and theories contrary to our nature have drawn Italian music. In this *chaos*, from which a new world may emerge (though not one we'd recognize), but more likely emptiness, I do not want to have a part. I most sincerely hope, however, that the orchestral branch of music will flourish, while hoping equally much that the other branch may also be cultivated, to the end that Italy one day again may have that art which was *ours* as opposed to that *other*.

It is right to educate the public to, as the cognoscenti say, high art, but it seems to me that the art of Palestrina and Marcello may also be high art . . . and it is *ours*.[27]

When nine months later the Orchestral Society and Franco Faccio, no doubt partly in response to Verdi's views, planned a concert entirely of vocal and choral music by Italian composers, Verdi could not help but be interested. And when he was invited to have the premieres of his two works serve as the event's capstone, he hardly could refuse; indeed, through Ricordi he had solicited the invitation to ensure an Italian premiere for his two works, for Hiller was pressing to present them at his Cologne Festival.[28] But in agreeing to the La Scala premiere under these circumstances he burdened the works with more weight than either comfortably could carry. In his eyes, and in the eyes of those close to him, I suspect, they ceased to be the minor works they are and became salvos in a patriotic cultural campaign. Given their simple, even slight natures, the beauty that Ricordi lavished on their first editions is almost too much, near to pomposity. Similarly, the decision to treat them like major works and market them like operas soon told against them. As the years passed, managers and performers relegated them to churches and recital halls, where the "Ave Maria" was accompanied by organ or piano and not by the string ensemble that Verdi intended.

Even from churches, however, at least from those that are Catholic, the "Ave Maria" in time was driven out. On 22 November 1903, roughly two and a half years after Verdi's death, Pope Pius X issued a statement, the *Motu Proprio*, on the proper function and form of music for use in Roman churches. The standard against which it should be measured was Gregorian chant, and Section 3 of the *Motu Proprio* laid down as a rule: "the more closely a composition for Church approaches in its movement, inspiration and savor the Gregorian form, the more sacred and liturgical it becomes; and the more out of harmony it is with the supreme model, the less worthy it is of the temple." This is still the basis of the Church's policy for judging the propriety of ecclesiastical music.

In Section 6 the *Motu Proprio* went on to advise: "Among the different kinds of modern music, that which appears less suitable [. . .] is the theatrical style, which was in the greatest vogue, especially in Italy, during the last century." And in later sections it prohibited the use of a piano in a church and forbade the employment of women in choirs or as soloists.

All of Verdi's published sacred works, including the *Requiem*, violate these requirements in some way, but this probably would not have surprised or disturbed him, for there is no evidence that he intended them for churches. Nevertheless, for some of them, including the "Ave Maria, 1880," the Church for many years provided a hospitable home where artists and audiences became aware, however dimly, of the works' existence. Gradually, however, the principles of the *Motu Proprio* began to penetrate daily practice in Catholic churches all over the world. The Society of St. Gregory of America, for example, following a convention in 1922 published a "White List" of approved music and a "Black List" of disapproved, and specifically on the latter were the Ave Marias of eight composers, one of them Verdi.[29] Also condemned were arrangements and adaptations "of operatic melodies, such as [the] Sextet from *Lucia di Lammermoor*, [and the] Quartet from *Rigoletto* [. . .]" and even more specifically a work of Verdi given new words and entitled "Jesu Dei Vivi." Of this the Society remarked: "Taken from the opera *Attila* [Trio, last Act]. This number is another favorite among Catholic choirs. Verdi did not write this for use in the church, but for one of his operas. He would have been the first to object to its use in its present form, since it is neither fitting nor appropriate."[30]

The Society reissued its lists from time to time, and the type of music sung in Catholic churches of the United States slowly changed. The chronology of this shift matches closely what appears to be the history of the "Ave Maria, 1880" in England: in 1897, a "cherished" work; in 1930, slipping from the repertory; and in 1940, gone. In both countries, and in Italy as well, the work seems to have disappeared for reasons having little to do with the quality of its music.

Certainly the "Ave Maria, 1880" is a work in Verdi's theatrical style; he knew no other. And perhaps that style, accepted and loved in the opera house, will not find favor today in the recital hall. But surely the time has come for Ricordi to publish a new edition of the work, discarding the attribution of the text to Dante and for the first time presenting the music complete, with the string accompaniment. Time, too, for some enterprising soprano to sing it in recital, as well as record it, with the string ensemble, so that finally the rest of us may hear it—probably for the first time—as Verdi wrote it.

APPENDICES

APPENDIX A
"IL CINQUE MAGGIO"
(THE FIFTH OF MAY)
by Alessandro Manzoni
(written 17–19 July 1821)

Translated by William Ewart Gladstone, 1861, then Chancellor of the Exchequer of Great Britain, as "Ode, On the Death of Napoleon"

1.

Ei fu; siccome immobile,
Dato il mortal sospiro,
Stette la spoglia immemore
Orba di tanto spiro,
Così percossa, attonita
La Terra al nunzio sta;
Muta pensando all' ultima
Ora dell' Uom fatale,
Nè sa quando una simile
Orma di piè mortale
La sua cruenta polvere
A calpestar verrà.

1.

He died; As in the senseless clay
No stir of life was left,
When, drawn the mortal sigh, it lay
Of such a soul bereft,
So, at the tidings thunderstruck
And pensive, Earth remains:
And muses o'er the dying hour
And o'er the Child of Fate,
Nor knows if ever such a Power
Again shall desolate
With like deep track of wounds and stains
Her blood-red plains.

2.

Lui sfolgorante in soglio
Vide il mio genio, e tacque;
Quando con voce assidua
Cadde, risorse, e giacque,
Di mille voci al sonito
Mista la sua non ha;
Vergin di servo encomio,
E di codardo oltraggio;
Sorge or commosso, al subito
Sparir di tanto raggio,
E scioglie all' urna un cantico
Che forse non morrà.

2.

Him, blazing from his throne, to see
My soul in silence bore;
When with quick change he fell, and
rose,
And fell to rise no more;
Amidst a thousand voices' throng,
Hers went not up on high,
No slavish adulation stored,
No dastard slander poured;
But stirs and wakes, when such a
light
Is quenched in sudden night,
And utters o'er his urn a song
That haply shall not die.

3.

Dall' Alpi alle Piramidi,
Dal Mansanare al Reno,
Di quel securo il fulmine
Tenea dietro al baleno;
Scoppiò da Scilla al Tanai,
Dall' uno al altro mar.
Fu vera gloria? Ai posteri
L' ardua sentenza. Nui
Chiniam la fronte al Massimo
Fattor, che volle in Lui
Del Creator Suo Spirito
Più vasta orma stampar.

3.

From Alp to farthest Pyramid,
From Rhine to Mansanar,
How sure his lightning's flash foretold
His thunderbolts of war!
To Don from Scilla's height they roar,
From North to Southern shore.
And this was glory? After-men,
Judge the dark problem. Low
We to the Mighty Maker bend
The while, Who planned to show
What vaster mould Creative Will
With him could fill.

4.

La procellosa e trepida
Gioja d' un gran disegno,
L' ansia d' un cuor, che indocile
Ferve pensando al regno,
E 'l giunge, e tiene un premio
Ch' era follia sperar,
Tutto ei provò: la gloria
Maggior dopo il periglio,
La fuga, e la vittoria,
La reggia, e 'l triste esiglio,
Due volte nella polvere,
Due volte su gli altar.

4.

The joy, that o'er some brave design
With thrill tumultuous yearns;
The craving of a heart that, wild
With thought of Empire, burns,
And gains, and holds, the prize it seemed
But madness to have dreamed;
He knew all this, and glory too,
By peril heightened, knew,
The Exile's gloom, the Victor's glare,
The palace or the hut his share,
Twice bit the dust, twice scaled in might
The altar's height.

5.

Ei si nomò: due secoli,
  L' un contro l' altro armato,
  Sommessi a lui si volsero
  Come aspettando il fato:
Ei fè' silenzio, ed arbitro
  S' assise in mezzo a lor;
    Ei sparve : e i dì nell' ozio
    Chiuse in sì breve sponda,
    Segno d' immensa invidia,
    E di pietà profonda,
D' inestinguibil' odio,
E d' indomato amor.

5.

He dawns; two Ages, armèd each
  Against the other, stand;
  To him they bend, their doom beseech
  Submissive from his hand;
He bids be still, and sits betwixt,
  The Arbiter of Fate:
    He wanes; an islet's bounds inclose
    His terrible repose;
    Him Envy's far-drawn arrows wound,
    Him Pity's gaze profound
Pursues, him Love unconquered, mixt
  With deathless Hate.

6.

Come sul capo al naufrago
  L' onda s' avvolve, e pesa,
  L' onda su cui del misero
  Alta pur dianzi e tesa
Scorrea la vista a scernere
Prode remote invan;
    Tal su quell' alma il cumulo
    Delle memorie scese;
    Oh! quante volte ai posteri
    Narrar se stesso imprese,
E sulle eterne pagine
Cadde la stanca man!

6.

As on the shipwrecked mariner
  The weltering wave's descent—
  The wave, o'er which, a moment since,
  For distant shores he bent
And bent in vain, his eager eye;
  So on that stricken head
  Came whelming down the mighty
    Past.
    How often did his pen
    Essay to tell the wondrous tale
    For after times and men,
And o'er the lines that could not die
  His hand lay dead.

7.

Oh! quante volte, al tacito
  Morir d' un giorno inerte,
  Chinati i rai fulminei,
  Le braccia al sen conserte,
Stette, e dei dì che furono
L' assalse il souvenir.
    Ei ripensò le mobili
    Tende, e i percossi valli,
    E il lampo dei manipoli,
    E l' onda dei cavalli,
    E il concitato imperio,
    E il celere obbedir.

7.

How often, as the listless day
  In silence died away,
  He stood with lightning eye deprest,
  And arms across his breast,
And bygone years, in rushing train,
Smote on his soul amain:
    The breezy tents he seemed to see,
    And the battering cannon's course,
    And the flashing of the infantry,
    And the torrent of the horse,
And, obeyed as soon as heard,
    Th' ecstatic word.

8.

Ahi! forse a tanto strazio
Cadde lo spirto anelo,
E disperò; ma valida
Venne un man dal cielo,
E in più spirabil aere
Pietosa il trasportò;
E l' avviò su i floridi
Sentier della speranza,
Ai campi eterni, al premio
Che i desiderii avanza,
Ov' è silenzio e tenebre
La gloria che passò.

9.

Bella, immortal, benefica
Fede, ai trionfi avvezza,
Scrivi ancor questo; allegrati:
Che più superba altezza
Al disonor del Golgota
Giammai non si chinò.
Tu dalle stanche ceneri
Sperdi ogni ria parola;
Il Dio, che atterra e suscita,
Che affanna e che consola,
Sulla deserta coltrice
Accanto a lui posò.

8.

Haply, by that wild struggle riven
The panting heart had failed
In cold despair; but help from Heaven
Descended and prevailed,
And raised him up, and pitying bare
Into a genial air,
And oared him on the flowery ways
Of Hope, and bade aspire
To those blest plains, and to the prize
That passes all desire,
Where darkly sinks in silence down
Earth's brief renown.

9.

O fair, O deathless, O benign,
O still victorious Faith,
This triumph reckon too for thine
With joy; for ne'er in Death
A sterner pride hath stooped to woo
The shame of Golgotha;
From his outwearied ashes warn
Each word of wrath and scorn:
The God, that gives or eases
pain,
That smites, and lifts again,
On that lone couch, in that dark day,
Beside him lay.

APPENDIX B
TEXT OF THE
MESSA DA REQUIEM

The lines that Verdi repeated, inserted, or added to the text used by Mozart are underlined. The words that he emphasized by a musical climax or repetition are set in capitals.

REQUIEM AND KYRIE

Requiem aeternam dona eis, Domine, et lux perpetua luceat eis. Te decet hymnus Deus in Sion, et tibi reddetur votum in Jerusalem. Exaudi orationem meam, ad te omnis caro veniet. Requiem aeternam dona eis, Domine, et lux perpetua luceat eis.

Kyrie eleison. Christe eleison. Kyrie eleison.

Give them eternal peace, Lord, and let perpetual light shine on them. A hymn becomes you God in Sion, and to you a vow will be made in Jerusalem. Hear my plea, to thee all flesh will come. Give them eternal peace, Lord, and let perpetual light shine on them.

Lord, have mercy upon us. Christ, have mercy upon us. Lord, have mercy upon us.

DIES IRAE

DIES IRAE, DIES ILLA *solvet saeclum in favilla,* *teste David cum Sibylla.*	*DAY OF WRATH, THAT DAY* *shall dissolve the world in ash* *as David and the Sibyl promise.*

Quantus tremor est futurus,	*How great the terror will be*
quando judex est venturus,	*when the judge is about to come*
cuncta stricte discussurus.	*on whose word everything hangs.*

TUBA MIRUM SPARGENS SO-NUM	*THE TRUMPET, SCATTERING ITS AWFUL SOUND*
per sepulchra regionum,	*through the graves of earth*
coget omnes ante thronum.	*drives all before the throne.*

MORS stupebit et natura	*DEATH and nature will be astounded*
cum resurget creatura	*when everything created will rise up*
judicanti responsura.	*to answer to the judge.*

Liber scriptus proferetur,	*The book of record will be brought out,*
in quo totum continetur	*in which everything is entered*
unde mundus judicetur.	*from which the world will be judged.*

Dies Irae	*Day of Wrath*
Judex ergo cum sedebit,	*Then when the judge takes his seat,*
quiquid latet,	*whatever is hidden, will appear;*
apparebit;	

Dies Irae	*Day of Wrath*
NIL inultum remanebit.	*NOTHING will go unpunished.*

Dies Irae	*Day of Wrath*

DIES IRAE, DIES ILLA	*DAY OF WRATH, THAT DAY*
solvet saeclum in favilla,	*shall dissolve the world in ash,*
teste David cum Sibylla,	*as David and the Sibyl promise.*

Quid sum, miser, tunc dicturus?	*What am I, miserable man, then to say?*
quem patronum rogaturus,	*to what protector will I turn,*
cum vix justus sit securus?	*when even the just man scarcely is safe?*

REX TREMENDAE MAJESTA-
    TIS,
   qui salvandos salvas gratis,
   SALVA ME, fons pietatis.

Recordare, Jesu pie,
   quod sum causa tuae viae,
   ne me perdas illa die.

Quaereus me sedisti lassus,
   redemisti crucem passus;
   tantus labor non sit cassus.

Juste judex ultionis,
   donum fac remissionis
   ante diem rationis.

Ingemisco tamquam reus,
   culpa rebet vultus meus;
   supplicanti parce Deus.

Qui Mariam absolvisti,
   et latronem exaudisti,
   mihi quoque spem dedisti.

Preces meae non sunt dignae,
   sed tu bonus fac benigne,
   ne perenni cremer igne.

Inter oves locum praesta,
   et ab haedis me sequestra
   statuens in parte dextra.

KING OF DREADFUL MAJESTY,
   who saves those needing it for
    nothing,
   SAVE ME, you fount of pity.

Remember, Jesus holy one,
   that I am the reason for your
    life,
   so that you won't destroy me on
    that day.

Seeking me you have sat down wea-
    ry;
   suffering on the cross you have
    bought me free.
   let not so much labor be for noth-
    ing.

You impartial judge of punish-
ment,
   make a gift of remission
   before the day of accounting.

I groan as when I'm guilty;
   my sins make my face red;
   God, spare the supplicant.

You who absolved Mary
   and listened to the thief,
   have also given me hope.

My prayers are not worthy,
   but you good Lord kindly make
    them so,
   lest I be burned in the everlasting
    fire.

Save me a place with the sheep,
   and take me away from the
    goats,
   putting me on your right-hand
    side.

Confutatis maledictis,	*When the wicked are overthrown*
flammis acrivus addictis,	*and given to the crackling flames,*
voca me cum benedictis.	*call me with the blessed.*

Oro supplex et acclinis,	*I beg as a suppliant and relying on you,*
cor contritum quasi cinis,	*my heart almost burned out with remorse;*
gere curam mei finis.	*take pity on my end.*

<u>*DIES IRAE, DIES ILLA*</u>	<u>*DAY OF WRATH, THAT DAY*</u>
<u>*solvet saeclum in favilla,*</u>	*shall dissolve the world in ash*
<u>*teste David cum Sibylla,*</u>	*as David and the Sibyl <u>prom-</u>* *<u>ise.</u>*

Lacrymosa dies illa,	*That tearful day*
qua resurget ex favilla	*in which shall rise out of the dust*
judicandus homo reus.	*the guilty man to be judged*

Huic ergo parce Deus.	*Spare him them, God.*
pie Jesu Domine,	*holy Jesus Lord*
dona eis REQUIEM.	*give them PEACE.*

Amen.	*Amen.*

(According to Alec Robertson, the poem "Dies Irae" properly ends with the stanza beginning "Oro supplex," which has been translated by an unknown: "Lord, this I beg on bended knee/With heart contrite as ashes be:/That thou take care both of my end and me." Thereafter, the lines beginning with "Lacrymosa" through "dona eis requiem" were added by another unknown who, horrified by the poem's use of the first person singular, fashioned these verses to bring it back to a more generalized prayer for the dead: "give them peace." [*Requiem, Music of Mourning and Consolation* (New York: Praeger, 1967), pp. 19–20])

DOMINE JESU

Domine Jesu Christe, Rex Gloriae, libera animas omnium fidelium defunctorum de poenis inferni, et de profundo lacu. Libera eas de ore leonis, ne absorbeat eas Tartarus, ne cadant in obscurum. Sed signifer sanctus Michael repraesentet eas in lucem sanctam; quam olim Abrahae promisisti et semini ejus.

Hostias et preces tibi, Domine, laudis offerimus: tu suscipe pro animabus illis quarum hodie memoriam facimus. Fac eas, Domine, de morte transire ad vitam; quam olim Abrahae promisisti et semini ejus.

Lord Jesus Christ, King of Glory, free the souls of all the faithful dead from the punishments of Hell and the bottomless pit. Free them from the mouth of the lion so that Hell will not gulp them down nor will they fall into darkness. But let holy Michael, the standard-bearer, lead them into the holy light; as you once promised to Abraham and his children.

Animals and prayers to you, Lord, we offer in praise; take them for the benefit of those souls whom we are remembering today. Make them, Lord, go from death to life; as you once promised to Abraham and his children.

SANCTUS

Sanctus, sanctus, sanctus Dominus Deus Sabaoth. Pleni sunt coeli et terra gloria tua. Hosanna in excelsis. Benedictus, qui venit in nomine Domini. Hosana in excelsis.

Holy, holy, holy Lord God of hosts. The heavens and earth are filled with your glory. Hosanna in the highest. Blessed is he who comes in the name of the Lord. Hosanna in the highest.

AGNUS DEI

Agnus Dei, qui tollis peccata mundi, dona eis requiem. Agnus Dei, qui tollis peccata mundi, dona eis requiem sempiternam.

Lamb of God, who takes away the sins of the world, give them peace. Lamb of God, who takes away the sins of the world, give them peace everlasting.

LUX AETERNA

Lux aeterna luceat eis, Domine, cum Sanctis tuis in aeternum, quia pius es. Requiem aeternam dona eis, Domine, et lux perpetua luceat eis.

Let eternal light shine on them, Lord, with your saints in eternity, because you are kind. Give them eternal peace, Lord, and let perpetual light shine on them.

LIBERA ME

Libera me, Domine, de morte aeterna, in die illa tremenda, quando coeli movendi sunt et terra; dum veneris judicare saeculum per ignem.

Tremens factus sum ego et timeo. dum discussio venerit atque ventura ira, quando coeli movendi sunt et terra.

DIES IRAE, DIES ILLA, calamitatis et miseriae, dies magna et amara valde; dum veneris judicare saeculum per ignem.

Requiem aeternam dona eis, Domine, et lux perpetua luceat eis.

LIBERA ME, Domine, de morte aeterna, in die illa tremenda, quando coeli movendi sunt et terra; dum veneris judicare saeculum per ignem.

LIBERA ME.

Free me, Lord, from eternal death on that terrifying day when the heavens and earth are shattered; when you will have come to judge the age with fire.

I tremble and am afraid at the judgment that will have come and the wrath to follow, when the heavens and earth are shattered.

DAY OF WRATH, THAT DAY of calamity and misery, the day so great and very bitter; when you will have come to judge the age with fire.

Give them eternal peace, Lord, and let perpetual light shine on them.

FREE ME, Lord, from eternal death on that terrifying day when the heavens and earth are shattered; when you will have come to judge the age with fire.

FREE ME.

APPENDIX C
NINE HITHERTO
UNPUBLISHED LETTERS
OF VERDI, WITH
TRANSLATIONS

The nine letters that follow, with one exception, I believe have not been published before. Some are trivial but amusing; a few are important; all nicely display facets of Verdi's personality. But claiming first publication of any Verdi letter is risky, and the exception here is an example of the danger.

The letter is one that Verdi wrote to Giulio Ricordi on 7 February 1880, about the initial publication of his "Ave Maria" that was to have its premiere at La Scala on 18 April. I have the autograph and gave its text to Pierluigi Petrobelli, director of the Istituto de Studi Verdiani, Parma, to include in the *Carteggio Verdi—Ricordi (1880–1881)*, vol. 1, of which he is the editor, and which possibly may appear before this book. Both of us thought the letter had never been published, and then in November 1986, Marisa Casati, on the editorial staff of the Istituto, discovered that the letter's postscript, only the postscript, had been published by Gino Monaldi in his *Verdi nella vita e nell' arte* (Milan: Ricordi, 1913), 127–28.

With that revelation as a caution, I believe that the other letters are hitherto unpublished and that this one, which is important, has not been published in English. At the moment the autographs of all these letters are in my possession.

In presenting them it seems pointless to repeat in English Verdi's signatures, farewells, dates, and addresses, so I have given these in the Italian text and omitted them in the translation. In both texts, however, Verdi's underlinings and dots are reproduced. Where a few explanations of his references seem in order I have placed them as an introduction to the letter rather than as a footnote.

*   *   *   *   *   *

In the Preface: Verdi, Letter, 20 August 1884, to [?] Beccaro. The envelope is addressed to Comm[endatore] Beccaro, Locanda Maggiore, Acqui, Montecatini. Beginning in 1882, Verdi and his wife went regularly to the spa at Montecatini, between Florence and Lucca, to take the waters, and Beccaro perhaps was an official of the Baths, or in some hotel. The Fedeli mentioned in the postscript is either Fedele Fedeli, a professor at the University of Pisa, who died in March 1888 and was at one time director of the Montecatini Baths, or his son Carlo, a doctor with an interest in music, who was Verdi's friend and perhaps had a son. Verdi addresses Beccaro with the formal "lei" instead of "voi" or the familiar "tu," but nevertheless with an easy familiarity.

(Busseto
(St Agata 20 agosto 1884

Eg[regio] Sig[nor] Beccaro
   Ho ricevuto la Panca Giardino e la sua lettera.
   La ringrazio moltissimo delle molte premure che si è dato, e credo doverle dire, <u>en passant,</u> che questo panca non è equale a quella di Montecatini. Non ha il doppio sedile, nè lo schienale mobile; non ha quella specie di ruota a cilindro di marmo per farla rotolare facilmente da un sito all' altro. È uno dei soliti canapè da giardino con un sottile macchinismo di ferro per sostenere la tenda. Communque sia, non è colpa nè mia, nè sua se siamo stati un po' canzonati.
   La ringrazio ancora e voglia credevimi
                                    dev.
                              G. Verdi

P. S. Mia moglie ringrazia e contraccambio i saluti, ed ambedue la preghiamo di salutare quello scellerato di Fedeli . . . col figlio. Questo non scellerato!

I have received the garden chair and your letter.

I thank you very much for all the attention you have given, and I think I should tell you, en passant, that this chair is not like the one at Montecatini. It does not have the double seat, nor the adjustable back; nor does it have that kind of cylindrical marble wheel that makes it easy to move from one place to another. It is one of those ordinary garden lounge chairs with a thin iron mechanism to support the awning. At any rate, it is neither my fault nor yours if we have been somewhat fooled.

I thank you again and believe me,

P. S. My wife thanks you for the good wishes and returns them, and we both beg you to greet that scoundrel Fedeli . . . with his son. That one is not a scoundrel!

In Chapter 1: Verdi, Letter, 25 March 1848, to Giovanni Ricordi. This letter reveals how slowly in 1848 news on occasion could travel, and it fixes Verdi's presence in Paris at least three days after the Cinque Giornate in Milan had ended. In those five days of fighting, 18–22 March 1848, the Milanesi succeeded in expelling the Austrian army from the city. Many patriots lost their lives, and when the Austrians in August retook the city, many more were imprisoned, exiled, or fined to the point of penury. Verdi, by arriving in Milan too late for an active part in the uprising, was not included in the reprisals, and his career could continue unbroken. Had he been in the city in March, his last operas might have been *Macbeth, I masnadieri,* and *Jérusalem.*

The music that he mentions sending to Ricordi, his publisher in Milan, is not identified, and he has written the names of several newspapers illegibly. Perhaps, too, for these he has used abbreviations, like "Trib" or "Tele." In any case he put his energy into underlining rather than writing the words clearly. The illegibility of a number of other words similarly suggests haste and agitation.

Parigi 25 Marzo 1848

Car[o] [Giovanni] Ricordi
   Ieri partiva colla Diligenza la musica col rispettivo costo che ho comprati per te. Ora ti mando le cambiale che ho dovuto far protestare perchè quantunque la Banca d' Eicthal paghi sempre, il cassiere [. . . ?] mi ha risposto che non hanno [. . . ?] da [. . . ?]
   Le spese che ho per te sono di fr. 21:70.
   Sento grande notizie de Milano ma nulla di certo, nissuno ha lettere direttamente e non si hanno che la notizia da nouveau [. . . ?] [. . . ?] etc. Sono nella più grande inquietudine, e dispiaciutissimo di trovarmi qui.
   Aspett[o] con impazienza lettere d' [. . . ?]
                    Add[io] add[io]
                          G. Verdi

With yesterday's stagecoach departed the music I have bought for you along with the relative expense. Now I am sending you the bank drafts that I have had to protest because, although the d' Eichthal Bank always pays, the [. . . ?] teller told me that they have not [. . . ?] [. . . ?]

The expenses I have for you are 21:70 francs. I hear great news of Milan but nothing for certain, no one has received letters directly, and there is news only in the Nouveau [. . . ?] [. . . ?] etc. I am in the greatest agitation and very unhappy to be here.

I await with impatience letters from [. . . ?]

In Chapter 7: Verdi, Letter, 27 April 1868, to Giovanni Maloberti. The following three short letters are all to the same man; the first is included because it gives his full name, which the others do not, and also because it suggests the variety of errands on which Verdi employed Maloberti. The address, on the letter's back, is Sig[nor] Giovanni Maloberti, Filarmonico, St. Maria dei Pagani, no. 5, Piacenza; and the letter, like a note, is written without any opening greeting. Maloberti is an obscure figure, but he seems to have been connected to the Philharmonic Society in Piacenza, perhaps as its secretary. Verdi addresses him with the familiar "tu" usually reserved for children, dogs, servants, and good friends.

Cremona 27 Ap[rile] 1868

Mercoledì prima delle 11 ore sarò a Piacenza. Disponi tutto per non perdere tempo e fammi vedere subito l' uno dopo l' altro i cocchieri.

In quanto ai cavalli se sono metri 1:70 sono troppo alti. Il mio cavallo e poco più di 1:60 . . .

Non vogli[o] polledri di 4 anni

Add[io] ad[dio]
G. Verdi

[written on the side of the letter] *Sappiami dire se vi sia un paravento (ossia [. . . ?]) antico e non di molto prezzo.*

Wednesday before 11 A.M. I will be in Piacenza. Plan everything in order not to lose time and arrange for me to see the coachmen, one right after the other.

As for the horses, if they are 1:70 meters they are too tall. My horse is little more than 1:60 · · ·

I do not wish colts of 4 years.

[on the side] Let me know if there may be a firescreen (or [. . . ?]) that is old and not too expensive.

The next note has no date or greeting. Its envelope is addressed to Eg[regio] Sig[nor] Maloberti, St. Maria dei Pagani, no. 10, Piacenza, and postmarked Busseto, 6 Mag[gio] [18] 73

Stà pur tranquillo che io non sono affatto in collera. Soltanto ho voluto dirti di non mandarmi mai quadri simili, e vedi in generale di lasciarmi un po' respirare . . . perchè francamente non mi lasci mai tranquillo ed io ho tante cose a fare a non posso talvolta nemmeno leggere le tue lettere.

Ad[dio]

G. Verdi

Be assured I am not angry. I only wished to tell you not to send me any such pictures, and try in general to give me some room to breathe . . . because frankly you never leave me in peace and I have many things to do and sometimes I cannot even read your letters.

St Agata 7 luglio 1875

C[aro] Maloberti

Dopo Vienna sono venuto subito qui, ne andrò a Venezia.

Non parlarmi ne di quadri ne di mobili. Ti ripeto ancora che non ne voglio, e desiderei che tu desistessi dallo scrivermene.

Io avrei bisogno d' altra cosa—più materiale, se vuoi, ma più necessaria. Ho bisogno di un Cuoco; ma lo vorrei onesto, e capace, molto capace. In quanto alle condizioni ci accomoderessimo facilmente . . . Ci sarebbe a Piacenza? . . . Bada che lo voglio buono, e non un fanfarone. Scrivimi. cord [ialmente]

G. Verdi

After Vienna I returned immediately here, and will not go to Venice.

Don't talk to me of pictures or furniture. I tell you again that I don't want any, and I would like you to stop writing to me about them.

I have need of something else—more material, if you like, but more necessary. I need a Cook; but I want one that's honest and capable, very capable. As for terms, we can come to an agreement easily enough . . . Would there be one at Piacenza? . . . Mind now, I want him good and not a boaster.

In this letter nothing more is known about the addressee, Signor Castignani, than what the letter tells: he had some sort of shop in Piacenza. Verdi, using "lei," addresses him more formally than he does Maloberti.

St Agata 15 Maggio 1887

Sig[nor] Castignani

La ringrazio di essersi occupato del Cuoco.

Ceresini è stato per due volte da me, e assolutamento <u>rinuncio</u> a Lui.

Restano dunque gli altri due.

Io sarò a Piacenza martedi mattina giorno 17. Mi mandi all' albergo l'uno dopo l'altro questi due cuochi, l'uno alle undici ore, l'altro alle dodici, e vedremo cosa si potrà combinare.

Desidero per altro parlare prima con Lei, ed io stesso verrò al suo negozio appena arrivato.

Prego non dir nulla a nissuno del mio arrivo a Piacenza; altrimenti non sarei quieto per tutta la giornata.

Mi credo Dev.

G. Verdi

I thank you for concerning yourself about the cook.

Ceresini has been over to my place twice, and I absolutely <u>renounce</u> him.

There remain the other two.

I will be in Piacenza Tuesday morning the 17th. Please send me at the hotel first one and then the other of the two cooks. The first at eleven o'clock, the other at twelve, and we shall see what can be arranged.

I also wish to talk with you beforehand, and I will come myself to your store the moment I have arrived.

I beg you not to tell anyone of my coming to Piacenza; otherwise I would not have peace the whole day.

In Chapter 8: The following two letters seem to confirm that Verdi composed ballet music for the Brussels premiere of *Nabucco* on 29 November 1848. The opera was performed, presumably with the ballet, at the Théâtre de la Monnaie in a French translation by Ferdinand Gravrand and Jules Guilliaume, to the former of whom the first letter is addressed. The ballet music has not yet been found. It may have been returned to Verdi, as he asks, and then, possibly, destroyed by him; or it may have been used, in part or whole, for the ballet music he composed for *Les Vêpres Siciliennes,* which had its premiere at the Paris Opéra, 13 June 1855; or it may lie in a trunk or drawer at the Monnaie, which is still Belgium's chief opera house.

Alphonse Royer and Gustave Vaez, to whom the letter refers, were two librettists in Paris who often worked together. Their most famous original work was *La Favorite* (1840) for Donizetti. More often, however, they translated foreign operas into French, such as *Lucia di Lammermoor* (1846), and in 1847 they had collaborated with Verdi in transforming his *I Lombardi* into *Jérusalem,* giving it a new story, French text, several new numbers, and a ballet. Its premiere at the Paris Opéra, on 26 November 1847, had been a success, and other French-speaking theatres were quick to pick it up, among them the Théâtre de la Monnaie, where it had a premiere on 15 July 1848.

The second of these letters lacks a date and probably precedes the first, but it can be better understood if read second.

Mons. Ferdinand Gravrand
Chausée de Zette 15
Faubourg de Flandre
Bruxelles

Parigi 10 Nov. 1848

Mio caro

Prima di tutto permettete che vi ringrazi per ogni cortese espresioni prodigatami nel vostro foglio e vogliate aggradire il sincero concambio che io vi offro di simpatia e di stima.

Io non ho nulla perdonarvi, perchè non siete colpevole di nulla! e mi sorprende che nella lettera che ho ricevuto ieri teniate un linguaggio di scusa come se io mi fossi lagnato di voi con qualcuno. Per vostra norma sappiate che io non ho tenuto parola con persona di questi nostri affari.

L'invito che mi fate di venire ad assistere alla prima rappresentazione di Nabucco me tenta moltissimo! Sono certo che passerei con voi, con Royer e Vaez qualche tempo deliziosamente, ma io sono incatenato fra il tavolo ed il piano forte senza tregua nè riposo. Sono quindi costretto di rinunziare all' offerta che voi mi fate con tanta delicatezza e cordialità.

Sono obligatissimo al capo d' orchestra del riguardo che m'usa di non voler intervertire l' ordine dei numeri nei balletti: nonostante diteli a mio nome che puo fare questa concessione al maestro di ballo purchè non si succedano Numeri *che siano dell'istesso tono oppure vi sia troppo urto da un tono all'altro.*

Quando rimanderete le arie di ballo, abbiate la bontà d' indirizzarle a me e non ad altri——

Mille cose a Royer e Vaez, e voi credetemi

Vostro aff.

G. Verdi

First of all permit me to thank you for every courteous remark you lavish on me in your letter and please accept in exchange those that I sincerely offer you in friendship and esteem.

I have nothing to forgive you, because you are guilty of nothing! and you surprise me in your letter that I received yesterday by using language of apology as if I might have complained of you to someone. For your information you should know that I have not said a word to anyone concerning our affairs.

Your invitation to come and attend the first performance of Nabucco tempts me very much! I am sure that I would spend with you, with Royer and Vaez some very delightful hours, but I am chained between the table and the piano without respite or repose. I am thus constrained to forego the chance you offer me with so much delicacy and cordiality.

I am most obliged to the leader of the orchestra for his consideration towards me in not wishing to change the order of the ballet's numbers: nevertheless, tell him, for me, that he can make this concession to the choreographer provided that successive Numbers are not in the same key or that there is not too great a clash from one key to the next.

When you return the dance numbers, have the kindness to address them to me and not to others.

A thousand good wishes to Royer and Vaez, and believe me

Something in the relationship, it would seem, had gone wrong. Verdi's diction, in its formality, is polite but cool.

The second letter is addressed to one of the two brothers, Marie and Léon Escudier, who served as Verdi's agents in Paris and French publishers. The former principally edited the firm's journal, *La France Musicale*, while the latter handled the business of publishing musical works. Because Verdi corresponded with the brothers chiefly about performance and publication rights, he wrote much more often to Léon than to Marie, and from the subject matter of this letter it seems clear that he was writing to Léon.

[No date, but circa early November 1848]

Car^mo [Léon] Escudier
    Se il Sig^r Gravrand in vece di partire stasera per Bruxelles potessere aspettare fino a domani io potrei darle la musica dei baletti perchè senza fallo domattina prima delle 12 ore io sarò a Parigi colla partitura terminata——Procurate di vedere il Sig^r Gravrand ed in ogni modo scrivetemi un bigliettino per la piccola posta.
                        Add [io]
                            G. Verdi

If Signor Gravrand, instead of leaving this evening for Brussels could wait until tomorrow, I would be able to give you the ballet music, because tomorrow morning without fail before noon I will be in Paris with the orchestral score finished——Try to see Signor Gravrand and in any event write me a short note by the small [afternoon?] post.

In Chapter 12: Verdi, Letter, 7 February 1880, to Giulio Ricordi, about the publication of the "Ave Maria" that would have its premiere at La Scala on 18 April. The Coro he mentions is his "Pater Noster" for five-part chorus, which had its premiere at the same concert. But the subject most on Verdi's mind at this time, as the letter reveals, was the increasing craze in Italy for all things German, and in music for symphonic rather than vocal works. Rightly or wrongly, he felt that Italy's younger musicians were cutting their roots to their native traditions, and would be the weaker for it.

Genova 7 Feb 1880

C[aro] Giulio
    Va benissimo l' ave. avrei peró voluto che nella riduzione riescissero più sensibili quelle note

dei 1^mi violoncelli   e quindi annetterci il fà dei primi violini. Voi vedrete come io l' ho indicato nella ultima pagina di questa riduzione, sperando anche che il traduttore troverà meglio. Sulla frase ora per me non credereste voi di mettere un accento sulla parola ora, per far capire bene che è verbo?

Distribuite le parti del Coro quando volete. Raccomando ancora sia ben impastato e ben equilibrato. Lo Stabat di Pergolesi è un capo d' opera (è convenuto) benchè a alcuni parti debole e senza carattere; ma appartiene al genere noiso. Ciò non vorrebbe dir nulla, se questa composizione fosse di un qualche vecchio tedesco venuto alla moda, ma essendo d' un Italiano bisogna ci sia un esecuzione perfetta a due voci simpatiche e sicure.

Non so dire quando partirò perchè all' Opéra sono tutti ammalati. Ve lo dirò più tardi.

Curate la salute, e scacciate la noia curandovi omeopaticamente similia similibus etc., prendendo una buona dose di quella tal musica etc etc. che forma ora il delirio dei vostri dilettanti . . . che bei matti! . . .

addio   vostro

G. Verdi

P . S . Fra le cose vecchie meno noiose vi è un motetto di Vittoria . . . proprio bello, sublime: eseguito bene senza i coloriti aggiunti dai maestri francesi, potrebbe fare grandissimo effetto. Se poi si potesse scambiare il nome di Vittoria in quello per es [empio] di Back voi otterreste un' esito di fanatismo. Ed il nome di Bach non sarebbe disonorato, perchè Egli il gigante, il colosso, l' indefinibile non ha mai saputo scrivere per le voci in quel modo! . . . Che bestemmia: È detta! — — —

Non saprei or indicarvi il mottetto, ma se volete ve lo saprò dire.

The ave is fine. I could have wished, however, that in the [piano] reduction those notes in

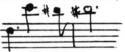

the first cellos   should have come out more distinctly, and then to attach there the F of the first violins. You will see how I indicated this on the last page of this reduction, hoping also that the arranger will find something better. Don't you think that in the phrase ora per me you should put an accent on the word ora to ensure that it is understood to be a verb?

Distribute the parts of the Chorus when you like. I stress once more that it should be well blended and well balanced. The Stabat of Pergolesi is a masterpiece (that is well established) although it is in some places weak and without character; but it belongs to the category of boring. That would not matter if this composition were by some old German who has come into fashion, but as it is by an Italian the execution must be perfect with two voices pleasant and true.

I cannot say when I shall leave, because at the Opéra they are all ill. I will tell you later.

Look after your health and drive away boredom by curing yourself homoeopathically similia similibus etc. by taking a good dose of that sort of music etc etc. which your cognoscenti rave about—some madmen!

P. S. Among the less boring old things, there is a Motet by Vittoria . . . really beautiful, sublime: well performed without the coloring added by the French masters, this could have a very great effect. If then one could substitute the name of Vittoria with that of Back [deliberately misspelled] you would have a fanatic success! And the name of Bach would not be dishonoured, because He, the giant, the colossus, the indefinable one, could never write for voices like that! What an awful thing to say: But I've said it!

I cannot now tell you which Motet it is, but if you like I will let you know.

APPENDIX D
VERDI'S OPERAS, WITH SOURCES, FIRST CASTS, THEATRES, AND DATES OF PREMIERES; AND OTHER WORKS

Opera	First Performance (Date, City, Theatre)	Librettist
OBERTO, CONTE DI SAN BONI-FACIO	17 Nov. 1839, Milan, Scala	Piazza, Merelli, Solera
UN GIORNO DI REGNO (*sometimes called* "Il finto Stanislao")	5 Sept. 1840, Milan, Scala	Romani
NABUCODONOSOR (*generally called* "Nabucco")	9 Mar. 1842, Milan, Scala	Solera
I LOMBARDI ALLA PRIMA CROCIATA (*see* "Jérusalem" below)	11 Feb. 1843, Milan, Scala	Solera
ERNANI	9 Mar. 1844, Venice, Fenice	Piave
I DUE FOSCARI	3 Nov. 1844, Rome, Argentina	Piave
GIOVANNA d'ARCO	15 Feb. 1845, Milan, Scala	Solera
ALZIRA	12 Aug. 1845, Naples, S. Carlo	Cammarano
ATTILA	17 Mar. 1846, Venice, Fenice	Solera
MACBETH (*see below*)	14 Mar. 1847, Florence, Pergola	Piave, Maffei
I MASNADIERI	22 July 1847, London, Her Majesty's	Maffei
JÉRUSALEM ("I Lombardi" *revised with new numbers and ballet added*)	26 Nov. 1847, Paris, Opéra	Royer, Vaez
IL CORSARO	25 Oct. 1848, Trieste, Grande	Piave
LA BATTAGLIA DI LEGNANO	27 Jan. 1849, Rome, Argentina	Cammarano
LUISA MILLER	8 Dec. 1849, Naples, S. Carlo	Cammarano
STIFFELIO (*see* "Aroldo" below)	16 Nov. 1850, Trieste, Grande	Piave
RIGOLETTO	11 Mar. 1851, Venice, Fenice	Piave
IL TROVATORE	19 Jan. 1853, Rome, Apollo	Cammarano, Bardare

	First Cast
Source	*(Women; Men)*
	Raineri, Shaw; Salvi, Marini
Pineau-Duval's play *Le Faux Stanislas*	Raineri, Abbadia; Salvi, Ferlotti, Scalese
Anicet-Bourgeois and Cornue's play *Nabucodonosor*	Strepponi, Bellinzaghi; Miraglia, Ronconi, Dérivis
Grossi's poem of the same name	Frezzolini; Guasco, Severi, Dérivis
Hugo's play *Hernani*	Loewe; Guasco, Superchi, Selva
Byron's play *The Two Foscari*	Barbieri-Nini; Roppa, De Bassini
Schiller's play *Die Jungfrau von Orléans*	Frezzolini; Poggi, Collini
Voltaire's play *Alzire*	Tadolini; Fraschini, Coletti
Werner's play *Attila*	Loewe; Guasco, Costantini, Marini
Shakespeare's play *Macbeth*	Barbieri-Nini; Brunacci, Varesi, Benedetti
Schiller's play *Die Rauber*	Lind; Gardoni, Coletti, Lablache, Bouché
	Julian-Vangelder; Duprez, Alizard, Prévôt, Brémont
Byron's poem *The Corsair*	Barbieri-Nini, Rampazzini; Fraschini, De Bassini
Méry's play *Battaille de Toulouse*	De Giuli; Fraschini, Collini
Schiller's play *Kabale und Liebe*	Gazzaniga, Salandri; Malvezzi, De Bassini, Arati, Selva
Souvestre and Bourgeois's play *Stiffelius*	Gazzaniga; Fraschini, Collini
Hugo's play *Le Roi s'amuse*	Brambilla (Teresa), Casaloni; Mirate, Varesi, Pons
Gutiérrez's play *El Trovador*	Penco, Goggi; Boucardé, Guicciardi, Balderi

Opera	First Performance (Date, City, Theatre)	Librettist
LA TRAVIATA	6 Mar. 1853, Venice, Fenice	Piave
(*2nd production*)	6 May 1854, Venice, S. Benedetto	
LES VÊPRES SICILIENNES (*generally called* "I Vespri Siciliani")	13 June 1855, Paris, Opéra	Scribe, Duveyrier
SIMON BOCCANEGRA (*see below*)	12 Mar. 1857, Venice, Fenice	Piave
AROLDO ("Stiffelio" *revised with new last act*)	16 Aug. 1857, Rimini, Nuovo	Piave
UN BALLO IN MASCHERA	17 Feb. 1859, Rome, Apollo	Somma
LA FORZA DEL DESTINO (*see below*)	10 Nov. 1862, St. Petersburg, Imperial	Piave
MACBETH (*orchestration revised, new numbers and ballet added*)	21 Apr. 1865, Paris, Lyrique	(Nuitter, Beaumont)
DON CARLOS (*see below*)	11 Mar. 1867, Paris, Opéra	Méry, Du Locle
LA FORZA DEL DESTINO (*numbers added; sequence of scenes and last act changed; prelude replaced by overture*)	27 Feb. 1869, Milan, Scala	(Ghislanzoni)
AIDA	24 Dec. 1871, Cairo, Opera	Ghislanzoni
(*2nd production*)	8 Feb. 1872, Milan, Scala	
SIMON BOCCANEGRA (*reorchestrated, text revised, and scenes added*)	24 Mar. 1881, Milan, Scala	Boito
DON CARLOS (*reduced from five to four acts*)	10 Jan. 1884, Milan, Scala	
OTELLO	5 Feb. 1887, Milan, Scala	Boito
FALSTAFF	9 Feb. 1893, Milan, Scala	Boito

	First Cast
Source	*(Women; Men)*
Dumas *fils's* play *La Dame aux Camélias*	Salvini-Donatelli; Graziani, Varesi
	Spezia; Landi, Coletti
Scribe and Duveyrier's play *Le Duc d'Albe*	Cruvelli, Sannier; Gueymard, Bonnehée, Obin
Gutiérrez's play of the same name	Bendazzi; Negrini, Giraldoni, Vercellini, Echeverria
	Lotti; Pancani, Poggiali, Ferri, Cornago
Scribe's libretto *Gustave III*	Julienne-Dejean, Scotti, Sbriscia; .Fraschini, Giraldoni, Bossi, Bernardoni
Duke of Rivas's play *Don Alvaro, o La fuerza de sino*	Barbot, Nantier-Didiée; Tamberlick, Graziani, De Bassini, Angelini
	Rey-Balla; Monjauze, Ismael, Petit
Schiller's play *Don Carlos*	Sax, Gueymard; Morère, Faure, Obin, David, Castelmary
	Stolz, Benza; Tiberini, Colonnese, Rota, Junca
	Pozzoni, Grossi; Mongini, Steller, Medini, Costa
	Stolz, Waldmann; Capponi, Pandolfini, Maini
	D'Angeri; Tamagno, Maurel, Salvati, E. de Reszke
	Bianchi-Chiatti, Pasqua; Tamagno, Lhérie, Silvestri
Shakespeare's play *Othello*	Pantaleoni; Tamagno, Maurel, Navarrini
Shakespeare's *Henry* plays and *The Merry Wives of Windsor*	Sthele, Zilli, Guerrini, Pasqua; Garbin, Pini-Corsi, Maurel

OTHER WORKS

Where the work was not published promptly, the first date in parentheses is the year of composition; the second, of publication.

Songs for Solo Voice and Piano

Brindisi (first version, 1835; 1935) (Andrea Maffei)

Sei Romanze (1838)

    1. Non t'accostar all'urna (Jacopo Vittorelli)
    2. More, Elisa, lo stanco poeta (Tommaso Bianchi)
    3. In solitaria stanza (Vittorelli)
    4. Nell' orror di notte oscura (Carlo Angiolini)
    5. Perduta ho la pace (from Goethe's *Faust*, trans. by Luigi Balestra)
    6. Deh, pietoso, o addolorata (from Goethe's *Faust*, trans. by Balestra)

L'esule (1839) (Temistocle Solera)

La seduzione (1839) (Balestra)

Chi i bei di m'adduce ancora (1842; 1948) (Goethe, trans. by Balestra)

È la vita un mar d'affanni (1844; 1951). Verdi's contribution to the autograph album of the Jacopo Ferretti family, Rome. (text?)

Il tramonto (first version, 1845; unpublished) (Maffei)

Album di Sei Romanze (1845)

    1. Il tramonto (second version, Maffei)
    2. La zingara (S. Manfredo Maggioni)
    3. Ad una stella (Maffei)
    4. Lo Spazzacamino (Maggioni)
    5. Il mistero (Felice Romani)
    6. Brindisi (second version, Maffei)

Il poveretto (1847) (Maggioni)

L'Abandonée (1849) (Marie or Léon Escudier?)

Barcarola: Fiorellin che sorge appena (1850; 1951) (Francesco Maria Piave)

La preghiera del poeta (1858; 1941) (N. Sole)

Il Brigidin (1863; 1941) (Dell' Ongaro)

Stornello (1869) (anon.) Verdi's contribution to the album for Piave's bene-fit.

Cupo è il sepolcro mutolo (1873; unpublished). Verdi's contribution to the autograph album of Conte Ludovici Belgiojoso, Milan. (text?)

Pietà Signor (1894) (Verdi and Boito; Verdi's contribution to an album for the benefit of victims of an earthquake in Sicily and Calabria, 16 Nov. 1894)

For Three Voices and Flute

Guarda che bianca luna: notturno (1839) (Vittorelli; for soprano, tenor, and bass, with flute *obbligato*)

Sacred Works

Messa da Requiem (1874) for four solo voices, chorus, and orchestra (to commemorate the first anniversary of the death of Alessandro Manzoni)

Pater Noster (1878–79?; 1880) for five-part chorus, SSCTB, unaccompanied (Italian text formerly attributed to Dante; now to Antonio da Ferrara)

Ave Maria (1878–79?; 1880) for soprano with string accompaniment (Italian text formerly attributed to Dante; now to Antonio da Ferrara)

Ave Maria, on a "scala enigmatica" (1889; 1895) for four soloists. Sometimes sung by a four-part chorus instead of soloists.

Stabat Mater (1896–97; 1898) for chorus and orchestra

Laudi alla Vergine Maria (1888; 1898) for four women's voices unaccompa-nied (text from Dante's *Paradiso*, Canto XXXIII). Sometimes sung by a four-part women's chorus instead of soloists.

Te Deum (1895–96; 1898) for double chorus and orchestra

The last four works are generally known as the *Quattro Pezzi Sacri*. But only the last three shared a common premiere.

Miscellaneous Works

La capricciosa (1825?; unpublished), sinfonietta. Performed at the opening of the tiny Teatro Verdi, Busseto, in 1868

La madre e la patria (1832?; 1988), sketch for complete work for voice and piano? or orchestra? (text?)

Marcia funebre (1832?; 1988), sketch for complete work for band or orchestra?

Io la vidi (1835?; 1977), aria for voice and orchestra; text from the opera *Il solitario ed Eloisa* (Calisto Bassi)

Tantum Ergo (1836; 1977), for voice, organ, and orchestra

Suona la tromba (1848), patriotic hymn (Giuseppe Mameli)

Waltz (1859; 1963), for pianoforte. Featured in the ball scene of Luchino Visconti's film *Il gattopardo* (The Leopard); hence sometimes called "The Gattopardo Waltz."

Inno delle Nazioni (1862), cantata (Arrigo Boito)

Romanza senza parole (1865), for pianoforte.

Aida, overture (1872; 1978). Verdi composed it to replace the opera's prelude and then decided against it.

String Quartet, E minor (1873; 1876)

There are a number of alternative arias that Verdi composed for soloists in his early operas. For an account of these, see David Lawton and David B. Rosen, "Verdi's Non-Definitive Revisions: the Early Operas," *Atti* (Parma: Istituto di Studi Verdiani, 1974), 3:189–237.

NOTES AND SOURCES
BIBLIOGRAPHY
INDEX

NOTES
AND
SOURCES

Where a source has been exceptionally important to an essay, I have listed it at the head of that essay's notes. Also, because the essays, with their notes, may be read independently and because the Bibliography lists only works in English, for each essay I have given full citations to all works, in whatever language, on each work's first appearance in the notes; thereafter the citation is abbreviated. For Verdi's letters quoted I generally have given citations to the large, fundamental collections published in Italian. Most of the letters, however, can be found in English translation in *Letters of Giuseppe Verdi* by Charles Osborne, *Verdi, A Documentary Study* by William Weaver, or *Verdi, The Man in His Letters*, eds. Franz Werfel and Paul Stefan, trans. Edward Downes (see Bibliography).

1. VERDI AND THE RISORGIMENTO

1. Verdi's birth date is uncertain chiefly because until 1876 he believed what his mother had told him: that he was born on 9 October 1814. In 1876 he learned that the parish baptismal register of Le Roncole, where he was born, recorded his baptism on 11 October 1813 with the statement that he was "born yesterday at eight hours." Verdi promptly acquiesced in the earlier year for birth, 1813, but held to the earlier day, 9 October. Then, in 1884, a certificate of birth in the registry of nearby Busseto was uncovered. The entry was made on 12 October 1813 and recorded the statement of Verdi's father, before the deputy mayor and witnesses, that his son had been "born the tenth day of the present month, at eight

o'clock in the evening." Two such documents in agreement—both are reproduced in William Weaver, *Verdi, a Documentary Study* (London: Thames & Hudson, 1977), plates 3 and 4— might seem conclusive, but evidently not to everyone. For a summary of the scholarly argument on this first fact of life, see Marcello Conati, ed., *Interviews and Encounters with Verdi*, trans. by Richard Stokes (London: Gollancz, 1984), 8, fn. 8.

2. The chorus, from Mercadante's opera *Donna Caritea* (1826) begins: "Chi per la patria muor, vissuto e assai" (He who dies for his country, has lived long enough). This sentiment, associated with an event that was reported all over Italy, imbues Verdi's patriotic opera, *La battaglia di Legnano*, whose libretto was written by a Neapolitan, Salvatore Cammarano. It echoes clearly throughout the final scene with its much repeated lines "Chi muore per la patria, alma si rea non ha!" (He who dies for his country, does not have such a guilty soul) and its appeal by the chorus "Apri, Signor, l' Empiro al tuo guerrier fedel!" (Open, O Lord, your heavenly kingdom to your faithful warrior).

3. Another passage in *Attila* that often sparked demonstrations in theatres occurs in the tenor's cabaletta in the Prologue: "Cara patria, già madre e reina di possenti magnanimi figli" (Dear country, one time mother and queen of powerful noble sons), which is "now a wasteland, desert, and ruin," but "will live again more proud, more lovely, the wonder of earth and sea." At the climax of this very rough and distant version of Leopardi's exquisite ode "All' Italia" Verdi does what the poet could not—he brings in the chorus with a sweep that must have been irresistible to Italian audiences. For an account of the opera's success at La Scala—"Furore! Furore! Furore!"—see *Giuseppe Verdi nelle lettere di Emanuele Muzio ad Antonio Barezzi*, edited by Luigi Agostino Garibaldi (Milan: Treves, 1931), 88–89. See also, Léon Escudier, *Mes Souvenirs* (Paris: Dentu, 1863), 71.

4. Vincenzo Marchesi, *Settant'anni di Storia Politica di Venezia, 1798–1866* (Turin: 1892), 73, 76.

5. William Weaver, "Verdi the Playgoer," *Musical Newsletter*, vol. 6, no. 1 (Winter 1976), 3–8, 24.

6. See "A Hundred Years of *Macbeth*, Annals compiled by Tom Kaufman and others," *Verdi's* Macbeth, *A Sourcebook*, edited by David Rosen and Andrew Porter (New York: W. W. Norton, 1984), 426–55; also "More About the Performance History of *Macbeth*" by Martin Chusid and Tom Kaufman, *Verdi Newsletter* (New York: American Institute for Verdi Studies), no. 13, 1985, 38–41.

7. Verdi, Letter, 25 March 1848, to [Giovanni] Ricordi. Author's collection (see Appendix C).

8. Verdi, Letter, 21 April 1848, to Francesco Maria Piave. Franco Abbiati, *Giuseppe Verdi*, 4 vols. (Milan: Ricordi, 1959), 1:745.

9. Verdi, Letter, 18 October 1848, to Giuseppe Mazzini. *I Copialettere di Giuseppe Verdi*, eds. Gaetano Cesari and Alessandro Luzio (Milan, 1913), 469: "I am sending you the hymn, and although it's a bit late, I hope it will reach you in time. I have tried to be as popular and easy as I can." He wrote for male chorus in three parts; first and second tenors and basses, in *allegro marziale*. The hymn, with a text by Goffredo Mameli, was too late for events in the Po Valley, which by October had been recaptured by the Austrians. It also had been preceded by a year by "Fratelli d'Italia" or "Mameli's Hymn" (text by Mameli, music by Michele Novaro), which became very popular and ultimately, when Italy became a republic in 1946, the country's national anthem.

10. Emilio Dandolo, *I Volontari ed i Bersaglieri Lombardi* (Milan: Albrighi, Segali, 1917), 218. The book first appeared in 1849, the year in which Manara died.

11. Sometime in the last quarter-century the statue was removed from the desk, presumably to avoid theft by any of the greatly increasing number of visitors to Sant' Agata. As old pictures of the desk show, it used to be crowded with bric-a-brac. Verdi, in his letter of thanks to Manara's son, states that he was an intimate friend of the father in the years 1844–47 and saw him for the last time at the premiere of *Macbeth,* in Florence. Verdi, Letter, 26 April 1880, to Luciano Manara (the son). *Carteggi Verdiani,* ed. Alessandro Luzio, 4 vols. (Rome: Accademia Nazionale dei Linci, 1935–47), 4:226–227. See also, Abbiati, *Verdi,* 1:630–631.

12. Verdi, Letter, 14 July 1849, to Vincenzo Luccardi. Abbiati, *Verdi,* 2:23.

13. Verdi, Letter, 29 January 1853, to Clarina Maffei. *Copialettere,* 532.

14. Verdi, Letter, 27 May 1860, to Angelo Mariani. *Carteggi Verdiani,* 2:204.

15. Verdi, Letter, 2 October 1860, to Angelo Mariani. *Carteggi Verdiani,* 2:204

16. Verdi, Letter, undated, to an unidentified friend. Annibale Alberti, ed., *Verdi Intimo, Carteggio di Giuseppe Verdi con Il Conte Opprandino Arrivabene* (Verona: Mondadori, 1931), 9: "I do not understand politics. So long as Cavour lived, I watched him in the Chamber, and I used to rise and approve or reject when he rose, because, doing exactly as he did, I was certain not to make a mistake. Now with these other gentlemen, who certainly are most worthy, I would not be able to make head or tail of it, and I would be afraid of making a blunder."

17. Bernard Shaw, *Shaw's Music, The Complete Musical Criticism in Three Volumes,* ed. Dan H. Laurence (New York: Dodd, Mead, 1981), 2:851.

18. Giuseppina Strepponi, Letter, 9 May 1872, to Cesare Vigna. *Copialettere,* 500.

19. Scholarship since his day has concluded that the two works, translations into *terza rima* from Latin texts, are definitely not by Dante. They appear in a poem sometimes titled "Dante's Credo" or "La professione di fede" and now ascribed to Antonio de' Beccari da Ferrara. See "Verdi's Second 'Ave Maria,' 1880."

20. Verdi, in a conversation, [?] September 1896, with Italo Pizzi, who was visiting him at Sant'Agata. Pizzi, *Ricordi Verdiani inediti* (Turin: Roux e Viarengo, 1901), 83. The remark originated in a discussion of the British in India. Verdi said: "Here is a great and ancient people now fallen prey to the English. But the English will regret it! Peoples allow themselves to be oppressed, vexed and maltreated—and the English are sons of bitches. Then comes the moment when national sentiment, which no one can resist, awakes. That is what we did with the Austrians. But now, unfortunately, we are in Africa playing the part of tyrants; we are in the wrong, and we will pay for it. They say we are going there to bring our civilization to those people. A fine civilization ours, with all the miseries it carries with it! Those people don't know what to do with it, and moreover in many ways they are more civilized than we!"

21. This essay, slightly shorter and without notes, was published first in *The Verdi Companion,* eds. William Weaver and Martin Chusid (New York: W. W. Norton, 1979), 13–41.

2. VERDI, MANZONI, AND THE *REQUIEM*

Chief sources on Manzoni other than his works published in Italian were:

Manzoni, Alessandro. *I Promessi Sposi*, trans. Archibald Colquhoun. *The Betrothed, A Tale of XVII Century Milan*. (London: Dent, 1951).

──────. *Del romanzo storico*, trans. Sandra Berman. *On the Historical Novel*. (Lincoln; University of Nebraska Press, 1984).

──────. *Il Cinque Maggio*, trans. William Ewart Gladstone (four times prime minister of Britain). "Ode on the Death of Napoleon," *Translations*, by Lord Lyttleton and W. E. Gladstone. (London: Quaritch, 2nd ed., 1863), 166–175.

Chandler, S. B. *Alessandro Manzoni, The Story of a Spiritual Quest*. (Edinburgh: University of Edinburgh Press, 1974).

Colquhoun, Archibald. *Manzoni and his Times, A Biography of the Author of The Betrothed*. (London: Dent, 1954).

Wall, Bernard. *Alessandro Manzoni*. (New Haven: Yale University Press, 1954).

Other sources were:

Hanslick, Eduard. "Verdi's Requiem" (1879), *Vienna's Golden Years of Music, 1850–1900*, trans. Henry Pleasants III (Freeport, N.Y.: Books for Libraries Press, 1969), 178–186.

Marchesi, Gustavo. "Verdi e Manzoni," *Atti del III° Congresso Internazionale di Studi Verdiani* (1972) (Parma: Istituto di Studi Verdiani, 1974), 274–84.

Pizzetti, Ildebrando. Preface to the manuscript facsimile edition of the *Messa da Requiem* (Milan: Museo Teatrale alla Scala, Casa di Riposo per Musicisti, Fondazione G. Verdi and the Casa Ricordi, 1941. Limited to 300 numbered copies).

Reynolds, Barbara. "Verdi and Manzoni, An Attempted Explanation," *Music and Letters*, vol. xxix, no. 1 (January 1948), 31–43.

Robertson, Alec. *Requiem, Music of Mourning and Consolation* (New York: Praeger, 1968).

Rosen, David B. *The Genesis of Verdi's Requiem* (Unpublished Ph.D. thesis, University of California, Berkeley, 1976).

1. Verdi, Letter, 24 May 1867, to Clarina Maffei. *Carteggi Verdiani*, ed. Alessandro Luzio, 4 vols. (Rome: Accademia Nazionale dei Linci, 1935–1947), 4:176.

2. Verdi, Letter, circa 1829–30, to [Francesco] Silva. Mary Jane Matz, "Flying with Verdi, The First Letter," in *Verdi Newsletter* (New York: American Institute for Verdi Studies), no. 6 (March 1979), 11–13.

3. Verdi, Letter, 1 April 1890, to Aldo Noseda. *I Copialettere di Giuseppe Verdi*, eds. Gaetano Cesari and Alessandro Luzio (Milan, 1913), 355. According to a note Verdi wrote in 1853 in response to an inquiry about his early works, the choruses were for three voices and the ode for solo voice. This note, addressed to Isidoro Cambiasi and reproduced in facsimile in a Numero Unico, *Nel primo centenario di Giuseppe Verdi* (Milan, 1913), concludes: "All

these [early works] are lost, and well lost, except for some overtures that still are performed there [Busseto], and the hymns of Manzoni which I have kept." The note is translated in full in "Gesù morì, an Unknown Early Verdi Manuscript" by Hans F. Redlich and Frank Walker, *The Music Review* (August/November 1959), 233, and is paraphrased in many later publications. The settings of the chorus from *Il Conte di Carmagnola* and of the Ode are mentioned by Giuseppe Demaldè, *Cenni Biografici del maestro di musica Giuseppe Verdi*, ed. and trans. Mary Jane Matz, in *Verdi Newsletter*, nos. 1, 2, and 3 (May and December 1976 and June 1977), 3:7. He states the chorus was for four solo voices and piano.

4. Italo Pizzi, *Ricordi Verdiani inediti* (Turin: Roux e Viarengo, 1901), 29.

5. Verdi, Letter, 22 April 1853, to Antonio Somma. *Verdi, The Man in His Letters*, eds. Franz Werfel and Paul Stefan, trans. Edward Downes (New York: Vienna House, 1973), 175. Downes trans. used.

6. Pizzi, *Ricordi Verdiani*, 43–44.

7. Verdi, Letter, 29 January 1853, to Clarina Maffei. *Copialettere*, 532. Verdi, Letter, 11 October 1883, to Clarina Maffei. Franco Abbiati, *Giuseppe Verdi*, 4 vols. (Milan: Ricordi, 1959), 4:226–27. See also two letters to Emilia Negroni-Prati. Werfel, *Verdi, The Man in His Letters*, 339, 432.

8. Verdi, Letter, 3 April 1861, to Clarina Maffei. *Copialettere*, 520.

9. Arturo Pougin, *Giuseppe Verdi, Vita Aneddotica* (Milan: Ricordi, 1881), 46. There have been many translations of this autobiographical account (see Werfel, *Verdi, the Man in His Letters*, 80–93). Verdi, Letter, 7 May 1893, to Edoardo Mascheroni. *Copialettere*, 717–18: "The most sensible thing is to be skeptical; it spares you new troubles."

10. Strepponi, Letter, 9 May 1872, to Cesare Vigna. *Copialettere*, 500.

11. Strepponi, Letter, [?] September 1872, to Clarina Maffei. *Copialettere*, 501.

12. Strepponi, Letter, 21 May 1867, to Clarina Maffei. Frank Walker's translation used of the draft in Strepponi's letter book, in Walker, *The Man Verdi* (New York: Knopf, 1962; Chicago: University of Chicago Press, 1983), 269.

13. Verdi, Letter, [?] July 1868, to Clarina Maffei. Abbiati, *Verdi*, 3:215.

14. Verdi, Letter, 23 May 1873, to Giulio Ricordi. *Copialettere*, 283.

15. Verdi, Letter, 29 May 1873, to Clarina Maffei. *Copialettere*, 283.

16. Verdi, Letter, 2 June 1873, to Clarina Maffei. *Copialettere*, 283.

17. Verdi, Letter, 9 June 1873, to the Mayor and Council of Milan. *Copialettere*, 283. Of course there always have been some who have hoped and argued that Verdi, in his heart, believed in Christianity, and for a brief discussion of these, see Walker, *The Man Verdi*, 280. To those Walker mentions now should be added Elena Cazzulani, *Giuseppina Strepponi* (Lodi: Lodigraf, 1984), 103, who states that Verdi "used to call [Manzoni] the 'Saint' [. . .] because he saw united in him the two qualities that he would have wished to be able to unite: art and faith.

18. According to Barbara Reynolds, in "Verdi and Manzoni, An Attempted Explanation," three of these hymns, "Natale," "Passione," and "Risurrezione," were set to music by Pietro Torrassi, and the verse drama *Adelchi*, by Giuseppe Apolloni (see Abbiati, *Verdi*, 2:391). According to Giuseppe de Amicis in *Pensando a Verdi, Note e Ricordi Personali*, published as part of *Verdi a Genova, Ricordi, Aneddoti ed Episodi*, ed. Ferdinando Resasco (Genoa: Fratelli Pagano, 1901), 99–100, Verdi intended to include among his *Pezzi Sacri* a setting of

Manzoni's sacred hymn "La Pentecoste" but was prevented by ill health from composing it. According to Julian Budden, *The Operas of Verdi*, vol. 2 (London: Cassell, 1978), 28, Verdi's librettist F. M. Piave in 1847 proposed an opera on *I promessi sposi*, but Verdi did not take up the idea. Though Verdi seems never to have considered setting the novel, at least six operas have been made of it, of which the three most famous are by Ponchielli (1856), Petrella (1869), and the Danish composer Franz Gläser (1849). Gläser's opera is entitled *Bryllupet vet Como-Søen (The Wedding by the Lake)* and has a libretto by Hans Christian Andersen. For a discussion of possible casting of roles in the novel, see Marchesi, "Verdi e Manzoni," 283.

19. Verdi, Letter, 17 November 1868, to [Tito] Ricordi. *Copialettere*, 210.

20. Ibid.

21. Verdi, Letter, 20 November 1868, to Clarina Maffei. *Copialettere*, 206. David B. Rosen, in *The Genesis of Verdi's Requiem*, 37–40, speculates on when Verdi began to think of a mass to honor Manzoni: probably a month or two *before* Manzoni died.

22. Verdi, Letter, 4 February 1871, to Alberto Mazzucato. *Copialettere*, 243.

23. Pizzetti, Preface to the manuscript facsimile edition of the *Requiem*.

24. See note 10.

25. Verdi, Letter, 11 October 1883, to Clarina Maffei. Abbiati, *Verdi*, 4:226.

26. See note 11.

27. Excerpt from Giovanni Tebaldini, "Ricordi verdiani," *Rassegna Dorica*, in Marcello Conati, *Interviews and Encounters with Verdi*, trans. Richard Stokes (London: Gollancz, 1984), 362. Stokes trans. used.

28. Leonard Garrison, "Verdi's Setting of the *Te Deum*," *Verdi Newsletter*, no. 11 (March 1983), 25–26.

29. Excerpt from Giuseppe Depanis, "Verdi a Torino—Una visita di Toscanini a Verdi," *I Concerti Popolari ed il Teatro Regio di Torino; Quindici anni di vita musicale; Appunti–Ricordi*; in Conatin, *Interviews with Verdi*, 307.

30. An entry in Strepponi's copybook for 12 June 1875. *Carteggi Verdiani*, 2:43. See Hanslick, "Verdi's Requiem," 179–82.

31. Cesare Vigna, Letter, 12 July 1875, to Strepponi. *Carteggi Verdiani*, 4:287.

32. Strepponi, Letter, 22 July 1875, to Cesare Vigna. Walker, *The Man Verdi*, 423. Walker trans. used.

3. FRANZ WERFEL AND THE "VERDI RENAISSANCE"

For this essay the chief sources were:

Werferl, Franz. *Verdi, A Novel of the Opera*, trans. Helen Jessiman (New York: Simon & Schuster, 1925; reissued New York: Allen, Towne & Heath, 1947). The most recent German reissue appears to be Frankfurt am Main: S. Fischer Verlag, 1962.

———. *Verdi, The Man in His Letters*, edited and selected by Franz Werfel and Paul Stefan, trans. Edward Downes (New York: L. B. Fischer, 1942; reissued Freeport, N.Y.: Books for Libraries Press, 1970; and with some minor corrections, New York: Vienna House, 1973).

_____. *Die Macht Des Schicksals* [vocal score of *La forza del destino*], edited and translated by Franz Werfel (Milan: Ricordi, 1926).

Other important sources were:

Gray, Cecil. "The Verdi Revival" (1931), *Contingencies and Other Essays* (London: Oxford University Press, 1947; reissued Freeport, N.Y.: Books for Libraries Press, 1971).

Gresch, Donald. "The Fact of Fiction, Franz Werfel's *Verdi, Roman der Oper*," *Current Musicology*, no. 28 (1979), 30–40.

Kuhner, Hans. "Franz Werfel and Giuseppe Verdi," *Verdi, Bolletino*, anno 1, no. 3 (December 1960) (Parma: Istituto di Studi Verdiani, 1960). Kuhner cites three Werfel articles on Verdi published in German journals.

Mila, Massimo. "L'unità stilistica nell'opera di Verdi," *Nuova Rivista Musicale Italiana* (January/February 1968), 62–75.

Polzer, Anne. "Leader of the Renaissance," *Opera News*, vol. 25, no. 15 (18 February 1961), 21–23. Polzer was Werfel's secretary for a decade. She quotes part of his speech on Verdi at the Mittlere Konzerthaussall, Vienna, 28 November 1934.

Rosenthal, Harold. "The Rediscovery of *Don Carlos* in Our Day," *Atti del II° Congresso Internazionale di Studi Verdiani* (Parma: Istituto di Studi Verdiani, 1971), 550–58.

Schmiedel, Gottfried. "Fritz Busch and the Dresden Opera," *Opera*, vol. 11, no. 3 (March 1960), 175–81.

Stefan, Paul. "A German Verdi Renaissance—Werfel Novel Instrumental in Making Revivals Possible," *Musical America*, vol. 48, no 7 (2 June 1928), 3.

Toye, Francis. *Giuseppe Verdi, His Life and Works* (London: Heinemann, 1931; first American edition, New York: Alfred A. Knopf, 1931; reissued New York: Knopf, 1946; Vienna House, 1972). Toye's preface has much to say about the Verdi renaissance; see also the references to Werfel in the text.

_____. "Verdi Over Fifty Years," in "Verdi—A Symposium," *Opera*, vol. 2, no. 3 (February 1951), 105–10. This issue, almost entirely devoted to Verdi, commemorated the fiftieth anniversary of his death on 27 January 1901. In addition to the article by Toye, it contains articles or statements by Lennox Berkeley, Arthur Bliss, Benjamin Britten, Cecil Gray, Harold Rosenthal, and Ralph Vaughan Williams.

1. Mila, "L'unità stilistica," 63; Toye, *Verdi, Life and Works*, 387; Julian Budden, *The Operas of Verdi*, vol. 3 (New York: Oxford University Press, 1981), 440–41, quoting several contemporary critics. Ferrucio Bonavia, *Verdi* (London: Oxford University Press, 1930), 107, quoting a letter without citation, from Verdi to Edoardo Mascheroni, the conductor of *Falstaff* on tour: "I am very prosaic in some things and regard the box office as the only infallible thermometer." For some statistics on the number of performances of the operas in various periods, see George Martin, *The Companion to Twentieth Century Opera* (New York: Dodd, Mead, 1984), 575–627.

2. Many Quartet and Orchestral Societies were founded in Italy during this decade, of which the most distinguished was the Orchestral Society of La Scala. Verdi's letters from about 1878 onward reflect his distress at what he felt was a mistaken turn in the development of Italian music: "We are all aiding, without wishing, in the destruction of our theatre [. . .]

Why the devil if we are living in Italy must we do German art? [. . .]" Verdi, Letter, to an unknown person, possibly April 1878. Giuseppe Verdi, *I Copialettere di Giuseppe Verdi*, eds. Gaetano Cesari and Alessandro Luzio (Milan, 1913), 626. Werfel, *Verdi, The Man in His Letters*, 343, states that the letter was written to Giulio Ricordi, 20 April 1878. See other letters translated in Werfel, 349 and 364. Some of these are quoted at length in "Verdi's Second 'Ave Maria,' 1880," with full citations.

3. Mila, "L'unità stilistica," 64.

4. Toye, *Verdi, Life and Works*, xii, xi. For echoes of the charges of vulgarity against *Aida*, see Dyneley Hussey, *Verdi* (London: Dent *Master Musician Series*, 1940), 186.

5. Walter Damrosch, *My Musical Life* (New York: Scribners, 1923), 65.

6. C. Hubert H. Parry, *Styles in Musical Art* (London: Macmillan, 1911), 167, 332. Almost every page offers similar statements. For a fellow Englishman puncturing Parry, see Gray, "The Verdi Revival," *Contingencies*, 153–54: "[. . .] his conception of the noble Teuton, puffing and blowing up the slopes of Mount Parnassus while the indolent and superficial Latin remained sitting at the foot strumming on his guitar [. . .]"

7. Polzer, "Leader of the Renaissance," 21.

8. Bruno Walter, *Theme and Variations, An Autobiography*, trans. James A. Galston (London: Hamish Hamilton, 1947), 139.

9. James G. Huneker, New York *World*, 24 December 1920, 11:5. Unsigned, New York *Herald*, same date, 9:3: "a forgotten opera [. . .] too much ponderous recitative [. . .] strained [. . .] unnatural [. . .] machine made." Gilbert W. Gabriel, New York *Sun*, same date, 5:1: "legitimate novelty [. . .] contains some noble arias [. . .] Verdi's a most careful, if uninspired, score."

10. Massimo Mila, *Giuseppe Verdi* (Bari: Laterza, 1958), 8.

11. Figures taken from Toye, *Verdi, His Life and Works*, xii-xiii, and from Schmiedel, "Fritz Busch and the Dresden Opera," 179.

12. Neville Cardus, *Conversations with Cardus*, ed. Robin Daniels (London: Gollancz, 1976), 192.

13. André Schaeffner, "Il 'ritorno a Verdi': La fine del Purgatorio," *La Rassegna Musicale*, anno xxi, no. 3 (July 1951), 225. This was a commemorative issue for the fiftieth anniversary of Verdi's death on 27 January 1901.

14. Mila, *Giuseppe Verdi*, 9.

15. Toye, *Verdi, His Life and Works*, xii.

16. Kuhner, "Werfel and Verdi," *Verdi, Bolletino*, 1793.

17. Polzer, "Leader of the Renaissance," 22.

18. Verdi, *Copialettere*.

19. Werfel, *Verdi, A Novel*, 11.

20. Ibid., 13.

21. Ibid., 15.

22. Ibid., 113.

23. Ibid., 291.

24. Ibid., 322.

25. Ibid., 419–22.

26. Verdi, Letter, 10 June 1884, to Opprandino Arrivabene. *Copialettere*, 629–30.

27. Unsigned review, *Cleveland Open Shelf*, February 1926, 24. Lloyd Morris, *Saturday Review of Literature*, 9 January 1926, 2:475: "It falls between exposition and narrative; it accomplishes neither." Louis Kronenberger, *International Book Review*, March 1926, 268: "Its elements of fact and fiction are not harmonized, and its numerous components are defiant of unity."

28. Edward Goldbeck, "Franz Werfel," *The Reflex*, vol. 2, no. 3 (March 1928), 33–39. Another detailed study of the novel, which is also an important, though unpublished, source on the Verdi renaissance, is James C. Davidheiser's doctoral thesis, "Franz Werfel and the Historical Novel, an Analytical Study of *Verdi: Roman der Opera, Die Vierzig Tage des Musa Dagh*, and *Das Lied von Bernadette*" (University of Pittsburgh, 1972). Davidheiser cites a number of more recent German articles and books on Verdi, Werfel, and the novel, including another novel, *Die Macht des Schicksals, Ein Verdi-Roman*, by Georg Nowak-Zivier (Frankfurt am Main, 1951). Davidheiser says of the latter: "This is indeed as much a novel of revolutionary struggle in Italy and even France as it is a biography of Verdi. It is far more historical and inclusive than Werfel's novel, embracing Verdi's life from the beginning to his composition of *La forza del destino*. The last chapter even quotes Verdi's death certificate and contrasts the political situation at the time of his death with that of his birth."

29. Werfel, *Verdi, The Man in His Letters*, 381, 389. Werfel and Stefan picked up both letters from an article in the *Berliner Tageblatt*, 19 March 1926.

4. VERDI'S IMITATION OF SHAKESPEARE: *LA FORZA DEL DESTINO*

1. Giuseppe Verdi, *I Copialettere di Giuseppe Verdi*, eds. Gaetano Cesari and Alessandro Luzio (Milan, 1913), 624.

2. August Wilhelm Schlegel, *Vorlesungen über dramatische Kunst und Literatur (Lectures on Dramatic Art and Literature)*, trans. John Black, 2d ed. rev. by A. J. W. Morrison (London: George Bell & Sons, 1984).

3. Samuel Johnson, preface to *The Plays of William Shakespeare*, 1765, in *Johnson on Shakespeare*, vol. 7 of *The Yale Edition of the Works of Samuel Johnson*, ed. Arthur Sherbo (New Haven, Conn.: Yale University Press, 1968), 59–113.

4. Gotthold Ephraim Lessing, *Hamburg Dramaturgy*, no. 96 (1 April 1768), quoted in Arthur M. Eastman, *A Short History of Shakespearean Criticism* (New York: Random House, 1968), 37.

5. Schlegel, Lecture XXII, in *Lectures*, 342.

6. Ibid., 344.

7. Verdi, *Copialettere*, 612.

8. Sophocles, *Oedipus the King*, trans. Stephen Berg and Diskin Clay (New York: Oxford University Press, 1978), 77.

9. S. H. Butcher, *Aristotle's Theory of Poetry and Fine Art with a Critical Text and Translation of the Poetics*, 3d ed. (London: Macmillan, 1902), 23. Aristotle's words are "ἀπὸ μίαν περίοδου ἡλίου εἶναι" or, word for word, "about one going-round of-the-sun-to-be." A

modern translator, Gerald F. Else, in his *Aristotle Poetics* (Ann Arbor: University of Michigan Press, 1967), 24, has rendered this as "tragedy tries as hard as it can to exist during a single daylight period, or to vary but little."

10. Schlegel, Lecture XXII, in *Lectures*, 245–46.

11. This is the definition offered, for example, in *The Oxford Companion to the Theatre*, ed. Phyllis Hartnoll, 2d ed. (London: Oxford University Press, 1957), 35.

12. Schlegel, Lecture XXII, in *Lectures*, 340.

13. Ibid.

14. Schlegel's lectures translated into Italian by Giovanni Gherardini: *Corso di letteratura dramatica: traduzione italiana con note di Giovanni Gherardini*, 3 vols. (Milan, 1817).

15. Franco Abbiati, *Giuseppe Verdi*, 4 vols. (Milan: Ricordi, 1959), 3:13.

16. Verdi, *Copialettere*, 482.

17. Carlo Rusconi, *Teatro completo di Shakespeare, voltano in prosa italiana*, 2 vols. (Padua, 1838).

18. For a list of books that Verdi kept at his bedside, including works by Rusconi, Carcano, and Maffei, see George Martin, *Verdi: His Music, Life and Times* (New York: Dodd, Mead & Co., 1963 [3d ed., 1983]), appendix B, 578–79.

19. Abbiati, *Verdi*, 4:289.

20. The fourteen plays are: *Macbeth, Romeo and Juliet, The Tempest, Othello, Hamlet, Antony and Cleopatra, King Lear, A Midsummer Night's Dream, Timon of Athens, King John, Richard II, Henry IV* Part 2, *Henry V*, and *The Merry Wives of Windsor*. I am grateful to Andrew Porter and David Rosen for alerting me to this point.

21. Schlegel, Lecture XXV, in *Lectures*, 407–11.

22. Franz Werfel and Paul Stefan, eds., *Verdi, The Man in His Letters*, trans. Edward Downes (New York: Vienna House, 1973), 175. Some other revealing letters to Somma, presented in the aforesaid but not quoted in this article, are those of 31 Mar. 1854 (p. 184), 4 Jan. 1855 (p. 186), and 7 Apr. 1856 (p. 190). For views in general, see letters on pp. 107, 140, 175, 195, and 262.

23. Abbiati, *Verdi*, 2:4–7.

24. Ibid.

25. Ibid., 3:235.

26. Schlegel, Lecture XXIII, in *Lectures*, 369.

27. Werfel and Stefan, *Verdi, The Man in His Letters*, 178.

28. The production book is quoted more fully by Julian Budden, *The Operas of Verdi*, Vol. 2 (London: Cassell, 1978), 443–44.

29. See the contemporary criticism quoted in the three-part article by Giorgio Gualerzi, "Il cammino dell'opera," *Verdi, Bolletino dell' Istituto di Studi Verdiani*, vols. 4, 5, and 6.

30. For example, the Metropolitan Opera from 1952 through 1972 presented a version in which the first scene of Act II was cut; the overture frequently was played as an intermezzo to join Act I to the truncated Act II; and the role of Preziosilla in Act III was reduced or restored depending, apparently, on the management's opinion of the singer's ability, which thus was announced publicly.

31. Title page of the vocal score: *La Force du destin*, Opéra en quatre actes de C. Du Locle & Ch. Nuitter, Musique de G. Verdi (Paris: Choudens, Père et Fils, Éditeurs), plate no. A.C. 5534. According to Budden, *The Operas of Verdi*, 2:516, the opera was performed in this version as late as October 1931 at the Théâtre de la Monnaie, Brussels, but today no orchestral score for the version can be found.

32. Verdi, *Copialettere*, 478.

33. Verdi, "Letters to Léon Escudier," *Music and Letters*, April 1923, letter no. 11, p. 184.

34. William Weaver, "Verdi the Playgoer," *Musical Newsletter*, vol. 4, no. 1 (Winter 1976), 3.

35. Johnson, *Johnson on Shakespeare*, 8:1048. This is the concluding sentence of the "Notes on *Othello*."

36. This essay, first published in *The Opera Quarterly*, vol. 3, no. 1 (Spring 1985), 19–29, originated in a slightly shorter version without notes as a speech to the Sixth International Verdi Congress held at the University of California, Irvine, California, April 24–26, 1980.

5. POSA IN *DON CARLOS:* THE FLAWED HERO

Chief sources were:

Passage, Charles E., translator of Friedrich von Schiller's *Don Carlos* (New York: Frederick Ungar, 1959), with an introduction; of *William Tell* (ibid., 1962), with introduction; and also of all the other important plays.

Sharpe, Lesley. *Schiller and the Historical Character, Presentation and Interpretation in the Historiographical Works and in the Historical Dramas* (Oxford: Oxford University Press, 1982). This work crystallized for me many thoughts about the play and opera. For an example of the kind of interpretation of Schiller that left me ready for Sharpe's analysis, see John Gassner, *Masters of the Drama* (New York: Random House, 1940; reissued New York: Dover Press, 1945), 322–26. For instance, of *The Maid of Orleans* Gassner concludes, "Schiller, for all his dabblings in history, philosophy and esthetic theory, possessed a diluted intellect." And of *William Tell*, "its elementary division of goats from sheep, of the perfect Tell from the melodramatic Austrian tyrant Gessler, produces Schiller's characteristic defects."

Steiner, George. *The Death of Tragedy* (London: Faber and Faber, 1961).

Other sources were:

Atti del II° Congresso Internazionale di Studi Verdiani. The Second International Congress of Verdi Studies, devoted to *Don Carlos*, was held in Verona, 1969, under the auspices of the Istituto di Studi Verdiani of Parma, which in 1971 published these papers. Many of them give information about performances of *Don Carlos* and other Verdi operas in various countries over the years. For this essay most important are "Un secolo di *Don Carlos*" by Giorgio Gualzeri, 494–504, and "The Rediscovery of *Don Carlos* in Our Day" by Harold Rosenthal, 550–58. No opera in the last fifty years has had a greater surge of popularity and critical interest; for dates of premieres and statistics on the number of performances of *Don Carlos* in some leading opera houses of the world, see George Martin, *The Companion to Twentieth Century Opera* (New York: Dodd, Mead, 2nd ed., 1984; London: Gollancz, 1980), 575–627.

1. Schiller, *William Tell*, Act V, scene 2, lines 3176–85, trans. Passage, 124–25.

2. Steiner, *The Death of Tragedy*, 176. Steiner's view was articulated forty years earlier by the New York critic James G. Huneker in reviewing the first Metropolitan production of the opera: "In fact Rodrigo [Posa] is the true protagonist." New York *World*, 24 December 1920, 11:5.

3. Julian Budden, *The Operas of Verdi*, vol. 3 (New York: Oxford University Press, 1981), 11.

4. Verdi, Letter, 19 February 1883, to Giulio Ricordi; Budden, *Operas of Verdi*, 3:37. See also Italo Pizzi, *Ricordi Verdiani inediti* (Turin: Roux e Viarengo, 1901), 26, 57.

5. Verdi, Letter, 12 January 1882, to Charles Nuitter; Budden, *Operas of Verdi*, 3:35.

6. In a summary of the opera's ending Verdi wrote, "Philip has nothing further to say. Elisabeth can only die and as quickly as possible." Verdi, Letter, 19 February 1883, to Giulio Ricordi; Budden, *Operas of Verdi*, 3:37.

7. Sharpe, *Schiller and the Historical Character*, 1.

8. Passage, Introduction to his translation of *Don Carlos*, xxiv.

9. Sharpe, *Schiller and the Historical Character*, 7, quoting H. Lindenberger, *Historical Drama, The Relation of Literature and Reality* (1975). Two other scholars whom Sharpe cites often for the newer interpretation of the plays are W. F. Mainland and G. W. McKay.

10. Verdi, *I Copialettere di Giuseppe Verdi*, eds. Gaetano Cesari and Alessandro Luzio (Milan, 1913), 104–6.

11. Budden, *Operas of Verdi*, 3:8

12. Verdi, Letter, 14 July 1859, to Clarina Maffei; *Copialettere*, 579–80: "I write under the impression of the deepest anger, and I don't know what you may think of me."

13. This history is recounted in a number of books, including my own *The Red Shirt and the Cross of Savoy, The Story of Italy's Risorgimento, 1748–1871* (New York: Dodd, Mead, 1969).

14. Verdi, Letter, 21 July 1865, to Emile Perrin; Budden, *Operas of Verdi*, 3:8.

15. Verdi, Letters of 6 and 14 July 1866, to Léon Escudier; Franco Abbiati, *Giuseppe Verdi*, 4 vols. (Milan: Ricordi, 1959), 3:93–94. Verdi, Letter, 22 July 1866, to Opprandino Arrivabene, *Verdi Intimo, Carteggio di Giuseppe Verdi con Il Conte Opprandino Arrivabene, 1861–1886*, ed. Annibale Alberti (Verona: Mondadori, 1931), 71–72.

16. "Britain" because, while France advanced toward democracy by successive revolutions, Britain did the same by reform bills in Parliament, of which the most famous were passed in 1832 and 1867. The latter was debated in the Houses of Parliament during February, in the month before the premiere of *Don Carlos*, and was widely reported in foreign papers.

17. Budden, *Operas of Verdi*, 3:25.

18. The episode is told by Folchetto (Jacopo Caponi) as one of his additions to the more complete, revised Italian edition of Pougin's biography (Arturo Pougin, *Giuseppe Verdi, Vita*

Aneddotica, con Note ed Aggiunte di Folchetto [Milan: Ricordi, 1881], 94). The empress reportedly also indicated displeasure with the Grand Inquisitor's role during the riot in the prison. Folchetto concludes, in a summary often paraphrased by later biographers: "With a court accustomed to follow the caprices and prejudices of its Empress, it is easy to understand how these incidents must have had a disastrous influence on the success of *Don Carlos.*" The empress's tie to the pope was direct and close, and Pius IX was godfather to her son, the prince imperial.

19. Gualzeri, "Un secolo di *Don Carlos,*" *Atti del II° Congresso,* 497.

20. Verdi, Letter, 14 December 1850, to Carlo D. Marzari. *Copialettere,* 109–11.

21. Verdi, Letter, 9 April, 1851, to Salvatore Cammarano. *Copialettere,* 118–21.

22. Verdi, Letter, 27 May 1860, to Angelo Mariani. *Carteggi Verdiani,* ed. Alessandro Luzio, 4 vols. (Rome: Accademia Nazionale dei Linci, 1935–1947), 2:204.

23. Verdi, Letter, 2 October 1860, to Angelo Mariani. *Carteggi Verdiani,* 2:204.

24. Giuseppina Strepponi, Letter, no date given, to Antonio Capecelatro. *Carteggi Verdiani,* 1:74

25. Strepponi, Letter, 3 January 1864, to Cesare De Sanctis. *Carteggi Verdiani,* 1:90.

26. A later judgment of Verdi on Garibaldi was that he was "a grand figure that will become still greater after another generation"; Verdi, Letter, 8 June 1882, to Giuseppe Perosio. *Carteggi Verdiani,* 4:99.

27. Verdi, Letter, 7 August 1869, to Giulio Ricordi. Abbiati, *Verdi,* 3:290.

28. Verdi, Letter, 17 March 1868, to Alberto Mazzucato; Frank V. De Bellis and Federico Ghisi, "Alcune Lettere Inedite dal Carteggio Verdi–Mazzucato, *Atti del II° Congresso,* 539.

29. Francis Toye, from an article in *Morning Post,* London, 25 May 1933, quoted at length by Rosenthal, "The Rediscovery of *Don Carlos,*" *Atti del II° Congresso,* 554–55.

30. Dyneley Hussey, *Verdi* (London: Dent *Master Musician Series;* reissued many times), 153.

31. Andrew Porter, "Musical Events," *The New Yorker,* 26 February 1979, 96; reprinted as "The Shakespearean Truth" in *Music of Three More Seasons* (New York: Knopf, 1981), 314.

32. E.g., Andrew Porter, "Musical Events," *The New Yorker,* 6 January 1973, 60.

33. This essay, in different form and without notes, originated as a speech, "The Topicality, Past and Present, of Verdi's *Don Carlos,*" delivered at the Pierpont Morgan Library, New York, 27 October 1983, in connection with its exhibit, *Four Centuries of Opera.*

6. *OTELLO,* MANZONI, AND THE CONCEPT OF "LA GLORIA"

1. Marvin Spevack, *The Harvard Concordance to Shakespeare* (Cambridge, Mass.: The Belknap Press of Harvard University Press, 1973).

2. The poem can be found in any edition of Manzoni's poetry. Goethe published one of the earliest translations, into German, in 1822; Gladstone, later the English Prime Minister, an English translation in 1863 (see Appendix A). According to Archibald Colquhoun, *Manzoni and his Times* (London: Dent, 1954), 160, for the inauguration of Manzoni's monument in

Milan in 1883, a collection of translations in twenty-seven languages was published, and the poem "outdid in popularity all the other odes on Napoleon, by Lamartine, Beranger, Wordsworth, and Byron."

3. Verdi, Letter, 1 April 1890, to Aldo Noseda; *I Copialettere di Giuseppe Verdi*, eds. Gaetano Cesari and Alessandro Luzio (Milan: 1913), 355. See also Mary Jane Matz, "Flying with Verdi, The First Letter," *Verdi Newsletter* (New York: American Institute for Verdi Studies), no. 6 (March 1979), 11–13, suggesting that Verdi set the ode when he was sixteen. See also Arthur Pougin, *Verdi: An Anecdotic History of his Life and Works*, trans. from the French by James E. Matthews (London: H. Grevel & Co., 1887), "Sundry Compositions" in Appendix, 298–99.

4. The poem is analyzed, with extensive quotations, in S. B. Chandler, *Manzoni* (Edinburgh: Edinburgh University Press, 1974), 48–53. See also Bernard Wall, *Alessandro Manzoni* (New Haven: Yale University Press, 1954), 18–20. Manzoni's question on Napoleon, *"Fu vera gloria?"* (Was it true glory?) continues to echo in Italian writing. A recent example in Verdian literature occurs in a biography of his wife by Elena Cazzulani, *Giuseppina Strepponi* (Lodi: Lodigraf, 1984), 158, in which Cazzulani, in describing the startling variety of Strepponi's roles as a soprano, states: "Non possiamo, con Manzoni, chiederci, 'se fu vera gloria,' e nemmeno se fu 'vera voce.' " (We cannot, with Manzoni, ask ourselves 'if it was true glory,' or even if it was a 'true voice.')

5. This essay, trimmed and without notes, first appeared in the program for the San Diego Opera, January 1986.

7. VERDI, FOOD, AND COOKS

1. Marcello Conati, ed., *Interviews and Encounters with Verdi*, trans. Richard Stokes (London: Gollancz, 1984), 310–16, quoting from an article published by Pietro Mascagni in "Verdi (ricordi personali)" in *La Lettura*, (Milan, XXX, 1: January 1931), 4–8; and another, "Una visita a Verdi" in *Scena Illustrata*, (Florence, XLIV, 21: 1 November 1913), 14.

2. Ibid., 280–85, quoting from the chapter "Giuseppe Verdi" in Arnaldo Bonaventura's book, *Ricordi e ritratti (fra quelli che ho conosciuto)*, (Quaderni dell' Accademia Chigiana, XXV, Siena, 1950).

3. Verdi, Letter, [envelope postmarked 6 May 1873], to Giovanni Maloberti. Author's collection (see Appendix C).

4. T. R. Ybarra, *Verdi, Miracle Man of the Opera* (New York: Harcourt, 1955), 275.

5. Giuseppina Strepponi, Letter, 21 May 1867, to Clarina Maffei. Frank Walker, *The Man Verdi* (New York: Knopf, 1962; Chicago: University of Chicago Press, 1983), 269–70. "Embonpoint" is Strepponi's word. In some photographs and cartoons she appears, however ungallant to say it, overweight.

6. Verdi, Letter, 23 December 1864, to Opprandino Arrivabene. Annibale Alberti, ed., *Verdi Intimo, Carteggio di Giuseppe Verdi con il Conte Opprandino Arrivabene* (Verona: Mondadori, 1931), 44. Today's *torroni* are spelt *"torrone"* and made of honey, almonds, sugar, wafers, egg whites, and natural flavors.

7. Elizabeth David, *Italian Food*, revised edition (London: Penguin Handbooks, 1963), 302, states: "Perhaps the most remarkable of Italian preserves is the fruit mustard, *mostarda*

di frutta, of Cremona. Made of whole fruits, pears, cherries, little oranges, figs, plums, apricots, and slices of melon and pumpkin, preserved in sugar syrup flavoured with mustard oil, this confection has an absolutely original flavour. Its origin I do not know, but it must be ancient, a survival from the days when sweet and sour were mingled in cookery with abandon. It was probably originally made with grape-must as a basis." It is served usually with meats, often with turkey, and eaten by some as a candy. Other towns in the Po valley have similar preserves or relishes, among them *la mostarda di Mantova* which uses of the fruits only apple and quince. David herself, however, prefers above all others a Venetian *mostarda*, whose recipe she keeps secret, 302.

8. Verdi, Letter, 13 March 1868, to Opprandino Arrivabene. Alberti, *Verdi Intimo*, 84. It is just possible that Verdi, in writing to Arrivabene about what was good in Cremona and naming three things in which the letter "t" is prominent, was making a sly reference to the popular saying that Cremona is the city of the three "t"s: in Cremona's dialect, "turon, turass, tatass"; in Italian, "torrone, torrazzo, tette delle donne," the last of which might be translated as the generous breasts of its women.

9. Verdi, Letter, 16 March 1868, to Opprandino Arrivabene. Ibid., 85.

10. Verdi, Letter, 9 April 1868, to Opprandino Arrivabene. Ibid.

11. Verdi, Letter, 13 December 1864, to Opprandino Arrivabene. Ibid., 43.

12. Mercede Mundula, *La Moglie di Verdi, Giuseppina Strepponi* (Milan: Garzanti, 1941), 150. Strepponi's letter: Ferruccio Botti, "Giuseppe Verdi e Italo Pizzi," *Spigolature d' Archivio: Nuove Spigolature Verdiane*, fifth series (Parma: Battei, 1971), 23.

13. Verdi, Letter, 27 May 1886, to Signor [Pasquale] Conti, in Alexander L. Ringer, "Giuseppe Verdi: Four Letters to his Wine Merchant," *Musical America*, vol. 71, no. 3 (February 1954), 4. The four letters were published first in *Orfeo*, 24 December 1912. See references to Conti in letters of Verdi to Giuseppe Piroli, 6 and 10 October 1875, *Carteggi Verdiani*, ed. Alessandro Luzio, 4 vols. (Rome: Accademia Nazionale dei Linci, 1935–47), 3:113–14. There reportedly are other letters to Signor Conti in the Biblioteca Nazionale, Florence.

14. Dr. Vitali, of San Secondo, reported the story to Italo Pizzi, who published it in *Ricordi Verdiani inediti* (Turin: Roux e Viarengo, 1901), 99.

15. Verdi, Letter, 9 April 1864, to Opprandino Arrivabene. Alberti, *Verdi Intimo*, 41.

16. In 1858 Verdi was in Naples roughly January through April and late October through early January 1859. In the first period, *Un ballo in maschera*, intended for the Teatro San Carlo, had difficulties with the censors and ultimately had its premiere shifted to Rome, 17 February 1859; in the second, Verdi produced *Simon Boccanegra* at the San Carlo. Delfico's cartoons, "Ricordi Napoletani," are reproduced in *Carteggi Verdiani*, ed. Alessandro Luzio, 4 vols. (Rome: Accademia Nazionale dei Linci, 1935–47), 1:323–83. See also Felice De Filippis, "Verdi and his Neapolitan Friends," *Verdi, Bolletino* (Parma: Istituto di Studi Verdiani), Anno I, no. 3, 1960, 1754–66.

17. Frank Walker, "Introduction to a biographical study," *Verdi, Bolletino* (Parma: Istituto di Studi Verdiani), Anno II, nos. 1–3, 1961, 9–10. Walker quotes the draft of Strepponi's reply to Barezzi from Strepponi's notebook. Walker's translation used.

18. Giuseppina Strepponi, Letter, 17 July 1861, to Mauro Corticelli. Franco Abbiati, *Giuseppe Verdi*, 4 vols. (Milan: Ricordi, 1959), 2:643.

19. Ibid.

20. Verdi, Letter, 12 August 1890, to Teresa Stolz. I have used William Weaver's translation, *Verdi, A Documentary Study* (London: Thames & Hudson, 1977), 246, in which, like most translators, eternally unsatisfied, he has changed two words. Verdi's similar instructions to Opprandino Arrivabene: Letter, 27 April 1872. Alberti, *Verdi Intimo*, 144.

21. Mario Medici, "Lettere sul *Re Lear*," *Verdi, Bolletino* (Parma: Istituto di Studi Verdiani), Anno I, no. 2, August 1960, 777.

22. Mundula, *La Moglie di Verdi*, 151.

23. Ferdinando Resasco, *Verdi a Genova, Ricordi, Aneddoti ed Episodi* (Genoa: Pagano, 1901), 18. This book includes *Pensando a Verdi, Note e Ricordi Personali* by Giuseppe de Amicis. This incident also was reported by Franco Ridella, "Giuseppe Verdi, Impressioni e ricordi," *Per l'Arte* (Parma), February and March 1902. Ridella's account, more sensational than Resasco's, is translated by Frank Walker in *The Man Verdi* (London: Dent, 1962), 283–84. Walker devotes an entire chapter, 283–393, to the "Breach with Mariani."

24. The descriptions of these two dishes are taken from Elizabeth David (see note 7). She describes the *cappon magro* as a "fish salad" and states, "The word *cappon* presumably has the same origin as the French *chapon*, the piece of oil and garlic soaked bread upon which a green salad is sometimes mixed. *Magro* denotes a *maigre* or fasting dish."

25. De Ferrari, 1824–85, had about a fifty years' success with his operas. The most popular, *Pipelè*, was based on Eugène Sue's novel *Les Mystères de Paris* (1842), in which two of the chief characters were concierges, "La mère Pipelet" and her husband. De Ferrari's musical style is reported to have been elegant, charming, and melodious but not very original.

26. Resasco, *Verdi a Genova*, 51–53.

27. Mundula, *La Moglie di Verdi*, 151–52.

28. Verdi, Letter, 7 July 1875, to Giovanni Maloberti. Author's collection (see Appendix C).

29. Mundula, *La Moglie di Verdi*, 151.

30. Edmondo De Amicis, "Giuseppina Verdi-Strepponi," *Verdi, Bolletino* (Parma: Istituto di Studi Verdiani), Anno I, no. 2, August 1960, 780.

31. Mundula, *La Moglie di Verdi*, 203, citing Giuseppe Perosio, *Ricordi verdiani* (Pinerolo: Sociale, 1928). Perosio, a Genovese, met Verdi in 1876, saw much of him and Strepponi in Genoa, and apparently heard the story from Strepponi.

32. Verdi, Letter, 15 May 1887, to [?] Castignani. Author's collection (see Appendix C).

33. Conati, ed., *Interviews and Encounters with Verdi*, 83–92, quoting an account ascribed to Stefano Sivelli and published as "L'origine d'un motivo dell' *Aida*," in *L'Italia*, Milan, 14 January 1941.

34. William Weaver, ed. and trans., *Seven Verdi Librettos* (New York: Norton, 1977), 499.

8. TWO UNPUBLISHED EARLY WORKS: "LA MADRE E LA PATRIA" AND "MARCIA FUNEBRE"

1. See Chapter 1, note 1.

2. Giuseppe Verdi, *I Copialettere di Giuseppe Verdi*, eds. Gaetano Cesari and Alessandro Luzio (Milan, 1913), 432, quoting a letter to Giuseppina Negroni Prati.

3. Verdi, Letter, 17 February 1889, to Arrigo Boito. *Copialettere*, 351–53.

4. The title page and first two pages of the autograph score of "Tantum Ergo" are reproduced in William Weaver, *Verdi, A Documentary Study* (London: Thames & Hudson, 1977), plates 38–40.

5. E.g., Hans F. Redlich and Frank Walker, "*Gesù morì,* An unknown early Verdi Manuscript," *The Music Review*, August/November 1959, 233–43, 235. Franco Abbiati, *Giuseppe Verdi*, 4 vols. (Milan: Ricordi, 1959), 1:125ff.

6. The first two pages of "Io la vidi" are reproduced in Weaver, *Verdi, A Documentary Study*, plates 35–36. The work was performed at a Clarion Concert in New York City, 8 February 1972, with Newell Jenkins conducting and Robert White, tenor, in a concert that consisted entirely of unpublished and unknown music from the Mary Flagler Cary Music Collection in the Pierpont Morgan Library. It was recorded at the time and later issued as one selection of several Verdi rarities on Side 6 of the recording of *Aroldo*, Voce Records #3. Presumably, this performance was the work's world premiere.

    The best description of "Io la vidi" is the short essay written for the Pierpont Morgan Library by Richard Macnutt, the English antiquarian music dealer from whom the library bought the score in 1969. In the course of his essay Macnutt gives his reasons for dating the work circa 1835 rather than 1833. As I have suggested, I think even 1835 is perhaps a bit early. See also Martin Chusid, *A Catalog of Verdi's Operas* (Hackensack, N.J.: Joseph Boonin, 1974), 18–19.

    The manuscript is on twelve oblong pages, recto and verso, and the instrumentation (reading from the top of the page) is as follows: first and second violins, violas, two flutes, two oboes, two clarinets, two horns, two trumpets, three trombones, two bassoons, and double basses. The neatness of the writing at the beginning suggests that Verdi intended to make a fair, perhaps final, copy of music already composed, and then began to make changes. At times, particularly on pages 9 recto verso and 10 recto, the handwriting begins to look too neat and regular for Verdi, as if possibly someone else—Macnutt discusses the possibility of Lavigna—had filled in or made additions to the manuscript. On the inside of the back wrapper (there is no front wrapper), a person whose name is not clearly written has stated: "Confrontato e indubitamente autografo di G. Verdi, 20/5/1901; E. Alb [ora?]ti [ad]detto ditta G. Ricordi & C." (Compared and without doubt the handwriting of G. Verdi, 20 May 1901; E. Alb[ora?]ti, employed in the firm of G. Ricordi & Co.). See note 19.

7. Programs for four concerts, on 4, 18, 25, and 27 February 1838, are reproduced in Weaver, *Verdi, A Documentary Study*, plates 41–44; the originals are in the Museo Comunale, Busseto. Gustavo Marchesi, "Verdi, merli e cucù: Cronache bussetane fra il 1819 e il 1839," Quaderno no. 1 of *Biblioteca 70* (Busseto, 1979), 122–23, prints a program of a concert on 12 October 1834, of which the original is in the archives of the Villa Verdi, Sant' Agata. The program lists six works by Verdi, two by Rossini, and one by the orchestra's conductor, Vincenzo Morganti. Verdi's works include two sinfonie to open and close the

program, a theme and variation for clarinet, a recitative and aria for soprano, another for tenor, and a capriccio for piano. This program is reprinted in *Con Verdi in casa Barezzi* (Busseto: Amici di Verdi, 1985), 16, in the essay of the same title by Corrado Mingardi. Some of Verdi's early works are mentioned by Giuseppe Demaldè, *Cenni Biografici del maestro di musica Giuseppe Verdi*, ed. and trans. Mary Jane Matz, in American Institute for Verdi Studies *Newsletter*, nos. 1, 2 and 3, May and December 1976 and June 1977.

8. Marcello Conati, *Interviews and Encounters with Verdi*, trans. Richard Stokes (London: Gollancz, 1984), 78 ff. 9, quoting the *Gazzetta di Parma*, 16 August 1868. From time to time the statement is made that many of Verdi's earliest works are preserved in the library of the Monte di Pietà e d' Abbondanza in Busseto. This is the library in which Verdi studied as a youth, and to some extent it is the town's archive. While it is always possible that among some of its uncataloged papers there may be a composition by Verdi, it seems by now unlikely. The present librarian, Corrado Mingardi, has told me that to his knowledge there is none.

9. A note addressed to Isidoro Cambiasi and reproduced in facsimile in Numero Unico *Nel primo centenario di Giuseppe Verdi* (Milan, 1913). It is translated in full in "Gesù morì, An unknown early Verdi Manuscript" by Hans F. Redlich and Frank Walker, *The Music Review*, August/November 1959, 233, and their translation is used here.

10. Léon Escudier, *Mes Souvenirs* (Paris: Dentu, 1863), 91–93.

11. Verdi, Letter, 30 January 1867, to Clarina Maffei. *Copialettere*, 521.

12. It is clear that some Verdi letters and documents were lent by Barezzi's granddaughter, Carolina Prayer-Galletti, to Franco Temistocle Garibaldi, who several years before Verdi's death started to collect material for a biography. How long before and the exact nature of the material is not clear. The book appeared in 1904: *Giuseppe Verdi* (Florence: B. Bemporad & Figlio). His son, Luigi Agostino Garibaldi, kept the material, showed it to others, and presumably used it in preparing his own book, *Giuseppe Verdi nelle lettere di Emanuele Muzio ad Antonio Barezzi* (Milan: Treves, 1931). He states the foregoing in his opening Acknowledgment to the granddaughter. The material now apparently is lost. The Garibaldi descendants reportedly have said that it was in the family's house in Genoa, which was destroyed by bombs during World War II.

13. Abbiati, *Verdi*, 4:666

14. Mary Jane Matz in "La famiglia Barezzo di Busseto e i suoi parenti," in *Con Verdi in Casa Barezzi*, 53, states that in 1800 the town had 1,658 persons in 416 families. Until well into the twentieth century it grew very slowly, if at all.

15. Abbiati, *Verdi*, 4:666.

16. Redlich and Walker, "Gesù morì, An unknown early Verdi Manuscript," *The Music Review*, August/November 1959, 233–43.

17. David Stivender, "The Composer of Gesù morì," American Institute of Verdi Studies *Newsletter*, no. 2, December 1976, 6–7.

18. For example, possibly his friend Dr. Luigi Balestra, a poet and lawyer from Busseto, who provided the text for a duet that Verdi intended to add to *Oberto* for a revival in Genoa, 1841, as well as translations of two Goethe poems that Verdi set to music and published in the *Sei romanze* (1838). Balestra also wrote the text for Verdi's song "La seduzione" (1839), which is as melodramatic as "La madre e la patria," and translated for him still another Goethe poem "Chi i bei di m' adduce ancora" (1842, 1948).

19. Redlich and Walker, in "Gesù morì," 234 and 234 ff 3, state that "Io la vidi" at that time was in the collection of Natale Gallini of Milan, and cite an article on it, "Il problema di uno sconosciuto autografo verdiano," in *Verdiana,* no. 6, 1951. I have not seen this article. According to Macnutt, the *Verdiana* series was "a news bulletin put out by the Scala Theatre at monthly intervals during 1950 and 1951 to document the activities of the Comitato Nazionale per le Onoranze a Giuseppe Verdi nel Cinquantenario della morte." See note 6.

The Music Division of the New York Public Library has a single, unsigned, undated sheet with musical sketches on both sides, and knows nothing of its history beyond the name of its donor to the library, Caroline Perera, of New York. She presumably had bought the sketches from a dealer. Scholars have conjectured that because they are for a father-daughter duet (there is a text), possibly they should be associated with Verdi's sketches (known once to have existed) for an opera on *King Lear*. Hence their offhand title "the *Lear* sketches." If this proves true, then they probably date from the early 1850s. Scholars also, however, have doubts about their authenticity: The writing, for example, is often too neat, too clear, too regular for Verdi. The sketches are reproduced in Weaver, *Verdi, A Documentary Study,* plates 159–60.

20. Franz Werfel and Paul Stefan, eds., *Verdi, The Man in his Letters,* trans. Edward Downes (New York: L. B. Fischer, 1942), 68.

21. Antonio Ghislanzoni, "Verdi's House at Sant' Agata" in Conati, *Interviews and Encounters with Verdi,* 74. Stokes trans. used. This development of Verdi's character appears clearly in Conati's collection of reports by visitors and journalists. In his final twenty-five years, roughly 1875–1900, Verdi, the Bear of Busseto, mellowed into a domesticated dog with little bark or bite. The journalist Blanche Roosevelt, for example, ended her account of an interview following the premiere of *Otello* (1887): "Verdi smiled—he smiled all over his face and eyes, as the children say." No one forty years earlier writes of him smiling. Ghislanzoni says of him then: "His entire appearance presented alarming symptoms. Whereas then his frail frame, pale face, sunken cheeks and deep-set eyes aroused ominous fears, today [1868] you find nothing in that countenance but the glowing health and stability of a man destined for a long career." The steady improvement in his health, which in old age was remarkably good, undoubtedly played a part in the softening of personality.

22. The upper right hand corner of the starting, recto page apparently was where Verdi usually signed his sketches or fair copies. In the autograph score of *Attila,* in the British Museum, each of the opera's numbers is signed in this corner.

NOTES TO THE ILLUSTRATION OF VERDI'S SIGNATURE

(a) Verdi, Letter, [c. 11 November 1848], to [Léon] Escudier. Author's collection (see Appendix C).

(b) Autograph sketch, signed, undated, for "Scena ed Aria, Rolando, No. 8" for *La battaglia di Legnano;* author's collection.

(c) Another forgery can be seen in an illustration in Peter Southwell-Sander, *Verdi, His Life and Times* (Tunbridge Wells: Midas Books, 1978), 154. The letter shown supposedly is from Verdi to the tenor Alessandro Bonci (1872–1942). It is discussed briefly in *Verdi's Macbeth, A Sourcebook,* eds. David Rosen and Andrew Porter (New York: Norton, 1984), 113 ff 3.

9. THE CURSE IN *RIGOLETTO*

In 1983, the University of Chicago Press and G. Ricordi & C., Milan, published jointly *Rigoletto Series I*, vol. 17, the first volume in a projected critical edition of all of Verdi's works. (The second volume, *Ernani, Series I*, vol. 5, was published in 1985.) Martin Chusid edited the *Rigoletto* and provided the orchestral score with an Introduction and a Critical Commentary (a separate volume) that discusses in detail the opera's conception, the first draft of its libretto, its preliminary musical sketch, and its final revision, as well as many related facts and issues. No other work on the background of *Rigoletto* is so extensive, and the "Critical Edition" was the main foundation of this chapter. Where I am citing multiple sources, this will be listed first.

Verdi's preliminary musical sketch for the opera was published by Ricordi in 1941 under the title *L'Abbozzo del Rigoletto di Giuseppe Verdi*. This was a facsimile edition, with an introduction by Carlo Gatti, and limited to 250 numbered copies. Hereafter I will refer to this as the Sketch.

The Istituto di Studi Verdiani, Parma, devoted three issues, nos. 7, 8 and 9, of its *Bolletino*, vol. 3, almost entirely to *Rigoletto*. These issues, in which all the articles are presented in both English and Italian, were published in 1969, 1973, and 1982 and contain, with a few articles on other subjects, twenty on the opera. For my purpose the two most important were "Rigoletto and Monterone: a Study in Musical Dramaturgy" 9:1544–58, by Martin Chusid; and "Tonal Structure and Dramatic Action in *Rigoletto*," 9:1559–81, by David Lawton. Another relevant essay, *"Rigoletto* as Drama," by Abraham Veinus and John Clarke Adams, was published by the Institute in *Atti del III° Congresso Internazionale di Studi Verdiani, 1972* (Parma, 1974), 464–94.

1. Joseph Kerman, "Verdi's Use of Recurring Themes," *Studies in Musical History, Essays for Oliver Strunk*, ed. Harold Powers (Princeton: Princeton University Press, 1968), 495–510. See also Dyneley Hussey, *Verdi* (London: Dent *Master Musician Series*, 1963), 140–42.

2. Critical Edition, Introduction, xvi, letter of the Chief of Police, Venice, to the management of the Teatro La Fenice, 28 November 1850, reporting the decision of the censors. Also in Verdi, *I Copialettere di Giuseppe Verdi*, eds. Gaetano Cesari and Alessandro Luzio (Milan, 1913), 487.

3. In his introduction to the Sketch, Carlo Gatti states that sketches for these other operas as well as some similar for the *Pezzi Sacri* are at the Villa Verdi, Sant' Agata. But Hans Busch reports: "Dr. Gabriella Carrara Verdi [the heir who deals with scholars on these matters] assures me that Verdi destroyed all the musical sketches he jotted down for *Aida* like any others." So there is doubt about what survives. *Verdi's Aida, The History of an Opera in Letters and Documents*, coll. and trans. Hans Busch (Minneapolis: University of Minnesota Press, 1978), xvii. See also David B. Rosen, *The Genesis of Verdi's Requiem*, Unpublished Ph.D. thesis, University of California, Berkeley (1976), 17 and ff 22.

Gatti, in *Verdi nelle immagini* (Milan: Garzanti, 1941), 64–65, published two pages of "the sketch for *Traviata*," without stating how many pages made up the sketch or whether these two represented first or revised thoughts. They seem, however, to be first thoughts for Act I, recorded by Verdi at an earlier stage even than those in the sketch for *Rigoletto*. The ideas here are fragmentary. They are discussed briefly by Julian Budden, *The Operas of Verdi*, vol. 2 (London: Cassell, 1978), 126–28.

4. Chusid gives a short description of the Sketch in the Critical Edition Introduction, xxii; and in greater detail in the Critical Commentary, 5–9.

5. Verdi, Letter, 3 June 1850, to F. M. Piave. Critical Edition, Introduction, xiii, citing Franco Abbiati, *Giuseppe Verdi*, 4 vols. (Milan: Ricordi, 1959), 2:63.

6. Verdi, Letter, 24 August 1850, to Carlo D. Marzari the President of La Fenice. Critical Edition, Introduction, xiv, citing Abbiati, *Verdi*, 2:68 and *Copialettere*, 106.

7. Verdi, Letter, 22 October, 1850, to F. M. Piave. Critical Edition, Introduction, xv, citing Abbiati, *Verdi*, 2:71.

8. *Copialettere*, 599, quoting Quintino Sella, to whom the statement was made. See also the letter cited in note 5. Also Gatti, in his introduction to the Sketch, quotes Verdi as saying: "To compose well one must do so almost in a single breath, reserving the right to adjust, dress up and repolish the general sketch; without that [breath], one risks producing an opera over a long period, with music like a mosaic, lacking style and character." See also, Léon Escudier, *Mes Souvenirs* (Paris: Dentu, 1863), 81.

9. The play was given its second performance—the French government having passed through several revolutions to become the Third Republic—on the fiftieth anniversary of its opening, 22 November 1882. It was staged by the Théâtre-Français (Comédie-Française) under the direction of Emile Perrin, with President of the Republic Jules Grévy, in his official capacity, in the stage box. Even so, it never remotely has approached the popularity or artistic eminence of the opera.

10. Victor Hugo, *Théâtre*, 3 vols. (Paris: Hachette, 1856), 2:168–71.

11. See note 5.

12. As Veinus and Adams point out in "*Rigoletto* as Drama," 478, the curse often is missung by baritones who put the stress on the first F and turn the first three notes into a triplet, "Sii maledet - to!" Singers with weak voices, anxious for the safety of orchestral support, are apt to do this, thus obliterating the tonal and rhythmic structure of the curse. Veinus and Adams have many interesting observations on the staging and singing of the opera.

13. In several librettos accompanying recordings, and even in one vocal score, this entrance line, "In testa che avete, Signor di Ceprano?" either out of misunderstanding or a desire to censor, is mistranslated, usually into some form of "What are you thinking?" Even Julian Budden, in *The Operas of Verdi*, vol. 1 (London: Cassell, 1973), 489, has "What thoughts are running through your head?"

14. Verdi, Letter, 2 February 1851, to Francesco Maria Piave. Abbiati, *Verdi*, 2:105. The ranges of the roles are: Rigoletto, B-flat to G, and Monterone, B-flat to F. At the premiere, the Fenice's "second baritone" sang Monterone (Chusid, Critical Edition, Critical Commentary, 12). It was listed for baritone in the first complete edition of a vocal score published, by Ricordi, Milan, 1852; in an early edition by Girard, Naples, 1853; in the first French edition with French text, by Escudier, Paris, 1859; and in an edition by Schirmer's, New York, 1902. Not long thereafter, apparently, basses succeeded in claiming the role, though most make a poor showing where it counts the most: the high Fs in delivering the curse.

15. Budden, *The Operas of Verdi*, 1:510, says of Monterone that "at each of his entrances his is the Voice of God." I doubt that many scholars would go so far. In the play, Saint-Vallier, having forced his daughter into marriage with an old man, was held by all at court to be a partial cause of her adultery and dishonor. In the opera there is no mention of the daughter's

marriage, but Monterone, as Rigoletto points out, has conspired against the Duke. He is not wholly pure.

16. Chusid in the Critical Edition, Critical Commentary, 63, points out that the meaningless syllables do not appear in the Sketch, and he considers their addition later to the musical line "an exceptionally powerful dramatic stroke." They offer some small problems, however, which he discusses. Verdi, in his final autograph score, sometimes wrote "la la" and sometimes left the accent off the second syllable. Pushing Chusid's cautious opinion farther than he might want to go, I would say that Verdi was merely forgetful, as he was working hurriedly. The easy thing to do would have been to write "la la" throughout, omitting all accents, which he did not do. For an example of a more typical use of "la la," see the Act II opening chorus of Ponchielli's *La Gioconda*.

17. Chusid, "Rigoletto and Monterone," 1549.

18. David R. B. Kimbell, *Verdi in the Age of Italian Romanticism* (Cambridge: Cambridge University Press, 1981), 439.

19. Verdi, Letter, 20 January 1851, to F. M. Piave. Critical Edition, Introduction, xviii, citing Abbiati, *Verdi*, 2:98.

20. The decasillabic (ten-syllable) meter is the strongest rhythmically that Verdi used in his operas, and in its power and rigidity it is very apt to smother any subtleties in the text. How Verdi felt about it can be seen in his letter of 4 November 1870 to Antonio Ghislanzoni, his librettist for *Aida*. He was discussing the text for the opening scene of Act IV. "[. . .] I would use decasillabic lines. On another occasion I suggested that you avoid that meter, because in allegros it inclines to be too jumpy; but in this situation that accent *three by three* would beat like a hammer and become terrifying." *Copialettere*, 664.

21. Chusid, "Rigoletto and Monterone," 1552, says that Rigoletto in Act II changes "into a dishonored and outraged parent openly challenging the licentious Duke. The latter role parallels exactly that of Monterone [. . .]" To my mind Rigoletto, *un*like Monterone, *never* openly challenges the Duke.

22. David Lawton, "Tonal Structure and Dramatic Action in *Rigoletto*," offers a number of ideas about Verdi's use of the keys of C, D and D-flat in the structure of the opera. Though intriguing, and arguably in support of my thesis, these ideas are more technical than I want to raise here.

23. Libretto published by Ricordi for the summer season 1852 at Sinigaglia, plate number 22757. Simultaneously the publisher issued an unbowdlerized text, p.n. 22752. In addition to the revisions already described, some towns further demanded that the abduction scene be canceled, and Ricordi had librettos available, p.n. 22757, with thick white blank paper pasted over everything in Act I, scene 2 following the conspirators' chorus. It is hard today, when the sexual abuse in *Rigoletto* is accepted without being deeply felt, to imagine the shock for those hearing it for the first time. Chusid, in the Critical Edition, Introduction, xxi, reports that the second performance of the opera in Bergamo, which was not in the Papal States, was stopped by the audience's protests, and the opera's run for the balance of the season was canceled. Abramo Basevi, the first scholar to write a book about Verdi, *Studio sulle opere di Giuseppe Verdi* (Florence: Tofani, 1859), 184, stated flatly that the opera was immoral because it depressed virtue and exalted vice, particularly in Gilda's death which was "a kind of suicide." Just why Verdi, beginning with *Luisa Miller* and progressing through *Stiffelio*, *Rigoletto*, and *Traviata*, chose a series of subjects that veer from sexual bullying toward sadism is a question not yet addressed by scholars.

24. In Italy in the mid-nineteenth century, public clocks, in most cases church clocks, still marked the day and night from 6 A.M. to 6 P.M. to 6 A.M. Noon or *mezzogiorno*, halfway through the day, was six strikes and midnight, *mezzanotte*, six strikes. The half hour was two short strikes, often on a different pitch. Thus 11:30—five long followed by two short.

25. In *Un ballo in maschera*, the clock strikes midnight with six strokes on middle C, but in *Falstaff*, with twelve strokes on the F below. In *Luisa Miller*, a clock sounds three strokes on a note of undetermined pitch. In *I due Foscari*, the bell of the Basilica of San Marco announces the election of a new doge, ringing on B-flat a ninth below middle C, and in *Les Vêpres Siciliennes* the bell signaling the uprising rings twenty-six times on the E directly above middle C. Perhaps the most famous bells in opera are, or were in the nineteenth century, those that initiate the St. Bartholomew's Eve Massacre in Meyerbeer's *Les Huguenots*. They alternate F and C two and three octaves below middle C.

26. In *Rigoletto*, to indicate any backstage music out of sight of the audience, Verdi consistently used the word "interna"; and to indicate music-making onstage, in sight except for darkness, he used "sul palcoscenico." In the opening scene where he intended three orchestras to play simultaneously, there is an orchestra in the pit, a "banda interna" (playing as the curtain rises), and a string band "sul palcoscenico" that plays the minuet—or is supposed to. Often it is omitted and its music played by the pit orchestra.

27. Budden, *The Operas of Verdi*, 1:509.

28. Verdi, Letter, 14 December 1850, to Carlo D. Marzari. Critical Edition, Introduction, xvi, citing *Copialettere*, 109.

10. THE ESSENCE OF *IL TROVATORE*

1. Giuseppe Verdi, *I Copialettere di Giuseppe Verdi*, eds. Gaetano Cesari and Alessandro Luzio (Milan, 1913), 106. Verdi, Letter, 24 August 1850, to Carlo D. Marzari about *Rigoletto:* "I was assured by Piave that there was no obstacle to this subject, and I, trusting the librettist, began to study it, to meditate profoundly on it, and the concept, the musical *tinta* were settled in my mind. I can say that for me the principal work was done." And in *Carteggi Verdiani*, ed. Alessandro Luzio, 4 vols. (Rome: Accademia Nazionale dei Linci, 1935–47), 1:25–26, Verdi, Letter, 6 July 1854, to Cesare De Sanctis, about preparing a new version of *La battaglia di Legnano:* "I want an altogether new subject, equally interesting and of the same character. It should not be difficult to find with regard to the plot and action, but very difficult with regard to the 'colorito.' To preserve all the emphasis on country and liberty, without speaking of country and liberty, is pretty hard; nevertheless, we can try." See also Verdi, Letter, 8 January 1881, to Arrigo Boito, talking of preserving in *Boccanegra* a scene's "colore"; Fritz Noske, *The Signifier and the Signified* (The Hague: Martinus Nijhoff, 1977), 354.

   Critics of the day also used the term "colorito"; see Abramo Basevi, *Studio sulle opere di Giuseppe Verdi* (Florence: Tofani, 1859): 4, 6, and 21, the "colorito sacro" of *Nabucco* and *I Lombardi;* and 63, in discussing *I due Foscari*, "il vero colorito" (its unique coloring), "e quell' unità che cercasi in ogni composizione" (and that unity one seeks in any composition).

2. His interest in settings, costumes, and stage action is displayed clearly in the letters concerning *Macbeth* (1847), particularly those he wrote to the leading artists, Felice Varese

and Marianna Barbieri-Ninni. These, as well as many other related letters and documents, are presented in both Italian and English translation in *Verdi's Macbeth, A Sourcebook*, eds. David Rosen and Andrew Porter (New York: W. W. Norton, 1984), 3–125. See also Verdi, Letter, 11 February 1846, to Vincenzo Luccardi, asking for a sketch of Attila's costume and hair in Raphael's fresco in the Vatican, *Copialettere*, 441; Verdi, Letter, 24 September 1881, to Domenico Morelli, about Iago's costume, *Copialettere*, 317; and Verdi, Letter, 18 September [1892], to Giulio Ricordi, on the sets and movements for *Falstaff, Copialettere*, 379. And, of course, the break with La Scala in 1845, which continued until 1869, was caused by Verdi's dissatisfaction with the productions. See also Léon Escudier, *Mes Souvenirs* (Paris: Dentu, 1863), 78–79.

3. Those who have seen the opera only on the stages of the world's larger theatres, where the party usually has all the principals and chorus standing, may not realize that Verdi intended it to be a dinner party with a table onstage at which Violetta seats her guests: Alfredo and Gastone beside herself, the Marchese and the Barone beside Flora, and the others where they will. These directions are in the orchestral and vocal scores.

4. Verdi, Letter, 19 August 1843, to Francesco Maria Piave, quoted in Franco Abbiati, *Giuseppe Verdi*, 4 vols. (Milan: Ricordi, 1959), 1:472.

5. Verdi, in conversation with Quintino Sella, reported in *Copialettere*, 599.

6. *L'Abbozzo del* Rigoletto *di Giuseppe Verdi* (Edizioni Fuori Commercio a cura del Maestro della Cultura Popolare, 1941). The facsimile reproduction, with an introductory essay by Carlo Gatti, was limited to 250 numbered copies. The original of the sketch remains in the possession of Verdi's heirs, at the Villa Verdi, Sant' Agata.

7. Verdi, Letter, 2 January 1850, to Salvatore Cammarano. Gino Monaldi, *Verdi, 1839–1898* (Turin: Fratelli Bocca, 2nd ed., 1926), 118. Julian Budden, *The Operas of Verdi*, vol. 2 (London: Cassel, 1978), 60, ff 1, thinks the date is too early and the letter, therefore, suspect. No one, however, doubts the authenticity of Verdi, Letter, 9 April 1851, to Cammarano, in which he gives a synopsis of how he thinks the opera should be structured. *Copialettere*, 118–21. Clearly, before April 1851 Verdi had done a great deal of work on the libretto.

8. Escudier, *Mes Souvenirs*, 80.

9. A short work in which it is easy to hear Verdi accelerating pace by shortening phrase lengths and increasing the frequency and suddenness of harmonic changes is the overture to *Luisa Miller*.

10. E.g., in Act II, scene 2, "Ah! vieni, vieni amor mio" and most of her lines in Act IV, scene 1. Likewise, Boccanegra has a vocal line in which the phrases frequently turn downward, e.g., in the Prologue, when he tells of his daughter's disappearance, and in Act II, scene 2, when he is alone and, going to the window, sings of the sea.

11. This melodic style of Verdi is not limited to soprano arias. A partial list for baritone would include: "Dagli immortali vertici" *(Attila)*, "Pietà, rispetto, onore" *(Macbeth)*, "Il balen del suo sorriso" *(Trovatore)*, "Eri tu" *(Ballo)*, and even "Per me giunto" *(Don Carlos)*. Similarly, Puccini's downward style permeates many of the most famous phrases and arias of *Manon Lescaut:* "In quelle trine morbide," "Manon Lescaut mi chiamo," "Nell'occhio tuo profondo," and "Guardate, pazzo son"; and in *Tosca*, "Vissi d'arte" and the orchestral march that underlies the execution.

12. Verdi, Letter [late 1852], to Vincenzo Jacovacci. Abbiati, *Verdi*, 2:177.

13. In the course of "Di quella pira" Manrico says to Leonora about Azucena: "I was her son before I loved you; your suffering cannot restrain me. Unhappy mother, I hasten to save you, or with you at least I hasten to die." During the Risorgimento, patriots, including supposedly even Cavour, sang the aria with *Italia* (the motherland), figuratively replacing Azucena.

14. Basevi, *Studio sulle opere di Giuseppe Verdi,* 218–20.

15. Verdi, Letter, 1 January 1853, to Cesare De Sanctis. *Carteggi Verdiani,* 1:16.

16. Julian Budden, "Verdi and the Contemporary Italian Scene," *The Verdi Companion,* ed. William Weaver and Martin Chusid (New York: W. W. Norton, 1979), 68–69, quoting Giovanni Pacini, *Le mie memorie artistiche* (Florence, 1875), 54.

17. The soprano was Sofia Loewe, who not only created the role of Elvira in *Ernani* but was also the first Odabella in *Attila* (1846). The tussle over the final number in *Ernani* is told in most biographies.

18. Verdi, Letter, 4 April 1851, to Salvatore Cammarano. Abbiati, *Verdi,* 2:122–23.

19. Verdi, Letter, 29 March 1851, to Cesare De Sanctis. *Carteggi Verdiani,* 1:4. See also Verdi, Letter, 1 January 1853, to Cesare De Sanctis. *Carteggi Verdiani,* 1:16.

20. The development of this central finale is well described by John Black, *The Italian Romantic Libretto, A Study of Salvatore Cammarano* (Edinburgh: The University Press, 1984), 202–04. See also Black, "Salvatore Cammarano's programma for *Il trovatore* and the Problem of the finale," *Studi Verdiani, 2* (Parma: Istituto di Studi Verdiani, 1983), 78–107. The article is more detailed than the book, printing in appendices the entire programma and four versions of the finale. See also the discussion in Julian Budden, *The Operas of Verdi,* vol. 2 (London: Cassell, 1978), 61–66, and Verdi's letters to De Sanctis, *Carteggi Verdiani,* 1:10–17.

21. Verdi, Letter, 14 December 1852, to Cesare Di Sanctis. *Carteggi Verdiani,* 1:14–16. Verdi's interest in brevity turns up constantly. He comes back to it again and again in writing to Antonio Somma about the libretto for the proposed *King Lear.* See the letters to Somma, 22 May and 29 June 1853, 31 March 1854, and 7 April 1856, in *Verdi, The Man in His Letters,* eds. Franz Werfel and Paul Stefan, trans. Edward Downes (New York: L. B. Fischer, 1942), 177, 178, 185, and 190: "In the theatre lengthy is synonymous with boring; and of all styles that of boredom is the worst." (Downes trans., 185.) And, of course, in his last opera, *Falstaff,* he has an aria, "Quand'ero paggio del Duca di Norfolk," that lasts about twenty-eight seconds.

22. Verdi, Letter, 20 October 1874, to Giulio Ricordi. Hans Busch, *Verdi's Aida, The History of an Opera in Letters and Documents* (Minneapolis: University of Minnesota Press, 1978), 371. Busch's translation used.

23. Verdi, Letter, 30 March 1875, to Giulio Ricordi. Ibid., 381. Busch's translation used.

24. This essay, very much shorter and without notes, was published as "*Il trovatore,* the Shape of the Melodies," in the San Francisco Opera Program, November 1981.

11. THE ORCHESTRATION OF *LA TRAVIATA*

1. Shaw probably picked up the phrase from Wagner's essay "Zukunftmusik" (Music of the Future), first published in 1861, in which Wagner asserted, "The orchestra [in Italian opera]

is nothing but a huge guitar for accompanying the Aria." *Richard Wagner's Prose Works*, 8 vols., ed. and trans. W. A. Eillis (London: Kegan Paul, 1892–99), 3:295–345, 338.

2. Bernard Shaw, *Shaw's Music, The Complete Musical Criticism in Three Volumes*, ed. Dan H. Laurence (New York: Dodd, Mead & Co., 1981), 3:581. See also 2:153, 3:540, 572–73, 688.

3. These figures are typical of the Teatro La Fenice in the early 1850s; see *Rigoletto, Series I*, vol. 17 of the Critical Edition of Verdi's works, ed. Martin Chusid (Chicago: University of Chicago Press, 1983), Introduction, xxviii. The Fenice, though a front-rank theatre at the time, was considerably smaller than either La Scala, Milan, or the San Carlo, Naples, and the figures probably are roughly correct for theatres in most of the larger towns. Opera houses in the small towns often had very reduced orchestras. By 1870, at La Scala the strings numbered 15 first violins, 12 second violins, 8 violas, 7 cellos, and 10 double basses; see Giulio Ricordi, Letter, 23 May 1871, to Verdi, in *Verdi's Aida, The History of an Opera in Letters and Documents*, coll. and trans. Hans Busch (Minneapolis: University of Minnesota Press, 1978), 160.

4. Hector Berlioz, *Treatise on Instrumentation*, enlarged and revised by Richard Strauss, trans. Theodore Front (New York: Edwin F. Kalmus, 1948), 145.

5. *Carteggi Verdiani*, ed. Alessandro Luzio, 4 vols. (Rome: Accademia Nazionale dei Linci, 1935–47), 4:255.

6. The labels of recordings constantly change, but casts, once recorded, remain constant, so I will identify these recordings by casts: Toscanini (Albanese, Peerce, Merrill); Giulini (Callas, Di Stefano, Bastianini); Pritchard (Sutherland, Bergonzi, Merrill); and Monteux (Carteri, Valletti, Warren).

7. Spike Hughes, *Famous Verdi Operas* (London: Robert Hale, 1968), 179–80.

8. Julian Budden, *The Operas of Verdi*, vol. 2 (London: Cassell, 1978), 136.

9. First quotation: Verdi, Letter, 11 April 1871, to Giulio Ricordi. Verdi, *I Copialettere di Giuseppe Verdi*, eds. Gaetano Cesari and Alessandro Luzio (Milan, 1913). Second: Verdi, Letter, (probably 1872), to Giulio Ricordi. *Verdi, The Man in His Letters*, eds. Franz Werfel and Paul Stefan, trans. Edward Downes (New York: Vienna House, 1973), 309; Downes translation used. See also Verdi, Letter, 19 August 1887 (because the footnote corrects mistaken date), to Franco Faccio. *Copialettere*, 701.

10. The only other *pausa lunga* in the score occurs in this same duet. Germont begins, "The sacrifice is indeed heavy," continues, "but hear me out calmly," and has the long pause before beginning "You are young and beautiful." Of course, throughout the opera there are many rests that are marked to be held, but apparently Verdi meant these two pauses to be especially noted.

11. Abramo Basevi, *Studio sulle opere di Giuseppe Verdi* (Florence: Tofani, 1859), 256.

12. Berlioz, *Treatise*, 392, says of the bass drum: "The pianissimo of the bass drum alone (if the instrument is well built and of large size) is gloomy and ominous; it resembles the distant sound of cannon." It also, when combined with kettledrums and an orchestration depicting anguish and terror, can "convey the idea of the strange and awful uproar accompanying great cataclysms of nature."

13. The orchestral and vocal scores mostly keep to Verdi's title "Scena and Aria," but whenever the introduction is played alone, and also frequently on record labels and in

librettos published with recordings, it is titled "Prelude"; and almost everyone talks of it as such.

14. Verdi, Letter, 11 March 1865, to Léon Escudier; published in full in both Italian and English translation in *Verdi's Macbeth, A Sourcebook*, eds. David Rosen and Andrew Porter (New York: Norton, 1984), 110–12.

15. Those who like the final act seem always to underestimate the portion taken by this scene and aria, usually gauging it at no more than a third; while those who dislike it will estimate it as high as two thirds. To be exact: on the Toscanini recording, which observes the usual cuts, the scene and aria require twelve of the act's twenty-seven minutes; on the Pritchard recording, without cuts, it takes sixteen and a half of thirty-four and a half.

16. This effect, though not associated with death, was much used later by Leoš Janáček in his operas, and harks back at least as far as Beethoven's late piano sonatas.

17. Verdi, Letter, 22 August 1870, to Antonio Ghislanzoni. *Copialettere*, 642. See also Verdi, Letter, 20 November 1880, to Giulio Ricordi. *Copialettere*, 559.

12. VERDI'S SECOND "AVE MARIA," 1880

An important source for this essay has been the beginning of a book not yet published, and I am grateful to Pierluigi Petrobelli, director of the Istituto di Studi Verdiani, Parma, for the chance to see these opening pages in galley proofs. The book presently is titled *Carteggio Verdi—Ricordi (1880–1881)*, vol. 1; it is edited by Petrobelli and is scheduled to be published by the Istituto sometime soon. In April 1880, at the start of the book's period, "Ave Maria" and "Pater Noster" had their premieres and their publication by Ricordi; hence much of the year's early correspondence concerns them. Many of the letters have not been published before, and almost as important as these will be Petrobelli's explanatory notes, which promise to be exhaustive. Taken together, letters and notes will make a remarkable cultural history.

1. Frederick J. Crowest, *Verdi, Man and Musician, His Biography with Especial Reference to his English Experiences* (Milne: London, 1897), 160.

2. Francis Toye, *Giuseppe Verdi, His Life and Works* (New York: Knopf, 1946), 392–93.

3. Dyneley Hussey, *Verdi* (London: Dent *Master Musician Series*, 1940), 310.

4. The director of the Istituto di Studi Verdiani, Parma, Prof. Pierluigi Petrobelli, in September 1986.

5. Two artists who have been adventurous with Verdi's songs and found success are Rita Streich, particularly with "Lo Spazzacamino," and Carlo Bergonzi, with "Stornello."

6. *Carteggi Verdiani*, ed. Alessandro Luzio, 4 vols. (Rome: Accademia Nazionale dei Lincei, 1935–47), 2:317–45.

7. Verdi, Letter, 31 July 1879, to Ferdinand Hiller. Ibid, 2:330–31.

8. Verdi, Letter, [late 1835], to Vincenzo Lavigna. Carlo Gatti, *Verdi*, 2 vols. (Milan: Edizione "Alpes" Milano, 1931), 1:111–12.

9. Verdi, Letter, 19 July 1896, to Giuseppina Negroni Prati Morosini. Verdi, *I Copialettere di Giuseppe Verdi*, eds. Gaetano Cesari and Alessandro Luzio (Milan, 1913), 372.

10. I have gathered this account of Antonio de' Beccari da Ferrara from various encyclo-
pedias and biographical dictionaries, chiefly the *Enciclopedia Dantesca* (1970), and from *Le
Rime di Antonio da Ferrara (Antonio Beccari)*, introduction, text, and comment by Laura
Bellucci (Bologna: Pàtron, 1972). In sum, the first serious challenge to the attribution to
Dante came in the seventeenth century, from Leone Allacci in *Poeti antichi* and Apostolo
Zeno in his *Lettere*. Both thought the poem was by Antonio da Ferrara. Then, in the present
century the philologist Ezio Levi (1884–1941) set out proof in his article "Il canzoniere di M.
Antonio da Ferrara," *Archivio storico italiano*, LXXV vol. 2, 93–128. The most decisive
reason was stylistic, but there was also some manuscript evidence. The tradition in the latter
favored Dante. Of the Florentine codices, for example, 13 did not indicate an author, 22
indicated Dante, and 5, Antonio. Yet Levi demonstrated that the most authoritative manuscripts, those with the clearest, most identifiable and reliable geneology, pointed to Antonio.
Thus, roughly forty years after Verdi set the prayers to music, their authorship was
changed.

It is possible to sense the increasingly stern rejection of the Dante attribution in
Thomas G. Bergin, *Dante* (New York: Orion Press, 1965), 212: "Definitely apocryphal are
the *Seven Penitential Psalms* and *Dante's Credo*, translations into *terza rima* from Latin texts.
Passerini printed them in volume VII of his edition of the minor works (Florence, 1912), and
they have been reprinted 'simply as a literary curiosity' in the Rime of the Biblioteca uni-
versale (Milan: Rizzoli, 1952)."

11. No doubt the chief reason many Verdi scholars have been slow to note the change in
attribution of the texts from Dante to Antonio da Ferrara is the obvious one: the two works,
compared with the operas, attract little attention, and the old attribution seems correct.
Indeed, most reference works, the mass of critical writing, and all of Verdi's letters support
it.

There is also, with the "Pater Noster," a confusion. Canto XI of the *Purgatorio* opens
with a paraphrase of the Lord's Prayer that has a first line identical to the *Pater Noster* in
"Dante's Credo"; thereafter, the lines are different. Plainly, Antonio da Ferrara hoped to stir
memories of Dante, and the reference was picked up by Verdi scholars, for whom it seems to
have reinforced the appearance of his authorship, e.g., Camille Bellaigue, *Verdi, Biografica
Critica* (Milan: Treves, 1913), 79, and Gatti, *Verdi*, 2:439, ff 1. Gatti, in this footnote, adds
to the confusion by suggesting that the "Pater Noster" is authentic Dante while the "Ave
Maria" is not, though he does not mention who might be the latter's author. Curiously, *New
Grove* reverses this, having the "Ave Maria" unequivocally by Dante, and the "Pater Noster"
merely "attributed" to him. But, of course, the two prayers, drawn from the same poem, must
stand or fall together as Dante's works.

12. Verdi, Letter, 7 January 1880, to Giulio Ricordi. *Carteggio Verdi—Ricordi (1880–
1881)* vol. 1 [as yet unpublished; see above]. See also Verdi, Letter, 10 February 1880, to
Giuseppe Piroli, stating that he had written both works "some time ago." *Carteggi Verdiani*,
3:144. Arthur Pougin, *Verdi, An Anecdotic History of his Life and Works*, trans. James E.
Matthew (London: Grevel, 1887), 239–40, tells of a Frenchman, August Emanuel Vaucor-
beil, who visited Verdi at Sant' Agata in September 1879 and, finding the "Pater Noster" on
the piano, played it.

13. I am grateful to Pierluigi Petrobelli for examining the autograph score for me, confirming
the instrumentation and Verdi's direction.

14. Verdi, Letter, 3 May 1880, to Ferdinand Hiller. *Carteggi Verdiani*, 2:335–36;

15. Everyone agrees on the size of the orchestra, 130. The historian of La Scala, G. Tintori, *Due cento anni del Teatro alla Scala, Cronologia opere—balletti—concerti, 1779–1977* (Milan: Grafica Gütenberg, 1979), 262, states the chorus numbered 300 and lists the various groups composing it. Verdi, in two letters, puts the total considerably higher, at 370 in a letter, 19 April 1880, to Opprandino Arrivabene. Annibale Alberti ed., *Verdi Intimo, Carteggio di Giuseppe Verdi con il Conte Opprandino Arrivabene* (Verona: Mondadori, 1931), 244–45; and 3 May 1880, to Ferdinand Hiller. *Carteggi Verdiani*, 2:335–36.

16. Verdi, Letter, 19 April 1880, to Opprandino Arrivabene. Alberti, *Verdi Intimo*, 244–45. Same date, to Giuseppe Piroli. *Carteggi Verdiani*, 3:145.

17. Reportedly 4,000 persons gathered in the street beneath the balcony, and Faccio led the orchestra in the Overture to *Nabucco*, the prelude to Act [?] of *La traviata*, and the Overture to *I Vespri Siciliani*. Tintori, *Duecento anni del Teatro alla Scala*, 262.

18. Filippi's review in *Perseveranza*, 19 April 1880, is given in full in Alberti, *Verdi Intimo*, 245–50; partially, in Franco Abbiati, *Giuseppe Verdi*, 4 vols. (Milan: Ricordi, 1959), 119–21; and probably in full in the book to be published, *Carteggio Verdi—Ricordi (1880–1881)*, vol. 1.

19. These editions are listed in Cecil Hopkinson, *Bibliography of Giuseppe Verdi*, 2 vols. (New York: Broude, 1973–78), 1:19–20. His description of each work's first edition, however, starts with the title page and does not include the wrapper. He also omits description of the sharply decreased inner ornamentation in later issues of the first edition.

20. Ferdinand Hiller, Letter, 21 May 1881, to Giuseppe Verdi. *Carteggi Verdiani*, 2:338–39.

21. Verdi, Letter, 30 [January] 1880, to Giulio Ricordi. *Carteggio Verdi—Ricordi (1880–1881)*, vol. 1, as yet unpaginated.

22. Verdi, Letter, 7 February 1880, to Giulio Ricordi. Author's collection and included in as yet unpublished *Carteggio Verdi—Ricordi (1880–1881)*, vol. 1. For full letter, see Appendix C.

23. Ibid.

24. Verdi, Letter, 11 February 1880, to Giulio Ricordi. *Carteggio Verdi—Ricordi (1880–1881)*, vol. 1.

25. Verdi, Letter, 19 March 1878, to Clarina Maffei; quoted by Julian Budden, *The Operas of Verdi* (New York: Oxford University Press, 1981), vol. 3, 299, citing Alessandro Luzio, *Profili biografici e bozzetti storici*, 2:541–42.

26. Verdi, Fragment of a Letter, [April 1878], [addressee unknown]. Copialettere, 305–06.

27. Verdi, Letter, 4 April 1879, to the La Scala Orchestral Society. *Copialettere*, 305–06.

28. Verdi, Letter, [date not given, but 1879], to Giulio Ricordi. Abbiati, *Verdi*, 4:104.

29. The eight are: Luzzi, Millard, Verdi, Bach–Gounod, Mascagni, RoSewig, Lambillote, and Kahn, with others indicated by "etc." *The White List of the Society of St. Gregory of America* (New York: Society of St. Gregory of America, 1939), 3rd & augmented edition, 73.

30. Ibid.

BIBLIOGRAPHY: BOOKS AND ARTICLES IN ENGLISH ABOUT VERDI

Plainly some sort of selection must be made. With the explosion in Verdi scholarship continuing undiminished, a complete bibliography, or even one close to it, no longer is feasible. The Institute for Verdi Studies, Parma, which periodically lists recent works on Verdi, reported for the years 1977–79 a total of 229 books and articles published; for 1980–82, 337; and for 1982–84, 231. And even the Institute, as its addenda attest, does not catch every work.

In the Notes I have given full bibliographical information for all sources used, regardless of language. Here I limit entries to works in English, thinking these will be the most useful for the majority of those who read this book; and to works about Verdi, having given citations in the Notes to books and articles primarily about others, such as Manzoni or Schiller. For books that have appeared in several editions I have tried to list the first, to show the date of origin and the most recent, preferring, if there is a choice in the matter, the paperback to the clothbound.

FOUR SERIES OF VERDI PUBLICATIONS

Atti, or *Reports* of three International Congresses of Verdi Studies sponsored by the Istituto di Studi Verdiani, Parma, in 1966, 1969, and 1972, with publication in 1969, 1972, and 1974. The papers are published in the language in which delivered, and some are in English. Of these, only those used in this book are listed below.

Verdi, Bolletino, a journal of the Istituto di Studi Verdiani, Parma. Nine issues were published, then the series was replaced by another journal, *Studi Verdiani*. All articles appeared at least in English and Italian, and most also in German. Vol. 1, nos. 1, 2, and 3, 1960, were devoted chiefly to *Un ballo in maschera*; Vol. 2, nos. 4, 5, and 6, 1961, 1962, 1966, to *La forza del destino*; Vol. 3, nos. 7, 8, and 9, 1969, 1973, 1982, to *Rigoletto*. Each issue typically contained seven to twelve articles on the particular opera as well as several on other subjects. Indexes to each of the three-number volumes were published in 1960, 1966, and 1982. Only those articles used in this book are listed below.

Studi Verdiani, a journal of the Istituto di Studi Verdiani that replaced *Verdi, Bolletino*. To date three issues have been published; Nos. 1, 2, and 3, in 1982, 1983, and 1985. Articles appear in the language in which submitted, and there have been more than a few in English. Of these, only those used in this book are listed below.

Verdi Newsletter, published by the American Institute for Verdi Studies, New York. From May 1976 through 1985 the Institute has issued thirteen, with all articles either written in or translated into English. Only those used in this book are listed below.

BOOKS

Baldini, Gabriele. *The Story of Giuseppe Verdi*, Oberto *to* Un ballo in maschera, ed. and trans. Roger Parker. Cambridge: Cambridge University Press, 1980, cloth and paperback.

Bonavia, Ferruccio. *Verdi*. London: Oxford University Press, 1930; Dennis Dobson, 1947.

Budden, Julian. *The Operas of Verdi*, 3 vols. London: Cassell, 1973, 1978, 1981; New York: Oxford University Press, 1984, paperback.

_____. *Verdi*. London: Dent *Master Musicians Series*, 1985; New York: Random House, 1987, paperback.

Busch, Hans. *Verdi's Aida, The History of an Opera in Letters and Documents*. Minneapolis: University of Minnesota Press, 1978 cloth and paperback.

Chusid, Martin. *A Catalog of Verdi's Operas*. Hackensack, N. J.: Joseph Boonin, 1974; No. 5 of Music Indexes and Bibliographies.

_____, ed. *Rigoletto*. Chicago: University of Chicago Press, 1983; being Series I, Operas, Vol. 17 of *The Works of Giuseppe Verdi*. (This consists of 2 vols.: The Orchestral Score with Introduction and the Critical Commentary.)

Conati, Marcello, ed. *Interviews and Encounters with Verdi*, trans. Richard Stokes. London: Gollancz, 1984.

Crowest, Frederick J. *Verdi, Man and Musician, His Biography with Especial Reference to his English Experiences*. London: John Milne, 1897.

Gatti, Carlo. *Verdi, The Man and His Music*, ed. and trans. Elisabeth Abbott. New York: Putnam's 1955. (This is a shortened version of Gatti's revision, 1951, of his 1931 biography, one of the landmarks of Verdi scholarship. Most scholars feel, however, that the revision, while interesting in its polemics, was not an improvement on the original, which has never been translated into English.)

Godefroy, Vincent. *The Dramatic Genius of Verdi*, 2 vols. London: Gollancz, 1975, 1977.

Hepokoski, James A. *Giuseppe Verdi*, Falstaff. Cambridge: Cambridge University Press, 1983.

_____. *Giuseppe Verdi*, Otello. Cambridge: Cambridge University Press, 1987.

Hopkinson, Cecil. *A Bibliography of the Works of Giuseppe Verdi*, 2 vols. New York: Broude Bros., 1973, 1978.

Hughes, Spike. *Famous Verdi Operas, An analytical guide for the opera-goer and armchair listener*. London, Robert Hale, 1968. *(Nabucco, Macbeth, Rigoletto, Trovatore, Traviata, Boccanegra, Ballo, Forza, Don Carlos, Aida, Otello,* and *Falstaff.)*

Hussey, Dyneley. *Verdi*. Master Musicians Series. London: Dent, 1940; revised, 1948; 1963.

Kimbell, David R. B. *Verdi in the Age of Italian Romanticism*. Cambridge: Cambridge University Press, 1981; 1985, paperback.

Martin, George. *Verdi, His Music, Life and Times*. New York: Dodd, Mead, 1963; 1983, paperback.

Noske, Frits. *The Signifier and the Signified, Studies in the Operas of Mozart and Verdi*. The Hague: Martinus Nijhoff, 1977. (This offers six chapters on aspects of Verdi and a translation of the Verdi–Boito correspondence concerning the revision of *Simon Boccanegra*.)

Osborne, Charles. *The Complete Operas of Verdi*. London: Gollancz, 1969; New York: Da Capo, 1985, paperback.

_____, ed. and trans. *Letters of Giuseppe Verdi*. London: Gollancz, 1971.

Pougin, Arthur. *Verdi, An Anecdotic History of His Life and Works*, trans. James E. Matthew. London: H. Grevel, 1887.

Rosen, David, and Andrew Porter, eds. *Verdi's* Macbeth, *A Sourcebook*. New York: Norton, 1984. (Contains many of the papers delivered at the Fifth International Verdi Congress, 1977. In connection with these it includes 186 letters concerning the opera, reviews of the premieres of its first and revised versions, a transcription of Verdi's working libretto, a chronology of *Macbeth* performances, and an annotated bibliography. All texts are in English; many also are presented in their original language.)

Shaw, G. Bernard. *Shaw's Music, The Complete Musical Criticism in Three Volumes*, ed. Dan H. Laurence. New York: Dodd, Mead, 1981.

Sheean, Vincent. *Orpheus at Eighty*. New York: Random House, 1958; Westport, Conn.: Greenwood Press, 1975.

Toye, Francis. *Giuseppe Verdi, His Life and Works*. London: Heinemann, 1931; New York: Vienna House, 1972, paperback.

Travis, Francis Irving. *Verdi's Orchestration*. Zurich: Juris–Verlag, 1956.

Walker, Frank. *The Man Verdi*. London: Dent, 1962; Chicago: University of Chicago Press, 1983, paperback.

Weaver, William, ed. and trans. *Verdi, A Documentary Study*. London: Thames & Hudson, 1977. (Contains 287 plates and 31 additional illustrations. It also presents in English translation selections from hundreds of letters and documents in chronological order so that they read like a biography. As a preface, the book also offers a translation of Verdi's own account of his early, crucial years in Milan.)

————, ed. and trans. *Seven Verdi Librettos*. New York: Norton, 1977, paperback. *(Rigoletto, Trovatore, Traviata, Ballo, Aida, Otello,* and *Falstaff.)*

————, and Martin Chusid, eds. *The Verdi Companion*. New York: Norton, 1979. (Contains essays by Isaiah Berlin, George Martin, Giampiero Tintori, Julian Budden, Bruno Cagli, William Weaver, Martin Chusid, Luigi Dallapiccola, and Rodolfo Celletti; also a bibliographical essay by Andrew Porter, a chronology by Elvidio Surian, and a *Dramatis Personae* of people associated with Verdi during his lifetime.)

————. *The Golden Century of Italian Opera from Rossini to Puccini*. London: Thames and Hudson, 1980.

Werfel, Franz. *Verdi, A Novel of the Opera*, trans. Helen Jessiman. New York: Simon & Schuster, 1925; New York: Allen, Towne & Heath, 1947.

————, and Paul Stefan, eds. *Verdi, The Man in His Letters*, trans. Edward O. Downes. New York: L. B. Fischer, 1942; New York: Vienna House, 1973, paperback.

Ybarra, T. R. *Verdi, Miracle Man of Opera*. New York: Harcourt, Brace, 1955.

UNPUBLISHED STUDIES

These are unpublished only in a technical sense. Photographic copies can be obtained by writing to University Microfilms International, Ann Arbor, Michigan, USA, 48106, and paying a fee.

Bloomers, Thomas J. "Rivas and Verdi, The Force of Destiny." Ph.D. Thesis, University of Iowa, 1978.

Moreen, Robert Anthony. "Integration of Text Forms and Musical Forms in Verdi's Early Operas." Ph.D. Thesis, Princeton University, 1975.

Rosen, David B. "The Genesis of Verdi's *Requiem*." Ph.D. Thesis, University of California, Berkeley, 1976.

ARTICLES

Adams, John Clarke, and Abraham Veinus. *"Rigoletto* as Drama," *Atti*. Parma: Istituto di Studi Verdiani, 1974. 3:464–94.

Bellaigue, Camille. "Italian Music and the Last Two Operas of Verdi," *Musical Studies and Silhouettes*, trans. Ellen Orr. New York: Dodd, Mead, 1900.

Black, John N. "Salvatore Cammarano's programma for *Il Trovatore* and the problems of the finale," *Studi Verdiani*. Parma: Istituto di Studi Verdiani, 1983. 2:78–107.

Budden, Julian. "Verdi and the Contemporary Italian Operatic Scene," in *The Verdi Companion*, eds. William Weaver and Martin Chusid. New York: Norton, 1979; 67–105.

Chusid, Martin. "Rigoletto and Monterone, A Study in Musical Dramaturgy," in *Verdi, Bolletino*, Vol. 3, no. 9. Parma: Istituto di Studi Verdiani, 1982; 1544–58.

De Amicis, Edmondo. "Giuseppina Verdi-Strepponi," *Verdi, Bolletino*, Vol. 1, no. 2. Parma: Istituto di Studi Verdiani, 1960; 1057–68.

De Filippis, Felice. "Verdi and his Neapolitan Friends," *Verdi, Bolletino*, Vol. 1, no. 3. Parma: Istituto di Studi Verdiani, 1960; 1754–66.

Demaldè, Giuseppe. "Cenni biografici del Maestro Verdi," ed. and trans. Mary Jane Matz and Gino Macchidani, *Verdi Newsletter*, no. 1 (May 1976); no. 2 (December 1976); no. 3 (June 1977). New York: American Institute for Verdi Studies.

Gray, Cecil. "The Verdi Revival" (1931), *Contingencies and Other Essays*. London: Oxford University Press, 1947; reissued Freeport, N.Y.: Books for Libraries Press, 1971.

Gresch, Donald. "The Fact of Fiction. Franz Werfel's *Verdi, Roman der Oper*," *Current Musicology*, no. 28, (1979); 30–40.

Hanslick, Eduard. "Verdi's *Requiem*" (1879), *Vienna's Golden Years of Music, 1850–1900*, trans. Henry Pleasants III. Freeport, N.Y.: Books for Libraries Press, 1969; 178–86.

Kaufman, Tom. "A Hundred Years of *Macbeth*, Annals compiled by Tom Kaufman and others," *Verdi's* Macbeth, *A Sourcebook*, eds. David Rosen and Andrew Porter. New York: W. W. Norton, 1984, 426–55; and "More about the Performance History of *Macbeth*" by Martin Chusid and Tom Kaufman, *Verdi Newsletter*, No. 13, (1985). New York: American Institute for Verdi Studies; 38–41.

Kerman, Joseph. "Verdi's Use of Recurring Themes," *Studies in Musical History, Essays for Oliver Strunk*, ed. Harold Powers. Princeton: Princeton University Press, 1968; 495–510.

Kimbell, David R. B. "*Il Trovatore:* Cammarano and Garcia Guttiérrez," *Atti*. Parma: Istituto di Studi Verdiani, 1974. 3:34–44.

Kuhner, Hans. "Franz Werfel and Giuseppe Verdi," *Verdi, Bolletino*, Vol. 1, no. 3. Parma: Istituto di Studi Verdiani, 1960; 1790–1804.

Lawton, David. "Tonal Structure and Dramatic Action in *Rigoletto*," *Verdi, Bolletino*, Vol. 3, no. 9. Parma: Istituto di Studi Verdiani, 1982; 1559–81.

Martin, George. "Unpublished Letters, A Contribution to the History of *La forza del destino*," *Verdi, Bolletino*, Vol. 2, no. 5. Parma: Istituto di Studi Verdiani, 1962; 1088–1102.

Matz, Mary Jane. "Verdi, The Roots of the Tree," *Verdi, Bolletino*, Vol. 1, no. 3. Parma: Istituto di Studi Verdiani, 1960; 333–64.

———. "The Verdi Family of S. Agata and Roncole, Legend and Truth," *Atti*. Parma: Istituto di Studi Verdiani, 1969. 1:216–21.

———. "Flying with Verdi," *Verdi Newsletter*, no. 6 (March 1979). New York: American Institute of Verdi Studies; 11–13.

Medici, Mario. "Letters about *King Lear*," *Verdi, Bolletino*, Vol. 1, no. 2. Parma: Istituto di Studi Verdiani, 1960. 1039–56.

Polzer, Anne. "Leader of the Renaissance," *Opera News*, Vol. 25, no. 15 (18 February 1961); 21–33.

Porter, Andrew. "*Don Carlos* and the Monk–Emperor," *Musical Newsletter*, Vol. 2, no. 4 (October 1972); 9–12, 23.

Reynolds, Barbara. "Verdi and Manzoni, An Attempted Explanation," *Music and Letters*, Vol. xxix, no. 1 (January 1948); 31–43.

Ringer, Alexander L. "Giuseppe Verdi: Four Letters to his Wine Merchant," *Musical America*, Vol. 71, no. 3 (February 1951); 4.

Rosenthal, Harold. "The Rediscovery of *Don Carlos* in Our Day," *Atti*. Parma: Istituto di studi Verdiani, 1971. 2:550–58.

Schmiedel, Gottfried. "Fritz Busch and the Dresden Opera," *Opera*, Vol. 11, no. 3 (March 1960); 175–81.

Stefan, Paul. "A German Verdi Renaissance—Werfel Novel Instrumental in Making Revivals Possible," *Musical America*, Vol. 48, no. 7 (2 June 1928). 3.

Toye, Francis. "Verdi Over Fifty Years," *Opera*, Vol. 2, no. 3 (February 1951). 105–10.

Walker, Frank, and Hans F. Redlich. "Gesù morì, An unknown early Verdi Manuscript," *The Music Review* (August/November 1959); 233. In connection with this, see "The Composer of 'Gesù Morì' " by David Stivender, *Verdi Newsletter*, no. 2, (December 1976); 6–7, which denies that the work is Verdi's.

———. "Introduction to a biographical study," *Verdi, Bolletino*, Vol. 2, no. 4. Parma: Istituto di Studi Verdiani, 1961; 1–16.

Weaver, William. "Verdi, the Playgoer," *Musical Newsletter*, Vol. 6, no. 1 (Winter 1976): 3–8, 24.

"Verdi—A Symposium," *Opera*, Vol. 2, no. 3 (February 1951). (This issue, almost entirely devoted to Verdi, commemorated the fiftieth anniversary of his death on 27 January 1901. It contains articles by Lennox Berkeley, Arthur Bliss, Benjamin Britten, Cecil Gray, Harold Rosenthal, Francis Toye, and Ralph Vaughan Williams.)

INDEX

The chief discussions of any subject or musical work are placed first in the entry and set in *italic type;* quotations from Verdi's letters are indicated by page references set in **boldface type;** superior figures refer to notes.

Entries concerning Verdi are listed in three sub-indexes under his name: first, "General," a sub-index of events, his characteristics, and his opinions, such as birth, his skepticism, and "on Dante"; second, "Operas," and third, "Other Works." Some references appear in more than one entry.

Books, poems, plays, and musical compositions are indexed under the author or composer's name; theatres and opera houses, under names of cities.